Composition in the Digital World

COMPOSITION IN THE DIGITAL WORLD

Conversations with 21st-Century American Composers

Robert Raines

OXFORD
UNIVERSITY PRESS

OXFORD
UNIVERSITY PRESS

Oxford University Press is a department of the University of
Oxford. It furthers the University's objective of excellence in research,
scholarship, and education by publishing worldwide.

Oxford   New York
Auckland   Cape Town   Dar es Salaam   Hong Kong   Karachi
Kuala Lumpur   Madrid   Melbourne   Mexico City   Nairobi
New Delhi   Shanghai   Taipei   Toronto

With offices in
Argentina   Austria   Brazil   Chile   Czech Republic   France   Greece
Guatemala   Hungary   Italy   Japan   Poland   Portugal   Singapore
South Korea   Switzerland   Thailand   Turkey   Ukraine   Vietnam

Oxford is a registered trademark of Oxford University Press
in the UK and certain other countries.

Published in the United States of America by
Oxford University Press
198 Madison Avenue, New York, NY 10016

Library of Congress Cataloging-in-Publication Data
Raines, Robert, 1954–author.
Composition in the digital world: conversations with 21st-century American
composers/Robert Raines.
  pages cm
Includes bibliographical references and index.
ISBN 978–0–19–935703–1 (alk. paper)
1. Composers—United States—Interviews.   2. Music—United States—21st century—
History and criticism.   I. Title.
ML390.R138 2015
780.92'273—dc23
2014020231

9 8 7 6 5 4 3 2 1
Printed in the United States of America
on acid-free paper

This book is dedicated to my father, Professor Charles Alanceson Raines, who demonstrated how to be a good man and father, and taught me that music is among the greatest joys of life.

CONTENTS

ABOUT THE COMPANION WEBSITE

⊙ www.oup.com/us/compositioninthedigitalworld

Oxford has created a website to accompany *Composition in the Digital World*. Some of the composers in this book have provided additional material for this companion website including excerpts of scores, web links, and interviews, as well as material that cannot be made available in a book, such as audio excerpts and videos. The reader is encouraged to consult this resource in conjunction with the book.

Composition in the Digital World

Introduction

What exactly is a composer? The answer may seem obvious, but the definition continues to evolve and in the 21st century encompasses a wider meaning than ever before. No longer bound by conventional constraints dictating a particular educational background, a specific instrumentation, or a formal performance setting, a contemporary composer may truly be defined by the broad phrase "an inventor of music," as Stravinsky described himself more than 100 years ago.

The field of concert music composition is on fire, reclaiming audiences with an extraordinary array of styles, panache, and innovation. There has been a noticeable turning of the heads in popular culture with regard to new art music. The dusty image has been shaken off and it's no longer "unhip" to be a composer—quite the opposite in fact, as exemplified by several of the stars in this book.

The diversity now evident in this formerly conservative and tight-knit club is striking. Less than a century ago, almost all well-known classical composers were white European males. They certainly made some wonderful music and I'm not knocking them, but I believe we are all benefiting from the much greater inclusiveness that is now the norm among music makers. While all of the composers who participated in this book are American citizens, many arrived here via other countries, drawn to the artistic mecca that the United States has become. With roots in China, Cuba, the Czech Republic, France, and Spain, these composers greatly enhance the current American music scene with the rich heritage they bring with them from their countries of origin. Similarly, while female composers struggled to be heard and recognized historically, women now form a solid cornerstone of the community of contemporary American composers. This is all good news for music lovers.

Thankfully, a number of the established composers included here continue to write for formal ensembles such as symphony orchestras and chamber ensembles, carrying on the tradition of Western art music and expanding the repertoire with some brilliant new works. At the same time, the range of today's music has unleashed an unprecedented variety of instrumental combinations and stylistic approaches. The influence of popular music like rock and jazz is readily apparent and freely acknowledged by many of the composers, something that was all but unheard of just a few generations ago. While it's true that in past decades experimentation with alternative instrumentation and electronic and taped sound took place, the use of varied instrumental combinations and electronics is no longer the exception but the norm. Electric guitars, amplified traditional instruments, taped and computer-generated sounds, synthesizers, homemade custom instruments, digitally modified voices, found objects, and a dazzling array of musical instruments from other cultures: All have been brought into the traditional setting of Western music. The works resulting from this "flinging open of the doors" is refreshing, colorful, and often breathtaking.

Then there is the language of the music itself. A quick perusal of music history confirms that styles and tastes continually evolve: Sound combinations that are considered horribly dissonant by one generation may sound trite to the next, as listeners grow accustomed to those previously daring sonorities. Case in point: Beethoven's music was considered radical and cacophonous by many of his contemporaries.

Just a few decades ago, the Second Vienna School had a very strong grip—some might say a stranglehold—on the world of composition. Those who formally studied the art of writing music were almost universally expected to create pieces that fit within the strict rules of serial composition. General audiences, however, did not react well to most of this music, and attending a concert of modern music was often looked upon as something akin to a visit to the dentist. It cannot be overemphasized how strongly the slavish adherence to a dogmatic set of musical rules affected the output of several generations of composers. Those who chose to write outside the bounds of serial music were generally disregarded and considered lightweights or worse in academic circles. Happily, any rigidly set style or system of composition is now pretty much out the window. In this heterogeneous and freewheeling atmosphere, almost anything goes: Latin rhythms, Indian or Chinese traditional instruments in an orchestral setting, digital computer sounds, tonal, modal, microtonal; all are acceptable.

There seems to be another sea change taking place in music education. While more than half of the composers in this book attended Ivy League schools, another sizable percentage were able to enter the field despite pursuing their musical higher education at institutions outside of that previously exclusive academic alliance. Additionally, almost all styles of music are now readily accepted as valid in even the most traditional of composition departments. The eclecticism of the sounds that students listen to, and in turn compose themselves, is in sharp contrast to the output of previous generations of student composers who were in many cases vigorously discouraged from venturing outside of academically acceptable styles of "serious music" of that time. These are important developments and, I believe, are a direct result of the diversification of the population of composers and the technology that has facilitated that diversification.

It is easy to see that the explosion of technology, specifically digital technology, has altered the very fabric of our lives. Computers, cell phones, and the Internet have changed not only the way we approach the most mundane of daily activities but also have had a profound impact on the way we work, communicate, and create. This issue of technology being a catalyst of fundamental change in contemporary life is an important focus of these composer interviews and is one of the primary reasons I felt this book needed to be written.

There is an interesting disparity among the composers in terms of how they use technology. At one end of the spectrum are those who have fully embraced all of the technologies available: They use the computer to compose, orchestrate, and create digital sound demos; digital sound in live performance settings; and computer software to create scores and parts. At the opposite end are those who stick to pencil and paper and never touch a computer music program. But even they use cell phones, have some form of web presence, interact with students electronically, and follow new music on the Internet. The two groups together provide a complete picture of how technology has altered the working process for composers. The bottom line is, it's impossible for us *not* to be transformed by the technology that surrounds us, and it's fascinating to see how differently these artists variously embrace or attempt to fend off the digital invasion.

Pedagogical practice itself also has been greatly altered as composition departments across the country embrace digital technology. The use of computers by students to compose, publish, and study music is ubiquitous; digital communication by e-mail and school websites is commonplace; and classroom (or virtual classroom) teaching methods often utilize digital technology to demonstrate concepts, present listening examples, and test pupils. Most tellingly, students almost always present their work either directly from their laptop or through some type of digital media delivery. The 21st-century teacher must be comfortable teaching in a digital setting, familiar with a myriad of technologies, and adept at keeping pace with new developments. To fail in any of those and continue as a mainstream contemporary music educator is not an option.

Inside and outside the classroom, the pervasiveness of the Internet has facilitated a music revolution. Just as the major record companies have lost their footing as purveyors of musical taste—digital downloads and music streaming have put that firmly back in the hands of consumers—so have traditional institutions such as music conservatories and orchestra halls lost their grip on what is being composed, and in turn, what audiences hear. Technology allows an ever-widening pool of composers the means to have their music realized and heard, and also makes it easy for potential audiences to quickly search and find this new music on the Internet, unhindered by programming restrictions of the symphony hall or corporate preference. It's not difficult these days to find a composer who matches one's personal taste by spending a bit of time exploring a few websites. I believe the reverberations from these changes are only just beginning to be felt.

As reflected by its very specific title, *Composition in the Digital World: Conversations with 21st-Century American Composers* aims to provide a focused snapshot of American composers and their art at the outset of our young century.

The word *Conversations* is used to stress that these are not academic essays but informal discussions meant to offer some insight "around the edges" into each of the unique personalities included in this collection. I have not attempted to provide a comprehensive biography of the composers but instead to create a humanistic portrait of each, highlighting the character and thought processes of these innovative and influential artists while uncovering information that is not easily gleaned from a formal biography. With this in mind, I have limited biographical information to a few lines in the short opening paragraphs that precede each interview. Similarly, this book is not intended to provide a complete catalog of the *works* of each composer. For one thing, these are active creators; their catalogs are constantly in flux as they add new pieces. For these interviews, I asked each composer to select just 12 of their pieces for a list of selected works at the end of each interview. Some fretted over this request: "How can I represent my life's work with only a dozen pieces? I need at least 40!" In the end, most agreed, if reluctantly, that selecting a limited number of works would help readers, students, and other composers see which pieces are among those of the most import *to their creators*. This seemed to me a useful and telling exercise. I do urge interested readers to explore each composer's website to find a more comprehensive biography and complete list of their works, and above all, to listen to their music.

Perhaps most important, this book is not limited to interviews with *famous* contemporary American composers, though many of them certainly fall into that category. Instead, this series of interviews offers a glimpse into the working process of contemporary American men and women who have devoted their lives to writing music; the vast majority of people who make that decision will not become famous or wealthy as a result of their efforts. While eight of the composers have won Grammy Awards and six have won Pulitzer Prizes, all of the artists included here create important music that reflects their diverse interests, influences, and strengths, and all offer inspirational advice and insights.

A note on the organization of the book: Early on I decided that I would not organize the chapters by the ages of the composers. This practice needs to be put to bed. It's a hangover from music history classes of the last century and was meant to help students memorize the names and eras of various composers (some of them obscure) of centuries past. Likewise, I wanted to put more thought into the sequencing of chapters than simply ordering them alphabetically by last name (Why should Ellen Zwilich always have to go last?). As a result, the book is informally divided into four sections, though there is a great deal of overlap among the groups, and some composers could comfortably have fit in anywhere. We begin by looking at the well-established composers who continue to create and influence the world of contemporary American music, then move on to those who have established themselves more recently. The third section includes the artists who have arrived here from other countries, and we close with the radical innovators, those who are pushing the limits of technology and challenging the traditional definition of a composer.

The musicians who participated in these conversations are as different from one another as might be hoped of guests at a particularly stimulating, if imaginary, dinner party, yet all share a passionate artistic drive that is both joyful and inspiring. While the idea of attending a gathering of all of these people is appealing, I feel fortunate to have been able instead to speak to the "guests" in one-on-one conversations. Each has so much to offer, such insightful perspectives on their art, that I'm afraid I would have missed their individual spirit in a collective conversation. And that benefit is what I hope to offer you here: the chance to eavesdrop on personal and impromptu conversations about music, composing, and the creative process.

Technologies aside, words of wisdom for aspiring composers are generously offered from each of the composers in this book, including these:

- Start an ensemble so that your music can be played.
- Work as much as possible and not only when you feel struck by inspiration.
- Take time to learn the business end of your craft, both in self-promotion and in money matters.

To me their most moving and universal advice is in regard to being one's self. All seem to agree that this is key. Perhaps the most reassuring words I've encountered along these lines came from the great dancer, choreographer, and artist Martha Graham. Although there are many variations on her exact words, I've found this quote to be a great inspiration and have it framed on the wall of my studio:

> There is a vitality, a life force, an energy . . . a quickening . . . that is translated through you into action, and because there is only one of you in all of time, this expression is unique. And if you block it, it will never exist through any other medium but will be lost. It's not your business to determine how good it is, nor how valuable, nor how it compares with other expressions. It is your business to keep it yours clearly and directly, to keep the channel open. Whether you choose to take an art class, keep a journal, record your dreams, dance your story, or live each day from your own creative source, above all else, keep the channel open.

All of the composers in this book are delightful conversationalists. They generously donated their time and knowledge to help student composers and to compare notes with their contemporaries. Famous and not-yet-famous alike, all embody that excitement and drive shared by devoted artists, whether composers, writers, dancers, visual artists, or those following any other creative pursuit.

This book is an homage to the artistic spirit and a celebration of a few inspiring examples of people whose creative channels are wide open.

Ellen Taaffe Zwilich

As recordings boomed in the mid-20th century, more people, not fewer, were exposed to music, to good performances, and to more kinds of music, and the musical level of performance rose significantly in places far from traditional musical centers. I expect the same kind of flowering (we're already seeing it) in our digital age. To me, it's all about new doors opening—you don't have to walk through every last one of them, but some of them will make a huge difference to you and each one offers a new contribution to our musical world.

Instantly striking about Ellen Taaffe Zwilich (b. Miami, 1939) are her genuinely warm smile, intense eye contact, and total presence in a conversation. Engaging, articulate, and intelligent, she is entirely consumed by her art, as quickly becomes apparent, and her love of writing music creates an infectious aura of enthusiasm about contemporary composition.

She is almost self-effacing about her meteoric rise to stardom as a composer. The first woman to win a Pulitzer Prize for music (1983) and the first female doctoral graduate in composition from the Juilliard School (studying with Roger Sessions and Elliott Carter), she also is the winner of an Academy Award, has had four Grammy nominations, and is the first-ever occupant of Carnegie Hall's Composer's Chair. Her collection of prestigious awards is too numerous to list. Yet she seems to be relatively blasé regarding these achievements and the fact that she is a champion female trailblazer in the typically all-male world of serious music composition. Rather, she is the consummate artist, passionately focused on taking her own art to the next level and on discovering and supporting the next generation of bright stars in the world of composition.

Zwilich has completely embraced modern technology and is as creative in her methods of teaching music as she is in her composing. During one composition lesson, I asked her for guidance in creating a ballet score. She suggested that I go into a room, close and lock the door, turn out the lights, and dance with arms outstretched until the music came to me. Such an unorthodox, free-spirited approach to her pedagogy is balanced by a solid foundation in the craft of her musical heritage.

Her stunning array of contemporary American concert compositions includes large-scale orchestral works, concertos for most of the spectrum of orchestral instruments, choral works, orchestra music for children, chamber music, and ballet. Her music is in great demand and is performed around the world. Audiences love her music. Critics love her music. Fellow composers love her music. Widely hailed as a modern master of composition, Ellen Zwilich is a tireless creative force in modern American music.

Do you have a process that you like to follow when composing?
I don't really have a set process. Sometimes things can go really quite quickly, and sometimes they go painfully slowly. I typically spend a lot of time sort of muddling around before a piece really grabs me and gets going. For instance, my string quartet *Voyage* was commissioned to honor the centennial of the original Galimir Quartet, which was formed in Vienna in 1927 by the members of the Galimir family, three sisters and a brother. They were very young when they started, and had quite an amazing career in the early 1930s, but then, thankfully, were able to leave Vienna in 1936. They headed in all different directions, though ultimately all four of them ended up in the United States.

In preparation for this piece, I spent a great deal of time thinking about the historical situation of this family, and these young people. The critical moment for my work came as I was going through all kinds of archival material. I saw a picture of the four of them, with their instruments in position, from a newspaper in the 1930s. They look so serious, and so innocent, and so full of life and hope. It just sort of knocked me off of my chair, and the piece just began to "go."

I generally do a lot of thinking about what I might do, and then I'll do some sketching and some improvising, but there comes a moment in my work when the piece says to me, "Okay, let's go." And sometimes it's something like that picture that sort of sets me off. That photograph started me on a kind of voyage and I let the piece take me on the journey. But then, that was the way this particular process went.

Had you created sketches before the inspiration, if you want to call it that . . .
Yes, yes, I do want to call it inspiration. We tend to shy away from using that term, but why? Because it is truly out of our total conscious control if we're doing it right. If we're just adding A to B, just following a system, it's not nearly as interesting as if we are pulling things together in our mind that are, in a sense, out of our immediate control. I think our minds are much more advanced than our way of theorizing about things, and so sometimes there is an important impetus like that. The idea of "informed intuition" is where it's at for me as a composer. In other words, I want to inform myself as much as possible about everything concerning the piece that's going to be, and then I want to trust my instincts. If I have a plan for a piece, and then as I'm writing, the piece wants to do something different, I will *always* go with the piece and throw away the plan. But it's never just total inspiration, or total reliance on intuition, it's a question of trusting yourself to make judgments that are beyond your emotional or intellectual grasp.

When you're composing do you create pencil sketches or work at the piano?
I work almost entirely at the computer now; I hardly use a pencil anymore. One of the things I have done for my entire composing life is to have a full score in front of me to sketch on. If I'm writing a string quartet, I have the four staves there in front of me. If I'm writing for full orchestra, I do the same thing. I want to have the immediate feeling of the ensemble at the end of the piece, so to speak. So I sketch in full score.

So you orchestrate as a part of your compositional process?

Oh certainly, but I don't like the word "orchestrate." That implies that you've written the piece at a piano and now you're going to apply it to an orchestra. I want to write directly "on" the orchestra, or the string quartet, or the septet, whatever ensemble it is I'm writing for. I want to write directly for those instruments.

Is hearing the MIDI (Musical Instrument Digital Interface) playback from the computer a good thing, or can it be a problem?

It can be a problem. There is so much more involved in making music come to life than just getting the notes right, and when I hear a simplistic MIDI playback I just want to throw the computer across the room. When good musicians are playing my music well, it's different every time. Not radically different, but just little touches of humanity—those moments make all the difference. I know you can spend a great deal of time and get pretty good MIDI playback, but I just don't want to focus on that, so I turn it off when I'm composing.

But I'll tell you what I do use MIDI playback for: It can be the most wonderful tool for proofreading. Because you certainly can't miss a wrong note when it's played at you. Sometimes it's very difficult to proofread your own material, whether it's language or music, because you know what you had in mind. So, I do use playback for proofreading. It can also be handy to quickly grasp a long span of a piece, but generally speaking, I shy away from using it.

Do you create all of your final scores and parts, or do you have someone do that for you?

It depends. Generally speaking I do the score, and then I have someone else do the parts so that I know they will look really, really good. For example, I had an engraver create the parts for the *Commedia dell'Arte*, because I did this crazy thing of having different string players play various percussion instruments like slapstick, tambourine, and bells, and I was worried about those parts looking right.

When you go into rehearsal does the piece pretty much stay the same, or does it continue to evolve?

I go to my first rehearsal with my eraser! I'm always open to tweaking things. In the case of the *Commedia dell'Arte*, which is my most recent premiere, I went over the solo violin part with Nadja Salerno-Sonnenberg[1] before it ever got to the final score stage. We tweaked a little bit of this and a little bit of that. Some things are very clear to me as a composer but they might not be so clear to every performer, so this is an opportunity to clarify things.

When I get into rehearsal, there are sometimes issues of dynamics, or articulations, or perhaps I've used a word that doesn't resonate with some of the performers, so I'll find another word that succeeds in resonating for everyone. It's not an exact science. Some of the most experienced composers struggle with this. Mahler, for example, who was also a wonderful conductor, used a lot of little directions in his scores, some of which sound like your grandmother's recipe for gravy, like "add some flour, but not too much."

Your *Septet for Piano Trio and String Quartet* is a great favorite of mine. Can you talk a little about how that piece came about?
It was written for people I know and love. Sharon Robinson, the cellist of the Kalichstein-Laredo-Robinson (KLR) Trio approached me and said that they had never been able to find a piece for piano trio and string quartet. Sharon's brother [Keith Robinson] is the cellist of the Miami String Quartet, but they had never played a piece that had them all on the stage at the same time. Would I be interested in writing a septet? I waited about a nanosecond and said, "I'd love it!"

One of the things I do as a composer, probably because I had so much experience as a player, is that I talk extensively with my performers. I always want to pick their brains, find out what they think about any number of subjects. In the case of this septet, when considering the instrumentation one might automatically think two violins, two violas, two cellos, and a piano to sort of balance it out. But my pre-compositional conversations with the performers helped to shape the piece in another direction.

The first thing that Jamie Laredo [violinist with the trio] said was "whatever you do, try not to write for viola." This was because it's such a pain to travel with the violin and a viola. Going through airport security with one instrument is a nightmare, but two? Forget about that. So I took that into consideration. And then in talking with Joseph Kalichstein [pianist with the trio], we were chatting about this and that, and he said, "Oh everything is fine, don't worry about it, you write it, we'll love it," but just before we hung up he said, "Just don't make it a piano concerto with string orchestra accompaniment." At that moment, a light bulb went off for me and I thought, "Hey wait a minute, I have two ensembles here, not just seven instruments. These are two ensembles with distinct personalities of their own." So I decided to make that part of the piece. In fact, I began the piece with a quote from my piano trio, like a gauntlet laid down by the KLR

Trio, answered by the Miami Quartet with a quote from my second string quartet. Of course, as the movement goes along, they all become one. That was a key impetus for me in the compositional process of this piece: Not only do I have seven virtuoso artists on the stage, I have two ensembles.

In the second movement I explored my interest in how well the historically informed performance tradition has evolved in the last few years. People are doing wonderful things using inventive instrumental techniques. So, the second movement goes back and forth between a very modern, robust virtuoso style and a more reserved style with little vibrato, the kind of sound the more historically informed performers are producing. That technique has a tremendous emotional impact on certain kinds of music. It's nice to be able to explore.

I like the idea of feeling free to do *whatever*. For many years there was a feeling that composers had someone looking over their shoulder saying, "You can't do this," and "You are supposed to do that." I don't like that. I want to feel free. Sometimes things turn out differently than I might have anticipated, but now I feel free to let it go. If, for instance, a jazz impulse (which is a part of my background) wants to come out, I go with it.

Do you feel that jazz is an organic part of who you are as a composer?
Our music incorporates everything about us, so in that respect my jazz background is an element. A lot of my concepts about composition came about because I spent many years playing different kinds of music. I loved playing. I was a violinist with the American Symphony Orchestra under Leopold Stokowski[2] for seven years and we played a lot of different music, particularly under our guest conductors, many of whom were European. It was really an amazing and wonderful experience. And so, as a player, it's been wonderful for me to write for strings. I've done quite a bit of it. However, I don't want to be limited by my technique, I want to be open to more than my capabilities as a string player. The string instruments are fascinating to me and I never get over my infatuation with them.

There is also a sense of karma about instruments that I'm very interested in exploring. When I was an undergraduate at Florida State University, I played jazz trumpet, big band and small combo stuff. That was something I enjoyed doing very, very much. It is a part of me. The Tallahassee area had a very interesting underground jazz scene with some wonderful players, Nat Adderley [brother of saxophonist "Cannonball" Adderley], for instance. I found that out during the first week of my freshman year.

Speaking of freshman, please talk about the BMI Student Composer awards.

It's one of my great pleasures to be able to hand out those awards once a year. I chair the final jury. I don't look at the materials until afterward though. They put together really, really good panels and everyone does a very conscientious job. I just moderate the final panel, and get to give out the prizes, which is a great treat.

And you started the "Making Music" series at Carnegie Hall. That's a major initiative, an effort to connect audiences and composers.

Yes, and the series is still going on I'm very happy to see. Originally it was a little different from the way they are doing it now. When I started the "Making Music" series, I wanted the lay audience to have contact with all kinds of contemporary music. The first season went from Ned Rorem[3] to Steve Reich—really very, very different composers. I wanted the audience to get an overview of contemporary music, and not tell them, "You're supposed to like this" or "You're supposed to like that." My feeling was that we should give people an insight into what was happening in the music world, and let them make up their own minds.

I have found that composers are able to speak much more easily about someone else's music than their own. This includes yours truly. And what I thought would be fun for the three or four years that I led this program, was to ask composers to bring to the table other people's music that meant something to them. We would talk about that as well as the pieces that were on the program. The interesting thing was that we had everything from a gamelan band to Beethoven. We had Bach, we had singers in the African tradition, Gunther Schuller brought really good small jazz combos, we had styles of music from all over the globe, it was really interesting. The audience never knew what they would be getting because the music the composers were interested in was not always what you might expect. It really created a window into the persona of the composer that was featured.

I know you have many musical interests, but please share some music you love that might be surprising to those who only know your classical music credentials.

For my "Making Music" concert I brought some Beethoven and Thelonious Monk.[4] It's really people outside the field who have rigid ideas of what should and shouldn't be interesting to composers, whereas I think people in the field are very open-minded. It's always a discovery when you're writing music. When you write something new you're discovering something new personally as well.

It's often commented that your music possesses a particularly strong personality, that your sound is immediately recognizable. Are you aware of your "voice" as you are composing, and do you pursue it?

No, I don't care about that. I mean, I'm happy to hear it, perhaps it makes you feel like your efforts are somehow authentic, but I'm just focused on the music, and as soon as possible on the results. As I write it, I'm hearing it and imagining it being performed.

When you were an undergraduate at Florida State University, what motivated you to move away from your original studies and become a composer?

Well, I was already writing, but when I went to university, the only major I knew of was music education, so that's what my major was. But I had already been writing music. I wrote for my high school band, for example. The gradual coming into focus of my musical life was like having a really good lens on a camera, and slowly sharpening the focus. When I was an undergraduate I was playing the trumpet, I was playing the violin, I was writing music, I was singing in a *collegium musica*, I was doing anything musical that wasn't nailed down.

I remember, I was playing violin in a Bartok quartet, and I was also playing trumpet in a jazz band, and there were people on both sides of the aisle, so to speak, each saying I shouldn't be doing the other. This never made sense to me. Through it all, I was always writing and I ultimately changed my major to composition in my second year, after I realized it was actually possible to *do* that as a major.

You work with a lot of student composers. Have you seen any changes in young composers over time, or are they still basically the same beast as they were in your student years?

Well, it's an odd beast and it's pretty much the same beast. I don't think we live in the age of the protégé. For example, Mozart evolved into a much deeper, more wonderful composer as an adult than he was at 10, but he was still pretty darn good at 10. If you have an existing style that everybody sort of takes for granted and works within, then that's the era of the protégé.

In the era we live in, we are exposed to so many different styles of music and we have so many different types of music at our beck and call, and we also have so many different experiences as a listener, composer, or performer, that this is not the age where you are going to be "ripe" at 18. I think people are approaching 30 at least before they really get a unique voice. So my main thing in working with young composers is that I try not to get in their way. It can be very difficult to predict who is going to do what.

How do you advise young composers to find and develop their unique voice?

I think it's important for young composers to try out everything that is available, but real composing is more about finding your own voice, following your heart as a musician rather than trying to go for whatever is the flavor of the moment. How you compose really depends on what you love. For example, if you are interested in electronic music, it's a wonderful time to be writing; there is just some incredibly interesting stuff going on. There are so many interesting possibilities now, with live instruments and electronic modification, for example. There is just a wonderful opening up of that field. Again, it depends on what the composer wants. I mean, nobody told me to be most interested in instrumental music. I just *am* most interested in that. It's what I love. We make our own voice by following our heart and the things that we are drawn to intellectually, emotionally, soulfully, kinesthetically. That individual, personal line is incredibly important. All of these influences are in our music and we have to go where our totality as a music lover takes us.

You are an extremely prolific and successful composer. Do you have any advice for young composers trying to deal with both the challenge of leading a creative life and the reality of having to make a living?

I almost hate to tell young composers my own story, which involved holding three jobs, getting my degree, and writing music while riding the cross-town bus. It is certainly a very difficult thing to balance out. Oddly, though, I found that many of the things I did just to make ends meet ended up providing a real advantage in my work. In my early years in New York, I was teaching music appreciation at a college. It was a course I was probably a bit overqualified to teach and yet it turned out to be an important experience. The students were great, but they had absolutely no experience with classical music at all. I had to learn how to talk to them and communicate the things I thought were really meaningful without debasing the subject. This was before the whole "Meet the Composer"[5] business came about and it turned out to be a wonderful experience that I was able to call on later.

There are situations where people can find a way to bring in income that frees them from those types of financial obligations, but they are rare and usually don't come when you most need them. It really comes down to doing whatever you have to do, and to your level of commitment. It's not so much *making* a commitment as finding out whether you are able to stop.

What about all of your music that can be heard without charge, without royalties being paid, on the Internet? Does that concern you?

I leave this up to my publishers and record companies. While I understand that YouTube is now paying royalties, it seems to me that there is a balance between getting a piece "out there" and having copyright control. After all, people could always go into a library and check out a score or recording and the composer didn't get paid. So I don't think it makes much difference in making a living as a composer.

Do you feel that digital technology has changed the artistic landscape? Has it had a great impact on "art music," or your music in particular?

The most exciting emerging technologies, to me, are the ones that marry live performance and digital technology. The creation of new instruments that do that is of particular interest to me. At every important juncture in musical technology, some people were upset and predicted dire consequences, for example, the Player Piano would mark the end of live piano playing; the recording would overtake live performance, et cetera. None of the dire predictions came true; in fact, just the opposite happened. For example, as recordings boomed in the mid-twentieth century, more people, not fewer, were exposed to music, to good performances, and to more kinds of music, and the musical level of performance rose significantly in places far from traditional musical centers. I expect the same kind of flowering (we're already seeing it) in our digital age. To me, it's all about new doors opening—you don't have to walk through every last one of them, but some of them will make a huge difference to you, and each one offers a new contribution to our musical world. And sometimes there is a surprise benefit. For example, since the advent of MIDI, I have become more acutely aware of how important the bodily elements of performance—breathing, pulse-like rubato, all of the kinesthetic elements—are to me. I had asked myself, "What is it about the MIDI in my computer that turns me off?" and my answers to my question deepened my understanding of what matters most to me.

You are so busy with performances and other obligations, are you able to compose every day? Is that even something you try to do?

A good thing that I've had in my life for a number of years is that my time is available to myself, both for those days where I sit for 10 or 12 hours composing and for those days that I just sit and look at a blank page. I have the freedom to go at my own pace, whatever that might be for any given day. I don't have a set pattern. I have always envied those writers who get up, say, at 7:00 in the morning, have a cup of coffee, go for a walk, write until noon, then stop for lunch and work again; I have never lived an orderly life like that.

That makes me feel better about my own work habits! What about deadlines? Do they help or hurt?

Oh, I love a deadline. In fact one of the things I feed into my psyche is a picture of the performers on the stage, maybe the New York Philharmonic Orchestra, and they are all looking out at me in the audience as if to say, "Where's our music?"

A good deadline is inspiring to me. I personally aim to be ready early because I never know what might come up that might delay the process and I hate the idea of writing the second movement while the performers are rehearsing the first one. That is more stress than I am equipped for.

I also love a commission. Not only is it something that enables me to take the time to write a piece, but it is also someone else's commitment to it. I particularly like a consortium commission because that ensures performances. It is a terrible shame for performers to go through all the effort to learn a piece, to master not just the notes but the style, the ideas, the persona of the piece, and then not to have more than one opportunity to play it.

Your music is performed a great deal; audiences, conductors, and musicians seem to really enjoy hearing and performing your pieces. That must be very gratifying.

That's the most fun of all. Getting that feedback, hearing your music played by wonderful performers. I have really lucked out with that. I have been very, very fortunate. Of course, it's funny that when we work really, really hard, and give 150 percent, and make sure that every little thing is just exactly as we want it to be, and we work, and we work, and we work . . . If, after all of that, everything comes off really well, if we're smart, we say, "Boy am I lucky!" rather than, "I've earned this."

Commedia dell'Arte (2012), Violin and String Orchestra
Quintet (2010), Violin, Viola, Cello, Contrabass, and Piano
Septet (2008), Piano Trio and String Quartet
Symphony No. 5, Concerto for Orchestra (2008)
Rituals (2003), Five Percussionists and Orchestra
Concerto for Clarinet and Orchestra (2002)
Symphony No. 4, The Gardens (1999), Mixed Chorus, Children's
    Chorus, and Orchestra
Concerto for Violin and Orchestra (1997)
Symphony No.3 (1992), Orchestra
Concerto for Bassoon and Orchestra (1992)
Symphony No. 2, Cello Symphony (1985), Orchestra
Symphony No. 1, Three Movements for Orchestra (1982), Orchestra

▶ To learn more about Ellen Taaffe Zwilich and her music, including program notes on her "Quintet," "Septet," and "Symphony No.5," visit www.oup.com/us/compositioninthedigitalworld.

NOTES
1. Nadja Salerno-Sonnenberg is an Italian-born violinist. She studied at the Curtis Institute and the Juilliard School.
2. Leopold Stokowski (1882–1977) was a British-born conductor who led numerous (primarily American) orchestras, and appeared in several films, including Walt Disney's *Fantasia*.
3. Ned Rorem is an American composer who won the Pulitzer Prize (1976), and has written extensively about music and the arts, and his personal relationships with other composers, including Samuel Barber, Leonard Bernstein, and Virgil Thompson.
4. Thelonious Monk (1917–1982) is considered one of the greatest jazz composers and pianists of all time.
5. Meet the Composer was formed in 1974 with a mission of supporting composers. In 2011 it merged with the American Music Center to form New Music USA.

Steve Reich

If you expect that the music you are writing is going to outlive you, if that is of the slightest interest to you, then the indications of that in your lifetime are as I said, two: First, the musical community, not everybody of course, but a large chunk of the musical community respects and likes what you've written and likes to play it; and second, they like to play it because the audiences they are playing to seem to enjoy listening to it. Those are two basic, human, musical realities and they will always be the case as long as we survive on this planet.

Whether referred to as "our greatest living composer" [*New York Times*] or "the most original music thinker of our time" [*The New Yorker*], Steve Reich (b. New York, 1936) is widely acknowledged as one of the most influential and revolutionary of contemporary American composers. Over decades of evolution, his music has journeyed from the experimental fringe to the mainstream of our culture's musical language, where it has forever altered the way we compose, perform, and hear music.

A long-standing admirer, I was greatly looking forward to our interview, only to have it begin on a most disastrous note: I missed it. I had written down the wrong date for our conversation. I was mortified and dreading our rescheduled interview, but he could not have been more congenial, and we were soon sharing memories of living in New York City and comparing notes on music education and composing. His comments came in rapid fire, as if verbalizing ideas is too slow and inefficient a method for communicating all that he means to say.

Raised in New York and California, Reich graduated with honors in philosophy from Cornell and studied composition at Juilliard and at Mills College. Rather than pursuing an academic career, he studied African drumming techniques in Ghana and experimented with tape recorders and phasing, which led to the development of his compositional language and his place as a pioneer of minimalism.

His numerous honors include two Grammy Awards (1989 and 1998), a Pulitzer Prize (2009), and membership in the American Academy of Arts and Letters. Not one to rest on these or any of his many other laurels, Reich continues to explore ever more original compositional forms, techniques, and instrumental combinations. Steve Reich remains at the forefront of contemporary American music, where he is captivating a whole new generation of musicians and audiences.

With the many demands on your time brought about by your success, this interview being an example, how do you find the time to continue composing? It must be difficult.

You're quite right. In some ways it may be harder to be successful than to be unsuccessful. For 40 years from 1966 to 2006, I ran my own ensemble, Steve Reich and Musicians, and although I had people helping me, there was an irreducible minimum of my time devoted to being involved in that. Now I've put that aside because I just can't manage that along with everything else. Obviously, everybody wants to be recognized and appreciated, but there's no free lunch. Part of my decision to move out of New York City was to remove myself from that constant flow of obligations. If I want to get work done, my best situation is to be in Vermont.

In what ways does living away from a major city affect your writing?

Well, it's simple: Less distraction means more time to write. One of the major centers for music in the world is New York City, and my whole career has been tied into that—still is—but to get work done, it is sometimes good to be as far away from that center as possible, to be some place where there is literally nothing going on. Many composers, including myself, have been attracted to that, and use it. It's an old tradition for composers to find a place to work out in the country.

Since the very beginning of your career as a composer you've embraced technology, and continue to do so. Several of your recent pieces incorporate the use of pre-recorded material in live performance, such as 2X5,[1] Double Sextet,[2] and WTC 9/11.[3] Are there particular technical challenges when working with pre-recorded elements plus live musicians in performance?
There is an important difference between pre-recorded non-musical sound like speech and pre-recorded musical parts played against in performance—like in 2X5 or Double Sextet. To me, the most interesting use of pre-recording and music is to use speech, as in Different Trains, The Cave, Three Tales, and, most recently, in WTC 9/11, which uses real pre-recorded speech material. The other pieces that use pre-recorded musical parts are better played live; I don't really like to hear them played with tape. I'd much rather hear Double Sextet played with 12 performers, as it usually is by the way. For 2X5, it's harder to find 10 players but it's much better that way. The only musical pieces that benefit from being played back from tape are the counterpart pieces. All of them. And Triple Quartet is better using tape and live players as well.

Why do you prefer to hear some of your pieces played with a recorded part and some with all live players?
The combination of tape and live has been going on forever and, in some cases, it is musically a benefit to play a piece that way, in all of the counterpoint pieces, for example. Vermont Counterpoint and New York Counterpoint are very commonly played all live at schools because they always have a lot of clarinetists and a lot of flute players, and they think, "Wow, isn't it wonderful to be able to play this piece live?" It isn't wonderful; it's always a mess. It's hard to get a really focused sound. The performance is never as good as a single player playing against a pre-recording of themselves, having made their own tape, or even using a rented tape from Boosey & Hawkes [Reich's publisher]. Those counterpoint works were meant to be recital pieces for soloists, where the attention is riveted on the single player, and if the live player plays the piece correctly, then the ensemble will be spot on. So psychologically, psycho-acoustically, and in terms of musical performance, it's better to have one player and a pre-recording.

Is that also true of a piece like the _Double Sextet_?

In the case of the _Double Sextet_, I simply couldn't write for their [ensemble eighth blackbird][4] instrumentation as it stands; I'd have to double the size of the ensemble so as to get all these unison canons that are the backbone of my music, and have been since _It's Gonna Rain_,[5] though if you heard _It's Gonna Rain_ and _Double Sextet_, you probably wouldn't think it was the same composer. In the case of eighth blackbird, they would much rather play _Double Sextet_ live. When they tour, and in particular if they are performing at a school, they will arrange to arrive a day or two early and play with three members of their ensemble and three students on one side, and three and three on the other side, because they would rather play it with all live performers. _Double Sextet_ is much, much better as a live piece. When they do play with a recording, the only difficulty is in hearing the playback. They have monitor speakers on the stage, and they have to go in before the performance and tweak the position of the monitor speakers, or perhaps the mix in the speakers, and it takes time to make sure that each player hears what he wants to hear. Of course, eighth blackbird travels with their own engineer, as do most good 21st-century chamber ensembles in the United States and Europe.

Is it common practice for modern ensembles to have their own sound engineer?

Bang on a Can[6] have their own engineer, Ensemble Modern[7] in Frankfurt have their own engineers, London Sinfonietta[8] in London have their own engineers. This is part of 21st-century performance practice. If you are using live musicians and playing with pre-recordings or electronic accompaniment that has to be done in a real situation, then you have to have an engineer who is part of the ensemble who is doing that, or you will end up with a mess and will have no control over what's happening. Kronos Quartet[9] started to perform this way and _Different Trains_ is what encouraged them to do just that, and now most of their repertoire involves electronics and live performance.

If the composers who are reading this book simply write for the orchestra all the time, well fine. I don't do that because for me it would be bad orchestration, I don't need it. I don't want 18 firsts and 16 seconds; I want one first, and one second so I can have the clarity that comes with having one or two players to a part, or at most, three players to a part. More than that, and the sound becomes thick and fat, and is inappropriate for my music. It would be like hearing Bach played in a Stokowski arrangement; the notes are there, they work, but it feels overinflated. You want to hear that music the way Bach intended.

You seem to truly embrace new technology while at the same time keeping it in the service of your art.

I think a lot of people are doing a lot of good music with electronics, and I think we are going to see a lot more of that. The influence of dance, house rock and electronic dance music and other types of popular music that really involve electronics—where these electronics really come from—is infiltrating more and more into the world of classical music or, as I prefer to categorize it, "notated" versus "non-notated" music. A lot of today's musicians are conservatory trained and they can read anything you put in front of them, but they also are genuine rock and rollers. Bryce Dessner [the National] went to Yale, Mark Stewart [Bang on a Can] came out of Eastman, Jonny Greenwood [Radiohead] went to Oxford, and of course they're also genuine rock stars. These are all people who are completely at home with technology; they don't even think about it. The use of technology in modern music is not the vision of some money-grubbing record producer who wants to make a crossover record; that's over and done with. Now we see a generation of musicians who *are* conservatory trained, and who like rock and want to play it.

Technology plays an integral part in your compositions, as opposed to being an afterthought or a gimmick.

I understand what you're getting at. You want to use technology because you have a musical *idea*. For instance, in the early 1970s, I was interested in slowing down a recording so you could [exaggerates pronunciation of the words] r-r-r-r-really hear every vowel as a glissando. I also wanted to do the sound equivalent of a freeze-frame in a stop-action film, where you might say, "They came from Bost-*on*," and the last syllable would be held indefinitely. Unfortunately, at that time, you couldn't do that; if you slowed down a tape you got [drops pitch of voice dramatically] Darth Vader. So I published this idea as a conceptual piece, in my book *Writings on Music 1965–2000*,[10] and lo and behold, with the development of computers, by the time we got to 2002, this concept was realizable. And I have subsequently used that idea. It was a very important part of *WTC 9/11*, where the last syllable of each speaker is sustained and leads to the next speaker. This is a case where I had an idea and used the technology to realize that idea—and I could not have done it any other way.

What I don't think is so good as a general practice is for someone to buy a piece of software and say, "Let's see what this thing can do and maybe I'll make a piece out of it." Maybe someone could come up with something worthwhile that way, but I think the odds are against it. They're more likely to come up with something that might be considered a gimmick.

In the '80s, there were the samplers, in the '90s the notation programs. Are there any new technologies that are particularly exciting to you right now?

In my studio right now I have an upright piano; I also have an electronic keyboard right next to my computer, because it doesn't go out of tune [laughs]; I have a Mac Retina, 15" MacPro, which is a fantastic machine, I have a 27" monitor. I also use Sibelius, which I think anyone reading this book will either use, or at least be familiar with. I don't like the samples in Sibelius; they're a little too 19th century for me, so I work with samples that I made myself. I use a software sampler called Reason,[11] which people might know. Sibelius triggers the score and it can be played back via Reason. I can be on an airplane with headphones on and hear a MIDI mockup of what I'm working on.

Do you sketch and develop all of your ideas on the computer?

I still use my music notebooks to work out the basic harmonies for whatever I'm doing in music notation, using pencil and paper. It's sitting right on top of my electric keyboard by my computer, so I'm back and forth with all of that. I'm in the generation that started out with pencil and paper and ended up with computers, but in the middle, I was using multi-track tape. *Drumming* and *Music for 18 Musicians* were created using multi-track tape to overdub myself drumming or singing, playing everything myself. If I couldn't play a certain instrument, a violin or cello, for example, I'd use a cheap synthesizer to sort of mock that up. Even *Tehillim* has a version with me singing all four women's voices, recorded at 7.5 ips [tape speed] and played back at 15 ips, so it's affectionately known as the chipmunk version [laughs]. And I sent this to Péter Eötvös,[12] a very distinguished, excellent conductor who worked with Stockhausen, and he said yes, it was funny, but it also was helpful because it gave him an idea of how I wanted the piece to go.

You sometimes provide computer or tape demos for conductors and performers who are learning a new piece?

Whenever I write a new piece, the musicians are sent a mockup along with their parts, even if it's through Boosey & Hawkes, my publishers. In the old days it was an overdubbed tape; now it's a MIDI mockup, but they always get something that they can play against when they are practicing on their own, just to give them some idea of the context, of what will be going on around them. So when they get to rehearsal, it's almost as if they have had a rehearsal or two before they start the real rehearsals.

Right before you wrote *Radio Rewrite*, you worked on a large piece that you were ultimately unhappy with. You said it was "flat, inelegant, a mess." What advice do you have for a young composer who has invested a lot of time in a piece, but finds it is just not working? Do you put it aside, work on something else for a while, struggle with it?

Trash it!

OK, well that's to the point [both laugh].

Did you always have a strong conviction, a belief in what you were doing as a composer? You've said you were ridiculed while in school for not wanting to compose 12-tone music.

Well, while I was at Juilliard (1958–61), most composers there were still finishing up Americana; it was very conservative. But I went to the library, to concerts. I heard Luciano Berio at the New School. I knew what was going on; it was clear that Juilliard was way behind the times. So the last piece I wrote while I was at Juilliard was my first 12-tone piece, but the way I dealt with the 12-tone row was to never invert it, never retrograde it, never transpose it, just repeat it! When I first went out to California to study with Berio, I showed that piece to him and he said, "Well, if you want to write tonal music, why don't you write tonal music?" He was a very flexible, sweet, non-doctrinaire type of guy; he was interested in jazz, in what was going on.

In that era, in the academic world at least, writing music other than 12-tone was generally frowned upon.

At that time, from about the late 1950s into the early '70s, to not write 12-tone music—or more correctly, serial music—was to be considered a fool. Really. It was so powerful an influence that even the titan of the age—Igor Stravinsky—felt obliged to try his hand at it. He may have used rows that had less than 12 tones and were more tonal, but he still got involved in the technique, and he produced masterpieces like *Agon* and *Canticum Sacrum*. As another example, and this is just my own personal theory, Aaron Copland wrote *Connotations* and, obviously, it wasn't the most wonderful Copland ever written, and I think he knew that. On the one hand, he couldn't write *Appalachian Spring* again, but he also knew he wasn't the kind of guy to write 12-tone music, so instead he began to just conduct and perform and give talks, and he stopped composing. There was just a huge musical-political impact from Boulez, Stockhausen, and even Cage in a way. Of course, Cage used a different way of getting there, but the result of his music was identical: no fixed pulse, no harmonic center, no melodic material that any postman could whistle, ever, and if you didn't write that way, you were not taken seriously to put it kindly. So I really began to get into what I was doing once I got *out* of Mills College, once I got my M.A. from Berio.

And you were listening to and influenced by many other styles of music in addition to the established "classical" repertoire?
There were a lot of things in the air at that time. Back in 1961 John Coltrane recorded *Africa/Brass*, which was 16 or 17 minutes on E. That sounds impossible. So what did he do? He had incredible melodic invention on the soprano saxophone, sometimes playing beautiful melodic material and sometimes just screaming through the instrument. Eric Dolphy was part of the project and he arranged all of the brass, including the French horns with glissandos that sounded like elephants coming through the jungle. Rhythmically, there was Elvin Jones, who is like having two or three drummers playing at the same time. So, if you have rhythmic complexity, you have timbral variety, and you have melodic invention, then you can stay on E for 17 minutes and end up with something successful. That's a real lesson, and I learned a great deal from it. If you look at my piece *Drumming*, that is exactly what it is: It's an hour on F-sharp major, with changes of timbre from drums to marimbas to glockenspiel, and incredible rhythmic complexity, and melodic resulting patterns coming out of all this rhythmic interlocking.

Also, speaking about the middle1960s and on, there was a great interest in Eastern music. Many people from the Beatles to Phil Glass to Terry Riley got involved with Indian music. Being a drummer, I got involved in Western African drumming and Balinese gamelan, because those two cultures are the place where the percussion is the dominant voice in the orchestra, as opposed to the strings, which are the dominant voice in our orchestra. So non-Western music was a real source of compositional ideas, not just an exotic sound, but how to organize music in repeating patterns interlocking in different ways, which is highly developed in West African drumming and in Balinese gamelan.

Jazz and what might be called "world" music today were big influences for you?
Influences were also coming from pop music: Junior Walker came out of Motown with a song called *Shotgun*, where the bass line just repeats without change; there's no release, no contrasting sound section. This was unique. Most pop material songs are basically ABA: you have a release, a bridge or something, so the tension that built up in *Shotgun* was enormous,

and it really gave the sense of something brand new. So, harmonic stasis, either staying put harmonically or moving very slowly, was in the air: It was in the air in Motown, it was in the air in Indian music, it was there in African and Balinese music. It was there in Pérotin[13] and 11th-century organum, in which I had a great interest. The music had long-held tenor notes, which are, if you will, the harmonic center of long chunks of the music before they change. It's this hugely augmented melodic line, which becomes not drones, but very long-held harmonies. So the idea of harmonic rhythm becoming extremely slow or actually having harmonic stasis is an idea that is coming at people from many, many different sources in the middle '60s, and that had a big effect on what I did once I got out of school.

You've said that non-jazz composers who continuously try to write a jazz piece end up nowhere because they are pretending to be something they are not. How would you advise young composers to go about finding their own unique voice?
Find your own voice? God knows. [Laughs]

Finding your own voice is writing something that you love to hear again; once you've written it you have to keep going back to listen to it again, and again. You'd rather hear it than the greatest music of the past, even if you know it's not as good. In other words, write what you really want to hear, what really moves you. And acquire the techniques necessary to do that by going to a good conservatory, a good music program. It's important to go to a music school where there are performers. You might go to a university where you sit around and *talk* about music until you're blue in the face, and you won't really learn anything. But if you are at a good school with a conservatory attached to it, you can go down to the lunchroom and put together a string quartet and write for them. And that's how you will learn how to do what you need to do. By writing as much as possible while you are a student, you will gradually evolve—probably not while you are actually a student, but shortly thereafter—you will begin to emerge with your own voice. You will find your own voice if you do what *you* want to do, and not just follow what is already being done. As a student, you are obliged to imitate to learn how a canon is written, how did Bach do the chorales, what is sonata allegro form, species counterpoint, and on and on. All the basics you need to know as a composer; it's very important. But at some point, when you feel reasonably fluent—you'll never master everything, you'll die needing to learn new techniques—you should start gravitating toward the music that you like, the music that most interests you. Then start developing your particular voice in that direction.

There seems to be a huge opening up of styles that interest today's student-composers.

When I was in school, maybe when you were in school as well, there was one way to write music: Boulez/Stockhausen/Cage. Take it or leave it. Now, when I'm asked to speak with students, I usually play them a piece of mine on tape and I show them the score. Then we start talking and I'll go around and ask them what they are doing and one kid might say, "I'm into neoromanticism, and I like John Adams, I'm getting into Sibelius," the next one might be interested in my music, or Terry Riley and Arvo Pärt, and the next is doing house and electronic dance music, and in every case the instructor is saying, "Well, isn't that nice, isn't that interesting?" Anything goes. One could scratch one's head and say, "Who's got it easier?" People like you and me who went to music school and were up against the wall in terms of learning to compose in one way, or students today who are essentially out on the ice, they can slide and slip and go anywhere. Frankly, I think in many ways, with all the problems, I think we had it easier. Right now we are in a very polyglot situation educationally. In the end, all that really matters is how well, how convincingly, you do what you do.

Your music and that of your peers has had a tremendous influence on today's young composers.

In the English-speaking world, here in America, in the U.K., in Canada and Australia, the kind of music I did and Riley did and Glass, Adams, and Pärt did, holds sway. It's really been the dominant direction. It's already sustained through a second generation, the "Bang on a Can generation," with David Lang, Julia Wolfe, and Michael Gordon; and now we are into a third generation. Look at Nico Muhly;[14] he's only in his early 30s. And I feel very good about that, that the kind of music I was involved in beginning has really taken root and has already produced three generations of composers, and I suspect that there will be many more. Why? Because it's based on musical basics, not necessarily functional harmony a la Mozart, but as Stravinsky said "poles of harmonic attraction." This is, I think, the dominant voice in "notated music" in the Western world today. There are some very fine, very learned composers in Europe who are still beating on their chest and [raises pitch of voice] *screaming!* about the angst of it all. I respect them, but I don't really want to listen to their music. I think it's going to be like Schoenberg, Webern, Boulez, and Stockhausen: it's really music for a dark corner. It's something you want once in a while, but not something you listen to every day. There's a stylistic division between English-speaking countries and the European world, and I'm an American.

That supports the idea that if musicians want to play your music, and audiences want to hear your music, you have succeeded.
Yes, I think that is absolutely the case. I'd call to witness Johann Sebastian Bach, Joseph Haydn, Ludwig Beethoven, Wolfgang Amadeus Mozart, and on and on, as examples of music that musicians like to play and audiences like to hear. If it's good for them it just might be good for you and me too. It doesn't mean you have to be on the hit parade [chuckles], but if you expect that the music you are writing is going to outlive you, if that is of the slightest interest to you, then the indications of that in your lifetime are as I said, two: First, the musical community, not everybody of course, but a large chunk of the musical community respects and likes what you've written and likes to play it; and second, they like to play it because the audiences they are playing to seem to enjoy listening to it. Those are two basic, human, musical realities and they will always be the case as long as we survive on this planet.

You've recently composed a piece for rock band instrumentation [2X5].
I wrote *ONE* piece like that, and I don't anticipate writing any others with that instrumentation. In fact, one of the things people miss about my music is that I never write for the same ensemble twice. And I've never written for a conventional ensemble, except for the orchestra pieces— which, truth be told, are not the greatest pieces I've ever written. I have to invent my ensemble: Instrumentation is my inspiration. *Double Sextet* is an ensemble of my own devising; *2X5* is an ensemble of my own devising; *Different Trains* is another ensemble, it's not a string quartet. I can't write for a string quartet: Where's the other viola? I want to have two violas interlocking. Where's the other cello? I need another cello. So I've never written for string quartet and I probably never will. Same with woodwind quintet; I just don't have any interest in doing that.

You don't typically orchestrate a piece after it's been composed then; the instrumentation is a part of the compositional process.
For me, the choice of instruments really sets up what will happen in the piece. Always, one of the major jobs I have is determining what my instrumentation will be. For example, people may refer to *The Cave* as my opera, but it isn't just mine, it's Beryl Korot[15] and Steve Reich, and it isn't really an opera in terms of traditional opera and operatic voices, though it is definitely a piece of music theater.

So *2X5* is a one-off, I don't think I will ever write again for electric guitar. The electric bass, however, I love. The first decision I made for *2X5* was that the drummer wouldn't keep time, he would just come in from time to time and the timekeeper, the rhythm section, would be the electric bass and the piano.

You've recently written a piece inspired by two songs of the British rock band Radiohead.
I also used the electric bass in *Radio Rewrite*. It's the only rock instrument in that piece, standing beside flute, clarinet, string quartet, two pianos, two vibes, and one electric bass. I think *Radio Rewrite* works very well. It's very satisfying, and I think it will be a piece of great general appeal. I know the musicians enjoy playing it! They just performed the first three movements up at the Guggenheim as part of their "Works in Progress" series.

I understand your newest piece is a quartet; can you talk about that new work that's in progress?
Yes, it's a quartet for two vibes and two pianos for Colin Currie[16] and his friends, and I'm about halfway through it. It's a hard piece to talk about, because in a way its atypical for me; it doesn't have constant motoric rhythms, it's *constantly* modulating. I feel like I'm feeling my way through this piece. It's very different and a little bit more complex than anything else I've done. I'm sure some people will think it's really, really interesting, and others will think, "Ugh. What else is new?" [Laughs]

I think it will be a little bit of a surprise for many people, and that's good too.

SELECTED WORKS OF STEVE REICH

WTC 9/11 (2010), String Quartet and Pre-Recorded Voices and Strings, or Three String Quartets and Pre-Recorded Voices
Double Sextet (2007), Ensemble or Ensemble and Pre-Recorded Tape
You Are (Variations) (2004), Amplified Ensemble and Voices
Triple Quartet (1998), Amplified String Quartet and Pre-Recorded Tape, or Three String Quartets, or String Orchestra
Proverb (1995), Voices and Ensemble
Different Trains (1988), String Quartet and Tape
Electric Counterpoint (1987), Electric Guitar, Amplified Acoustic Guitar, and Tape, or Amplified Guitar Soloist and Tape, or Guitar Ensemble
Sextet (1984), Percussion and Keyboards
The Desert Music (1984), Amplified Voices and Woodwinds, Orchestra

Tehillim (1981), Voices and Ensemble (Amplified Woodwinds, Voices and Strings)

Music for 18 Musicians (1974–1976), Amplified Ensemble and Voices

Drumming (1970–1971), Amplified Ensemble and Voices

⊙ To learn more about Steve Reich and his music, visit www.oup.com/us/compositioninthedigitalworld.

NOTES

1. *2X5* (2008) is scored for electric guitar, electric bass, keyboards, drums, and pre-recorded tape. The piece can also be performed with two quintets of the same instrumentation minus the pre-recorded material.
2. *Double Sextet* won the 2009 Pulitzer Prize for Music.
3. *WTC 9/11* premiered 2011 by the Kronos Quartet. The piece uses pre-recorded dialogue related to the events of September 11, 2001.
4. The contemporary music sextet eighth blackbird is known for commissioning and performing contemporary works.
5. *It's Gonna Rain* was composed in 1965 and is a seminal minimalist work. Using recordings of a preacher's looped speech and street sounds, two tape decks were slightly out of sync on playback creating phase shifting. Mr. Reich exploited this phase phenomenon in this piece and expanded upon it on others that would follow, to great compositional effect.
6. Bang on a Can is based in New York and was formed in 1987 by Michael Gordon, David Lang, and Julia Wolfe. The organization presents concerts and recordings featuring new American art music.
7. Based in Frankfurt, Germany, Ensemble Modern is a chamber ensemble formed in 1980 in order to perform and support contemporary music.
8. Formed in 1968, the London Sinfonietta is an English chamber orchestra dedicated to the performance and promotion of contemporary classical music.
9. The Kronos Quartet, formed in 1978, has won numerous awards, including a Grammy (2004), and is know for its superb performances and support of contemporary art music.
10. *Writings on Music 1965–2000* (2004) by Steve Reich (Author), Paul Hillier (Editor). Oxford University Press.
11. Reason is a Swedish computer music software program that provides a digital emulation of a music studio.
12. Péter Eötvös is a Hungarian composer, conductor, and educator and was part of the Notre Dame School of polyphony.
13. Pérotin was a European composer from the early 13th century.
14. Nico Muhly is a contemporary American composer who works with both rock and classical musicians.
15. Beryl Korot is a pioneering video artist, Guggenheim Fellow, and the spouse of Steve Reich. The couple collaborated on *The Cave* (1993) and *Three Tales* (2002).
16. Colin Currie is a Scottish percussionist. In 2010, his recording of Jennifer Higdon's *Percussion Concerto* won a Grammy.

Christopher Rouse

Photo Credit: Jeffrey Herman

Everything seems to be geared toward "making it in the business" and a glib answer like, "Write good music" is not what students are looking for. They want a 10-step program as to how to be a success in this business. It's worrisome. If you are going into composing with the intent of making a financial success of it, you are probably better off going into commercial music, if you have the chops for it. I've been incredibly fortunate, but certainly you don't pursue a career in concert music for financial gain. You have to do it because you love it and are impelled to do it, and you may well find success if your music is good enough.

By his own account, Christopher Rouse (b. Maryland, 1949) first became interested in music by listening to rock and roll, including Little Richard and Elvis Presley. Then his mother gave him a recording of Beethoven's *Symphony No.5* and he was set on his life's path: to be a composer.

I had expected that Rouse might be formal and reserved for our interview, but instead found him to be extremely affable, earthy, and unpretentious. Our conversation quickly grew animated as we discovered a mutual love not only of classical music but also of classic rock and roll.

Rouse studied at Oberlin and Cornell universities. His teachers included Karel Husa and George Crumb. Recognized by the BMI Student Composer Awards when he was only 23 years old, he has since received innumerable prestigious awards, including election to the American Academy of Arts and Letters, the Kennedy Center's Friedheim Award, a Grammy Award, and the Pulitzer Prize. He has taught at the University of Michigan, the Eastman School of Music, and now teaches at Juilliard. Rouse's term as the Marie-Josée Kravis Composer-in-Residence has been extended to a third year by the New York Philharmonic.

He is constantly working on new commissions and his works, lauded by musicians, composers, conductors, and audiences, have been performed by many of the world's greatest orchestras. Rouse personifies the heritage of the great orchestral composers; he is the quintessential combination of consummate craftsman and sublime artist. His music can in turns be violent, heartbreaking, invigorating, and comforting, but it always provokes an emotional and visceral response from his audience. He has secured a permanent place in the firmament of great composers.

Why don't we start by discussing your recent *Symphony No. 3*, how you came to compose the piece, and how the performances have been going. Please talk a bit about the process of composing this particular work.

There are two things I have to figure out at the very beginning when composing a new piece. The first is what the piece is trying to say or achieve on an expressive level. Second, what the overall form of the piece is. My first two symphonies were very intense and personal, so I decided this third symphony would be less autobiographical. In terms of the form, I looked at what I had done before. My first symphony was a one-movement symphony, in four connected parts, and my second was a pretty standard three-movement symphony. So in casting about for something different for this third one, I looked to Prokofiev's *Second Symphony*, my favorite of his symphonies, but one that is rarely played. That piece is in two movements, a pretty savage, ferocious, toccata-like opening movement, followed by a theme and variations. So I thought, "Well that is certainly an unusual form; I think I'll take a crack at it." I didn't want to actually quote too much from it, but I did want to refer to it. The Prokofiev starts with trumpet blasts on D, and his first movement is very loud and very harsh, and tends to scare people away. I decided to refer to that for my symphony, though for my purposes I needed an F, so up it goes a minor third. And then, at the end of the first movement there's an exact quote from a passage just for percussion near the end of his first movement that I put in at the end, as a sort of overt tip of the cap. Otherwise, I don't really quote anything from his symphony. So many of my pieces are consciously meant as "crypto-homages" to other composers, so this is my "Prokofiev piece." Although I don't use any of his notes, there are passages in the variations that are intentionally evocative of Prokofiev, and I think anyone familiar with his work would hear that connection.

So the form was the most important thing. And, since I don't sketch— well, I sketch mentally, but not on paper—when I felt I had enough of a sense of what each variation would be in the second movement and what I wanted from the piece, I just started to put it on paper.

I find it intriguing that you sketch your compositions mentally. So you visualize the piece rather than working it out on the piano or manuscript paper?
Well, I don't play the piano, so it isn't a very useful tool for me. Not being an instrumentalist of any kind, I really have to rely more on my inner ear. Berlioz said that when he got an idea, it was already an oboe melody, or a viola melody; and that is true for me as well. Ideas tend to occur to me already orchestrated, so when I hear it in my head, it is already inextricably linked to the scoring itself. I don't consider orchestration to be something that can be glommed on to an idea later; it is all part of the same process.

Have you ever personally experienced any prejudice for not being a pianist, or an instrumentalist?
I don't think people tend to care. There are some who say they don't understand how I can write for an instrument without being able to play it, but really it is just part of our job as composers. Even composers who do play an instrument still have to be able to hear the whole piece in their head.

Some composers have told me that they have started out to write an homage to a particular piece or composer and then found their own work overwhelmed by the original. Is that something you've encountered?
I can only say that it hasn't happened to me. But in my work, I may pay homage to a composer's entire body of work, not necessarily to one piece.

I can't imagine trying to do a new *Rite of Spring*, for example. That is Stravinsky's piece, his music. It came from where he was at the time, and the idea of redoing that seems ridiculous. I would even disagree that the definitive recording of *Rite of Spring* is Stravinsky's own recording that he did in the 1960s. I'd argue that he was, at that time, reinterpreting the music through the veil of a much older, neoclassical composer. It's really not at all what he put on the page in 1913. He emasculated it, made it very precise and underplayed the savagery of it. I think even he couldn't remember how it *felt* to write that piece 50 years earlier.

When I was a student studying privately with George Crumb,[1] I went through a period of writing a lot of "pseudo-Crumb" music. It took me several years to realize that what was working for him was not working for me. I had to sort of "de-Crumb" myself, find my own way.

What was it like to study composition with George Crumb?
He's a lovely, gentle soul, much like you would expect from listening to his music. The most educational conversations we had were about his music, and about music in general. He was always nurturing and supportive of whatever I was doing in my own music, so absolutely not a harsh critic as a teacher.

What do you advise your own students regarding finding their own musical voice?
I actually tell them not to worry about finding their own voice. If they are lucky, it will find them. I think most composers never really find a voice, or don't "get" a voice, and the more they hunt for it the more elusive it becomes. So I only advise them to listen to an enormous amount of music, because you may find inspiration, or an answer to a problem, in the work of a composer who isn't necessarily one of the big names. Some of the music that has had the biggest effect on me has come from lesser-known composers. I tell students, "Just listen to everything."

Do you agree that the Internet has allowed students to be exposed to a wider range of music than they might previously have been able to easily experience?
Yes, as long as they can hear it on decent speakers! If they are listening on generic computer speakers, they aren't getting a sense of the piece. It used to be that we heard music primarily through recordings, and before that it was only heard if it was played live. Of course, the opportunity in the 19th century to hear a live performance of a Brahms symphony, for example, was comparatively limited. People who wanted to hear it would likely have

to learn to play it in a piano reduction. So it has gotten easier and easier to hear different kinds of music, but that can be either a blessing or a curse; it really depends on what you do with it.

I look at your schedule and I'm struck by how incredibly busy you are. With all of your obligations as a very successful composer, how do you find time to continue composing?
Ha! Well, I wish I had more, but there it is. For one thing, I only do one piece a year. I don't work quickly, and I don't work on teaching days. I find that teaching is so energy-consuming and requires so much focus on the students' work that I can't then turn around later in the day and look at my own music. I say "no" to a lot of things, whether commissions or other requests, because I know enough about my own work habits to make sure to leave enough time to do the writing I've agreed to do.

Speaking of work habits, do you have a certain regimen or routine you like to follow when you work?
I can only compose at home. I have to feel that I am in very comfortable and familiar surroundings, so I always work in my living room: at a card table with a pad of music paper and a #2 lead pencil—so, the old-fashioned way. I usually work with the TV on, and almost always in the afternoon. It's rare that I work in the morning and I never work at night, so I'm generally a lunch-to-dinner composer. As I said, I don't work on teaching days, so the summer is my main time to get things done, when teaching is not an issue.

Do you use any of the new technological tools available today, such as computer notation programs or digital sound libraries?
I really don't. I use a pencil, paper, a straight-edged ruler. Well, actually, I have custom music paper made for me, but that is about it. Not too exciting.

It's said that some students can become seduced by all of the technological advancements available, to the detriment of the development of their ability to hear the sounds of instruments and the orchestra in their head.
It's true. With MIDI capabilities, you can just write any old thing and it will be played back to you. It does make it easier to not train your ear. Certainly, I have seen more than a few pieces that look fabulous on the page, the student has a beautiful printout and so forth, but you wonder

if they are really hearing any of it and if they have an ear good enough to judge its quality. That's the cursed side of the technology.

It is definitely a boon in terms of editing. If you want to change something, take out a measure or whatnot, it's not like the old days of engraving. For example, in my third symphony I removed a measure and I added a measure to the last movement. Usually I don't do any revising, but in this case I did. And the computer made that task easy! If the score has been engraved, that sort of change is horrible. Computer programs undoubtedly make that a much happier process for everyone concerned.

Personally, I use computer music programs, but I prefer to create my initial sketches with pencil and paper. For me, it's much faster than composing directly to the computer because I have my own shorthand.
Yes! There is the speed issue. A lot of people think it is faster to use a computer, but it's not necessarily. I still like the feeling of holding that implement and pressing the note into the page. I like that physical, tactile kind of relationship with the music rather than moving a mouse around, clicking, and seeing something appear on a monitor. To me, that just doesn't appeal.

Do you see a different mindset in today's students compared to when you were in school?
Certainly, today's students all use laptops or computers, and they all know how to use computer music programs, Sibelius [computer music notation program] or what have you. That technological savvy is an absolute must now. No publisher is going to give the time of day to young composers who don't submit their music as computer files. My publishers are patient with me and allow me to send a written manuscript that they then have converted into computer files. But for composers just starting out, it's mandatory that they know how to use current digital technology or they won't get a foot in the door. On a more general note, I think the overall education level is not as good now as it was, and I also see a disturbing lack of intellectual curiosity. Everything seems to be geared toward "making it in the business" and a glib answer like "write good music" is not what students are looking for. They want a 10-step program as to how to be a success in this business. It's worrisome. If you are going into composing with the intent of making a financial success of it, you are probably better off going into commercial music, if you have the chops for it. I've been incredibly fortunate, but certainly you don't pursue a career in concert music for

financial gain. You have to do it because you love it and are impelled to do it, and you may well find success if your music is good enough.

Do you believe that if the music is good enough, if the talent is there, it will be discovered and appreciated? Or are there wonderful composers out there who will never be heard due to lack of promotional savvy or social skills?

I have come over time to agree with Bill Schuman, who said years ago that it is extremely unlikely that there is some great, unwashed master out in the middle of nowhere and that the cream will "rise to the top," so to speak. I don't think I believed that at the time, but I have found that the composers who are becoming successful are the ones writing the best music. It isn't because of all their networking or because they are sucking up to the right people. Of course, there's a happy medium. You can't just hide in the shadows and hope someone discovers you, but neither is it all right to shove your music in everybody's face. There's nothing wrong with networking, with meeting people, going to concerts, seizing an opportunity that presents itself. But I think it is better to let people who can help you ask for your music, and then let the music speak for itself.

I'm interested in how you made the transition from being a rock drummer to becoming a concert composer.

It's funny, but I don't know how that story got started. I was never a drummer in a rock band. [Laughs] The only connection I had to rock drumming was a piece I wrote called *Bonham*, a reference to John Bonham, the drummer for the rock band Led Zeppelin. I did play some percussion when I was in school, but I was never a drummer.

Well, that particular legend is dashed! But I must say, *Bonham* is a wonderful piece of music. I believe you taught a course surveying the history of rock, didn't you? Do you think it's unusual for a contemporary concert composer to openly enjoy popular music, especially rock?

I don't think it is unusual for a composer to be interested in the vernacular music of his time; a lot of my teachers were very knowledgeable about jazz. Rock was the music I grew up with, and certainly with the Beatles, the Rolling Stones, the Byrds, and on and on. There were a lot of amazing rock musicians making great music, especially in the '60s and early '70s. It was no longer "beach party" sort of music from the later '50s, Frankie Avalon and such. It was a very exciting time for music in general. I'm not saying I don't make any distinction between rock and concert music. I do; they have different purposes. And I must admit I've never come to jazz. It's never called me, unlike a lot of other people that I know. There are still times when nothing will do for me but to listen to some particular rock song; no piece of concert music will do.

What was the arc of your transition like— from being a young, student musician to becoming a professional composer? Was that a path you planned and pursued?

To a degree, it's the sort of thing you can't really control. It was being in the right place at the right time. Anyone who says there is no such thing as luck in these matters is totally wrong. I guess I was writing music that was decent enough that the people I knew felt it was worth supporting, and they introduced me to other people who asked me to write something for them, and it went from there. There's a sense that you are a student until you get that doctoral degree and that then you're suddenly a professional, but that dividing line is pretty ridiculous. I have actually withdrawn a lot of the music I wrote in those first few years after I graduated with my doctorate because it just wasn't good enough yet.

Do you have a different compositional approach when you are writing, say, a concerto compared to writing a symphony?

Aside from balancing the soloist with the orchestra, deciding on the role of the solo instrument, whether it will be a battle of soloist against the orchestra or some other type of interplay, not really. I may be writing for a particular musician, but I don't tailor a piece for a given performer's unique abilities if it means that no one else will be comfortable picking up the music. I want people to play my music.

I was thinking in particular of your guitar concerto, premiered by Sharon Isbin.[2] As a guitarist myself I can attest to the fact that it's easy to learn to strum a few folk songs on the guitar, but it is a difficult instrument to write for at an advanced level.

That was a unique experience. For all other concerti I've written, I felt that I could just go off and write it without having to consult with the player much, if at all. But for that piece I did have to get together with Sharon every six weeks or so and go over it with her to see what worked and what couldn't work. That instrument has a lot of idiosyncrasies, and unless someone has grown up playing in a rock band, I don't think a lot of composers have much understanding of the instrument. After having worked on that piece for a year, I can confidently say that I still didn't understand the instrument any better than I had at the beginning. Fortunately, she plays the piece beautifully.

Congratulations on your appointment as Composer-in-Residence with the New York Philharmonic.[3]
They've been wonderful to work with, and of course it's a great orchestra. I grew up in the Baltimore area and always admired them from afar. They have always played with a lot of excitement, such spirit, and they still do. And of course they have been very supportive of me, playing a lot of my music, and there's a commission every year.

And you are advising for their new music series CONTACT![4]
I'm certainly doing what I can to further the cause of composers, whenever and wherever I can, particularly American composers, and am happy with the number of pieces that have been played at the CONTACT! concerts, particularly from American composers.

I believe you have begun working on your Symphony No. 4. Can you talk about that at all?
I can say that every once in a while, you have to write a piece that is really a private communication. This new symphony is not really a showpiece; it's a little grim maybe, in a whispering kind of way. When asked what his Symphony Pathétique was about, Tchaikovsky said, "Let them guess." So, that will be my program note for this piece: "Let Them Guess."

SELECTED WORKS OF CHRISTOPHER ROUSE

Symphony No. 4 (2013), Orchestra
Prospero's Rooms (2012), Orchestra
Symphony No. 3 (2011), Orchestra
String Quartet No.3 (2009)
Friandises (2005), Ballet scored for Full Orchestra
Requiem (2001-2002), Baritone solo, Children's Choir, SATB Chorus
    and Large Orchestra
Concert de Gaudi (1999), Guitar and Orchestra
Symphony No. 2 (1994), Orchestra
Flute Concerto (1993), Flute and Orchestra
Trombone Concerto (1991), Trombone and Orchestra
Symphony No. 1 (1986), Orchestra

Gorgon (1984), Orchestra
The Infernal Machine (1981), Orchestra

▶ To learn more about Christopher Rouse and his music, including audio excerpts from his *Violin Concerto, Flute Concerto*, and *Phaethon*, visit www.oup.com/us/compositioninthedigitalworld.

NOTES

1. George Crumb is an American composer known for his extended techniques, unusual timbres, and unique notation. He was awarded the Pulitzer Prize for Music in 1968, and a Grammy Award in 2001.
2. Sharon Isbin is a multi-Grammy award–winning American guitarist. Her teachers included Andrés Segovia and she created the guitar department at the Juilliard School in 1989 and is the director of the guitar department at the Aspen Music Festival. She has commissioned works by many contemporary composers.
3. Christopher Rouse was named the Marie-Josée Kravis Composer-in-Residence at the New York Philharmonic for three seasons. He is only the second composer to hold this title.
4. Mr. Rouse served as advisor for *CONTACT!*, the New York Philharmonic's new music series with performances at the Metropolitan Museum of Art and Peter Norton Symphony Space.

Martin Bresnick

We begin to realize that we live on one planet of music making, and that there is no exotic music, there is no esoteric music. All of us humans who are making music are involved in a very similar journey.

Any conversation with Martin Bresnick (b. New York, 1946) almost immediately gravitates toward the subject of music. Cheerfully obsessive about his vocation, he is not only a preeminent American composer of 21st-century music but also one of our most influential educators of modern American composition, guiding the way for dozens of notable young composers.

Bresnick's musical interests began early with the guitar and were subsequently nourished by the public school system and a remarkable series of exposures and educational experiences that he credits with his development. It is, however, immediately apparent to those who hear his music that his ferocious talent drove the opportunities that were presented to him. His compositions are exceptionally robust, rhythmic, and masculine. He embraces rock, jazz, and blues—good music in any style—and then fluently incorporates their essence into his own unique brew. Experimental, fearless, and forward-looking, his music seems more immediate and relevant than ever.

Winner of the first Charles Ives Living Award, the Rome Prize, the Berlin Prize, a Guggenheim Fellowship, and a Koussevitzky Commission, his compositions include computer music, chamber music, and symphonic works. He also has had success as a composer of music for film, including *Arthur and Lillie* (1975) and *The Day after Trinity* (1981), both nominated for Academy Awards.

Some composers lament that teaching can be a drain on their own creative juices, but Bresnick seems to thrive on the give-and-take of working with young composers. Widely recognized as an exceptional and dedicated teacher, he has helped to shape and direct the talents of many of the most prominent composers of our time. While he continues to lead and inspire new generations of composition students at Yale, as he has for decades, Bresnick is increasingly focused on his own art, setting a new standard for American musical composers in the process.

You've said that your piece *Willy's Way* was inspired by Cream's album *Wheels of Fire*. I wore that record out learning to play the guitar. Have genres like rock and jazz had an ongoing influence on your music?

Guitar was actually my first instrument, though I didn't start by playing rock guitar, which is what I had in mind. When I said I wanted a guitar, my father insisted that I take lessons and he found me a neighborhood teacher, Thomas Sokoloff, a Russian guitarist who actually had a guitar, mandolin, and balalaika orchestra. So I ended up learning to play pieces like *Swan Lake* and Borodin's *On the Steppes of Central Asia* on the guitar. Of course eventually I did learn folk and rock guitar just by listening to other people play.

My family wasn't particularly clued in to classical music per se. They had a pretty random collection of classical "hits" so to speak, but they did know folk music. My own training really started with the New York City public school system. At that time, when I was about 11 years old, the public schools let kids play instruments, and since nobody else seemed to want to play the oboe and I loved the sound of it, they gave me an oboe. I also started to write my own little pieces around that time. That was an era when kids were skipped ahead a grade in school if they were quick, so I ended up getting into a specialty high school called the High School of Music and Art, in Manhattan. I actually entered as a sophomore at age 13. Kind of nuts. But the advantage of that was that my childish efforts at composition were taken quite seriously by the teachers there, and I was admitted to a special class designated for people who wanted to study composition.

How has the introduction of technology affected your students over time? Do you see differences in how your students think, or compose, or work from when you were a student?

There's no question that the computer has made an incredible difference, and not necessarily in ways that could have been predicted. I first started doing computer music as a graduate student at Stanford under the tutelage, or mentorship, of John Chowning. We were at the very beginning of digital reproduction in music and there were two strands going on simultaneously: One was a kind of an inquiry into the acoustics of music and how computers could make very precise inroads into the world of synthetic sound production that were not available to analog equipment users, and on the other side were people who were working in software programs to develop printing programs and sequencers. Now, I don't think I have a single student who hands me a handwritten score any more, and also a lot of what we listen to when we discuss their work is MIDI versions of what they are doing, which is very effective from the standpoint of large formal questions. It's less effective in the world of acoustical reality because these sequencer programs don't always have the very best sound reproduction, though I don't think it's as bad as some people think.

Is the ubiquitous use of computer technology by composition students a positive thing? Some composers have mentioned to me that they are worried about their students relying too much on computer playback while not developing their ear properly. Do you think that's a valid concern?

Yes, there are issues there for sure. Students who don't actually vigorously play an instrument can sometimes get the wrong idea about what is possible in the real world. One of the typical problems I find is that while music composed using a sequencer can be played back on a computer, it may actually be written at speeds that no human being could achieve. So yes, there can be problems, but I think most alert composers overcome them.

Has the technology changed the way that you work personally? Do you only work at the computer now or do you still use a pencil and paper?

It's funny that you ask me that, because despite the fact that I knew a fair amount about computers and processing, I didn't get to the computer sequencer side of things until fairly late. My students started saying, "Seriously, Martin, what are you doing? Why are you still using a pencil?" So slowly but surely, I became more accomplished at it, but then I had to teach myself a new way to work. Sketching on a computer is much different from sketching out ideas with a pad and pencil, or trying something on the piano over and over. So now I really do a mix. I might sketch some ideas with a pencil and paper then enter them into the computer to work on them there, or I might play the ideas on the piano a few times. I have noticed, though, that as I get more adept at the computer, I make sketches of what I want on the computer now. I am tending to work that way more and more. I do have a pencil and paper in front of me all the time, and I use that to make annotations of little things I think need to be fixed or changed, but the actual creative side is more inside the computer now than I would ever have imagined 10 years ago.

Do you think that the end result might be different if a piece were composed using a computer as opposed to a more traditional method of composition like pencil and paper and piano?

In a way, it's similar to the fears that people had when they changed from writing manuscripts by hand to using a typewriter or word processor. It's possible that there is some effect there, but I think that a good composer can overcome the propensity of the computer to alter the music. A computer can be bent to your needs if it is handled correctly. You just have to learn the technique. It's a slightly different way of working.

What about a piece like *Conspiracies*, where you use a lot of extended techniques? Does that pose any particular challenges when notating on the computer?

Conspiracies in some sense is one of the descendants of a bunch of pieces that I had considered making back at Stanford in the early 1970s, when we were experimenting with all sorts of quadraphonic, spatial simulations.

Chowning had developed this remarkable program that would actually move sounds in space and make them swing around in different directions by incorporating Doppler shift and other details of the quadraphonic system. And *Conspiracies* is really a descendant of that, where it takes live instruments and, by notation, simulates Doppler shifts and changes and complicated spectra. I lost interest a little bit in purely electronic music, where people sat around in a room and stared at . . . well, nothing really . . . a tape recorder, loudspeakers. It just didn't seem like a worthy social event. On the other hand, a recent flute concerto I wrote called *Pan Penseroso*, played by the great Robert Dick, is just now being finalized after very careful editing by Margaret Lancaster to make sure that every one of these multiphonic structures is correctly notated. But not every player wants to put in that kind of time, so I also made a version for two flutes. The wonderful flute player and conductor Paul Dunkel told me, "I don't do windows and I don't play multiphonics." I remain interested but I am very picky. There is a lot of multiphonic music that is left to chance in terms of the player's choice among other variables, and I am much too obsessive for that. I want what I want, and I work very hard to specify precisely what that is. I think it comes out of those years of working so carefully on computer music where you really actually do that.

Please talk about your piece *Every Thing Must Go*.
In the middle movement of that there's a series of just intonation[1] passages, both linear and vertical, and when I wrote the piece, I knew in my ear exactly what I wanted, and I took a lot of trouble to make sure that the expression of that just intonation was derived from a really audible fundamental, so you could hear how it worked. The guys in the Prism Saxophone Quartet are truly wonderful players and they were very conscientious about pursuing this. Amusingly enough, I could almost not bear to play that one back on the computer. The kind of tuning that I intended would have taken a lot of time to get the sequencer to play them, but I took a lot of pains to notate them anyway, which gave the program some trouble. The sequencer does not really understand a quarter-tone very well. Inputting is tedious and doesn't quite work.

It is actually pretty easy now to find, for example, how many cents off the 7th or the 11th partial is. I give that precise information in the instructions on how to play the piece. And the result has been very gratifying. I did not expect this, but that piece has sort of become my *Bolero*. There are a lot of saxophone players. They don't have a tremendous amount of repertoire and they got very excited about *Every Thing Must Go*.

A piece of music is a little bit like a beacon, and if you write a piece of music that players are interested in, they will seek it out and they will glom onto it, because wonderful musicians are eager, maybe more eager than the composer, to make a world that includes those kinds of things. And this piece has been that kind of a beacon.

What was it like to have György Ligeti[2] as a composition teacher?
It was completely transformative. Ligeti himself was the beacon for me. His work has always illuminated terrains and places that I never imagined. Some of those musical places I couldn't go; they were not congenial to me personally, but they were always something I felt I needed to know about the universe of sound and the universe of musical potential. I was always very honored to be illuminated by that light that he cast. I still miss him. I can't deny that I always think, "Why isn't there another great Ligeti piece?" I'd like to hear some more. In a sense, I studied with him before I ever met him. It took me a while to work out a way to be with him. When he first accepted me as a student, I went over to Europe on a Fullbright, and he couldn't teach me because he had a grant of his own. It wasn't until two years later that Chowning and I conspired to bring him to Stanford and I was able to study with him in a private circumstance. By the time I studied with him, I was already 23 or 24 and, while I wasn't finished, I was on my way to becoming a formed composer. Many of the ideas that I needed to learn from him I had already learned by studying his scores. That being said, sitting next to him while he looked at a score, sometimes mine, sometimes his own or someone else's, was a privilege. He understood with remarkable alacrity what the strategy of any composition was. It didn't take him long to figure out what you were trying to do. He got that very, very fast and he could make very salient and sometimes trenchant comments about what the procedure or strategy was in any given work. If that was all, that would have been enough, but he would also see in your music the sonic picture of what it was that the music was trying to realize, and he could tell you to a calibration that still staggers me, what the proper instrumentation should be for what it was that you were trying to do. And he would never, ever permit a musical idea to trump the possibility of its realization. If I was trying to do something and was not realizing it because I hadn't paid sufficient attention to how it was being set in the world of sound, he would say, "This is no good. Don't do *this*, this has to *sound* like something. There's no justification for anything you do that doesn't sound like what it should sound like." I think that probably accounts for why his music is going to be with us for a long time, because it never fails to sound.

And what was the music that inspired him? Did he share that with you?

He would shake his head with admiration about someone like Debussy, for example, and he would say, "It's astounding that this composer, who in some ways has the most genial and mild surface to his music, it's never upsetting, is at the same time as experimental as any composer who ever lived. But you don't always know it because he sort of sneaks it by you with music that is incredibly beautiful. He sort of picks your pocket." Debussy is remarkable in that way, and I think Ligeti admired that very much, that ability to absolutely mystify and delight with the world of sound, without neglecting the formal intensity and rigor of which he was such a master.

Please talk about your own composing process. Do you have a routine that you follow?

Still referencing Ligeti, you can look back and see pretty clear directions that he took, but he always said, "I'm like a pig looking for truffles, snuffling around until I find the one I want." And my routine is sort of like that too. My method of working is to try to find the context and circumstance that the piece provides for me, either by commission or by some other detail of constraint. And if I have a constraint, I am happy because then I will search out what I consider to be the best realization of the work that will allow the constraint to be a building block and not a stumbling block.

Somewhat atypically for modern concert composers, you have written film scores. What has your experience been working in the world of film music?

I have been a very lucky guy and I think luck plays a major part in anybody's career, for good or ill. When I was at Stanford, I put up a sort of "will work for food" sign and by doing that I met a bunch of young Stanford filmmakers and started writing music for them, some very small things and later some more substantial things, and most dramatically, became a friend of the great documentary filmmaker John Else, who I admire beyond words. He just set me free on his wonderful documentary films, among them, *The Day after Trinity, Arthur and Lillie*, and a lesser known work called *Cadillac Desert: Water and the Transformation of Nature*, a four-film sequence that included the flagship film, *Mulholland's Dream* about how Mulholland stole a river from the mountains of the Sierras to create the modern city of Los Angeles.

Ah, sounds like the plot of the film *Chinatown*.
Yes, it really is the true story of Chinatown. Meeting John was a lucky stroke, just the fact that we found each other and he thought my music was really good and wanted it in his movies, when another composer would have given him something much more traditional. Through him I met a lot of other distinguished and very courageous filmmakers who also wanted music that was more daring than the conventional score. With most of them I was given the green light to follow my judgment as to what I thought should be done.

Some composers I've spoken to have experienced difficulties working in film, but it doesn't sound like that was your experience.
Well, I'm sort of soft-pedaling my difficulties because in comparison to the experiences of some composers I know, my problems were small. Good stories to tell over a beer. [Laughs]

Some of the tales told by my contemporaries make me think, "Well, if that were me I would be out of the business."

Your wife [Lisa Moore] is a wonderful pianist; it must be great to have not only a life partner but also an art partner.
Yes, it's fantastic. She has tuned up my piano music a lot. I'm not a pianist, and playing piano with her is like playing tennis with Nadal. I'll be the ball boy! But she's not afraid to tell me when something is not working. She'll edit for me, or she'll tell me, "You shouldn't do it that way," and she will show me fingerings or tell me why something will work better one way than another. That piece *Willy's Way*? That's actually a condensation of a piece for a larger ensemble, and I put a whole lot of counterpoint and lines from that larger work, and she makes that sound much better than it is!

What was your thinking process when you explored that simple but wonderful Willie Dixon theme and unfolded it into *Willy's Way*?
I was teaching a course for many years at Yale called Composition for Performers, which was for performers who were interested in writing music, but had no experience in it. I would put them through a series of exercises, not necessarily to turn them into composers, but to introduce them to the same problems that composers face. I didn't want them to learn to imitate without understanding. The Willie Dixon tune, and specifically the Cream version on *Wheels of Fire*, starts with a very conventional blues subject and moves into live improvisation that takes you for about 17 minutes through a really amazing variety of rhythms and imaginative

melodic ideas. It doesn't change keys or even have much of a dominant, even a flat-seven dominant, and I think the performers in the class get a feeling for what intelligent improvisation can be, given a narrow and significant point of departure. So I wanted to show, in my way, how I might go about treating that.

What are some of the challenges of leading a creative life while dealing with the realities of making a living?

Some of our European colleagues, as well as some American colleagues, felt that having to have a job or be an academic was a detriment to your creativity as a musician and a composer, and it may be true. But if you don't have the church or the state to support you, you have to work for somebody. In the case of Charles Ives, for example, I don't think it would have been congenial for him to become a music teacher; he did what worked for him by becoming an insurance agent. But it took a tremendous toll too. I think he had to work terribly hard to be the great insurance guy that he was and come home and write music all night. He burned out pretty fast. Teaching is congenial for me and it is a way to give back to the community that was so generous to me. When I won the Charles Ives Living prize[3] and had to stop teaching for three years, it was traumatic for me, but in a good way. I saw very clearly what the value of my creative life had been as a mixture of a teacher and a composer, but I also saw, sort of standing on the shores of that temporal Walden Pond, some ideas in my mind and my heart that would not be possible unless I really began to restrict my time with others to give more time to my own ideas. When I got back to full-time teaching in 2001, I had a reservoir of things to work on, and I became somewhat more jealous of my time to work on them.

Allen Ginsberg was really shrewd about this. He said that in this very commercial, rough-shouldered economy that we live in, it's hard to keep one's sensibility as fresh and responsive to the world as it might have been before you had to grow up and work and accept responsibilities. *Ich grolle nicht*, as Heinrich Heine says in the great poem that Schumann set: "I don't complain." And really, I shouldn't complain. So many people have had it much, much harder than me. But now as I'm entering my *Opus Posthumous Period*, I'd like to have a little more time away from school to work on my own stuff.

What do you have planned for the foreseeable future?

I'm working on an opera—who isn't? And I'm working on one piece for two pianos, and I have another for eight trombones on order.

Digital technology affects contemporary composers in many ways. For instance, your music is all over the web; on Spotify, and YouTube, and many other sites. Does it concern you that your music is available for free?

Yeah, well, it does concern me somewhat. I don't know where anyone is getting the money anymore to create a really fine recording, because you're not going to get your money back when it's played for free all over the Internet. So it's a troubling situation. I actually had no real contact with Spotify until a few weeks ago when I went on Spotify myself. I saw, to my astonishment, that they have almost everything of mine that has ever been recorded, and even pieces that have not been officially recorded and released by me! Did they get them off of my iTunes site? I don't know how they got them, or who got them. So yeah, I'm concerned about that.

Some composers are convinced that it's going to make it a lot harder, even harder than it already is, to exist and make a living as a composer.

I think that's right. The royalty situation is very difficult. Nobody really knows what to do next. I think this question is very complicated right now.

On the positive side, it seems that digital technology has opened up a whole world of new sounds that composers can exploit.

As a sound source, computer manipulation is definitely adding to the palette: available sounds, pre-recorded sounds, and sounds that you can create in the computer yourself. The reservoir of available materials has grown very, very wide as a result of computers and access to the sounds of other faraway cultures, as well as very exotic sounds that we can make ourselves. It's really an exciting part of what the new technology has to offer.

It seems to me that the Internet has made it easier for composers to be exposed to esoteric instruments and music of other cultures. Do you find that to be the case?

There's no question. The access through the computer, not just in terms of writing music, but the library, in a sense, of world music that is available through YouTube, for example, or any of these other electronic devices and media, is kind of a bewildering, overwhelming warehouse of musical genres, types, and characters that were never accessible before. You used to have to be able to sit at the piano and go through an orchestral score to sort of "whack out" music that you could not hear any other way. Now I can go online and find four different versions of Prokofiev's quintet, for example, with completely different players. It's astounding. I think my students have been profoundly decentered by this. I'm not saying this is a bad thing, it's just a different educational paradigm than the one I grew up with. I think that the salutary part of that is that we begin to realize that we live on one planet of music making, and that there is no exotic music, there is no esoteric music. All of us humans who are making music are involved in a very similar journey.

SELECTED WORKS OF MARTIN BRESNICK

My Friend's Story (2013), Opera in Three Scenes, a Prologue and Epilogue, J. D. McClatchy Libretto (based on a story by Anton Chekhov)

Ishi's Song (2012), Piano Solo

Prayers Remain Forever (2011), Cello and Piano

Pan Penseroso (2009), Concerto for Flute and Orchestra

The Botany of Desire (2009), Film Score

Caprichos Enfáticos (2007), Piano Solo and Percussion Quartet

Every Thing Must Go (2007), Saxophone Quartet

Fantasia on a Theme by Willie Dixon (2001), Piano and Amplified Ensemble

Mulholland's Dream (1997), Film Score

Woodstock (1993), SATB a cappella, Psalm Texts

Pontoosuc (1989), Orchestra

The Day after Trinity (1981), Film Score, nominated for an Academy Award

▶ To learn more about Martin Bresnick and his music, visit www.oup.com/us/compositioninthedigitalworld.

NOTES

1. Just intonation is a system of tuning based on ratios and the harmonic series as compared to equal temperament, which is most common in modern Western music.
2. György Ligeti (1923–2006) was a composer born in Transylvania. His students include Martin Bresnick, Mohammed Fairouz, and Michael Daugherty. His music is extremely influential, but may be best known to the general public by its use in films by Stanley Kubrick, including *2001 A Space Odyssey*.
3. In 1998, the American Academy of Arts and Letters inaugurated the Charles Ives Living, which Mr. Bresnick was awarded. The award gives an American composer $100,000 a year for two years.

Joan Tower

Photo Credit: Bernie Mindich

I believe there is a huge vulnerability when composers share a piece at a premiere. Because you put all of this heart and soul, and work, and time into this new music. Now it's being shared by other people, other ears. So it's sort of like your soul, your guts, everything is out on display for everybody. And for me it's painful, because I'm not always sure what I have. I'm not sure if it's really working right. So I sort of go the other way. I create a huge shield around me that says, "That's okay, you can't hurt me because I know it's a terrible piece."

I was a student when I first heard the music of Joan Tower (b. New York, 1938). At the time, I knew nothing of her fascinating story; I just knew that her music jumped out and grabbed me. I soon learned that she is not only one of the pioneers of American *women* composers; she is one of the most important and influential creators of new music living today. Colorful, robust, and surprising, her music projects a distinctively American originality, immediacy, and gutsiness.

Following a childhood in South America, Tower was schooled at Bennington College and Columbia University, although she considers herself a self-taught composer. She is also an extremely accomplished pianist and educator.

Tower eschewed the world of Ivy League academia in favor of pursuing her performance career and was a founding member of the Da Capo Chamber Players. During the course of our interview, I learned that we were formerly neighbors in Greenwich Village and, in fact, some of my early music studies were at the Greenwich House School, where she taught at the time.

Her many honors include three Grammy Awards, finalist for a Pulitzer Prize, and a Guggenheim fellowship. In 1990, Tower became the first woman to win the prestigious Grawemeyer Award, for her composition *Silver Ladders,* and was the first composer chosen for a Ford Made in America consortium commission. She teaches at Bard College and is a member of both the Artistic Advisory Panel of BMI and the Academy of Arts and Letters.

Upbeat and impassioned, Tower also has a wonderful sense of humor and is a fluid conversationalist. After speaking with her, I found myself exhilarated and inspired but also rueful that our paths hadn't crossed much earlier; I wish I'd had the opportunity to study with her back in Greenwich Village.

You've gone through many challenging transitions in your musical career—living in South America, attending Bennington College[1] and then Columbia University, and performing in the Da Capo Chamber Players.[2] Then you became a full-time composer and went through a major style change in the 1970s. How did you manage those difficult transitions?

I think life tends to be a series of coincidences, as well as motivated actions. It was extremely traumatic when I first moved to South America when my father got a job down there. I was changing cultures, languages, schools, everything, and I was just nine years old. I remember that as being a very, very difficult transition. But, it turned out to be one of the best things that ever happened to me because my horizons were widened considerably culturally, and I developed a more international perspective on America. Coming back to the United States was not easy either. I had to go to a private school that I did not like at all. I was very free and wild and this was a very reserved upper-class school, so that was a traumatic event as well. Another difficult transition was leaving Bennington. I loved Bennington, which opened up a whole bunch of musical doors for me personally and allowed me to explore who I was. In fact, they're the ones who got me going on composition. I did not want to leave. But they did me a favor and sort of said, "You've got to get out of here." So they helped me to get a position at Greenwich House[3] in New York.

I grew up in Greenwich Village and as a young music student studied at the Greenwich House School of Music, I know it well.
A wonderful place isn't it? I was there for 10 years and that was an amazing training ground for me. I taught piano there, developed young composers, and started a series of contemporary music concerts, which became very successful. So that was a terrific experience for me. At the time, I was also going to Columbia University trying very hard to be scholastic. I got a master's degree and a doctorate, but it took me 14 years. I was not very involved and I had to do it very slowly. It was not my particular cup of tea. I was the kind of person who wanted to make music, not talk about it. So that was another difficult transition for me. But I did it; I persevered, because everyone told me I needed to get those degrees in order to teach. So I did it, kicking and screaming.

But the other side of my life in New York, making music, was the most exciting. I started meeting players and producing and writing a lot of music. So that balanced things out.

Speaking of difficult situations, how about the challenges of becoming a woman composer? At that time in the 1960s and '70s it was not the easiest process in the world. In fact, becoming a composer is not ever easy, as you know. Having your work performed and received positively, which is your food (it's my life food anyway), is not easy. It's a long path, and it takes a lot of time to find your own voice. And to me that is the goal, to find your own voice. Because, if you don't have your own voice, you don't have much of an identity. You may be very good chops-wise, but if you don't have a voice, the music doesn't always "sit up." I developed my voice very intuitively and very unconsciously. I planted my own little garden. I planted my own flowers and watched them grow.

My life has been an uphill climb. Around me were all of these very successful people. I didn't think I was ever going to be noticed the way they were. (Laughs) Eventually it happened, over a long period of time. I also love to teach, I have really good students. They're like my kids and I adore them, so it's been a very rewarding life.

Would you give your 21st-century composition students different advice than you received when you were starting out?

Things are not the same. Students these days are much more advanced than they were in the '60s and '70s. They come in from high school with orchestra pieces they have written on their laptops. I think that is primarily due to the technology, which has been so helpful to them. But they still have many of the same challenges. They have to find their own voice, and to set up shop for their compositional life.

My advice is always to form a group of some kind, either to play in, or conduct, or present. That allows them to have their own structure without being rejected. Then they can work on their musical life on their terms, and can hear their music played. The world is not particularly interested in composers, so I think this is a wonderful way to go. We have examples of extraordinary groups, and they all do it very differently depending on their vision. Bang on a Can does one thing, Kronos Quartet does another, Common Sense Collective[4] does their thing. They've all created very unique ways of presenting music stylistically, et cetera.

So I always say to my students, the first thing you've got to do in order to survive musically is form your own group. It's important to create your own environment where you can grow, uninhibited by other people's choices, like institutional choices for example. I formed my own group, the Da Capo Chamber Players, and that turned out to be a huge educational experience for me. Huge. Steve Reich and Philip Glass did it, and a whole bunch of other composers of my generation did it as well. That's the way we could follow our own vision.

How important is it for composition students to attend a certain school? It seems as though a large number of composers who have received major awards have graduated from a handful of particular universities.

I don't follow the advice that many of the credentialed schools give to young composers: "You should apply here and there," and "talk to so and so," "win this award and win that award." I'm not of that school. Of course it's important where you go to school, but the awards and all of that? Very ephemeral, very elusive, very temporary, and very political.

Very political?

And very political. We have many Pulitzer composers who are not heard from at all. I don't think that prizes make your career. I think the *music* makes your career.

If, for example, you write a good piece for solo flute, it will take off like wildfire. This is because all of the flautists know each other and are very aware of what the other flautists are doing.

I've had wonderful experiences writing music for flute players. As a rule, they seem to be so open and eager to embrace new music.
The flute world happens to be a very composer friendly world, more so than any other instrument. They should get the Nobel Prize for the number of commissions they are responsible for. They incorporate young composers, older composers, and the styles are all over the place, it's not just one style. They hear a new piece for flute they like and everyone in that community wants to play it. It's an amazing world of opportunity for composers.

You have a piece being played at the upcoming National Flute Association convention entitled _Rising_.
I was terrified of that piece. _Rising_ was a hard piece to write because combining the flute and string quartet is not easy. The flute keeps running into the violin. They're in the same register and you have to be very careful how that interaction works. And of course writing for Carol Wincenc,[5] who is a dear friend, and knowing that she was going to play it many times, there was more pressure on me. "Oh my God! I've got to make this work." It's not going to be just played and then shelved; it's going to have a life. But when it was finished, I didn't like it at all.

Really? I think it's a wonderful piece. You weren't happy with it?
At the premiere I just wanted to go and hide. There were 500 people at Juilliard with the Juilliard Quartet[6] performing. I just wanted to go into a hole and die. People kept coming up to me and saying, "What a great piece," and I was thinking you're just saying that because you like me, you're a friend of mine, whatever. Now it's been proven, my perspective was wrong. My perspective was completely off the wall.

And that happens to composers doesn't it? Sometimes we finish a piece and then think, "What have I done? This is worthless."
I believe there is a huge vulnerability when composers share a piece at a premier. Because you put all of this heart and soul, and work, and time into this new music. Now it's being shared by other people, other ears. So it's sort of like your soul, your guts, everything is out on display for everybody. And for me it's painful, because I'm not always sure what I have. I'm not sure if it's really working right. So I sort of go the other way. I create a huge shield around me that says, "That's okay, you can't

hurt me because I know it's a terrible piece." [Both laugh] I've been doing this for so long, sometimes I'm right. But more often I'm wrong. And it takes a few years, and a few performances to convince me that I'm wrong.

It's refreshing to hear someone of your stature be so honest about those insecurities, because I know exactly what you're talking about, and I think most people who create art know those feelings as well.
I'm old enough now to be honest publicly about what I do, because why hide it? And I know that there are composers like you and others that feel the same way. Most composers are pretty humble, but then on the other hand some composers think they are the cat's pajamas. [Laughs]

You've had some amazing teachers[7] but I've seen you quoted as considering yourself self-taught.
I really believe that composition cannot be taught. It's too complex. You can't teach a student how to compose because there are just too many parameters that go into making a piece of music. You can teach them about a lot of outside things, like, "That's not going to work in that register on the flute" or, "I think this harmonic rhythm may be a little too slow." You can bring in suggestions based on the context of what you are hearing. But if a student composer doesn't believe in what you are telling them, it's sort of like talking to a therapist who says, "Have you thought about your mother in relationship to this problem"? And the student looks at the teacher totally perplexed and thinks: "What is she talking about? I don't know how my mother has anything to do with this." And the student does not understand the implications because it does not reverberate with them. That's teaching composition. It's mostly a hit-and-miss thing.

Any intelligent student will listen to the facts that you present to them. For example, when you say, "This combination of instruments will not work." They will listen to what you say because they know that *you* have the experience in this area. If you as the teacher say, "The harmony is too slow here," that is a hit-or-miss comment. Because they might really like slow music and you don't. So I feel that composition, except for the external things, is almost impossible to teach. I think most really good composers are self-taught. They figure it out for themselves, somehow. They get a lot of information along the way, but it's outside information, not inside information. So that's why I say I'm self-taught.

Do you consider the compositional process to be mystical, or at least indescribable?

That's absolutely true, because it's so complex. You can't pin it down verbally, and I think a big mistake we make is concentrating solely on pitch as a pinning-down thing. We say, okay I can talk about the pitch in this piece, yeah, because you can analyze it. But what about all of the other parameters that make this piece what it is? We sidestep the complexity of the issue by focusing on pitch.

Do you use the computer or MIDI in your compositional process?

No, I'm a pretty good pianist. I love the real sound of the piano and the immediacy of what a dotted half note actually sounds like when I play it. The immediacy of that experience is important to me. I'm about to be 75 and probably a "dinosaur" of sorts, but I do use an iPhone and iPad regularly!

Well those devices certainly count as technology. Do your students use music software like notation and sequencing programs?

Oh yeah, they come in with their pieces on the laptop and play them for me, and we make changes right on the spot using their computer. Oh, it's amazing.

Do you think that digital technology helps them as young composers or hinders them?

Both. There are several drawbacks, but let me first address the positives. They can write something and hear it back immediately. However, the computer programs do not perform dynamics very well, which is a huge part of music. And the technology does not manage timbres very well unless you're really high-tech with expensive samplers, et cetera. which some of my students can manage. But you're still not getting the real thing. Not even close unless you're in the business of composing for movies and have all of that sophisticated and expensive equipment.

You have an intimate knowledge of every instrument, and I suspect you are also familiar with the nuances of the individual performers who will perform in a premiere of a new piece.

I learned a lot from performing and writing for the Da Capo Players. That experience taught me a lot about winds and strings, the violin, cello, flute, and clarinet. It was a huge education, and a real one, a hands-on one. But later when it came to writing for brass I was kind of out of the loop. I had not been around brass players. So I started writing fanfares for brass and I learned pretty fast. I just finished a bassoon concerto, which is sort of a new instrument for me. I've featured it in pieces for orchestra, for instance in a piece called *Stroke* that I wrote for the Pittsburgh Symphony. I still don't know a lot about the bass, the tuba, and the piccolo, but I'll get to those instruments. I'm working my way around the orchestra.

You rearranged *Amazon I*, which had been written for the Da Capo Players, for full orchestra. The resulting piece, *Amazon II*, was your first work for large orchestra. Was that a daunting experience?

It was daunting for me. In fact, I had previously turned down a commission from the American Composers Orchestra.[8] I told them I was not ready to write for full orchestra, but they said, "Oh yes you are," and insisted. That's when I wrote *Sequoia*, which was a torturous experience because there was so much guesswork involved for me. Particularly the combination of all of those instruments, that was just mind-boggling. So I decided to write the piece at the piano, then orchestrate it, and hope that it worked.

So you usually orchestrate after you have composed a piece?

I'm much more experienced with writing for the orchestra now, so my guesswork is considerably less. Now I often think in terms of groups of instruments when composing. But I still think that a piece has to have a solid musical format. Orchestration does not make the piece, even if you are a great orchestrator that talent alone is not going to make the piece work.

You have given a nod to some of the great composers in your own pieces. For instance *Petroushskates* captures the essence of Stravinsky's *Petrushka* and *Tres Lent (Hommage a Messiaen)* perhaps takes a bow to Messiaen's *Quartet for the End of Time*. Are there any particular challenges when your piece is influenced by another composer's work?

That's one of the hardest things to figure out because we're all surrounded by great music, and the more vulnerable we are, the more influenced we are by others' work. I've noticed over the years that some of my colleagues have gotten lost in someone else's music. These are talented and wonderful musicians; they just couldn't get out from under these big powerful voices. But I had to figure this out on my own. When I wrote *Petroushskates* I decided to go toward *Petrushka* rather than away from it. The first part of the first section is more Stravinsky than Tower, but then I got out of it pretty gracefully. [Laughs] I learned an important lesson there. I tell my students you can be influenced, but you can be drowned sometimes by powerful pieces. Instead of running from it, use it! But keep listening very carefully to how you're going to work through it and come out the other side of the piece with your particular voice intact.

The latest piece you have been working on is *White Water* for string quartet?

Yes, commissioned by the Monterey Chamber Festival in California.

They wanted to tie the commissioned work in with a video artist Bill Viola. I wanted to write a string quartet so I said, okay. But I thought to myself, "I'm going to do my own thing." Then they sent me some of his videos and some of them are very powerful. I like his work, but connecting music and videos is not easy. I was intrigued by his images of water and light, this glowing feeling that I found in a lot of his work. This suggested masses of sound to me. Luckily, in the performance they did not show the videos at the same time as my music was being played. That's something I really don't like at all. The videos were shown at intermission, which worked well. I worked with the Daedalus Quartet[9] who played beautifully. They perform the piece a lot, which is very nourishing. They will record it this year.

And what else is on the horizon, any other new pieces you can discuss?

Well, I just finished the bassoon concerto. And there's an older piece of mine called *Rapids* for piano and orchestra that I'm revisiting. Frankly, it was a piece I was not sure about when I first completed it. Then it was recently performed with great success. It was very exciting. And I thought to myself, you know what? You've been treating this child like a delinquent. And he's/she's not a delinquent! But it needed an introduction. So I just finished a five-minute introduction to that piece which is very calm and the opposite of rapids. I think it's going to be called *Still Waters* but I'm not sure quite yet. And I'm revising a song I wrote for Dawn Upshaw.[10] She's singing it at my 75th birthday concert this fall. I'm thinking of writing another song for her because she is just so fantastic, and I need to improve my vocal writing. I'm sort of new to the vocal world (laughs). There are many other projects coming up but those are a few.

You are very busy, and you're so prolific. I understand you have a regular working schedule?

Oh yeah. I like to go to work every day. I compose from one to five pretty religiously unless I'm teaching or traveling.

How important is fame, and how do you deal with the challenges of leading a creative life while balancing that with the realities of making a living as a composer? Because it's so difficult . . .

Yes, I know. Just this week I was at the Academy of Arts and Letters. There is this composer who I've known a long time, and he has struggled interminably. We gave him an award. My God, you would think we had given him the earth he was so happy to be given this award. Not only financially, but also musically and everything. It just showed me how hungry and how desperate some composers are. It's very sad. I think it's very hard today to be a composer.

On the other hand, you have a wonderful career as a composer. So, it can be done.

I've been very, very fortunate. Because I have a terrific job, I'm paid well, and I love to teach. And yet, I have created a kind of a split life for myself. I teach on specific days, and compose on specific days. I've done that many years because I know that I have to do it that way. I can't just compose whenever I happen to get around to it. I have colleagues who teach way too much and say, "The only time I can compose is in the summer." I say that's not good enough! You need to do it throughout the year. If you have to get up at 6 AM to compose, get up at 6 AM!

And then there are those who don't even have a job, so I am totally blessed. But I didn't go through my career as much for the credentials as I did for the music. And that paid off in reverse for my finances, because as I became better known, I got better compensation and leverage with jobs et cetera. The music should always be at the base of the whole thing. I am a very strong believer that the music is controlling the career, the life, the finances, everything. Not the credentials so much, the credentials are elusive.

There are tons and tons of talented composers that the general public will never know about, especially women composers. Okay, so the question is why? I guess if you're living on a mountaintop in Montana and you don't see anybody, people are probably not going to know about you unless you have a very strong website. See, that's where the Internet comes in handy. You can publicize your stuff and people can have access to it immediately. Of course, I don't do much of that. People say, "Joan, you should be on Facebook"! But I just don't have time to do that. I probably will go on eventually, but right now I've got too much to do.

Your music is all over the Internet…

Oh good. But I almost don't want to know. Especially what people think of it! [Laughs heartily]

SELECTED WORKS OF JOAN TOWER

Descending (2012), Chorus
Stroke (2011), Orchestra
White Water (2011), String Quartet
String Force (2010), Violin
Rising (2009), Flute and String Quartet
Ivory and Ebony (2009), Piano
DNA (2003), Percussion Quintet
Wild Purple (1998), Viola
Rainwaves (1997), Clarinet, Violin, Piano
Night Fields (1994), String Quartet
Concerto for Orchestra (1991)
Tres Lent (1980), Cello, Piano

⊙ To learn more about Joan Tower and her music, visit www.oup.com/us/compositioninthedigitalworld.

NOTES

1. Bennington College is located in Vermont and is a women's liberal arts college that became co-educational in 1969.
2. The American contemporary music ensemble, the Da Capo Chamber Players, was formed in 1970. The ensemble has commissioned many new works from composers including John Harbison, Shulamit Ran, Mohammed Fairouz, Milton Babbitt, Martin Bresnick, and David Lang.
3. Greenwich House is located in New York's Greenwich Village and was formed in 1902. Its music and arts program is particularly renowned.
4. Common Sense Collective was formed in 1993. The eight composers of Common Sense seek out and collaborate with different performing groups.
5. Carol Wincenc is an award-winning flautist. She has been featured by many composers including Christopher Rouse, Joan Tower, and Peter Schickele. She has been a professor at Juilliard since 1988.
6. The Juilliard Quartet was founded in 1946. The Quartet's awards include four Grammys and the NARAS Lifetime Achievement Award.
7. Joan Tower's teachers at Columbia University include Jack Beeson, Otto Luening, and Vladimir Ussachevsky.
8. The American Composers Orchestra is based in New York City and is dedicated to the encouragement, preservation, and performance of music by American composers.

9. The Daedalus Quartet (Min-Young Kim and Matilda Kaul, violins; Jessica Thompson, viola; and Thomas Kraines, cello) has performed in many of the world's leading musical venues and to widespread acclaim.

10. Dawn Upshaw is a highly celebrated and sought after American soprano, known for a wide-ranging repertoire of opera, concert music, and sacred works as well as contemporary art music. Nonesuch Records says she is a "favored partner" of many musicians, including Richard Goode, Kronos Quartet, James Levine, and Esa-Pekka Salonen. Several composers in addition to Joan Tower have written pieces for her. A four-time Grammy Award winner, she is featured on more than 50 recordings, including the million-selling Symphony No. 3 by Henryk Górecki.

William Averitt

Photo Credit: Karla Collegman

In the end, teaching is all about rendering oneself redundant. You want to set the students free to become themselves. As composers, we have to become our own guides and find what it is we are trying to say. I think that at a certain point, very individual, and very particular help is useful. But it becomes less and less useful as the student gets older and more experienced. Ultimately they have to become their own teacher.

In the long-standing tradition of the composer/educator, William Averitt (b. Kentucky, 1948) is a talented composer who has divided his time between composition of his own music and a heartfelt dedication to help-ing upcoming composers learn their craft. Despite the demands of his teaching schedule, Averitt also was an active conductor for many years and has amassed an impressive body of work for chorus, voice, chamber groups, flute, and orchestra. Among the most gracious and cultured of gentlemen, his music has enriched audiences from Washington to Paris, where he has traditionally spent his sabbaticals absorbing the European influences that color his music.

In his manner, Averitt is serious, thoughtful, sincere, and passionate, whether discussing world events, lofty ideas, or his favorite subject, music. These same terms also describe his music, which defies compartmentalization. One of his most popular works is *Afro-American Fragments*, a piece for chorus and piano set to the poems of Langston Hughes, that has been hailed for its authentic soulfulness. In contrast, his two-hour *St. Matthew Passion* (2009) for soloists, two choruses, and orchestra has an epic sweep true to the best traditions of Western concert music.

Averitt's honors include grants from the National Endowment for the Arts and Meet the Composer, a fellowship from the Virginia Commission for the Arts, and ASCAPlus Standard Awards. The Shenandoah University, where he is Professor Emeritus of Music and was formerly Coordinator of Composition, presented him with the Wilkins Appreciation Award for Faculty Excellence.

I studied composition with William Averitt for several years, and became fast friends with him. I not only learned a great deal about music from him, but also much about how to live a life enriched by art. Now retired from teaching and happily immersed in creating new music, Averitt is an exemplary model of the pure artist dedicated to, and in love with, his work.

How did you become interested in becoming a composer? You started as a singer, I believe.
That's right. I began by singing in a high school choir. I went to college as a music education major, although even in high school I already knew I wanted to write music and be a choral conductor. I wanted to conduct, but mostly I wanted to write music.

I grew up in Paducah, a small town in western Kentucky, and there was really no situation where I could study composition. In college, there was a composition teacher, James Woodard,[1] that I wanted to study with. At the end of my first year, I went up to him with considerable temerity and asked if he would accept students. Fortunately, he said yes. He turned out to be someone who basically gave me the life I have had. He was wonderfully cultured, musically literate, a brilliant pianist, and a wonderful composer. He was never famous, but he was a very fine, what we would now call a neoromantic composer. But this was the late '60s and that was very out of fashion, so he never enjoyed the career I think his music merited.

And so you set out on a career as a composer. How did you envision your future at that point?

Most everyone in my generation believed that if we were fortunate enough to be composers, we would teach. That was pretty much the accepted pathway for making a living. Very few people at that point in time were able to make a living at all from writing concert music. So I always assumed I was going to be a university teacher, which I was, for 38 years.

I studied at Murray State University in western Kentucky. When I finished my composition degree there, I went to Florida State University and worked with John Boda.[2] It turned out that he was the perfect next step for me. Dr. Boda was this fabulously gifted man who allowed me a great deal more freedom, which was exactly what I needed at that point. That worked very well for me, and I have always felt very lucky to have had those two fellows in my life as teachers. As a teacher myself, I tried to emulate the specific work that Jim [Woodard] did with me as an undergraduate. He guided me so carefully, and I tried to do the same thing with all of the undergraduates I taught over all those years: to point out very specific things, to offer what I hoped were good alternatives for approaching what they were writing, to give them detailed guidance. With the master's students I had, who obviously had experience, I tried to offer reasonable guidance of course, but in a way that allowed them to come to their own conclusions and solve problems for themselves.

In the end, teaching is all about rendering oneself redundant. You want to set the students free to become themselves. As composers, we have to become our own guides and find what it is we are trying to say. I think that at a certain point, very individual, and very particular help is useful. But it becomes less and less useful as the student becomes older and more experienced. Ultimately, they have to become their own teacher. We all have to do this as we write pieces beyond academic programs.

When you graduated from Florida State University you started teaching. I'm curious what that experience was like. How did you find time to compose music? Being an educator is a very demanding job.

It is that! Especially back in the early 1970s. At Florida State, I met my wife, Frances Lapp Averitt[3] (as she is now). We married and we both got jobs at the same school, which was an unexpected thing because often schools wouldn't hire couples. So we felt lucky to get jobs, both of us, at the

Shenandoah Conservatory of Music. When we joined the faculty in 1973, it was relatively small, recently moved to a new town and just beginning to find its legs. Financially, it was a very poor school; we made very, very low salaries for the first half of our tenure there. It was enough to live on, so I am not complaining—we were glad to have jobs! But our teaching loads were quite heavy and our salaries were quite low.

The Shenandoah Conservatory is not located in a major metropolitan area. How did you stay in touch with the community of composers and have your work performed?
I am intrigued by the way in which composers of a generation younger than I have such an interesting interconnectedness with each other. Obviously, this is facilitated by the Internet and by the kinds of communications that have evolved over the last 40 years or so. I think this has had a dramatic effect on things like commissioning new works. Back then, even applying for grants or commissions tended to be a slow process. You got a flyer in the mail, which everybody now calls "snail mail." You might apply for it, but of course there was every likelihood that you wouldn't get the commission or the prize or whatever it was that was being advertised. But everything operated at such a slow pace, and being connected to other people was, I think, far more difficult and time-consuming.

So technology has impacted that aspect of being a working composer: making contacts and applying for grants and commissions.
Technology has allowed us to become connected in a very much more ongoing way than we ever were before. I just read a review of a book of letters to and from Leonard Bernstein. It made a very interesting point: The reviewer was so happy that there had not been e-mail for Bernstein's generation. Because his letters, both letters to and from people with whom he corresponded, have such invaluable insights into the way they thought. On some level that no longer exists, and it is never going to exist again, at least not in the same way. I write dozens of e-mails in any given week, but I almost never write a letter. I don't know anybody who actually writes letters anymore. I think there is a certain kind of loss, a certain kind of permanence if you will, that a piece of paper holds with the thoughts that someone has put down. You don't really get that clarity of thinking in most e-mails, even the ones you think through and try to craft carefully: They don't seem to have the level of importance that a written letter holds. It is a tragedy that subsequent generations won't have the benefit of reading the intimate thoughts of some of the deeply gifted and important composers who are living now as translated through letters. Of course, people

have websites and blogs and do tweets, but I think it's pretty unusual for anyone to share a truly intimate musing on a topic in the way one would feel comfortable doing in a letter to a close friend or colleague.

Do you use the Internet to communicate with colleagues and performers?

Yes. In fact, virtually every commission that I have been fortunate enough to get in the past few years has involved communication with somebody who located me as a composer either by finding my website or a piece of my music that is published, liked it, and decided to commission me.

There is an ambiguity in one of my most performed pieces, and at least two commissions have come about as a result of conductors writing to me about this one note that's missing an accidental. [Laughs] Ultimately, those initial questions led to an online correspondence and then commissions.

You've composed for many different combinations of instruments, including full orchestra, but choral music seems to hold a particular affinity for you. Is this accurate?

My very first love, my deepest love, was choral music. That said, I've spent most of my career as a composer *not* writing very much choral music. I did go through a period when I organized and conducted a fine choral group, Winchester Musica Viva, that's actually still going, although I haven't been with it for over 20 years. When I had that outlet, I did write choral pieces over those 10 years; but that aside, I didn't really have many opportunities to write choral music in any consistent way. But interestingly, correspondences I had via e-mail put me in touch with choral conductors around the country, so commissions and opportunities to hear performances and interact with the conductors and choirs have materialized more recently because of that immediacy of contact and being able to connect with colleagues at a considerable distance.

I think that the recent generation of composers take all of that for granted because it has always been a reality in their lives, whereas for my generation the computer and the Internet happened in middle age.

I am not technologically savvy; I use an iPhone, I use a computer a thousand times a day, and I copy my music into Finale [computer music notation program], but . . .

Do you use Finale exclusively as a publishing tool, or do you also actually compose your work with the program?

Therein lies a tale. I mentioned Jim Woodard, who was my undergraduate composition teacher until 1970. In 1987, my wife and I visited him and his wife, and he looked at me and said in his glorious North Carolina accent, "So, Willie, what music program are you using?" I said, "Music program? You mean a computer program? We don't even own a computer; we can't figure out what we would do with a computer." Can you imagine anyone saying that all these years later? [Laughs] Well, he took me down to his basement where he had a Mac computer and a program called Professional Composer.[4] Here, the most nineteenth-century man I probably ever have met was using a computer and a music program, well before that was so common. Also back then, most people, if they even had a personal printer, were using a dot matrix printer, which, when you printed out music, made everything all "jiggidy-jaggedy." But I was never a particularly gifted calligrapher, so even this seemed like absolute magic. I immediately ordered a computer and Professional Composer. I worked with that for maybe three or four years. Then in the early 1990s Finale came out. In its earliest edition, Finale was—for somebody technologically insecure like me—nearly imponderable. You had to specify practically everything! There was almost nothing that simply defaulted. It was a nightmare. Did you use it?

Yes, in fact, I ran out and bought it as soon as it was available. I was so excited, but it was terribly expensive and really didn't work very well at all in its first incarnations.
Yes, it was expensive. But at the time, Professional Composer had so many limitations, and this program offered so many advantages that were obvious even in its most primitive state. But I think the very first thing I attempted with it was, of all senseless things, an orchestral score. Extracting the parts was beyond comprehension for me; without assistance, I had no idea how to make it do what I needed it to do. Of course, nowadays, it handles things with such ease, at least it does if you know which button to select!

Music computer software has come so far in such a short amount of time that it's difficult to remember how cumbersome the programs were when they first came out.
Yes. It's come such a fantastic distance in 25 years, or whatever it's been. I was so un-technological, but I think I was the very first person at my university to use Finale. It's funny: I got into using Finale all those years ago, but I really used it only as a copy program. I still wrote all of my music with pencil and paper at the piano, although I'm not really much of a pianist. Then the next step was putting it into the computer to create a score and, finally, extracting the parts. Now, when my laser printer spits

out perfect-looking pages of music, it feels like a miracle to me. I still can hardly believe it.

On the other hand, for years I never listened to anything by playing it back on the computer. I just strictly used it as my copyist. I did the proofing and all of that without benefit of listening to anything. I think that was partly because the program required so much memory, and the playbacks were not that fabulous. It didn't impress me very much, not only because the sound was terrible, but also because the playback would start and stop, sort of choke up for lack of sufficient computer memory.

Eventually, my computer got better, and I guess I got a bit more savvy and began at least to proof scores by listening to the computer playback; because it's easy to overlook a miscopied rhythm or something like that, it is a particularly great help for that task. Finally, about five years ago, I screwed up my courage and tried to write a piece directly into the computer, which I never had done before. At first it felt very strange because, you know, it is so easy to erase this and add that. In the end, there is something quite different about working directly in the computer, although it's hard for me to explain exactly what. I still do sketches with pencil and paper, you know, the preliminaries. But now I usually put them into the computer and begin to work with them there almost from the beginning.

Many composers who started out by composing at the piano or with pencil and paper have commented that the experience of writing directly into the computer is somehow less satisfying. There is a tactile experience missing. Have you found that to be true?
You can waste a great deal of time staring at a blank computer screen. It's a pretty empty feeling. My very first ideas rarely come to me at the computer. They still come when I am either sitting in a chair sketching in a notebook or sitting at the piano.

But I made a great discovery for myself. As I said, I am not a pianist, which means everything I write other than slow movements depends entirely on my inner ear and my best guess with respect to timing. Music is all about the passage of time after all. I think the greatest gift, in a way, that Finale has given me is the opportunity to hear a piece with lots of voices that I could not reproduce on the piano, or at a speed that I couldn't begin to perform. With this software I can hear my ideas in time and, perhaps, make better judgments about what is and is not working. For me, that has been one of the real gifts that computer music software has provided: the chance to hear things moving in real time.

Do you think that the outcome of a finished piece is affected by whether it was composed using a computer or a more traditional process, such as pencil and paper or a piano?

Yes. I really think it does. While nothing substitutes for hearing your music live, this can be the next best thing: hearing the notes and rhythms and textures that you have tried to create in real time. A computer version doesn't sound like actual people playing or singing my music, but it can be enormously helpful, and I don't think that the pieces would be quite the same had I just written them directly in manuscript at the piano.

However, using a computer presents a lot of temptations. The copy-and-paste function is one of the definite pitfalls that can be very difficult to resist. If you are a composer who often uses repeating sections, it's very easy simply to copy 10 measures and then slap them into a spot later in the piece.

Some composers have commented that the very thing you are discussing, the cut-and-paste procedure, has fundamentally affected some composers' music.

Many students find the copy-and-paste procedure irresistible as a method for expanding their music into larger, if not more substantial, creations. Music that has a recurrence of recognizable ideas, for most audiences, is going to be a stronger listening experience. But simply repeating things without growth, without change of some sort, isn't particularly interesting, at least not to me. This is something I've tried to teach my students: Figure out a way to make your ideas happen, but let them grow by being re-presented in different ways: a different register, a different instrument, a different context. This seems to be one of the basics of artistic expression. Art does use recurrence, but I think generally it makes a stronger statement if the recurrence is varied, rather than simply repeated. Development, in other words. Of course, notation programs make it tempting just to copy something and stick it back in, but there is greater value in bringing an idea back in such a way that it has a little bit something different to say.

It concerns some composer-educators that students no longer seem to put an emphasis on learning their basics: ear training, orchestration, et cetera, because they are relying on instant computer playback, which can be unrealistic and not idiomatic. Is this a valid concern?

It is decidedly a concern. I think it's up to a teacher to point out that you can't put the flute on low C and expect it to balance with the trombone section at forte just because Finale or Sibelius allows you to do that. Neither program can provide a substitute for solid information and discretion about the choices that you make. Again, I think we have to try to guide our students and their awareness of what is musically effective.

Because of the Internet, students listen to an incredible variety of music now, so young composers are influenced by many different types of composition. Some composers have told me, "Well, that's good, but it's also bad. It's good because they are hearing all different kinds of music, but it's bad because they are not really getting down into the music. It's just superficial listening."

I think that's a valid point. Yes, students now have the opportunity to experience a gargantuan array of styles and composers. For students in the 1960s, there were recordings around, but nothing like the panoply of possibilities that exists nowadays online. I would share the same sentiment: It's hard perhaps to be discriminating if you are bombarded by so many different things. On the other hand, it may be very thrilling and enlivening!

Did you compose while you were teaching? For instance, Christopher Rouse told me, "I can't compose when I'm teaching, I have to do it in the summer."

Oh yes, I did compose when I was teaching, but . . . Christopher Rouse? He is a genius. He only writes in the summers? Oh my God, he ought to quit teaching. He is a fabulous composer. Somebody ought to give him a grant to just live and write music.

He said it was draining creatively for him to teach a class or to give private lessons and then he doesn't feel like doing anything when he gets home.

It is musically distracting. I used to have days when I had mostly half-hour lessons, splitting hour lessons up into two half-hours, so I could see students twice a week on Monday and Thursday. At the end of Monday or Thursday, I had probably seen 10 or more student pieces.

And you have to apply your creative energy to each student.

Exactly, or try to. I could never have written at the end of those long days of teaching.

But you would compose on days when you were not teaching?

Yes, usually. Both then and now in retirement, I usually start in the morning and if I have something going well, I can often take a break for lunch and come back and work in the afternoons as well. I don't like working at night, and I never have.

The most sustained writing I have ever done was when my wife and I were on sabbatical and living in Paris. I was writing my *Saint Matthew Passion,* and it was a huge effort: It's a great big, two-hour piece for soloists, choirs, and orchestra. I was able to get up, eat breakfast, work in the morning, have lunch, work in the afternoon, have dinner, and sometimes I'd even work in the evening. I did this basically seven days a week. I'm okay as long as I am feeling good about the piece. If I get stuck on the piece, it is hard to keep plugging away—counterproductive actually.

What do you do if you get stuck on a piece?
Well, I don't think there is any magic formula for getting unstuck. Writer's block affects a large percentage of people who write music or write words because it's just normal to not always have the kind of immediacy of knowing what should happen next. I find that, for me, starting a piece is the most difficult moment, not knowing exactly where I want the piece to go or what I want it to do. I have to make certain kinds of decisions, and then once I get into the piece I don't usually get terribly stuck. I might have a few false starts in a movement. I might write maybe 20 bars or 40 bars and decide this just isn't really what I want to do. So I start over again.

So you just reject that idea that you feel is not working and start over?
Well, most of the time. But sometimes there will be an element in that start that I think is okay, and I will find a way of developing something out of that original idea. But everybody is just so different; I don't think there is any single method for getting unstuck. I know there are people who have a graceful facility and are able to do their work without ever hitting a blank space. That isn't me for sure, although if it is a piece that I'm really engaged in, usually I can find a way to restart the process.

With the Internet we can now instantly send our music, ideas, audio files, et cetera, anywhere in the world. Is there really a center of music anymore? Or has technology made it unnecessary for a composer to live in a Paris or a New York in order to pursue their career?
Even with the Internet, e-mail, Skype, and all of that, there is still a great deal to be said for one-on-one personal contact and simply knowing somebody on a face-to-face basis. I don't know that anything substitutes for that.

I suspect the mechanics of being a composer, of taking care of details and all of that, can be done from anywhere. That in itself is certainly possible. Whether the things that big careers depend upon, aside from talent, can be achieved from a remote location is the question.

Does talent alone make for a successful career? Whether one is a composer, writer, or painter, isn't there a lot more that has to go into creating a successful career?
I certainly think there probably are fine talented people who simply don't have a huge career in their field. Is it possible to accomplish that and the things that facilitate a career outside of the big cities? My initial thought is that it probably isn't possible, because those with significant careers depend so much upon the contacts that they have, the people who promote them and their music.

It's interesting though. I do wonder if New York itself is as compelling as it once was in American musical life, if it hasn't lost its absolute centrality, due in no small measure to the connectivity everywhere. I guess being performed in New York and all of that is still a big deal. But I'm not so sure; there seem to be really fine composers living everywhere in the country now.

Some composers have commented that the compositional process is mystical, religious, or that they sometimes are surprised by the inspirations that come to them and have no idea of their origin. Comments?
The process of creation certainly is something ineffable. Somehow, it probably begins with the music a composer has experienced. In turn, musical experience is transformed into something new and, ideally, fresh through the combination of intrinsic talent and learned technique. It seems to me that the greatest talents always possess the strongest musical personalities, voices that are their own and no one else's, wedded to the skills that allow those personalities to come through definitively. On a much humbler level, I find there is something thrilling about working my way through a score, finding what I hope are solid solutions to the challenges that always arise and, on the best days, finding the notes, rhythms, harmonies, textures, and colors that best express what I want to say in my music. I am reluctant to claim anything as grand as inspiration, but I always am excited when something turns out well in a score. Perhaps it really is inspiration only in the greatest composers; so, sometimes I wonder if creating a good moment isn't just dumb luck for the rest of us! Who knows where such things come from?

From These Honored Dead (2013), Soprano, Violin, Viola, Cello, Piano

The Deepness of the Blue (2012), SATB, Piano Four Hands

From Dreams (2012), SSA, Flute, Viola

Traveling Home: An American Requiem (2011), SSAATTBB

The Dream Keeper (2009), SATB, Piano Four Hands

Tunebook (2004–2008), Woodwind Quintet

Symphony (2003–2004), Orchestra

Wind Play (2002), Flute, Bassoon, Piano

The Passion of Our Lord Jesus Christ According to St. Matthew (1997–2009), Soloists, SATB Choir, SSA Choir, Orchestra

Sonata (1992), Flute, Piano

Afro-American Fragments (1991), SATB Choir, Piano Four Hands

Tripartita (1989), Violin, Clarinet, Piano

▶ To learn more about William Averitt and his music, including audio excerpts from *Afro-American Fragments, The Dream Keeper, The Deepness of the Blue, Tunebook, Tripartita, Wind Play*, and *Traveling Home*, visit www.oup.com/us/compositioninthedigitalworld.

NOTES

1. James Woodard was an American composer and music professor at Murray State University and Southern Illinois University. He studied piano at the Juilliard School and composition at Florida State University.
2. John Boda (1922–2002) was an American composer, and music professor at Florida State University. He studied at the Eastman School of Music. He served as assistant conductor to George Szell, and played the piano in a performance of *Petrushka* with Stravinsky conducting.
3. Frances Lapp Averitt is an American flautist and spouse of William Averitt. She is Professor Emeritus at the Shenandoah Conservatory of Music and has performed with numerous orchestras.
4. The software Professional Composer was released in 1984 by the company Mark of the Unicorn. It was one of the very first Macintosh music-notation programs.

Michael Torke

If the digital revolution had never happened, we would still have six major record companies deciding which pop songs get recorded and played and what classical music they might deign to put out. Probably none of us classical people would have much of a recorded presence at all any more. Even if the digital revolution is going to kill us all in the end, at least in the short term it has been very helpful to musicians and classical music in particular.

Michael Torke (b. Wisconsin, 1961) is not only one of the most prolific, well-known, and often-performed American composers but also a savvy businessman, articulate and humorous speaker, and avid poker player. He has style in spades and a satisfyingly eccentric wit. Talking with Torke feels like having a conversation with an old college friend, or a rock band teammate. He is direct, unapologetic, earthy, and confident, yet he remains refreshingly humble as he questions the certainty of his future as a composer.

From the very beginning of his career, Torke showed himself to be somewhat of a rebel: He left Yale before completing his studies to move to New York City to pursue his composing career, flew in the face of convention by securing the rights to his own music, launched his own recording company, and took on wildly divergent commissions in service to his muse.

Educated at the Eastman School of Music as well as at Yale, Torke studied with some of America's preeminent composers, including Joseph Schwantner, Christopher Rouse, and Martin Bresnick. In 1985, following his Yale-to-New York move, the Brooklyn Philharmonic premiered his piece *Ecstatic Orange*, with Lukas Foss conducting. Hailed as a terrifically talented composer, a publishing deal with Boosey & Hawkes quickly followed. He then spent a year living and composing in Italy after winning the Rome prize, was awarded a fellowship from the National Endowment for the Arts, and wrote several ballets for the New York City ballet—all while he was still in his 20s.

Torke's music, often referred to as post-minimalist, is smart and fresh, with a vivid palette and robust sense of rhythm supported by his exceptional gift for compositional imagination and orchestration. Working in genres as divergent as ballet, opera, music for the Olympics, rock, and a series of orchestral pieces based on the color palette, he shows no sign of slowing down.

In the finest tradition of financially and artistically successful composers of the past, Torke aims to avoid the impoverished fate of artists such as Mozart. His goal is to make uncompromisingly great music, and to make a comfortable living doing it.

Do you have a particular process that you follow when you're composing a new piece? A set schedule, for example, or a particular setting or time of day that works best for you?
I remember as a teenager trying to devour books on this very subject. What do composers do? How do they compose? What are their schedules? I was so curious, but I never found a really interesting answer. So here I am on the other side, trying to give my own answer. For me, I compose full time. I don't have any other positions that take up my time or bring in money, and so I need to work, not around the clock (although sometimes I do), but I get up every morning and I work. I work through the day as if it

is a regular job. I look at one of the projects in front of me, see what needs to be done, and I attack it. Sometimes with relish, sometimes with dread.

It's the dream vocation: I have no boss. I have no administrative responsibilities; I'm the envy of all. And yet it sometimes doesn't feel that way. The world is changing all the time, and regardless of economic swings up and down, I have to stay afloat. And so it comes down to commissions and royalties. That's it. And what happens if people decide they're just going to stop playing my music? That could happen any day. What happens when no one wants to commission any new music, no one has any money? I'm always trying to think of ways to stay ahead. One example is that I have my own record label.

Doesn't managing your own record label take a lot of time away from your composing?

Yes, it takes a good deal of time, but that diversification is an important part of my business strategy. For example, I was extremely lucky that in the CD boom of the late 1980s and early 1990s, I got the opportunity to have a lot of my music recorded commercially. But then of course the world changes. Ten years later, all the independent labels fold, and then 10 years after that all the majors fold, and finally there is really no recording industry at all per se. It's just complete suicide and collapse. Hah! How stunning it is to see all of that disappear in a matter of 20 years. It's really, really interesting and amazing.

If that is how you describe the state of the record industry in the 21st century, how and why did you come to own a record label yourself?

Fortunately for me, in the early 2000s the executive producer of all of my Argo/Decca recordings said, "I can help you get all the rights to your music, so you can release them on your own." I had already seen how difficult that was. No one at record companies would take a phone call, answer an e-mail, or even had an online presence I could write to, if I had a legal question. So it was a huge benefit to have that supportive connection. The deal was done in 2002–2003, and so now I have the right to manufacture and distribute all of my own recordings worldwide.

And then that expanded into doing new releases. Recordings are hugely expensive. The latest release, which came out in the fall of 2011, is called *Tahiti*. That release was made possible by doing a project with the Liverpool Philharmonic, where Andrew Cornall was the executive director at the time. It went really well. I said to him, "If I write you another piece, free, to fill out an album, would you record both pieces, and hand over the rights to me?" We did a handshake deal. And that's how that album came about. So there I was sacrificing a commission so that I could go further into debt and bring out an album that I could self-finance.

Is releasing a CD still important?
Because of recorded music, I have at least a certain minimal presence on classical radio, in this country and worldwide. Music directors are enthusiastic when I have a new release. They play it, and now you can track all of this online. When I saw how everyone was playing the new album as well as all of the old stuff, I realized the value. Those radio performances do generate income from BMI. And recordings are still an important marketing tool.

Have digital recordings and the web changed the life of composers?
Absolutely. The technology of the 20th century made recorded music possible, but the digital revolution killed analog recorded music. Which meant that it democratized it, so that the little guy like me can now have total control of his recordings. If the digital revolution had never happened, we would still have six major record companies deciding which pop songs get recorded and played and what classical music they might deign to put out. Probably none of us classical people would have much of a recorded presence at all any more. Even if the digital revolution is going to kill us all in the end, at least in the short term it has been very helpful to musicians and classical music in particular.

Despite your anxieties about your career, you are widely recognized as a success in your field. How did you begin your career as a composer?
I started as a professional composer circa 1985, when I walked out of Yale, and I've been able to maintain this lifestyle through 2012. But I'm constantly paranoid. I always think it's all going to be over tomorrow. It seems as much a struggle today as it was in the 1980s when I started, or the 1990s, or the 2000s. One can never really coast along.

How do you balance the challenges of leading a creative life while dealing with the realities of making a living as a composer?
In the early 1980s when I got started, an orchestra would call and say, "Can you write a 10-minute orchestra opener for us? We will commission you." And I would say, "Great! Hey, that's exactly what I wanted to do, write a 10-minute piece for orchestra." So the commissioning wishes were in line with my desires. Then later on, I started getting interested

in theater. When the New York City ballet commissioned me in the late 1980s to write a ballet, it was in the Balanchine tradition of a 30-minute piece of abstract music for abstract dance. At the time I didn't believe music was capable of doing any kind of narrative so again, that was right in line with what my wishes were.

Still later, I became very interested in telling a story on stage and guess what? In the early 2000s, the national ballet of Canada commissioned me to write two story ballets. So once again what I wanted to do was right in line with what I was being asked. When I decided I wanted to write some opera, along came some opera commissions. It's all been kind of weird and uncanny.

At age 50, though, I'm looking at life in a different way and think all of it has been just luck. Now I ask myself what do I, over my whole life, want to accomplish? What have I done? What do I still want to do? And what if I want to write a major concerto for orchestra that lasts for 35 minutes? Well, where's the commission for that? Do I wait for the commission? And so, the challenge now is to find ways to write exactly what I want to write and still find ways to monetize it, either on the backend or just through promoting performances, or maybe just struggling more with a higher artistic vision.

I certainly think it's become more of a challenge. My piece *House and Home*, which I wrote for the American Opera Center, is a good example. When that came along I first thought, "Well, they're asking me to write a song for $1,000, not a lot of money, although it's generous for writing a song." I realized that in fact I had lots of song ideas, and I could per- haps do this with a kind of facility and joy, writing it in maybe a week or even a weekend. Which is what I did and I'm very proud of it. I'm think- ing of making some arrangements for other instruments because I was so pleased with the way it came out, and hey, guess what? There was $1,000 attached to it too.

I like your website. What role does it play in promoting your music?
Frankly, I don't know whether having a website helps or not anymore. It takes a lot of time and maintenance. It constantly needs updating, it's important to me that it's clean. When the Internet first became something that everyone was getting involved with in the late 1990s, people tended to react by saying, "Wow, you have a website?" It was probably similar to the time when people started handing out business cards. What if you had been the first person to hand out a business card? You would have had an edge because then other people would have your credentials right at their fingertips. Once everyone had a business card, it evened out the playing

field. And so of course that's what has happened with the Internet. You can't *not* have a website anymore, because people want and expect to know everything about you immediately. But does it help? It helps to the extent that it helps everyone. But, if an orchestra has one slot in its next season, and they're going to select one contemporary piece, they look around online to see what they can find on the Internet. They expect you to have a website and may look at your website to see what you are doing, but your website is not going to get you that slot, what you need is a recommendation. In a certain way, the Internet is a zero sum game.

I understand, but it does seem that the Internet has had a huge impact on music and the business of being a composer. What about YouTube and social media? Do these new technological innovations help or hurt?

YouTube, which is owned by Google, is going to be the end of all entertainment and art. Maybe it already is the end. First, they were brought to the lawmakers who said, "You're not paying any royalties." So they took however long, three months or three years, working out all the details so as to comply with copyright law and pay the composers whenever their music is played on a YouTube video. So then, everybody's all excited, oh boy! And then earlier this year I got my first statement, and every month since I get a new statement. And it's weird because, and I'm not exaggerating, every line is $0.00. Finally, after five months of getting statements, I earned one penny.

I was speaking to a young composer friend of mine who is working in Korea right now on an opera. She was telling me how inspiring the YouTube phenomenon is. But then I asked her, "Can you buy those DVDs in Korea?" No, she just watched the music on YouTube. There is no income for the composer coming from there. So everything becomes free. The broadcast and publishing industries are going to collapse. Hollywood will be one of the first to go, then television will follow, and then the music industry. However, what's great about the music industry and the theater is that they still depend on live performance. And that can't be digitized. The experience of live performance is the anathema to making a copy of it, so that's what's going to save us. When Hollywood collapses, theater will rise again. It will be a different world.

So, the fact that your music is available for free on the Internet is a big concern?

People naturally think that the frustration of YouTube is the loss of income. To me it is the loss of control. You meet a random person at a dinner party; and they are curious about your music. These days their default behavior (if they care to follow up) is a search on YouTube, listening to whatever uploaded performances first appear on the screen. And what do they find? Fourth-rate, uncoached performances by third-rate amateur musicians so proud to post *their* performance to show off to their friends. It's the bad performances that are uploaded, not the good, because the good musicians don't need the immediate psychological reinforcement the lesser-experienced musicians crave. My music does not render well if it is not played accurately or musically. So most newcomers to my music are developing incorrect opinions about what my music is. What's the answer? "Start your own YouTube channel!!" Even the Harry Fox Agency is promoting this idea. Talk about throwing the towel in! Now all of my commercial music will be essentially free. OK, I will earn .0003 cents per year in Google royalties. Again, the digital revolution has been suicide for the music industry.

All of this must be disturbing to you as a composer and a business-person.

It is disturbing, in the literal sense that it disturbs the status quo. But the world is always shifting. Right now, I'm reading the four-volume biography on Tchaikovsky by David Brown. And it's made me think: When Tchaikovsky was establishing himself, he did not have recordings. I mean that's an obvious statement, but we forget, they didn't have television or movies then, and classical music meant much more to the culture in the 1800s than it does today. So if movies, television, recording—all of that—collapses, we should still have a thriving classical music scene because it's already been proven that it can be done. That's a hopeful position.

Another way to look at all of this is that our current situation is really a continuum of 20th-century technological influences on the music industry. First there was the piano roll, and then radio, and then 78-RPM recordings, then the real boom of the record industry, television, and movies—that's the whole 20th-century arc of technology taking over the arts. That inflated the value of popular music. The Beatles became the kings of the entire universe. Okay, they wrote great songs, but they weren't *that* great. Their achievement is not more than Beethoven or Bach, come on! It made me think, "How come that got so distorted?" It's because people were making way, way too much money and the economic harnessing of that particular 20th-century technology artificially drove up the value of that particular form of music. It was a kind of bubble economy for popular music. And then there was this feeling that the only way any kind of serious music could be done in an intellectually responsible way was to have some kind of connection to this huge wave that was taking over the universe. Now that's all collapsing, and there's kind of a *schadenfreude* [pleasure derived from the misfortunes of others] going on, which is kind of interesting. All of the true starving artists today are the rockers. I know this from personal experience. I was just in Paris working with all these London rockers, and they don't have any work. They're lucky if they get a $5 bill for their efforts. They are the starving artists. And those classical folks who are in circulation, we're doing okay, relatively speaking. It's kind of nice to see the correction of that bubble. This is all technology-based; the technology of the 20th century has shifted.

On the positive side, digital technology has created some incredible opportunities for composers, and removed some old barriers, sometimes in unexpected places.
One impact of technology is on geography. It would be cumbersome and unwieldy for me to maintain two homes (one in Las Vegas, the other in New York) if I had to cart pages of scores and sketches along with the corresponding tapes of recordings back and forth as I work on a project. Now everything can be stored and sent efficiently (and quite invisibly!), such that all I need to pack when I travel is a toothbrush! True, if this were 150 years ago, when what you wrote down in ink could not be duplicated, I would be traveling with only a few pages of manuscript. So it's funny that 20th-century technology made composers increasingly a slave to their studio, while 21st-century technology frees him up again.

Take the example of Eric Whitacre's "virtual choirs." Without technology of social media, how could he have united the thousands of individual submissions [of vocalists] and coordinate all the disparate parts to make his beautiful unified wholes? Impossible. I feel very inspired by these advances.

Do you use technology when you're composing? For example, do you write at the computer or do you use the piano and pencil and paper?
Technology really saved me, especially the development of notation programs. And why did that transform everything? Because the real reason that composers gave their copyrights to the big publishers, which is like giving away valuable real estate, was because copying all of the parts for a big orchestra piece, or an oratorio or opera, was tremendously time-consuming and/or expensive. The publishers would step in and say, "Hey, we've got deep pockets, we can do all of this for you, but in exchange, give us the copyright because we're taking such a big risk on you." It was

highway robbery. Well, the notation programs came along, and now we don't need the publishers. We can do it ourselves. The score is digitized, and now the parts can be generated fairly easily. Once I could take over my notation, I could really control my copyrights and my expenses.

I remember how it was when I left Boosey & Hawkes. I had an administration deal with them that started in 1992, so that I could retain my copyrights. In 1996, I composed an oratorio called *Book of Proverbs*. I remember that the commission fee was approximately $20,000. I did not have a notation program, so I hired a guy to engrave it. His total bill was $20,000. So in effect, I wrote a free piece just so that I could get good-looking parts and a score. Today the parts can be done over the weekend. So notation technology drastically changed the economics of composing for me.

Now, that's the business side, but there is also the composing side where technology changed the process. And this is both good and bad. It's labor intensive to write notes with ink or with pencil, so you think a lot before you put the notes down. When you have these notation programs at your disposal, and they have playback, you write in a different way. You slap things down, you listen to it, then you revise, and then you listen to it again, and then you revise some more. And it's always about cleaning away the dirt or getting it into focus. Now, is that a better or worse way to write? I don't know. My dad was an architect, and I remember watching him work. He would do a sketch, and he would put a piece of yellow tracing paper over his sketch, and he would revise that sketch, and then he would put another piece of tracing paper over that, and revise it again. That's how a draftsman worked. So you could say that the new notation programs make me work more like an architect. That's the good side. The bad side is that I think that all of that hard thinking that I used to do before actually committing notes to the page was actually really good. I was doing multi-level thinking as I was doing that. And I feel I've sacrificed some of that.

Do you create MIDI demos as a rehearsal aid for new pieces? I'm wondering if technology affected your interaction with performers in a positive way.

Again, there are pluses and minuses. On the plus side, when you go to the first rehearsal of a premiere, there is not one mistake in the parts. Now that's 60 percent technology and 40 percent me being obsessive-compulsive. Proofing the score and parts is much more accurate now than when the work was done by a bunch of hand copyists. And that goes a long way. I remember in the early days, the first rehearsal would typically be spent answering questions like, "Is that a G or a G sharp in the trumpet part?" You got nothing done, and it was so humiliating and such a waste of time. So those days are over, now you go in with absolutely perfect parts.

On the other hand, it can induce a kind of laziness on the part of the musicians. They may say, "Do you have a MIDI file of the new piece?" And, of course we do. So we send them off one of these stupid MIDI files, and they listen to it. Now some conductors and musicians say, "Oh, now I know the piece." But there are two problems with this: First, the musicians don't dig into the music with the study, the passion, and the zeal that they formally had to use to study the score from scratch, and second, the MIDI playback demonstrations are run by a computer and they don't have the right kind of musicality even if the composer has taken the time to program in rubatos, et cetera. Of course, the best musicians and conductors don't fall into that trap. In fact, a lot of good musicians simply refuse to listen to these MIDI demos. The role of the MIDI demo is decreasing by the year and I'm happy to see that.

Do you take a different approach when writing for ballet or opera as opposed to pure instrumental music?
I think the primary difference is that when I write instrumental music, I am thinking about form. Foreground, mid-ground, background, everything is about form. How do I organize these abstract vibrations in the air to make sense and be expressive? When I'm dealing with ballet and opera, I am dealing with a libretto, with narrative. I'm telling a story. The mathematics of music are really good to depend on when you write purely instrumental music. But when it comes to having a story to tell, a lot of those mathematics and those formal considerations are thrown away in the service of the singer or the story. Unless you're a genius, or at least really clever, that sacrifice of what I call "the math," or the structure, is a big price to pay. And I still sometimes struggle. How can you ever write a truly durable and good piece of theater music? Is it possible? Maybe if I had some huge theatrical successes, I would be espousing a whole different theory. Maybe these thoughts are all just a rationalization, but that's what I grapple with.

It's been said that jazz, rock, and popular music are part of your sound. What are your thoughts on your musical style?
At one point I went to my Wikipedia page, and whoever wrote it said, "He is a jazz and rock inspired composer." And I thought, okay take any one of my pieces and point to any bar you like and tell me where the jazz is or tell me where the rock is. This is partly because there is

a solipsism going on. I'm the composer, so I don't know how others see me in an accurate way. When I listen to my music, I don't hear any rock or jazz. I know what rock is—I listen to it. I know what jazz is—I listen to it. My music doesn't fall into either of these areas. I don't get it. And yet, close, trusted friends, say, "No, we hear it! What are you talking about? That's very accurate." I've had people say of a student, "He's imitating you," so then I want to listen to the piece, but when I do, I hear nothing that has any relation or bearing to anything I have done, so I have no idea what they're talking about. There is a blindness there I suppose. It's kind of a metaphysical problem, not being able to see myself the way others do, or understand what people mean when they refer to a "Torke style." I'm flattered, though, that there might be such a notion.

In the 1990s, the *New York Times* ran an editorial making a big intellectual deal out of classical concert composers using popular rock and jazz influences, as if this was somehow a huge intellectual breakthrough. And a lot of us got a lot of press, and of course it was a good way to get a lot of attention, like we were riding on the coattails of some kind of movement. But even that didn't make sense to me. Obviously, this had been going on long before in the 1980s, and in fact all through American music. Every American composer seems to have been influenced by some popular style. In other centuries, folk music was the popular music of the day, and that was always influential. So there is nothing new under the sun.

You live near Las Vegas. We've talked about the fact that you love playing cards. Do you see any parallels between poker and writing music?
Absolutely! There is a huge parallel because both music and poker are mathematically based and deal with human psychology. Human psychology in the broadest sense involves all of the feelings we have, which music addresses, and of course music also is very mathematical. It's similar with poker. The game is extremely mathematical but there is also the uncertainty involved in the "imperfect information" aspect of the game, so then you're dealing with human psychology. It's game theory. Is this guy lying, is he telling the truth? Is he representing, is he not? So the part of my brain that gets excited writing music is very close to the part of my brain that gets excited playing poker. Of course they are different enough so that after a long day of writing music I enjoy the recreation of going out and playing poker. It's a really nice way to switch gears.

Does a "serious" composer have to be located in New York at all anymore? For that matter, is there a world center of music now that we have the Internet?

Well, I love to be in New York, because New York still is the center of culture. It's hugely stimulating and I'm a person who needs lots of stimulation. The danger of being out here in the desert, even though I have Las Vegas nearby, is the lack of cultural stimulation. And that's a problem for me; so going back to New York is like getting my medicine, or filling up with gas.

That said, you *can* compose anywhere. But if you're working on a collaborative piece such as an opera, having face-to-face meetings is absolutely essential. You just can't successfully realize an artistic collaboration without these meetings. To have meetings in New York is commonplace, not so much out here in Nevada. So sometimes I have to be in New York for my work.

Do deadlines help you with your work? Do you hate them or consider them a positive tool?

I'm an organizational and deadline enthusiast. I find it incredibly stimulating, but I think I've overdone it over the years, and it's not as stimulating as it once was. Now I like to imagine two different scenarios. First: What if I suddenly came into $50 million, and had no economic concerns whatsoever. How would I think about what projects I would write, and then how would I get them performed? That's liberating to think about. But then there's the converse of that: What if everything dries up and I make no more money at my music? What would I do then? That tends to take my mind away from, "Oh, here's the next commission, when is the deadline?" I'm getting kind of tired of that.

Do you think there are great artists, composers, whom the general public will never hear of because they've had bad luck, or lack marketing savvy? Or do you believe that if you have the talent, you're going to be heard?

The consensus answer is that because of the way information is disseminated today, no one can remain obscure. Of course, someone could write a great symphony, lock it in a trunk, and prevent even the lawyers from getting at it, but what artist would want to do that? If that's what you want to do, to purposely remain in obscurity, then you might get your wish. But if someone does something creative, it may take a while, and it may be misunderstood for decades, but eventually it will get out there. I don't think you can hide anymore.

Oracle (2013), Orchestra
Fiji (2007), Large Ensemble
Rapture (2000), Percussion Concerto
Strawberry Fields (1999), Opera in One Act
July (1995), Saxophone Quartet
Four Proverbs (1993), Soprano and Ensemble
Javelin (1994), Orchestra
Ash (1988), Orchestra
Green (1986), Orchestra
Ecstatic Orange (1985), Orchestra
The Yellow Pages (1985), Flute, Clarinet, Violin, Cello, and Piano

▶ To learn more about Michael Torke and his music, including score and audio excerpts from his *Iphigenia, Oracle*, and *Bliss,* visit www.oup.com/us/compositioninthedigitalworld.

Libby Larsen

My search began a long time ago.. I'm working on finding the sound palette that I believe actually relates to human beings. I'm looking to become 100 percent fluid in many combinations of technologies that form our musical ears. That's what I'm looking to do. Life's a playground!

With several irons in the fire at all times, Libby Larsen (b. Delaware, 1950) is busier than ever before in her creative work. Despite her hectic schedule, however, she projects an air of relaxed confidence and I found her to be both laid back and very funny. She is smart and extremely articulate, and our conversations were peppered with her razor-sharp observations on contemporary music, technology, and a variety of general subjects, including the current state of church music and the crisis in the US educational system.

Larsen began her musical career as a young girl singing Gregorian chants under the direction of the nuns at her Catholic school. Later, during her tenure studying composition and theory at the University of Minnesota, she co-founded (with fellow students, including Stephen Paulus) the Minnesota Composers Forum, which ultimately grew into the American Composers Forum, which has been providing significant support for composers for over 40 years.

Larsen held the Papamarkou Chair in Education and Technology at John W. Kluge Center of the Library of Congress. Her awards include a Grammy, the George Peabody Medal, induction into the Minnesota Music Hall of Fame, and a Lifetime Achievement Award from the American Academy of Arts and Letters.[1]

A prolific composer with over 500 works covering a wide variety of genres, Larsen cites an eclectic mix of influences ranging from Chuck Berry and Big Mamma Thornton to Lutosławski and Bach. It's difficult to describe her music in a single paragraph; if a label must be applied to her sound, a new one will have to be concocted just for her. Her compositions encompass elements of ragtime, post-modernism, boogie-woogie, New Orleans jazz, and minimalism. Add to that her unique blend of imagination, heart, talent, and sonic perspective and you might come close to understanding the dazzling sound that is distinctively Larsen's own.

You have an extremely extensive list of compositions. How do you find time to compose so much music?

I elected not to join the faculty when I completed my doctorate in the 1970s. I had a retreat with myself in order to determine exactly what it is that I would need in order to compose all of the music that was unformed in my head, basically an infinite well of music. I decided not to join a music faculty for many, many reasons, including gender and faculty politics. I always wanted good energy around me if I could possibly have it. As years have gone on, I've come to understand that there is a particular rigidity about faculty life. The classes you teach, the meetings you must attend, the syllabi you must prepare. Much of that life is very linear. My own brain is not linear. It's continuous thinking, a type of thinking that eventually finds itself in an art form that appears to be linear but is not. At that point in time I didn't have any money and I didn't have any job prospects in the traditional sense, so I decided to try to form my life in a way that would facilitate using my brain in the way that it best functions. There are macro things about my daily life that pertain to music. I think about the pieces that I'm working on all of the time in one part of my brain. I usually work on more than one piece at a time (although the pieces need to be in different stages of development in order for me to work on them simultaneously). For instance, today I am working on the second act of my new opera *A Wrinkle in Time*, and in fact that piece is well on its way. It has its language, its architecture, and it has a life.

Is the opera *A Wrinkle in Time* based on the children's story of the same title? [2] **I remember reading and enjoying that book as a child.**
Yes, isn't it a wonderful book? I'm not done, but the piece is pretty well formed. Then I'm working on another piece for four-hand piano. For that one, I have only about four minutes of music so far. I already know the architecture, I know the energy of the piece, and I know what I need to create, but the piece is still in the creative stage. And then a concept for another piece just came this week, and that's a piece for baritone instruments and interactive graphic novel. That piece just occurred to my brain, let's see, is today Tuesday? So yesterday. I'm in the earliest stages of that piece.

And so I go about my days in a domestic way that looks relatively normal. We are cleaning up after a tornado recently hit our neighborhood, so I spent the morning chopping up a tree in our front yard and I put a wash in, and I walked the dog. While I'm doing the domestic work of everyday living other parts of my brain are working on these pieces. I take my brain very seriously and I always have. The way for me to work is to be as vigilant as I can with all of the techniques that are available compositionally, and then put those techniques in the service of my instincts. In service of the "eureka moments." That way, my entire day feels like a big compositional playground. The technical and mechanical processes of transferring the music into readable and/or reproducible "scores" is what appears to most people as "composing." But for me, this part of the process is about refining what is already relatively complete and residing in my head.

So you always work on more than one piece at a time? That's interesting.
Yes I do unless I'm depressed, which is very rare. For instance, after 9/11 I could not activate any of the joyous, creative parts of my brain for quite a while. Otherwise, ever since I was quite young this has been the way that my brain works. I can work on many different problems or challenges at a time and have always been able to do that. In my life, it's been a matter of becoming cognizant of how to take advantage of this.

How do you capture your musical ideas? Do you keep notebooks?

I do not keep notebooks. I keep the ideas in my head until it's time for me to begin getting them out. I have special paper made for this purpose. It's an 11 x 17 pad of paper with 20 staves on each page. The ideas are all in my head, like a big beauty pageant with 1,000 entries. They're all parading around saying, "Is it time for me now?" [Laughs]

The first pages of sketches for a new piece might be in my own short-hand: some numbers that are indecipherable to anyone but me, like 1 times 4 or A over 3. So, on that page I sketch basic language: the architecture of the piece, the energy of the piece, and maybe just a tiny little fragment of how the piece begins to unfold in what we call linear time. Then I just start writing the piece out as it is in my head. I lie on the piano bench and begin to write the piece out, and then I will check on the piano to confirm that what I'm writing down is actually what is in my head.

Do you take those ideas to a computer for notation, or for any other reasons?

I have two people that I have worked with since graduate school who transcribe my music for me. I write by hand and they transcribe it into computer notation. I much, much prefer writing by hand because it's a different physicality than sitting at a computer, and I am a very physically active and kinetic kind of person. I hear all of the music that I write fully orchestrated in my ear. I have a traditionally trained ear and can read a full orchestral score and hear it as I read. That's traditional ear training. I'm in mourning for our young composers who have been given the idea that to hear music on a computer is to hear music. I worry mightily for their inner ear. Mightily, because it's the inner ear training that makes the musician, whether as a performer or as a composer.

I've heard several composers comment that although they feel the computer has done much for music education, and in aiding the work of creating parts and scores, the immediate gratification a student gets when hearing a playback from a computer is undermining the necessary work involved in developing one's musical ear. Do you feel that this is a serious problem?

I do. Have you noticed that some younger composers who are training themselves to hear solely by listening to computer playback are actually training themselves to think that they hear things that cannot actually be performed, much less heard? Also breath. Breath is becoming a big issue I think.

Are you referring to musical phrasing and the danger of writing lines on the computer that are not physically possible on an actual instrument?
Yes, exactly.

You've discussed forming and shaping your music around language and the human voice. I think that is very important. Would you talk a little bit about that concept?
Oh, I would love to talk about that! [Laughs] One of the questions that I have always been interested in is, "Where does music come from?" If I am conducting a master class, I ask the composers to tell me where music comes from.

I went to a Catholic school and from first through fifth grade we regularly sang all the Latin chants in the choirs for the church. And communication happened: spiritual and mystical communication. This was clear to all of us who were singing in the choir, even at that young age. Then in sixth grade, the Vatican II Council happened, and the Latin chants were eliminated from worship services. They were replaced with what I like to refer to as " folk-nun music." [Sings a snippet of "Dominique"]³ Basically, it's spaghetti western music that became part of what is now the church liturgy. Terrible, unsophisticated music with a flat 7 everywhere [Laughs], with really unskilled musicians playing the guitar badly, and singing over microphones in cathedrals. The sound was just so incompatible with the simultaneous evolution of the acoustics of churches and the Gregorian chant. To me this evolution brought about a perfectly harmonious, 1,000-year-old development of expression of the soul of the human being. When Gregorian chant was suppressed, it was, to me, a true offense.

So I began to think that, perhaps, one place music springs from is the language spoken by the people. The question is, what music comes from this language? I pursued this idea most vigorously in trying to understand what is physical about language. I keep transcriptions in notebooks of people speaking. I listen to you speaking and I can go to my notebook and write "Robert Raines" and I will "rhythmate" your speech, meaning I will take rhythmic dictation of your unique speaking pattern. I'll give you your pitch range (with most people it's about a perfect 4th, at least for English speakers) and apply it to your rhythmic profile. So the basis of my music often begins with language profiles. I now think that that is the way to be accessible. If you approximate the language that your audience speaks, it doesn't matter what you do with pitches or even timbre. You can immediately open the audiences' ears to the music that you are presenting if you know how people speak.

I found this concept to be useful in teaching students phrasing and cadences by referring and comparing those techniques to spoken vocal inflections, so I know what you mean. Of course, your concept goes much further.

I've begun to present these methods to young composers, and at first it confuses them, but then they often grasp it and begin to use it. For instance, I often use a phrase from Lou Gehrig's farewell speech, "I consider myself the luckiest man on the face of the earth." I will play that on my laptop for my students over and over again until the class can hear the pulse. Everybody has a pulse when they speak—you have a pulse, I have a pulse. We take one line and add hash marks to indicate where the pulses occur. Then we rhythmate everything that is said between the pulses. What we find is that in rhythmated speech there is a paucity of the dance meters that we have convinced ourselves are the meters of music. There is only pulse and the speaker's unique rhythmic presentation within that pulse. Interesting. It's made me think that in our music education system music offers us infinite possibilities but we spend at least 12 years impoverishing ourselves by defining music through a narrow set of parameters that are merely cultural perceptions. Terrible, isn't it? See why I can't be on a faculty?

You held the Harissios Papamarkou Chair[4] in Education at the Library of Congress in 2003–2004.

I joined the John W. Kluge Center, a think-tank on education and technology. Each fellow at the Kluge Center was to pursue a cultural theory. I had two charges, one was to look at the Library of Congress's technological practices and make suggestions about archival techniques, and the other was to do original thinking involving technology and education. What I found is typical in many large institutions that archive a lot of material: the same library system that existed when I was young. Still the Dewey decimal system, boxes full of paper, and stacks of books—the same retrieval system used when I was born in 1950. The library administrators understand what's needed in order to update accessibility so that this generation of students might use their technological devices to tap into the Library of Congress and research and retrieve the information that they need instantly. Their goal is, of course, to accomplish this as quickly as possible. Where the library is today in meeting that goal, however, is at about 1972 technology. Someone needs to give the Library of Congress a multi-billion-dollar grant so that they can come up to speed. Every 10 years or so the technology changes radically, but the budget to update does not keep up.

I have a theory about how those changes affect creativity: Every time the culture at large changes its major mode of transportation, it also changes its preference for the most effective delivery system for music, speeches, sermons, et cetera. I researched that theory, looking at 1750 to 2006. Using the resources of several divisions of the Library of Congress, I studied the simultaneous development of transportation and communication technologies, looking for correlations to the development of concert halls. I discovered, or confirmed, that there is a strong correlation—in fact, the three areas are inextricably intertwined. So I discovered quite by accident where our traditional classical canon comes from and realized that the place for us, American composers, is limited at best.

How has the development of technology directly impacted the compositions of the composers who were writing during those respective periods of change?

A few years back, the American Symphony Orchestra League brought about six composers together (including me) to talk about how to best get young people to attend concerts. Our conclusion: You have to update your sound palette. You've got to give to the ears of people what they hear in the air. We talked about sound from the perspective of a composer's ears. If the composer has a really well-trained ear, you project the sound that's in your thoughts into the delivery system for that sound. Take Wagner, for instance. He knew the sound that he wanted and so he essentially built a great big old megaphone to project the sound the way he heard it in his head.

A delivery system for music has clear and identifiable acoustic properties. These delivery systems all rely on technology. Every civilization that needs point-to-mass communication in order to function smoothly has evolved an amplification system to facilitate delivering its message. Greek theater design (Epidaurus), the Swiss alphorn, and African talking drums are examples. If you are the creator of the message, you are naturally influenced by the technology you are using. As a composer, you are influenced by the sound of your delivery. If you are cognizant and vigilant, you design the object you are making for its delivery system.

In *A Wrinkle in Time*, which I'm working on right now (and just having a blast), it is a mix of acoustic and technological sound. It's to be premiered in Bass Hall in Fort Worth, Texas. Though Bass Hall opened its doors in 1998, its acousticians designed the hall to embrace both purely acoustic and heavily mixed productions. That hall is just a huge speaker with acoustic properties. So, for this opera, I'm using the acoustic hall and the acoustic operatic voice. I'm also integrating technological sounds, so I need a full surround-sound speaker system. Two of the characters in the opera have to be body-mic'd in order to be heard. The hall's sound delivery systems are an important part of my creative process. Part of my job as a composer is to know my acoustics for any given composition. I am influenced by these delivery systems at the very core of my creativity.

So, yes, the technology does influence the creator.

You were in your 20s when you formed the Minnesota Composers Forum.[5] I'm curious about the impetus for forming that organization. Was finding a way to get your music performed one of the reasons that you thought of putting that group together and would you advise young composers to be thinking in those terms; trying to create performance opportunities for themselves?

When I was in my early 20s, studying at the University of Minnesota, I found myself in one of those vortexes where the right energy, and the right people, are in the same space at the same time. There was a group of us, 12 or 15 graduate students including, among others, Stephen Paulus, Steve and Carol Barnett, Charles Lilienfeld, Darrel Newell, Marjorie Rusche, Uri Barnea, and Lynn Dixon who all got along. We each had a unique voice and we had a faculty that supported the development of our individual voices. If you were composing a piece for, say, oboe, bass, and oscilloscope, the only way you could study with your professor was to plunk it out on a piano. We were dissatisfied with this. We were writing pieces for varied instruments, not just the piano. We wanted to hear our pieces on the instruments that we were writing for. So we asked ourselves, how can we do that?

And so we said okay here's what we're going to do: Let's gather the performers and put on some concerts. We went after the idea of developing an audience that would come to the hall curious about the music, not necessarily family or friends attending out of loyalty and friendship. So we began to organize ourselves.

We met with the Suzanne Weil, Director of Performing Arts at the Walker Art Center, and she said, "Okay, you can put a concert on here. If you can fill the hall, I'll give you a concert series." In the process, we realized that we needed to become a legitimate organization for many reasons, chief among them, a need to raise funds. That's when a few of us formed the Minnesota Composers Forum. The first thing we did was get letterhead and envelopes. We figured if we called someone up, and we could follow up that call with a note on letterhead, we would be taken seriously. Then we realized that we needed to become a nonprofit organization. So we researched how to apply for nonprofit status with advice from my then boyfriend (who is now my husband) and who was in law school at the time. I walked the incorporation papers over to the state government and said, "I'll wait here while you approve it," and sat down. In retrospect, it must've been hilarious watching us walk through this process with such optimism. [Laughs] We were approved, and from that point on we were an organization with a board of directors. We started writing grants and putting on concerts. We discovered we were not alone in the world of composers, not only all over the state, but also all over the country. A community was needed, and so that has developed into what is now the American Composers Forum.

Would I recommend young composers to organize? Absolutely. I think young composers now should look at groups like eighth blackbird, Nexus, the King's Singers, Cantus, and others who have figured out how to survive in a world that doesn't actually have a place for them. I would say to young composers, "Find all the models you can of people of your own generation. What are they doing and how are they surviving? Figure it out." For some people it might be one composer creating a performing group, like Philip Glass did; for other composers it might be forming a group of composers who are also performers. The Academy now is looking at young composers and ensembles with an eye toward developing courses in entrepreneurship. They may not have a clue of how to teach it, by the way, but that's what I would say to young composers: Look outside, figure out who your audience is, who's going to listen to what you have to say, and go get them.

In addition to Bach you mention Chuck Berry and other popular artists as part of your musical influence. When I was attending music school I would have been ostracized for mentioning any interest in music other than what was prescribed for me. Do you think that attitude has changed?

Oh boy, me, too. When I started college, I learned rather quickly that referencing my musical interests outside of the canon was strongly discouraged. That was part of my decision to not pursue a faculty position at that time. I would not have been able to write the music that I wanted to write and expect to earn tenure. I think that attitude is changing, but slowly. There are schools where you can learn the craft of composition and apply that knowledge to whatever your ear is interested in pursuing. Recently, I was speaking with Dan Kellogg of the University of Boulder, Colorado. He is one of the great teachers there, and that particular school is very forward thinking. We were talking about why, for most American music schools, it's so hard to find women graduate students who aren't from Asia. UC Boulder has a really healthy number of women graduate students, and he attributes that in part to the fact that students are free to pursue their individual musical interests without fear of ridicule. If you want to write hip-hop on Monday, temporal music on Tuesday, and pop songs on Wednesday, that's great. That's the modern definition of a young American composer; they have a range of repertoire that interests their ear. Student composers need to seek out a school where they can learn compositional techniques, and yet still be allowed to explore music universally rather than specifically. However, things are still quite stringent at some schools. These are schools where if you don't pursue the prescribed approach to composition you can't even get into the school. And so it is really an interesting point in time for students to define for themselves what composition is.

How would you advise a young composer to find and develop his or her voice?

An excellent question. I want to say one word: analysis. What I mean by this is that young composers should, early on, study the techniques of musical analysis. If a composer shows up at my door to study composition, I get out the Ravel string quartet and we spend about two months analyzing the piece. The younger students will often say, "I can analyze that, there's a one chord, and there's a four chord." and I say, "Well, that's just the harmonic organization; it's only one aspect among many that make this piece work." So we analyze the piece at various levels of analysis. I'm concerned that the study of theory has pretty much replaced the study of analysis. One of the best ways for young composers to find their own voice is to learn how to analyze music. Really thoroughly analyze it. For pitch, for structure, for motivic development if there is any, for dynamic levels, for tempo plots, for articulation plots, all of the various elements that make a piece feel whole and satisfying. Once I have taken a student through analyzing one piece at the highest graduate level, it's amazing to see what happens. It's just amazing, amazing! Two months later, this whole different composer shows up saying, "look at this piece I just wrote." I look at the new piece and I just never would've believed that this music would have come out of that composer. So, whole analysis should be taught in the freshman year of college, if not in high school.

I was lucky. Both of my major composition teachers are composers and taught me in that way, through thorough and deep analysis of music.

I was lucky too. Both composer Lloyd Ultan and musicologist Donna Cardamone Jackson were fabulous teachers of analysis.

Looking into the future, what do you hope to achieve as a composer, an artist?

I'm working on it. [Laughs] My search began a long time ago. I'm working on finding the sound palette that I believe actually relates to human beings. I'm looking to become 100 percent fluid in many combinations of technologies that form our musical ears.

That's what I'm looking to do. Life's a playground!

SELECTED WORKS OF LIBBY LARSEN

A Wrinkle in Time (2015), Opera
Evening in the Palace of Reason (2008), String Quartet and String
    Orchestra
Strut (2003), Concert Band
The Womanly Song of God (2003), SSSSAAAA
Try Me, Good King: Last Words of the Wives of Henry VIII (2000),
    Soprano, Piano
Symphony No. 5: "Solo Symphony" (1999), Orchestra
Holy Roller (1997), Saxophone, Piano
Sonnets from the Portuguese (1991), Soprano and Chamber Ensemble
The Art of Arlene Augér (1994), Soprano and Orchestra
Frankenstein: The Modern Prometheus (1990), Music Drama
    with Libretto by Ms. Larsen
The Settling Years (1988), SATB, Woodwind Quintet
Symphony No. 1: "Water Music" (1985), Orchestra
Deep Water Music (1982), Orchestra

▶ To learn more about Libby Larsen and her music, including video performances of *Concert Piece for Bassoon and Piano III, Cowboy Songs Bucking Bronco,* and audio excerpts from *Holy Roller, String Symphony (Symphony No. 4): II,* and *Try Me Good King: Last Words of the Wives of Henry VIII,* visit www.oup.com/us/compositioninthedigitalworld.

NOTES

1. In 1994, a Grammy was awarded to Ms. Larsen as producer, Best Classical Vocal Performance; *The Art of Arlene Augér,* which features *Sonnets from the Portuguese.*
2. *A Wrinkle in Time,* published in 1962, is a science fiction novel by American writer Madeleine L'Engle.
3. "Dominique," was a number 1 song in the United States in November 1963, from the movie *The Singing Nun.*

4. The Library of Congress established the John W. Kluge Center in 2000 to bring together the world's best thinkers to stimulate, energize, and distill wisdom from the Library's rich resources and to interact with policymakers in Washington, D.C. [from the Library of Congress website www.loc.gov]
5. From the web site of the American Composers Forum: ". . . We provide new opportunities for composers and their music to flourish, and engage communities in the creation, performance and enjoyment of new music."

Aaron J. Kernis

As busy as a young composer may become with schoolwork, family, and all of the other things in life, you must make time to compose. That's a fundamental point, and it's easy for composers to get wrapped up in making a living, and everything else that distracts. Making time for working at your art—every day if at all possible—is a baseline.

A prolific composer, with dozens of orchestral, choral, and chamber works to his credit, Aaron J. Kernis (b. Pennsylvania, 1960) is noted for his colorful orchestration and rhythmic intensity. Speaking with me from his home in New York City, our conversation was punctuated by long, perfectly comfortable pauses while he reflected on a question before providing a well-constructed and carefully considered answer.

In some ways, Kernis's story mirrors that of some of the great classical composers: From a young age he was an accomplished violinist and pianist and began garnering recognition early, earning the first of three BMI Foundation Student Composers Awards at the age of 13. Recognition as a composer followed quickly and went hand in hand with a self-confidence that allowed him to defend his music in circumstances that might have wilted others.

He studied at the San Francisco Conservatory, the Manhattan School of Music, and Yale University, with such distinguished teachers as John Adams and Martin Subotnick.

The youngest composer to win the Pulitzer Prize (in 1998 for his String Quartet No.2, *Musica Instrumentalis*), Kernis also has been awarded the prestigious Grawemeyer award (2002), the Nemmers prize (2012), and the Rome Prize, as well as tributes from the National Endowment for the Arts and the Guggenheim Foundation. He has taught composition at Yale since 2003 and is the director of the Minnesota Orchestra's Composer Institute.

His music is strikingly visual and fiercely rhythmic. His wry sense of humor is evident in titles such as *Super Star Etudes, Dance Party on the Disco* (which calls for the ensemble to yell "dance party!" near the end), and *Too Hot Toccata*, but the music is not to be taken lightly. At times emotionally lush and sweetly melodic, it also can be violently angry, verging on the barbaric. Parallels have been drawn between his sound and that of Leonard Bernstein and Igor Stravinsky. Such comparisons have been the kiss of death for some composers in the past, but Kernis and his music are right at home in such celebrated company.

You're a prolific composer. How do you find time to compose with such a busy schedule?

It's a funny thing; I feel that I was more prolific about 10 years ago. Since then I've had children (it's not only that, but that's played a big part) and felt a slowing of my productivity, which happily is revving up again. For a number of years there would be one big piece with a few little ones in a year, or even a few pieces that took nearly a year and a half to complete. It's gotten harder to figure out how to best use time, to make it my friend.

Your wife [Evelyne Luest] is also a musician, a pianist?

That's right, so between the two of us we manage the house and parenting. Certainly one of the biggest differences in my use of time now is that I used to be primarily an afternoon-to-late evening composer. I would regularly work until 2 AM or so. Now most of my work takes place from around 10 in the morning until 4 or 5 in the afternoon, then the late evening is used for editing, proofreading, or other work that is less mentally taxing.

I teach a full day each week at Yale. For the last few years I've been able to keep my energy going longer so that I can compose on the days before and after I teach, and that's been really helpful. When school is in session I'm able to compose four days a week and then for a few hours on each day of the weekend as well.

You have a space of your own that you compose in? Do you try to keep a regular schedule, composing at a particular time?
Yes. I have a studio in our apartment that has a lot of windows and lets in a lot of light. It's a space that I feel great in. In fact, as time goes on, I let fewer and fewer people in there. [Laughs]

It's really private and is my primary space for creating music. Generally, I work from the time the kids are in school until the time they get home. When a deadline is approaching and the work becomes more intense, I'll lock myself in and be constantly working into the evening.

Do you focus on one piece at a time, or do you work on several at once?
My attention is always focused on the single piece at hand, and developing the thread of that work. Occasionally, I'll come up with a starting idea or some vague ideas for a future piece. I might write a few sketches or have a glimpse of that next piece. I'll hold onto those thoughts while finishing the current piece.

Many composers keep a notebook, either on the computer or on paper, in order to capture those kinds of ideas for later development. Is this true for you as well?
I do. I keep a very messy, scribbly, large pad of music paper for my rough ideas. I also write out larger images, structures, concepts, or shorthand for timbres in words on a large yellow pad or small pocket notebook.

Is the process for each piece similar or is every piece different?
I've been thinking a lot about that, especially over the last year. I just began to notice how much my compositional materials and processes have changed since my early years. In my first pieces as a teenager, I was writing things that sounded good to me, that I intuitively found. I had no idea what a structure could be. I used cinematic elements or text to give me the shape of the piece. Once I was in school, I felt the urgency to develop very strict formal constraints on rhythm, pitch, harmony, and phrasing. At that time, I was particularly interested in minimalism and thinking about building various layers of processes

that developed into larger forms. That was very, very important for me until I was about 23.

It seems like I've worked in five-year cycles, making groups of pieces that developed in a singular direction. Then, after five years or so, something would significantly change at the end of a group of pieces. My interests would shift and I would say, "I'm done with that, I've got to move on and break that mold." For one or two groups I developed a conceptual way of thinking, where I was creating musical relationships through metaphors. When I wrote my cycle of war pieces, there were certain core metaphors that I would use to create musical pitch, chordal, and coloristic timbral relationships. There wasn't a story per se, but there was a kind of dramatic progression in the sense of relating themes, harmonies, and sonic density to an emotional character. Later I started drawing vague shapes of form on notepads, or trying to capture a progression in words. There was another period when traditional forms were very important to me. My focus on sonata form and 19th-century and 18th-century forms came to the fore. So really, at each successive stage, I dropped something I had done previously, went into another area, and kept accumulating information and experiences in these different formal worlds.

Now I've let go of formal processes and pre-compositional work almost completely. I'm letting the material I come up with dictate my next steps. I'm following continually transformative and varying processes in the piece I'm composing right now, which I find quite fascinating. I never know quite where the piece is going until I get there and take stock of what's arisen. That being said, I don't take any old idea that comes and feel it's finished. I wind up re-shaping a great deal of it as I go. I'm very interested in all of these experiences, especially in not knowing what's going to happen next. That's very compelling to me at this point.

Many composers describe the compositional process as a mystical one. Does that resonate with you?
Very much so. I've always felt a particular resonance with the mystery of creativity. Constraints can be very helpful in creating limits, and often there can be tremendous growth within constraints. At some point I started to feel that those limits were holding me back. I had to let them go in order to make my way toward a kind of process that was more unpredictable, less intellectualized, and felt more freeing. I've always had the experience that when a work starts really going, most of those constraints or constructs of the pre-compositional work just fall away. The work develops a flow—usually in the middle and hopefully through to the

end—where it's just kind of humming along. When I reach that point in the process, there's less of an intellectual construct in the foreground of the experience of writing, and most importantly, there's a change in the self-critical internal voice, which is nearly always at play.

Speaking of musical voices, how do you advise your students to seek and develop a voice of their own?

It's something I think about a lot, but I do not want to define their voice for them or create a sense of pressure or expectation in terms of finding their voice in my studio. Every student comes in at a different stage of development, and focusing too intensively on voice at the wrong time can create strong internal pressure. I honestly believe that everyone has their own compositional voice, though some may be more distinct at first and others more syncretic. Certainly I look for many things in students' work; we talk about aspects that are stronger and areas that need attention, and I try to capture a sense of their compositional process so I can experience it (in part) through their sensibility. We try to focus the intention of each piece, but I won't try to guide them to define their voice too early if the time isn't right.

What were your experiences with teachers like John Adams and Morton Subotnick like? Did they have a similar pedagogical approach?

All of my teachers had very different styles, one of the strongest dichotomies being between Adams and Wuorinen.[1] They all had incredibly different voices and not a single one of them imposed a dogma on me or gave me the idea that I should write in a particular way. They were all wonderfully generous and open in their commentaries. This had an extremely positive influence on the way I think about teaching and nurturing young composers.

Please discuss the Minnesota Orchestra Composer Institute.[2]

I believe the program has helped many, many talented composers. For one thing, it demystifies working with an orchestra for emerging composers. To bring young composers into a place where they can see professionals who are working hard to understand their music and then performing it at the highest level is a wonderful thing.

It's a unique program.

Completely. Every year I have assisted in the process of choosing composers and working with panels, usually looking at about 150 scores each season. Some years I would begin to feel very frustrated at the mid-point of the screening, but when it came down to those last 20 or 30 scores, I saw so much extremely high-level work coming out through that process. It's very inspiring to see how much talent there is today.

Do you see any difference between student composers of today, compared to when you were studying?

I think one of the biggest changes I've seen is in the diversity of music that is available, and how large the conversation about music is today. There are so many varied styles, sounds, and worldviews available now. Young composers come into school without that sense (that I know I certainly had) of a "great divide" between musical approaches. When I was a student there was a whole lot of music that we as students were interested in and listening to, but that "other music" was always at the edges, and not to be discussed with our mentors.

My sense is that now the lines between different musics are extremely fluid. Students have an ability to shift between different musics as players, as listeners, as composers, often as all three. They come into their studies with different skill sets and compose without drawing sharp boundaries between styles. I think it's tremendous.

I do too. It's a wonderful thing to see the doors open so that a student's love of all kinds of music can be acknowledged and valued. That's a sea change from the time I was in music school, and I think this open attitude will help to enrich the new music of this century. Are your compositions influenced by popular music, like blues, rock, or jazz?

I'm highly influenced by jazz, which I grew up hearing around my family's home. Also, American popular songs that became the standards of the '40s, '50s, and '60s—the music my parents loved. Rock and roll was never really a big part of my early life; that interest came when I was in my 20s. Other than Frank Zappa,[3] punk was actually the first rock and roll music I was interested in. In Philadelphia, where I grew up, there was a college radio station I listened to. I heard world music, Irish music, early jazz and big band, rock, and minimalism, again, without the sense of any boundaries dividing them.

Back in the '90s, I created some work that I can say was influenced by hip-hop, disco, or salsa. It was like trying on different clothes, and it was a lot of fun. Those influences have kind of receded in my writing, in part because of the organic flow between musics that I see now with young composers. Influence from a variety of styles is part of the language that they speak. I'm concentrating now on the variety of music that I feel is really at my core and again looking outwards toward world music. But the jazz influence keeps coming back.

Is there a center of new music today, or has the Internet made that a dated concept?

Something I've found to be especially stimulating over the last few years has been students who feel comfortable coming to a lesson and talking about a wide variety of things that have influenced them. Sometimes that influence will be from a rock band I have never heard, other times students come in and say "listen to this amazing Sciarrino[4] piece," and they'll give me the link for YouTube. The Internet has made that exploration a much easier process. I've begun to feel that the interchange of music on the Internet is that new center.

For example, an element of the original plan for the cello concerto [*Dreamsongs*] that I just finished was for me to look at music from cultures that I was not familiar with. I wanted to delve into that music and see what struck a nerve. And so I began looking around on YouTube, which is so powerful and immediately accessible. I started looking at music from Africa, music from Azerbaijan, from the Balkans.

What an inspiring experience to hear a huge range of musical styles right in your home, and it's all constantly changing. Sometimes you may not immediately find the best work with an Internet search. You can't always tell with Google if you are getting the complete and accurate picture, so in some instances you may need to get down to the music library and find your answers in "old-fashioned ways," like spending time doing research. But for the armchair explorer, the Internet is powerful and invigorating.

It is wonderful to be able to just wander on the Internet and find music that you might not be exposed to otherwise.

Right. So while it [the Internet] may not be an actual physical center of music, it is a powerful way to explore and witness things that one might not otherwise have access to. And people are sharing their passions and creativity (and bad taste!) to a degree I've never seen before.

Are there pieces that were particularly influenced by what you were able to find?

Absolutely. For example, when writing the new cello concerto I just spoke about, I started to focus on the African instrument the kora.[5] I began to look on the Internet at various bands or individual musicians who play that instrument, and I started thinking about ways that I might relate the solo cello to the kora. I probably never would have come up with that concept without such immediate access to that music and seeing performers via the Internet. I think I'm going to do the same thing with one movement of the viola concerto that I'm going on to now. I'm fascinated with some Azerbaijani music. I have no knowledge of that style of music, so I've started looking it up on Wikipedia, various essays about it, that kind of thing. After writing many, many pieces that were coming primarily from exploring the personal and emotional things I needed to express from inside myself, this may be a new period where I'm more focused on looking outside, finding new sounds and new inspiration.

How do you feel about your music being digitally available, free of charge, on the Internet?

A complicated issue. I believe fundamentally that artists should be paid for their work. Yet we're quickly moving into a time where the expectations of free music are radically changing the artistic economy and expectations. While that availability can provide important promotion for our work, someone is out there earning billions from free or extremely low remuneration of intellectual property, and it's been galling to see, for example, the head of Spotify asking for further reduction in payments to musical artists. I'm more supportive of YouTube's posting of live performances than of Spotify's use of pre-existing recordings. If all recording companies and musical artists banded together, and as a large group refused to allow their work to be used in this way, those Internet companies would have nothing to play, and eventually a more equitable situation would have to arise. Instead, composers earn next to nothing from Internet availability.[6]

Do you feel that digital technology has made it easier, harder, or had no effect on your ability to earn a living as a composer?

I don't think it's made a big dent in earnings yet, but if the current system holds, it could have a strong impact later. I've heard of significantly fewer CD sales, both through the Internet and at live performances, so I think the expectation of paying very little to nothing for streaming, MP3, or through file-sharing seems to be increasingly the norm. There are few viral contemporary classical music videos (that I know of), and so far I have not seen artists able to leverage even moderate-to-good use of their music on the Internet into income.

In what other ways do you employ the computer in your compositional process?

For the most part it's pretty simple. I work at the piano; I'm a pianist, and the piano for me is a neutral instrument where I can "hear" the orchestra while I play. I sketch on paper for the most part, and then typically when I'm happy with the sketch, I'll enter my ideas into Sibelius [computer notation software]. I'll keep on doing that for a while, and then I'll start working more at the computer, entering more music, printing that work out and refining the ideas by hand in further iterations. And that will eventually become a finished work.

Lately, I've had a couple of interesting experiences using technology in my compositional process. There was one movement of a new piece that consisted of very fast music for a solid three minutes. This was very hard to capture through improvisation and a motivic development process. So I actually improvised the entire movement on the keyboard via MIDI to the computer. I had never done this successfully before. Then I refined that music working at the computer over the next three weeks. This enabled me to get a lot of material out; three minutes of 16th notes at 160 [beats per minute], and the intensive revision process enabled me to make a piece I was happy with.

Even more recently than that, I've started to actually play the piano and then sketch directly into the computer rather than writing a sketch and then waiting, waiting, waiting, until I'm happy. There is continually a lot of refinement, but this allows the critical voice to be held at bay a bit longer without getting in the way of sketching as much, and this process allows me to get the sketches down into the computer much faster.

Do you feel that the presence of the computer in that process somehow alters the outcome of the music in its final form?

I don't feel that it's much more than a tool in the sketching process, except for that one instance that I just mentioned. I'm sure many other composers share the love/hate relationship I have with MIDI. I haven't been in many situations where someone urgently needed a demo that sounded as close as possible to the sound of the final piece in order to study it, or in order to use it for some sort of promotional pre-premiere use. So I just create MIDI mockups (when I need to) with the mediocre sounds that are available in the basic notation software setup I use.

I'm always conscious of the confusing and acoustically false result of MIDI. It can be so seductive—it's hard to *not* listen. I like to use it to check counterpoint, and to make sure that verticalities are exactly the way I want them, that I didn't miss a harmonic crash for even a microsecond.

But, in terms of hearing a group of instruments or an orchestra, it's *so* off, it's *so* not like the real thing.

I'm always cautioning my students to not give too much credence to what they hear out of the computer and stressing using their ears and developing their inner sonic imagination. But we barely use the piano anymore in lessons. Students bring in their orchestrations or sketches using MIDI, and that allows us to address issues (such as balance) that we need to work through more immediately. But I still prefer to slowly work my hands around their notes and harmonies, so we usually sit down to do so after getting the overview of the work on their computers.

So again, MIDI is a tool that I've seen younger composers get wrapped up in, especially those who haven't had enough life experience as musicians. They can write music that sounds great on the computer but that oftentimes is impossible to play. With students writing for larger groups, as I listen to their work I'm always trying to get them to step away from that falseness of computer-generated sound, and try to imagine the work in a real acoustic setting, and in their ears, as it really sounds.

Many of the composers I've spoken with agree with you totally on this point; there's a deep concern that some young composers may not give enough credence to the importance of developing that "inner ear." Aside from the inherent dangers of relying too much on MIDI, are there benefits as well? For instance, when you are premiering a new piece and you're delivering the music to an orchestra or chamber group that is going to perform it, do you provide them with a MIDI rendition, a demo, or do you simply give them the score and parts?

I will give out a MIDI demo only under great duress. I don't think I would feel so uncomfortable giving something like that out if I could spend the time making a mock-up sound beautiful and perfectly balanced. I always make it clear that I don't want a rough demo to be heard beyond the small circle of people that need it, whether it's needed for an audition performance, or to help the conductor study the new work. I tend to be very protective about that.

As sophisticated and seductive as sampled sounds may be, many composers feel that they fall far short of the nuances that a human being brings to a live instrument in performance.

Very true, but those poor sounds in basic MIDI are at the sonic low-end of recording techniques. In film and TV, one has the resources to create a sophisticated virtual balance that I wish were possible to reproduce in live situations.

Hollywood and composers with high-end electronics can, at their best, create balances by bringing up the instruments that would otherwise be buried.

It's so hard for young composers to get started and to believe in themselves. This brings to mind the famous story of when your piece *Dream of a Morning Sky* was performed by the New York Philharmonic. Your defense of your music was very courageous, especially considering that you were only 23 years old.[7]

When I stood up in front of that orchestra and spoke to the conductor and players about playing what was in the score, I was just being myself and was speaking up about what was important to me. I knew that I'd spent a great deal of time writing that work, and felt certain that I'd set down what I'd intended to hear. I frequently stress that need for certainty to young composers, knowing when to and not to back down from one's intentions—along with the need to experience the music fully and learn from each performance and acoustic situation (along with studying scores and hearing live performances of existing and new repertoire).

I also stress that, as busy as a young composer may become with schoolwork, family, and all of the other things in life, you *must* make time to compose. That's a fundamental point, and it's easy for composers to get wrapped up in making a living, and everything else that distracts. Making time for working at your art—every day if at all possible—is a baseline that I really emphasize to my students.

By the point young composers have been accepted into the program at Yale, although they may not yet have their voice completely formed yet, they've gotten there because they intensely believe in what they are trying to do and they are deeply motivated. I try to provide an environment for these young composers at the Minnesota Institute and at Yale where they can follow their intensity through and confirm the commitment to their art, while trying to help them realize their intentions: to feel encouraged and strong about themselves, yet ask difficult questions of themselves, of music and about life. To not be brought down by the critical voice (or by critics at large) or lose one's confidence as a composer is so important.

SELECTED WORKS OF AARON J. KERNIS

Dreamsongs (2013), Solo Cello and Orchestra
Perpetual Chaconne (2012), Clarinet and String Quartet
Pieces of Winter Sky (2011–2012), Flute (Piccolo), Clarinet, Violin (Viola), Cello, Piano, Percussion

Symphony of Meditations (Symphony No. 3) (2009), Soprano, Tenor
and Baritone Soloists, Chorus and Orchestra

Valentines (2000), Soprano and Orchestra or Soprano and Piano

String Quartet No. 2 (Musica Instrumentalis) (1997)

Goblin Market (1995), Narrator and Thirteen Players

Lament and Prayer (1995), Violin, Oboe, Two Harps, Percussion, and
String Orchestra

Still Movement with Hymn (1993), Violin, Viola, Cello, Piano

Colored Field (1994–2000), English Horn or Cello Solo, Orchestra

Second Symphony (1991), Orchestra

Musica Celestis (1991), String Orchestra

▶ To learn more about Aaron J. Kernis and his music, including score
excerpts from *Dreamsong I, Danssar,* and *Pieces of Winter Sky,* visit
www.oup.com/us/compositioninthedigitalworld.

NOTES

1. Charles Wuorinen is an American composer, pianist, and educator. His awards
   include four BMI Student Composer Awards, the Lili Boulanger Award, and a
   Pulitzer Prize.
2. Founded by Mr. Kernis in 2002, the Minnesota Orchestra Composer Institute
   provides orchestral rehearsals, public performance, and numerous targeted
   workshops for emerging composers. Mr. Kernis served as the orchestra's new
   music advisor for 10 seasons.
3. Frank Zappa (1940–1993), was an American rock musician and composer. His
   styles crossed over into jazz, avant-garde, orchestral, and musique concrète. His
   influences include Edgard Varèse, Igor Stravinsky, and rhythm and blues from
   the 1950s. Zappa and his music are highly revered by many musicians ranging
   from Pierre Boulez to Bill Frisell and Nicolas Slonimsky.
4. Salvatore Sciarrino is an Italian avant-garde composer of contemporary art
   music.
5. A kora is a West African stringed instrument similar to a harp. It has 21 strings
   with a neck and a bridge. Some models resemble a banjo without frets.
6. Mr. Kernis: "See Jaron Lanier's fascinating article—'Fixing the Digital
   Economy,' *New York Times,* 7/8/2013" as well as his book, *Who Owns the Future?,*
   Simon and Schuster (2014).
7. In 1983, *Dream of the Morning Sky,* Mr. Kernis's first orchestral work, was premiered at a public sight-reading session as part of the Horizons Festival by Zubin
   Metha and the New York Philharmonic Orchestra. When the conductor com-
   plained about a particular passage in the score, Kernis (then just 23 years old)
   quietly but firmly told him to "perform it as written in the score," to applause
   from the audience.

Jennifer Higdon

Successful careers often come down to a combination of extraordinarily hard work and luck. I never exhibited any kind of talent as a kid, I don't have perfect pitch, no one ever thought I was a prodigy.... But I was always a hard worker. I was not one to give up on anything, even when people told me I couldn't succeed. And that made all of the difference.

Jennifer Higdon (b. New York, 1962) is a beacon of inspiration, especially for those who may fear they've started too late to pursue a career as a composer. Higdon did not even start listening to classical music in a serious way until her college years. Initially self-taught on flute and percussion, her career gained momentum despite a steep learning curve and some early teachers who were, shall we say, less than supportive of her ambitions. Ignoring her detractors, Higdon focused her unwavering attention on learning composition, setting her sights ever higher, and ultimately studying at Bowling Green State University, the Curtis Institute of Music, and the University of Pennsylvania, with teachers including David Loeb and George Crumb.

Born in Brooklyn, Higdon spent most of her formative years in Atlanta and Tennessee, and spoke to me from her current home in Philadelphia. Down-to-earth, unpretentious, and unabashedly upbeat, she speaks matter-of-factly about her bumpy journey from novice musician to the well-loved master composer she is today. She also displays a savvy business side and talks about the importance of having a web presence in today's marketplace and about having her own publishing company, which rents scores and parts for performances. Winner of both a Grammy Award and the Pulitzer Prize, her work reverberates with audiences and performers alike and is widely performed to enthusiastic response. Her music constantly pushes tonal boundaries and is endlessly inventive, colorful, exciting, and emotional.

Touting the critical importance of hard work, Higdon freely admits that she was not considered particularly talented as a child, but that she was singularly driven once she decided what she wanted to do. In many ways, Jennifer Higdon personifies the power of the creative spirit.

You started your musical career playing the flute, and only later turned to composing classical music. Please share some details of the unique path that led you to become a composer.
I grew up in a household where a lot of '60s rock and folk music was played. My dad is a commercial artist and worked at home, so when he was in his studio you could hear music playing. I would occasionally get a snatch of something unusual. For instance, I remember hearing a recording called *Snowflakes Are Dancing* by Tomita,[1] but we really didn't have any classical music or a piano in the house. When I was in high school I found a flute my mom had bought, and I decided to take the beginning band books she had and I began to teach myself how to play. I didn't know how to read music, so I had to teach myself how to read from that elementary book. I started playing flute; we're talking extraordinarily basic stuff. I eventually ended up joining the high school band, and that turned out to be quite an influential thing for me, but really my early education was from this band method handbook for flute. It is kind of a little unreal!

Actually that's where I started too, with the flute band method. I'm with you.

Great! It is good to meet someone else who understands! [Both laugh]

I went back and forth between playing percussion and the flute in the band. Then a flute teacher recommended I go to a high school flute camp at Bowling Green State University in Ohio. During my junior and senior year I went to this camp, and it was an eye-opening experience for me. Suddenly, there were all these people making music who were as serious about music as I was. I learned about the profession of making music. I decided to go to college there. I had applied to six or seven schools, but Bowling Green State University was the only school where I was accepted. I didn't know any basic theory, how to spell a chord, what intervals were, and I had zero keyboard skills. I basically started from the very, very beginning. Most of the people I started school with were far more advanced than I was, and I had an extraordinary amount of catching up to do.

That's a powerful and all too familiar story. It must have taken a great deal of courage for you to forge on.

Well, I had such a good time I didn't let the fact that I was so far behind intimidate me too much. I had teachers tell me that there was no way I was going to be able to do this because I was starting so late. But I loved music so I ignored them.

Yet despite that discouragement, you devoted your life to composition. How did that transpire?

Part of the way through earning my undergraduate degree in performance, my flute teacher gave me an assignment to write a flute and piano piece for a master class with Harvey Sollberger,[2] so I wrote a simple flute and piano piece. From that point I started writing on my own. I kept on playing flute, but I was writing more and more for friends or for the flute choir that we all played in. My flute teacher at Bowling Green State University was a phenomenal teacher, and I learned how to put music together from her. I still consider her one of my quintessential composition teachers. I also studied with Robert Spano,[3] who is currently the music director of the Atlanta Symphony.

So you were off and running with the composing bug. How did you transition from being a relatively inexperienced composer to someone who was ready to undertake the serious work of learning your craft?

I applied to quite a few graduate programs for composition, and it was a similar experience to my undergraduate applications, quite a few rejections. But I *was* accepted at the Curtis Institute of Music. Now that I teach there I'm shocked that I was accepted and wonder how it happened. The musicians are superb and I learned a lot from my colleagues, absorbing their high level of music making. Sometimes I played with the orchestra under fantastic conductors like Simon Rattle, and I had master classes with amazing composers such as Lutosławski[4] and Penderecki.[5] I tried to absorb as much as I possibly could. In theory, ear training, and music history I was still catching up. Keyboard skills, solfege: still catching up. I studied at Curtis for two years. I then applied to a couple of different graduate schools including the University of Pennsylvania, where I was rejected on my first attempt. Since I wanted to stay in Philadelphia, I took a year off and did music copying, flute performing, and a little theory teaching. Then I reapplied to the University of Pennsylvania and completed my master's and doctorate there.

Despite all of those ups and downs, you kept at your pursuit of learning your craft. Ultimately your determination paid off, and you attended some wonderful schools.

It was interesting because the three schools I attended present an amazing contrast. I went to a state school, an elite music conservatory, and an Ivy League university. I don't think those schools could have been any more different from each other. It was incredible. I kept playing the flute, kept writing a lot of music, and getting performances of my work. Because I was in Philadelphia, I was around the Curtis performers, so I could ask them to perform my pieces. That actually turned out to be a really good thing.

You also studied with George Crumb didn't you?

Yes I did. I also studied with David Loeb[6] and Ned Rorem. Crumb may have had the biggest influence on me, but Rorem and Crumb are the most extraordinary contrasts; they approach music so differently. That contrast can teach you a lot about how music is put together and how each individual can provide a different perspective to problem solving. I use that aspect of my learning experience, that knowledge of contrasts, in my composing.

Your schedule is so demanding; you teach, and you have an extraordinary number of performances, yet you are very prolific. How do you find the time to write music?

The teaching only takes two hours per week for me. Curtis is set up a bit differently than other music conservatories. Just about everyone who teaches at Curtis is a professional musician, playing in orchestras or touring. If I were teaching full time it would be much trickier to balance my time. I have to admit that the traveling is hard; I used to be able to compose in hotel rooms, but it has gotten harder to do that. Now I try my best to keep myself in my studio to write. I just finished writing an opera: I was writing eight hours a day, every day, seven days a week. When I'm not writing something that intensely my normal day includes between four and six hours of composing, about six days a week. After a really intense day of composing I come out of the studio drawing blanks. It's really obvious when I've used every bit of brainpower that I can muster in a day.

I've heard you talk about walking around doing everyday things while composing in your head, constantly thinking about the music you are creating. I think people who aren't musicians don't realize that many composers do a lot of creative work throughout the day, not just when they are in front of a piano or computer.
It's very, very true. There have been times when I would have a composition problem, go to sleep, wake up the next day and the answer was there. It's surprising when it happens, but when I'm having a massive moment of anxiety about a composition, I try to keep these miraculous events in mind. The fact that I compose so much actually makes it easier, though, because my brain is constantly working on composition problems.

I enjoyed the article you wrote for NPR, *Dinner with the Dead: Jennifer Higdon's Date with Beethoven*.[7] You describe an imaginary dinner with him and ask, "What did he do when he got stuck?" It's scary when you're composing, hit a wall, and think, "I don't know if I'm ever going to solve this."
Right, and I think every composer experiences this. Anyone who does anything creative, whether it's painting, creating film, or writing short stories or poems, faces this at some point. It's helpful to remember that it's a common thing that all creative people share.

One of the things that helps me is that I work so consistently. This means that I write enough so that I know I will eventually get myself out of a situation. I take the approach of taking it one note at a time.

When I started writing this recent opera I thought, "Good grief, I can't envision writing this many hours of music." How would I encapsulate the entire story, create a strong basis for each of the characters, and convey the general arc of the drama as it unfolds? It seemed like a completely impossible task. But then I said to myself, "You just have to start. Every journey is one step at a time, and you have to trust that you will eventually get to the end." And that's what I did. I frequently didn't have any idea how the thing was going to unfold, sometimes even just a few measures ahead of where I was.

Your new opera is based on the book *Cold Mountain*.[8] It occurs to me that the composing process that you just described mirrors the journey of the main character in that book. Taking one day, or even one step at a time. Similar to the journey Odysseus took in Homer's *Odyssey*.

I have to admit, not having written an opera before this, I thought that the entire process of composing so much music was a little daunting. When I set out to write this much music I knew the task was going to take way more than a year, and being on one project for so long is hard. There's no way to see the general arc of something so huge, dramatic, and wonderful, and have all the answers at the start. But by trusting that the ideas would come, I was able to begin. At times, I would become afraid when the ideas were slow to come to me. At times, the steps were incremental, while at other times the music came quickly. Sometimes the music would really surprise me. There was a certain amount of trust that went with that as well, to kind of follow the line and know that I could back up and do something differently. Giving oneself permission to erase or delete or not use an idea at all is important. Nothing is set in concrete. There were times where I wrote two or three versions of an idea, and then decided which one of the themes worked the best.

Did you begin working on *Cold Mountain* by creating sketches of the entire work, or did you start by focusing on key, individual scenes?

The piece is so big that I decided to start from the beginning with the libretto. When I'm not sure how to begin a new piece this is how I work: I'll just start with anything I can get on the page, knowing I can always go back later on as the piece develops and readjust that material.

I've asked other composers who have written operas how the heck they tackled getting started. Some people told me they had taken the approach of writing the highlights first, the emotional peaks. But I started from the beginning in this case, something I don't always do when writing instrumental music. It took 20 months of writing daily.

Do you keep sketchbooks, or do you work with a computer?

Sometimes I draw graphs in sketchbooks to figure out the shape of something, or I'll make mental notes to myself about a sound that I want to incorporate into the composition. I also work on the computer with Finale [notation program].

Do you use your computer to listen to the playback, or to create MIDI demos for new works?
I don't have my computer set up to play back. I became used to hearing scores in my imagination when I was in school, and I've stayed with that. Performers have to be able to breathe; they have to be able to bow effectively. Having been a performer myself, I'm acutely aware of the things a human performer cannot do that a computer can do. Everything from the range of instruments, the sound, how easy or hard it is to play something in certain ranges, how quiet or loud, how much control, and how those ranges for the different instruments affect the timbre.

One of your most often performed works is *blue cathedral*.
That's been an amazing juggernaut of a piece. So many orchestras have performed it: high school groups and honors orchestras, as well as amateur and professional orchestras. I'm really fortunate that it happens to work so well for so many different levels of players. I didn't originally set out to write something that would fit all of these bills; it was just by accident. The nice thing about *blue cathedral* is that there are a lot of orchestras that will program it that have never programmed anything by a living composer.

You publish your own music. How do you feel about the fact that so much of your music can be listened to for free on the Internet?
It's probably not an ideal situation for any living composer, although you could consider it advertising. I probably have the same mixed feelings that most composers have; it's nice to have your music out there, but other people are making money off of the music that you worked so hard to produce.

Many composers are right there with you, but there doesn't seem to be an immediate solution. Perhaps there is a promotional upside, but it does seem wrong to use people's music without proper compensation.
I've been on enough music committees to know that it can end up costing composers a lot more than one might imagine. But what is really the worst are people who think all music should be free. People who create deserve to make a living from it.

Congratulations on winning a Grammy for your _Percussion Concerto_![9]

Thank you! That's a fun piece. The percussion repertoire has grown in classical music and audiences absolutely love it. At first I wasn't sure if the music worked. Now I kind of laugh and think my judgment must have really been off. The work has been so popular with wonderful audience reactions: they really get down with it. It really surprises me; I'm kind of floored!

Other composers have made similar comments to me about their feelings when premiering a particular new piece of theirs: "Oh I am so embarrassed, this is no good." When they discover that everyone loves the new work they say, "I guess it is great and I just didn't realize it!"

I guess it may be a common thing. [Laughs]

I'm finding a lot of audiences want to hear new music, even to the point of audience members asking the administration why they aren't playing new music. A lot of people stopped going to classical concerts because they are tired of hearing the same old music. Over the past couple of years there has been a sea change: Now I get stopped on the street by people asking when I'm going to have another performance. People are enthusiastic about new music in general.

Congratulations are also in order for winning the Pulitzer Prize for your _Violin Concerto_.[10]

Thank you. It is a hard piece; not only is the solo part difficult, but the orchestra part is not so easy either. Sometimes when a piece is written specifically for someone, as I wrote in this case for Hilary Hahn,[11] who is an incredible violinist, there can be a concern that no one else will be able to perform the work. I've been really pleased at how many other orchestras and soloists have taken it up. It's great to see that the piece is moving out into the world and other soloists are taking it on. Learning and performing the piece is a lot of hard work; the person who is soloing really has to put in some serious woodshedding time.

When you were writing the piece did you work closely with Hilary Hahn?

I know Hilary pretty well because she was a student of mine when I taught classes on 20th-century music at Curtis. She's on the road a lot, so I went off and wrote the piece, and I sent each movement to her after I finished it. She would look it over and let me know if there were any problems. But in Hilary's case she kept saying, "You know, you can make it harder." Now this concerto is extremely difficult. It doesn't look that hard on the page, but it's actually quite tricky to execute. But she kept challenging me to make each movement harder. The cadenza in the first movement was the last thing I wrote in the concerto, I wasn't absolutely sure it was going to be playable, so I wrote a note to Hilary: "Look, if this is too hard, let me know and I'll write another cadenza." She said it was hard, but she could do it, that it was her job to learn it. I think every composer's dream is to have the opportunity to work with soloists like that, and have a player say, "Yes, it's hard but it is my job to do it."

Did winning the Pulitzer Prize change your life and/or career?
Yes! It is amazing. People return my calls now! [Both laugh]

It's like the Good Housekeeping Seal of Approval! It's also helped the ensembles that I've been working with to get publicity. And I receive even more commission offers that I can't accommodate, but now I am able to say, "If you like my music, check out this composer." So I know some other composers got commissions and that's one of the best outcomes of winning. It also gave me the chance to thank all of those people who had helped me along the way. A Pulitzer Prize shouldn't just honor the individual who writes the music. It should be something that goes to all the people who have been involved in that person's life.

I think it's great that you are so supportive of other musicians. Do you think there are really wonderful composers who remain unknown due to, maybe, bad luck or lack of self-promotion?
I think there are people who make all kinds of wonderful art that the public doesn't know about, although it's easier to promote one's work now that we have the Internet.

Theoretically, I shouldn't have a career. I'm not with one of the major publishing houses, and I started really late and was mostly self-taught.

Careers often come down to a combination of extraordinarily hard work and luck. I never exhibited any kind of talent as a kid, I don't have perfect pitch, no one ever thought I was a prodigy, and in fact a lot of my previous school teachers say, "We don't even remember you coming through here." But I was always a hard worker. I was not one to give up on anything, even when people told me I couldn't succeed. And that made all of the difference.

My dad is a commercial artist who worked at home, so for me that kind of life seems very normal. But it freaked out a lot of my teachers who said, "What do you mean you want to be a freelance composer?" But I was willing to get in there and keep working, even though people said, "You've started too late, there's no way." But I kept at it. It wasn't until I won the Pulitzer that I thought, "Holy cow, I guess I've caught up and figured this out!"

You mention promoting oneself on the Internet. Having a presence on the Internet is an important aspect of the business of being a contemporary composer now. You have a website and a Facebook page. Doesn't that take an enormous amount of time and effort to keep all of that updated?

I have someone who does that now, because it got to where I was handling all of the publishing stuff myself, and it was overtaking my life. I was either going to be a composer or I was going to be a publisher. So my partner, who is an experienced meeting planner, took over. She runs the business and it's a full-time job. It's a lot of work, but just having an Internet presence can really accomplish some major things. The first performance I had with the Cleveland Orchestra came about because I had a very basic website. The Cleveland Orchestra was trying to program a concert, and they found me on the web and sent me an e-mail saying, "We heard a little orchestra piece you have on your site. If you can ship it tonight to the Cleveland Orchestra, we will perform your piece." I said, "Yes, I'll ship the score and parts overnight!" To me that's a strong argument right there for having a website.

When I was in school, many of the students, including myself, listened to rock, jazz, and blues, but there was no way that I would have felt comfortable mentioning those interests in my composition lessons. Do you think that attitude has changed in recent years?

Yes, absolutely. I often ask students, "What's on your iPhone?" The kids who are studying music are listening to all kinds of music. In fact, oftentimes there is little classical music on their iPhones. They're listening to just about everything else, so I don't know how that is going to affect classical music per se in the long run; it's kind of an interesting switch. But you're right. When I was in school it was right at the tail end of the era in which you weren't supposed to be talking about that stuff. I know exactly what you are talking about.

You wrote a piece for Ned Rorem's 90th birthday, for clarinet and piano.

That's right. I squeezed that in late at night after a day of writing opera. I was working on it night after night. Ned is such an amazing character; it was hard to find a way to honor him.

Is it unusual for you to work on more than one piece at a time?

Yes. I almost always do one piece at a time. It is very rare, but occasionally there will be one small piece that I will work on literally from like 11:00 at night till 1:00 in the morning. I've done that on a few occasions, and it is actually pretty hard. Normally at that time of the day, I'm really tired and my creative brain is drained, and I'm not thinking clearly. But they had asked for the piece for Ned's birthday very specifically from me, so I couldn't say no. We just had that concert, and it was fun to see him and honor him in general. We owe so much to our elders; I think sometimes we forget to tell them, "Thank you."

There is the romantic vision of creative inspiration hitting an artist like a lightning bolt. I believe that in reality, inspiration is mostly a product of a lot of hard work. That said, I've spoken with a surprising number of composers who feel there is some transcendent, spiritual aspect to the process of creating. I've felt this. Have you experienced this yourself?

I've always thought that, despite all of our training, there are times where it comes down to pure magic. There is something going on that we can't explain.

I often think of writing music as a very spiritual experience, moments of incredible pure inspiration. Based on my pieces, people ask me about my sense of spirituality. It's totally relevant, and it completely makes sense. As I said, there is something there that we cannot explain but boy, when those moments happen, it's like, "Where did that come from?" It's part of the magic of what we do, but I also think you have to be showing up every day and working for that to occur.

Students often ask me, "Should I wait until I am inspired?" No, you should be sitting there writing every day to get the inspiration in the first place.

Looking forward, what do you hope to achieve in the decades ahead? What is your ambition for your future?

That's a good question. I'm always trying to expand my language, and I'm always trying to explore different things. At some point, I think I would like to take a crack at film scoring, but I also would like to explore the "Downtown Music Scene." I find that fascinating. So I'm always hoping that my art will continue to grow and I am always pushing myself to do something different, to explore something I have not explored before. One of the most important lessons I've learned is that it's really important to support fellow composers. So when people ask for help, or ask for service on panels or boards, it's worth taking that time to help. The better we make this for all of us, the better all around it is for the entire field. Be a good musical citizen; help your fellow artists.

SELECTED WORKS OF JENNIFER HIGDON

Cold Mountain (2012–2014), Opera
Violin Concerto (2008), Violin, Orchestra
Concerto 4-3 (2007), Two Violins, Double Bass, Orchestra
String Poetic (2006), Violin, Piano
Percussion Concerto (2005), Percussion, Orchestra
Piano Trio (2003), Violin, Cello, Piano
O magnum mysterium (2002), Two Flutes, Glasses, Chimes, Choir
Concerto for Orchestra (2002), Orchestra
Dash (2001), Two Soprano Instruments, Piano
blue cathedral (1999), Orchestra
Autumn Music (1995), Flute, Oboe, Clarinet, Horn, Bassoon
rapid.fire (1992), Flute

▶ To learn more about Jennifer Higdon and her music, visit www.oup.com/us/compositioninthedigitalworld.

NOTES

1. Isao Tomita is a Japanese composer and synthesist. On his 1974 album *Snowflakes Are Dancing*, he performs arrangements of works by Debussy on the Moog Synthesizer. It was nominated for four Grammy awards.
2. Harvey Sollberger is an American flautist, composer, and conductor. He co-founded the Group for Contemporary Music with Charles Wuorinen in 1962.
3. Robert Spano is an American conductor and pianist, and is the music director of the Atlanta Symphony Orchestra and of the Aspen Music Festival and School. He was formerly the assistant conductor of the Boston Symphony Orchestra under Seiji Ozawa. His awards include three Grammys.
4. Roman Lutosławski (1913–1994) was a Polish composer, pianist, and conductor. His music received numerous awards and was extremely influential to many composers.
5. Krzysztof Penderecki is a Polish composer and conductor. His *Threnody to the Victims of Hiroshima*, and *St. Luke Passion* are among the most well known of his works. His many awards include three Grammys.
6. David Loeb is an American composer. He has taught at the Mannes College, the New School, and at the Curtis Institute of Music.
7. The article *Dinner with the Dead: Jennifer Higdon's Date with Beethoven*, can be found on the National Public Radio (NPR) website.
8. *Cold Mountain* is a novel by American author Charles Frazier. It was released in 1997 and won the National Book Award for Fiction. The story takes place during the American Civil War, and has many parallels with Homer's *Odyssey*.

9. In 2010, Higdon received a Grammy for Best Contemporary Classical Composition for her *Percussion Concerto*.
10. Higdon's *Violin Concerto* premiered in 2010, and was written for Hilary Hahn. It was awarded the Pulitzer Prize in Music, and the recording by Hahn and the Royal Liverpool Philharmonic Orchestra won a Grammy.
11. Hilary Hahn is an American violinist. She has performed with many of the world's foremost symphony orchestras and is considered among the greatest of contemporary violinists. In 2014 she completed a project called "In 27 Pieces: The Hilary Hahn Encores." The project commissioned 27 short pieces for violin and piano from contemporary composers.

John Anthony Lennon

*It's such a wonderful experience when a piece starts to write itself; there is proba-
bly no more sublime time that can be had. It is one of the great human experiences.
Then it is so hard to say that it is just me creating alone.*

During my several conversations with John Anthony Lennon (b. North
Carolina, 1950), I came to know and admire this quiet, thoughtful, and
spiritual man. Raised in California, he is based now in Georgia, where
he teaches composition at Emory University in Atlanta. Lennon actually
began his education studying literature and philosophy before turning his
attention to music and composing and his love of language is clearly still
with him; quite a few of his pieces are informed by literature and poetry.

He has chosen a life out of the spotlight, focusing his energies on teaching and composing rather than celebrity, and seems genuinely at peace with the world and his place in it.

Lennon has written extensively for orchestra and chamber ensembles, including several works that feature the classical saxophone, and also has created a distinctive catalogue of works for the classical guitar. His writing for guitar is original, modern, rhythmically exciting, vibrantly colorful, and filled with virtuoso passages. As a guitarist myself, I can attest to the fact that his writing for the instrument is particularly effective. He clearly knows the guitar well and writes music that makes the most of its complex and beautiful voice.

Lennon's awards include Guggenheim and Tanglewood Fellowships, a residency at the MacDowell Colony, a Kennedy Center Friedheim Award, the Charles Ives Prize from the American Academy and Institute of Arts and Letters, and the Rome Prize.

Melodic, and to an extent tonal, his music has been described as romantic and passionate, yet modern. His hour-long lyric and dramatic work *Eternal Gates*, scored for chorus and full orchestra, is based on the Egyptian Book of the Dead and offers a poignant reflection of the man himself: resonant, lyrical, and original.

How do you find time to compose music?
I tend to be very habitual and try to work every morning. That habit becomes a ritual, and that ritual becomes a kind of meditation. I like to work in a Ralph Waldo Emerson-esque world without anything in my study that might distract me, like a clock or a telephone. I like to compose by natural morning light away from unnatural sounds. I do most of my work using Sibelius [computer notation software], although I do have a piano and a guitar in my studio so I compose on those instruments as well.

So you have a separate space that you can go to where you're not distracted when composing?
My wife and I live in an older house in Atlanta and we each have a space for our work, so there are no distractions. My studio has natural wood with large windows that overlook a fountain. It has furniture from my grandparents' home in San Francisco. I have pieces of art collected from travels. I play with juggling balls for a diversion. I drink green tea—it's part of my ritual.

To lead a creative life, I have learned how to isolate myself and be cautious about how I expend my time and energy. I need long stretches of uninterrupted time with a steady work routine. In this context I can hear sound better and consider what I am composing with more care. There are periods now when I don't listen to other music, particularly in the same medium in which I am working.

To make a living, I teach in the university. This suits me well. My classes are small and I am able to teach topics that I like. I've found a quiet and seamless connection between my home and the department to maintain a balance. It's taken time and experience to reach this continuum.

Do you compose one piece at a time or do you work on several at once?

I share a process with a lot of other composers in that at any given time I'm writing full steam on a new piece, but at the same time, on the off hours, I'm planning pieces that are coming up in the future. Then there are the pieces I'm editing for publication and the like. There is this sort of ongoing continuum of events and projects.

How do you gather and develop ideas for your pieces? Specifically, do you use pencil and paper, a notebook, or a computer?

All of the above. I came of age before the computer, and my training was to write with a pencil and paper at the piano, and then to go through many revisions of the work. These days the computer is so beneficial with editing and parts, and it has a sort of natural gravity of its own that pulls me into it. Of course, I still keep notebooks with ideas, and also compose at the piano or on the guitar, and then sometimes I just get away from instruments all together.

I have one computer file that I call a "garden file" where I keep ideas that don't fit the current piece I am working on, but that I don't want to delete. I save these ideas in that file so I can come back to them later and see if they still interest me. I call it the garden file in hopes that things will grow in there. I also have a written file of titles. I gather titles because they may inspire me, and I work on that actively. And of course we all have our mental sound files.

To develop ideas, I use the computer, the piano, the guitar, silence, or whatever works. Sometimes a novel will give me ideas about organization, or a painting may suggest contrasts. (I like to listen to groups of people talking because the natural but ametric flow of counterpoint is so interesting.) The computer allows me to sketch and to retain the sketches at the same time, whereas, with an instrument the notation process can be at odds with capturing the idea.

My pencil-and-paper sketches are essentially architectural, tracking pitch centers, pitch groups and registers, when instruments are in and when they are out, high points, low points, slow places, when thematic material comes back around. So I am cognizant of what is going on in the terrain.

That's a really interesting way of analyzing your own music. One of my composition teachers devoted much of our lessons to teaching me to draw informational pictures, graphic representations, of the music I was working on. It's a powerful tool, and it sounds like, to some extent, you also use that technique.
Yes, but it isn't like I am trying to adhere to any specific form, I just want to keep track of events. For instance, if I see that the piece is hovering around the pitch "A" too much and I've never really explored "F#," then maybe it will be a good time to try some new material. I have tried my share of compositional systems and they have changed as time and my tastes have changed. Recently, the "systems" I've employed involve modal chromaticism, tempo and rhythm cycles, partial coloring/doublings, fractured phrase attacks among instruments, large cadence points, and hyper-rhythms. These compositional aspects help make my music more visceral and human. I want the audience to feel the music in their body and move to it while they ponder it. This aesthetic probably has to do with my early experience playing rock and roll and popular music in contrast later to a waning interest in overly cerebral, modernist music.

You've composed for a variety of instruments, in particular the guitar. That can be a challenging instrument to write for. Are you a guitarist yourself?
When I was young, I played [guitar] and then played through my school years. In graduate school, I played in a new-music ensemble, but then after that my guitar playing kind of faded into the background. Right now I am on sabbatical for one year, and my wife and I plan to visit California, where I grew up. I'm going to bring my guitar and get together with some of my friends that I used to play with when I was much younger. I'm writing some rock and roll and jazz pieces to play with them. I'm hoping it will be like a composition lab with players who wouldn't try to read music but who have good ears and hands.

As a young man I loved Beethoven and Stravinsky, but I also was very excited by rock and roll and jazz. However, when I was in

music school that "other" music was frowned upon to say the least, and we didn't talk to our teachers about our interest in any other styles of music outside of the curriculum.

I'm interested in the world of performance versus the academic world. Schoenberg said he would influence music for a hundred years, but younger people are listening to popular music, even rock oldies, but they don't want to listen to Schoenberg, and it's hard to entice them to listen. I've come to the conclusion that getting the physical body into the rhythm and meter of a piece, getting the listener into a kind of emotional animalistic frame of mind, is an important part of music. This is something that a lot of new music has evaded for so long, wanting to be intellectual. We have generated so many generations of composers, one writing more apocryphal-sounding pieces than the last.

I recall when I was applying to graduate schools to study composition. I visited a number of different schools, one of them being Eastman. I talked to Joseph Schwantner and we got on really well; he liked what he saw, what I was writing, and he actually took me down to the admissions office to help me with application materials. The lady at the desk asked about my primary instrument, and I said "guitar" and she said, "Well you can't apply unless the piano is your main instrument or you can show piano proficiency." The guitar was not one of those instruments that counted, and I never applied.

The computer really lends itself to the keyboard, but there is now technology that allows you to capture your guitar playing directly to the computer via MIDI. Have you used this technique in your compositions?

I haven't done it yet but I am very tempted to try it. I'm not a natural improviser, so I tend to meticulously polish and change my music note by note. Sometimes I want to go to the piano and just rip something off and then have it go right to the computer. It's so hard to take some mellifluous idea and try to slow it down by a hundred times and try to navigate through editing it; it's a real barrier.

A recent composition that I think of as a crossover piece is a kind of rock and roll work that uses technology in the form of amplification. There is a guitar and a bass that can be amplified, and alto sax, piano, vibraphone, and cello. The sensibility of the piece is such that it is hard to say it is purely classical or popular.

I am all for amplification when it is needed. Instruments aren't equal dynamically and neither are music halls. With more balance control, composers can obtain colors that are otherwise lost. This opens many more sonic possibilities for the creative process. Purists will argue. My reply is that I can't imagine Beethoven turning down the experience of hearing his music played in perfect balance, or for that matter with the intonation and sound produced by modern instruments and today's players.

This is a piece that is in progress right now?
It's called *Passing Future Past* and I finished it very recently. It is about perception. When the composer first hears the idea and writes it down, there is a future perception to it, a projection of the future. The piece is different at its end and can never be the same again. When the players get the piece and begin working on it, they have an experience in the present, and when the audience hears the music for the first time it is from the past. So there are these different perception points.

Besides amplification, did digital technology play any other part in the development of that piece?
I received a request from the bass player for a new part transposed down a major second, which was a new one to me. He was working on a scordatura [open tuning] part and didn't want to have to retune his bass and so forth. Within an hour or so, I edited the part on my computer and sent it off by e-mail as a PDF. In the old days, this would have been a task that would have taken an entire day.

Do you create a MIDI demo or some sort of recorded version of what you intend the piece to sound like in its finished form?
I do make MP3 recordings but with great trepidation. If performers want a copy to help with score preparation, I am glad to comply. Other performers won't listen even if I send a copy. MP3s are better than no sound version at all, but sound samples like voices can do more damage (because they sound so horridly inhuman) for the composer than not.

When preparing *Passing Future Past* I sent MP3s for purposes of practice before the live rehearsal and performance because the players didn't live near each other. So they practiced independently, using these MP3s, until they showed up and we had one big three-hour rehearsal. They did really well, and a lot of that was due to the use of technology.

One aspect of my interaction with the computer is that I was trained before it came to the fore. I find this to be an advantage because I don't rely on the computer for the actual sound of live instruments and what they can do well or how human beings will react to the music I place in front of them. These can be difficult lessons to learn for student composers.

You started out majoring in English, literature, and philosophy. Then you made the transition to studying music and composition. How did that come to be and what motivated you to make a change in your studies?

When I was in high school in the '60s, things were pretty wild, a lot of idealism, particularly in the San Francisco Bay area. There were so many rock and roll bands doing and playing great art. There was a sense that you did not have to go to school, that musicians could create exciting music outside of the system. However, I felt that I should really go to college because there was so much I didn't know, like counterpoint and orchestration, and music literature. There was a synthesis.

I always had an interest in literature and writing, so I studied those subjects along with philosophy at the University of San Francisco, which was at the time a good Jesuit school. At the same time I started taking music courses—theory, counterpoint, and chorus. I started becoming less interested in rock, folk, and popular at that point. Even though I didn't abandon my interest in those styles altogether, my musical attention went in another direction. I started notating music for instruments, and I decided, "Yes, this is what I want to do."

You have had some outstanding composition teachers.

In particular, William Bolcom[1] and Leslie Basset.[2] They took a personal interest in me, sometimes an antagonistic one, but in a good way. They were supportive and helped me to learn important skills such as notating music accurately, knowing what Bach wrote, and encouraging me to know my operas. Leslie Bassett lives close by in Flowery Branch. He is 90 years old this year. When I visit he still wants to see my music.

How important is the fame that those composers achieved?

When I was young and idealistic, I learned about all of the great composers and how they were famous. They were placed on an altar. Today that image of fame is largely antiquated and has shifted to fame for fame itself. It is for Hollywood or sports stars, rock musicians, or politicians and talking heads.

I am a shy and reclusive person and would not enjoy being recognized by strangers (at the Copland house people came up the driveway to stare into the windows, I suppose to see if Aaron was still there). I do want to have my music known and performed, but I enjoy the role of being an obscure chamber composer so that I may live quietly. I have a wonderful freedom.

Do your current students have a different perspective of composing and music in general as compared with the student bodies that you and I were members of? In part, I'm thinking technology may have changed the perspective of contemporary music students as compared with that of past generations.

I agree, I think one big difference is the technology. Whereas you and I were trained to rely on our ear, many of the students now haven't had to internalize their musical skills to the degree that we did via ear training et cetera. Instead, they can instantly bring an array of computer-generated sounds up. Sometimes those sounds are unrealistic, like putting the trumpets two octaves up. But they are complete whizzes at this technology, and it's surely not reached the end of its development, so who knows what the future will bring? I think that another aspect to consider is that the curriculum we were given years ago—all of the assumptions of history, literature, and the organization of sound—are vanishing. That approach to learning music is just out the window for most of the young people I see coming in. All they really care about is what happened since maybe 1980. Where I teach students are not required to take 21st-century theory courses; instead they can take a substitute. So their perspective is very different from what ours was.

What advice would you give to young composers?

It would depend on their musical interest. If they were interested in rock or popular music, I would tell them to spend a minimal amount of time in school, and just get out there and do it. If their interest is classical music, they need to go to a school of music and learn the literature and techniques.

I might be the last person to offer advice to a young person who wants to become a composer. The world of composition has changed since I was a student. Aesthetics have changed. Students' musical orientations are different. The old curricula are reaching obsolescence. New technology has probably created the largest shift.

It seems that no two composers had the exact path in the past. The era of classical modern music has probably shifted, but exactly to what, I am not sure. Being in school until the age of 30 may no longer be the right solution, whereas networking and possessing excellent musical skills may be what it takes. To paraphrase Cage, "Find your audience and write for it."

Speaking of networking, the global revolution in communication technology has certainly had a huge impact on the way a composer may make his or her career successful.

Yes, it's easy from one's basement to get into the middle of it, so that's great. The creative opportunities are really unlimited. Somebody out in the middle of nowhere can create and get their music out there.

I have mixed feelings about music being digitally available, free of charge. The easy and wide access is a wonderful new benefit for composers, but at the same time, artists should have a method to be rewarded for their works. For most "classical" composers, or whatever it is we are, it seems that the financial rewards are less important than success of the music. Remuneration hasn't been my motivation, but I am fortunate to have a university that supports me, somewhat like the old guild system.

Is there a center of music anymore, now that the technology has made it possible, at least theoretically, to work from almost anywhere? Has technology changed the geography of the musical world for composers?

If I lived in New York or Boston, I would be writing different music than I do living where I live now. I can find out who I am and not be disturbed by too many other composers, or disturbed by things. For me, this is a much better environment in which to find my own voice, outside of any hotspot, and I like that very much.

Do deadlines affect your process?

I try to avoid deadlines at all costs. I recall a time when I had three simultaneous commissions. Really good commissions, but all due at the same time. In hindsight, two of the three pieces were really just not something I was happy with when I was finished. Now I will not release a piece unless I have had sufficient time to live with it and stand by it. After that experience, I've always tried negotiating around difficult deadlines. I'll say, "Well if I get it this season, I'll get to it eventually." That seems to work for the most part.

Eternal Gates is a recent and very large piece.

I was reading the Egyptian Book of the Dead[3] and started getting ideas for a large piece based on that text. When I was very young, my father would tell me about the Egyptian pyramids and other interesting historical things that would tend to get the attention of a young child. Years later, when I was studying religion and philosophy, I became aware of the Egyptian Book of the Dead. There were so many wonderful lines. I read the text and studied it for a long time, and I gradually separated out lines into 12 different movements, put them in order, and developed the primary characters. There are different themes about the creation, about how the world began, what happens on the earth, and so forth. The opportunity to have the piece performed was there so I went ahead and spent the time on it and got it performed.

How long did it take you to research and compose the piece?

Maybe six or seven years. I spent time researching text and then working on sketches on Sibelius. Then I worked on it full time for at least a year, with the last six months devoted to brutal editing, not really creative work. The 12 movements of this piece exist in more than 100 files on my computer. I have a file for the conductor, a version with cues for part extraction, combined percussion parts, vocal parts, and a piano version. Then there are the files for the title page and so forth. And so all in all, a gazillion files. I would like to write more large pieces like this, but it's very difficult to get them performed, and the organization is a nightmare. I can see what opera composers go through—in a way intriguing but really intimidating.

Does working with technology change the process of composing, and if so, is the piece in its final form a different work because of the fact that it was created using technology?

I think technology, in fact, has already done that. I have a theory: Minimalism started when "r" [repeat] was pressed on the keyboard. A whole new musical world started in that way. Digital technology has reduced costs and time for score and parts preparation and for postage. (Of course, this has rendered most copyists obsolete.) It also allows editing to be a simple task. Now that these processes are in place, there is more time to compose more pieces.

For performers, computer technology has forced a growth in their virtuosic techniques, in the ability to read difficult rhythms, for example, and in handling new devices like metronomes that can be set to all increments. They struggle to interpret their new parts artistically. This evolution will come back to influence composers who are always ready to take artistic advantage when they hear new possibilities.

From this process with musicians, new styles and aesthetics will emerge.

There are some composers left who have not adapted these new technologies. This has become a disadvantage for them. It is ironic that they may have an excellent ear and craft, but the process of the digital world may stymie them, whereas a technically adept composer can flourish with other strengths.

Some composers have commented that the process of composing is mystical or at least indescribable to them. Do you find that to be the case with your composing or is it more analytical?

I am sympathetic to this idea. I am a theist, so I guess we are products of our background. For me there is a sense that I am not on my own when composing. I'm very cognizant of that. There is sometimes a mystery as to how the sounds arrive. At times, musical ideas emerge that are surprising, and I don't feel solely responsible for creating those sounds. For that reason, I approach music purely as an intuitive endeavor and try to not be dogmatic in any way. I follow my instincts when I am sketching and try to trust them to see where they take me. I strive to trust the intuition in my ear rather than being too analytical or too mechanical. It's such a wonderful experience when a piece starts to write itself; there is probably no more sublime time that can be had. It is one of the great human experiences. Then it is so hard to say that it is just me creating alone.

SELECTED WORKS OF JOHN ANTHONY LENNON

Passing Future Past (2013), Band
Eternal Gates (2011), Orchestra and Chorus
Elysian Bridges (2011), Saxophone Quartet
Spiral Mirrors (2009), Saxophone Duo
The Fortunels (1998), Guitar
Gigolo (1996), Guitar
Symphonic Rhapsody (1992), Concerto for Alto Saxophone
    and Orchestra
Zingari (1991), Concerto for Guitar and Orchestra
Seven Translations (1988), Soprano, Clarinet, Violin and Piano
Concert Etudes (1983–1984), Guitar
Another's Fandango (1981), Guitar
Distances Within Me (1979), Saxophone and Piano

▶ To learn more about John Anthony Lennon and his music, including score excerpts from *At the Trace, Blue on Blue, Fabled Wings, Misericordia, Passing Future Past*, and *Quick Is the Twilight*, visit www.oup.com/us/compositioninthedigitalworld.

NOTES

1. American composer William Bolcom studied with Darius Milhaud and Olivier Messiaen, and has been awarded the Pulitzer Prize, two Grammy Awards, and the National Medal of Arts.
2. Leslie Bassett is an American composer and winner of the 1966 Pulitzer Prize for Music.
3. The Book of the Dead is an ancient Egyptian funerary text consisting of spells to assist the dead on their journey to the afterlife.

David T. Little

My generation came up at a time when we felt really hopeless about our profession. We felt like there was nothing left for us. The orchestras were dying, the industry as a whole was collapsing, the record industry was fading, downloads started taking over, and everything felt really dire. . . but there are other options: Start your own group, perform your own works, start a concert series. Let's build the next thing, take control of our means of production, and decide when our works are played and who plays them.

While many of his contemporaries similarly honed their love of music performing in rock bands, David T. Little (b. 1978) is keeping his first love with him as he grows into his career as a contemporary composer. He is the founder, drummer, and artistic director of the amplified chamber ensemble Newspeak, which he describes as "exploring the boundaries between rock and classical music."

Holding master's and doctoral degrees from the University of Michigan and Princeton University, respectively, Little's primary teachers included William Bolcom and Michael Daugherty. He has already amassed an impressive list of honors and awards, including recognition by the American Academy of Arts and Letters, Meet the Composer, the American Music Center, BMI, and ASCAP.

His works have been presented all over the world, with performances by a notable array of new-music ensembles including the London Sinfonietta, Alarm Will Sound, eighth blackbird, So Percussion, PRISM Quartet, the New World Symphony, the New York City Opera, and the Baltimore Symphony Orchestra and at such high-profile venues as the Tanglewood, Aspen, and Cabrillo Festivals.

Incorporating digital technology into all aspects of his music, Little has written a sizable body of works for chamber and orchestra and is becoming well known for his theatrical flair and the pictorial and visceral overtones of his music. After receiving extraordinarily positive press for his first opera, *Dog Days*, he is for the moment focused on composing for that genre, currently working on an opera tentatively titled *JFK*. In person, David T. Little seems a little larger than life, and the scope and grandeur of opera seem to suit him perfectly; he gives the impression of a man teeming with ideas both sweeping and dramatic.

You're an active performer and teacher. How do you find the time to sit down and compose? Do you have a regular schedule or ritual you like to follow?

Over the years I've settled into something of a pattern with my work habits. Some people like to compose from 6 AM to noon everyday, for instance, but for me that doesn't really work. I need to work in fairly large blocks of time. I need to have three or four days open in a row, which can be difficult to schedule, but that's what I need to get anything accomplished. Once I go in to compose, I am in. I produce a lot in that time. Generally, the first day is not spent actually writing anything, but instead, getting into the right mindset. I read or clean my office, just taking time to get into the right frame of mind. Then, usually by the evening of the first day, I'm starting to look at the music file I am working with, playing with ideas and the like. By the time I go to sleep that first night, my mind is in the right place. Then, starting the next morning I'll get up and I'm ready to go. I do take breaks. If my brain feels kind of fried from composing, I pause and watch 20 minutes of a movie or something. Then I will go back to work. I can usually do about three days of that kind of work and then I need to stop.

Do you use a notation program, or do you write your scores by hand?

I usually use Sibelius, but sometimes I'll do things by hand. The hand-drawn notations are mostly drawings and shapes rather than musical notation. These drawings refer to whole movements, whole pieces.

Is that a typical starting point in your process: drawing abstract shapes or graphic representations of various parameters of a given piece? I ask because I actually do this myself, as do several other composers I've spoken with.

Yeah, exactly. My opera *Dog Days* is an example of that method at work: I drew a very specific sketch and then kind of forgot about it. After the piece was written, I went back and compared it to the sketch, and they were almost identical, which was really strange, really unexpected. Even the timing of events and intervals was right on.

I see you have a piano here in your studio. Do you play piano regularly or use it to compose?

I'm a percussionist, but a very poor pianist. I took piano lessons when I was younger, but I never really clicked with it as an instrument.

In the past it was expected that a composer should also be a proficient pianist. Did you experience this as a student?

I always felt guilty for being a bad pianist. I was a little jealous of colleagues who could sit down and play their music. I still am. For instance, friends at parties who could sit down and play *The Rite of Spring* at the piano with other composers. That's a party trick that I just can't do. But I could play note for note what John Bonham [drummer for the rock band Led Zeppelin] plays on *Immigrant Song*.

Many contemporary composers I've spoken with are influenced by a wide variety of musical styles, including rock. For instance, you have a group that you have put together [Newspeak].[1] You are melding classical and rock music in that ensemble.

I grew up as a drummer, not really reading pitches. I could *kind of* read rhythms, but I played in a fife-and-drum corps, so I pretty much learned everything by rote. It was collective music making, where there were 40 of us marching down the street playing Revolutionary

War or Civil War songs. At the same time, I was playing drums in rock bands.

There aren't a whole lot of classical composers who grew up only playing drums and no pitched instrument. I didn't really know classical music existed until I was probably 16. Then I got into classical music through film scoring, which is a whole other story. So after I'd already been composing for while, I hit a point where I needed, for my own music, to find a group of musicians I could work with regularly, who understood the same kind of musical language that I understood. I began to wonder, "What makes John Bonham sound like John Bonham?" It's not necessarily the notes that he is playing; you can transcribe what he played and have someone else play it and it won't sound the same: it's something in the way *he* played it. So, if you're playing rock guitar, there is a certain way that you approach notes that is specific to that music. It isn't necessarily something that you can notate traditionally.

It sounds like you set out to explore how to apply the nuances of the musical styles that excited you in a classical setting by gathering like-minded musicians.

Right. I decided to put together a group of musicians who would understand the performance practices I was interested in, but were also top-notch, classically trained players. I wanted to work with musicians who would be able to play music written by me and other composers with similar backgrounds who wanted to bring that rock element into concert music in a way that felt authentic. Just putting a drum set in an orchestra never works. Sonically it's wrong.

That group is called Newspeak. The group evolved a lot at the start, but has had the same lineup, with one exception, since about 2007. It's had a huge influence on my compositional approach and the way my musical voice was able to blossom. Because I had this group of people I could work with often, with feedback from the other members, it was a kind of workshop for me compositionally. Early on, I wasn't playing with the group, just composing, but in 2007 I started playing drums with them as well. Once I started performing other composers' music, my own thoughts on music composition really solidified.

Making the transition from student to working composer is a mysterious, difficult, and fickle process. Most composers have told me success is a combination of luck, persistence, contacts, and, by the way, talent. [Laughs from both] One strategy that seems to have

helped many composers is to form or join an ensemble that will perform their music. So you followed that path as well?

Yes. It gives you some control. It is really difficult and requires a lot of work and a different set of skills than composing. With Newspeak, we had to go through the 501(c)(3) process [setting up a nonprofit organization] and learn how to deal with the IRS and all of that. I remember at the time feeling like, "Oh my God, this is awful. I'm reading these tax codes, when I just want to write music." But creating an apparatus so that your organization can thrive is really important.

I think my generation came up at a time when we felt really hopeless about our profession. We felt like there was nothing left for us. The orchestras were dying, the industry as a whole was collapsing, the record industry was fading, downloads started taking over, and everything felt really dire. I remember having a discussion at the University of Michigan, where colleagues of mine, fellow grad students, were really freaked out and frustrated and saying, "Well, what are we going to do? I guess we keep going to school, and then we get a teaching job." That's fine, you know, but there are other options: start your own group, perform your own works, start a concert series. Let's build the next thing, take control of our means of production, and decide when our works are played and who plays them. It's great if other people are going to play our music too, and that's ideal, but if they're not, we can at least make sure our work is out there, in a way that we think is appropriate and can believe in.

You mentioned the collapse of the traditional record companies and the decline of orchestras. What is the significance of the fact that so much music is available for free on the Internet now? As a composer, does that concern you?

It is sort of tricky. Thom Yorke[2] just pulled all of his music off of Spotify, but when I'm teaching lessons, Spotify and YouTube are my best friends. I can say to my students, "There's this piece you've got to know about,'" and I can play it for them instantly from the Internet. So, as a teaching tool, it is really valuable.

Why buy a CD of David T. Little's music if you can just go online and listen to it for free? Do you think people are still paying for music?

I think people do. I had this interesting experience the other night; I was formatting parts, proofreading a score, and I thought, "I'm going to listen to some music," so I went to YouTube and I found this whole channel of complete albums. I listened to a bunch of old Smashing Pumpkins [rock band] records, which I own, but it was so instantly accessible on the Internet that I listened to them that way. I think that's part of the psychological appeal: it is just so available. At the same time, there are so many labels that aren't available online, and so when I want that stuff, I go buy it.

Also, I've discovered a lot of new artists on Spotify that I would not have discovered otherwise, and the likelihood that I will in some way contribute to their project financially, either by buying a recording or making a donation or going to a show, is increased because of that first interaction. So it depends on how you look at it.

But somehow I feel less excitement when I download a piece of music as opposed to buying an object like a CD. When I download music, there's nothing to hold, nothing to add to my wall of music! [Both laugh]

I had a teacher who decided he was just going to give away all of the pieces he had written. He wasn't going to sell it; he just put it all up for download on his website. He found it didn't actually work the way he thought it was going to. I think there was a perception on the part of the audience that "if it's free, can it be good?" which is too bad because his music is great. I think he sells it again now. It's interesting that the way we listen to music has changed because of how quickly we can consume the material. The days of taking an LP out of its jacket, putting it on the record player, and sitting back—that's such a great experience. I haven't had that experience in a long time because I am online, even if it is just on iTunes, or a CD I am putting into my computer. It is still on the computer. It's less ritualized than it once was.

Well, here's another ritual that may be on its way out: Many composers who learned to write their music by hand (and I've found examples of this in all age groups) enjoy the tactile experience of composing by putting pencil to paper as opposed to entering their music into a computer program. Do you think there is a comparable ritual, where some composers feel most fluid and comfortable in front of a computer screen?

The process that I described earlier of blocking out a couple of days does have a kind of ritualistic quality to it, in terms of how I work generally. Working with the software is something that is evolving; I feel like I am at the beginning of a big shift in how I work with software. Part of this is because while I use Sibelius, I also now use Ableton Live[3] to do electronic stuff and also as an editing tool. That's been really interesting, as it's pushed my work to new places because of the sounds I can access [via

Ableton Live]. That goes back to my point about using a drum set in a classical ensemble. It ends up sounding kind of goofy. It doesn't really have the impact, and that's partially because the drummer can't play loud enough to sound like a drum set sounds in our musical memory without obliterating the string section. If you're working with sampled instruments or pre-recorded sounds, it can sound right and still have a controllable volume level. I'm moving in the direction of using more electronic sounds. With one exception, all of the pieces I'm writing this year have electronic components to them, which was not the case five years ago.

What do you mean by electronic components? Digital or pre-recorded sounds produced for live performances of the piece?
Yes, tracks backing the live performers. I'm planning to write a big piece for Todd Reynolds,[4] who is a big Ableton user. When we work together to develop his instrument—which means his violin, *and* his computer, *and* music software—I think we will imagine a new instrument for the piece that will do all kinds of different things. My programming chops aren't where his are, so working with him will be really great for me, and I will learn a lot from him. Pretty much everything I know about Ableton I have learned from working on projects like this.

So the approach of composing by creating sketches with traditional notation is not something you practice.
I don't ever start a piece writing by hand, or at least very rarely. I open a new file in Sibelius, and I start working. Because I don't use a MIDI controller, I've also developed a sort of weird process where I do a lot of typing and copying and transforming.[5] In a way, the piece is really generated from that first material, or what becomes the primary material. That's then transformed and altered digitally, in an almost very traditional, German-counterpoint sort of way. But it's all done in the software.

How do you approach helping your composition students in developing their own voice? Is that a focus of your teaching?
I try to be supportive and not squash anyone's voice. I focus on technical things, while trying to observe broader aesthetic issues. For example, if I think a student would benefit from hearing a certain Lou Harrison[6] piece, I'll make sure the student knows that piece.

I try to be very open to the direction that they want to go. For instance, I have one student who writes a lot of pieces that incorporate noise; he buys these handmade, hacked noise machines that are a part of a lot of his pieces. Another student writes very traditional orchestral music and has an interest in pursuing film scoring. So I try to provide each of these composers with what they need in terms of examples, but also make sure that they understand that you still need to think about music as "sound in time," that there are implications to events in time, and that they need to look at the relationship of those events. Even when working with a student who does a lot of stuff with noise, I try to talk about that in the same way you would talk about a tonal piece, using issues of harmonic tension and harmonic rhythm, and very traditional techniques as models. It can work the other way too, showing how a traditional work could benefit from noise.

I love the music of Bach and Beethoven, but I also love the Beatles, John Coltrane, and the MC5. If a student comes to you and is influenced by hip-hop, is that okay?
Totally. My theory is that not every rule applies to every type of music. I think that you can have interesting and productive conversations about music that will help a student discover something about, say a string quartet, via Jay-Z. I think that because that is the way I am. Listening to a Smashing Pumpkins record the other night, I thought, "Oh, that's a cool thing that could probably apply to this orchestration idea I'm working on."

What are you working on now?
The most recent piece I finished was *Dog Days*, which was very well received. It was nice because it was a piece that I really felt good about. I felt I accomplished everything I wanted to do, and I was able to make it work. As a bonus, audiences liked it, which was really satisfying. But also it was a huge undertaking; it kind of knocked me out for a while. After that I didn't start really writing again for six months.

Do you work on more than one piece at a time?
Sometimes I have to, but I prefer not to. It's hard to go into that intense writing isolation if I have two pieces, or three pieces, going at once. I'm currently in that sort of situation, not my favorite place to be, but I'm working through it.

Do you usually orchestrate in full score as you compose?
I'm really excited about the JFK opera that's my next big piece on the horizon, but I don't think I will be able to write it in full score; it's just too unwieldy with the delivery schedule from the company. So I think I'm going to do a short score piano reduction for that. For *Dog Days* I wrote in full score and the piano reduction happened after the fact.

What are some other projects that are on your horizon?

Right now I'm writing a piece for the Kronos Quartet. It incorporates a backing track and distortion pedals. That's more in my Newspeak world, where everything is amplified and the effects pedals are written into the score.

Do you use the standard sounds in your notation program or more advanced sound samples?

I want to start moving toward using better sounds, but so far I've just been using the default notation program sounds.

This question reminds me of an interesting experience I had as a student: I was 21, and it was my first day as a fellow at Tanglewood. I was feeling really brave, so I decided to present my orchestra piece, playing a MIDI mockup for the class. There was something I wrote in it that was acoustically impossible, but sounded great using MIDI. I got kind of scolded for this. The teacher said, "That's got to be the loudest clarinet in the universe." Being called out on that made me no longer trust MIDI or sampled sounds in the same way. I retrained myself after that moment to still use MIDI, but to "hear through it" and to not necessarily trust what the MIDI sounds like coming from my computer. For that reason I haven't really felt the need to have fancier sounds.

Do you create MIDI demos or mockups of new pieces for your performers and the conductor?

Oh, yeah, I do that. With *Dog Days*, I sent MIDI mockups to all the singers with their parts soloed, so they could check their rhythms.

You've had some very distinguished composers for teachers. Are there any particularly significant experiences you had with them you can share?

I studied with some teachers who were very open, including William Bolcom, Michael Daugherty, and Steve Mackey.[7] One of the most powerful "teaching moments" that I had was with Bright Sheng. I was writing something atonal, though I think it was a piece that ended up getting scrapped. He just said, "You know, some day you're going to need to deal with harmony. It doesn't mean you have to write tonal music, but you need to deal with harmony in a way that you're not." I didn't really know how to process that at the time, but I didn't forget it. The change in my music from that point until now has been significant, and I think very informed by that comment. Another really powerful moment was when I got to Princeton. I had a meeting with Paul Lansky[8] who went on to be my advisor and good friend. I was telling him about a piece I was working on, saying things like, "In this piece, this element is challenging this other thing," and I was putting out this very confrontational energy. He said, "There is really no one here to fight against but yourself." And it was totally true; the next couple of years were spent thinking about what I believed artistically. Not fighting the way I had been up to that point. So those were two really interesting moments.

Another great lesson was from Steve Mackey. I was writing *Soldier Songs*, and at the really big climax of the piece, there was a big C major pedal that went on for minutes: it's epic. He listened and said, "This is a great moment, but you haven't earned that yet. You need to go back to the three minutes before it, and you need to earn that moment, because the balance isn't right; it's not really working." I try to pass that concept of "earning moments" on to my students. I find myself saying, "This is a really cool idea, but first you need to earn it."

SELECTED WORKS OF DAVID T. LITTLE

AGENCY (2013), String Quartet and Electronics
Haunted Topography (2013), Orchestra
Dog Days (2012), Opera
AM I BORN (2012), Oratorio for Soprano Soloist, Choir,
    and Orchestra
Soldier Songs (2006–2011), Opera
CHARM (2011), Orchestra
Haunt of Last Nightfall (2010), Percussion Quartet and Electronics
and the sky was still there (2010), Violin and Electronics
sweet light crude (2007), Soprano and Amplified Ensemble
Electric Proletariat (2005), Amplified Ensemble
Songs of Love, Death, Friends, and Government (2004), for Soprano,
    Violin, and Clarinet
Piano Trio (2004), Violin, Violoncello, and Piano

▶ To learn more about David T. Little and his music, including score excerpts from his *AGENCY, AM I BORN*, and *Soldier Songs*, visit www.oup.com/us/compositioninthedigitalworld.

NOTES
1. Newspeak is an amplified octet formed by Mr. Little in 2004. He plays drums and is the artistic director. The ensemble aims to explore the combination of the traditions of classical and rock music.

2. Thomas Yorke is the lead singer, guitarist, and songwriter for the rock band Radiohead. He has been an outspoken opponent of major record labels and companies like Spotify that stream music on the Internet, citing unfair royalty payments to musicians.
3. Ableton Live is a digital music program that functions as a music sequencer and digital audio workstation.
4. Todd Reynolds is a violinist, conductor, and composer. He has worked with artists as varied as Steve Reich, Bang on a Can, Todd Rundgren, Yo-Yo Ma, and R. Luke DuBois.
5. Copying and transforming is a process in which sections of music in a notation program or sequencer can be copied and pasted into the document, thus repeating previously composed music. These sections can then be transformed using computer functions.
6. Lou Silver Harrison, an American composer (1917—2003), studied with Arnold Schoenberg and Henry Cowell, among others.
7. Steve Mackey is an American guitarist, composer, and educator. His awards include a Charles Ives Scholarship, a Guggenheim fellowship, and two awards from the Kennedy Center for the performing arts.
8. Paul Lansky is a composer and professor at Princeton University. He studied with Milton Babbitt and is particularly noted for his work with computer music and algorithmic composition.

Kevin Puts

It's an absurd place that we've gotten to when a composer cannot, or will not, even acknowledge the fact that what we are doing is entertainment. Certainly Beethoven wasn't shy of that concept. He was clearly trying to knock people out of their seats, trying to knock their socks off; that's what Beethoven was trying to do. I think it's what we're all trying to do.

For quite some time opera has been the odd child out in the world of modern music, but that appears to be changing. Kevin Puts (b. Missouri, 1972) is one of a growing number of contemporary composers who are reviving the art form with a new wave of creativity, shot through with a fresh vitality that is helping to make it truly popular again. One factor in opera's renewal is digital technology, which has made it possible to stage affordable productions in smaller and more informal venues, in turn making it viable for composers and opera companies to take creative chances.

Puts began his career with a focus on piano performance but moved to composition during his college years. He studied with William Bolcom and Bernard Rands at the Tanglewood Music Festival and earned degrees from the Eastman School of Music and Yale under the tutelage of a host of eminent teachers including Samuel Adler, Martin Bresnick, Jacob Druckman, David Lang, Christopher Rouse, and Joseph Schwantner.

His career took off with performances of his works by top artists and orchestras and commissions and awards including the Rome Prize, a Guggenheim Fellowship, and the Pulitzer Prize. Prior to his first opera, *Silent Night*, Puts had already produced an impressive body of orchestral and chamber works including four symphonies and seven concertos. His music is sensuous, emotional, and brilliantly crafted, particularly in its orchestration.

In talking to Puts, I found an extremely unassuming and amiable fellow who seems genuinely humble about his recent successes, expressing both astonishment and elation at learning he'd been awarded the 2012 Pulitzer Prize for *Silent Night*. No longer on the list of "up-and-coming composers to watch," Puts has firmly established himself as one of Americas most prominent composers and that calls for celebration, particularly among current and future opera lovers everywhere.

You put a tremendous amount of time and effort into developing your chops as a concert pianist. What made you want to focus on composition instead, and how did you make that transition?

I spent most of my time at Eastman playing the piano: I would play new pieces, and spent a lot of time learning those big war-horse piano concertos by Beethoven, Rachmaninoff, and Mozart. I was really motivated to play as well as my classmates, but then I decided that I wouldn't pursue a master's degree in piano but in composition instead. I became more interested in the musical unknown than the athletics of playing the piano. I thought, "There are so many people who can play these pieces as well as I can, but there is only one person who can compose them." I was more interested in discovering a piece as it unfolded as I composed it: the "personality" of the piece, the mystery of searching for the next note or the next phrase, to define a new piece from the ground up. That was far more exciting to me and it really wasn't a tough decision to focus on composing.

And then you sought out composition teachers who could help you pursue that passion with composing. What were your next steps?

I was interested in Yale because so many composers I admired, whose music I really loved, including Aaron J. Kernis, Michael Torke, David Lang,[1] and my friend Chris Theofanidis [2] who was just a few years ahead of me at Eastman, had gone to Yale. So I thought that must be the place to go. I visited the school and I just loved the feel of it. The two main instructors there at the time were Jacob Druckman[3] and Martin Bresnick. I liked the vibe between the two of them; they approached composition very differently but were complementary to each other as teachers.

When I went to Yale my other class work was much lighter than it had been during my undergraduate studies at Eastman, so there was suddenly time to think about the music I was writing and I wrote a lot more of it.

You had some exceptional teachers: Martin Bresnick, Joseph Schwantner, William Bolcom, Samuel Adler,[4] and Christopher Rouse among them.

I *have* had some great teachers. At Eastman, students had to switch teachers every year, so it allowed me to come into contact with many talents. In fact, I was at a concert just last night at Julliard, and Samuel Adler, my first teacher at Eastman when I was 18, had his 85th Birthday Concert at Julliard. Chris Rouse was there, and I was trying to count all the teachers I had, including those two. Kind of amazing. But for me, composition is so much about finding who *you* are. I think it's important to keep changing, keep taking a lot of different approaches, because then you can pile all of your experiences together and push them away, and have the confidence to be who *you* really are.

How does one find an individual voice as a composer? Is that something that just naturally develops as you work and progress as a composer?

As a student, you might write one kind of music that is supported enthusiastically by one teacher, while another teacher might think the same music is not worthwhile. You have to find what feels the most real, natural, and unique to *you*. You'll know when you've gotten to that place because then composing is easy. It doesn't require any kind of calculation or "hedging your bets." You'll say, "This is it, this what I am going to write." Eventually, you shed the things that aren't of interest to you, that don't feel as personal.

I was in my last year of study at Yale when Jacob Druckman heard one of my pieces and said, "This sounds very close to Copland." I remember that was the first time anybody had really made that comparison. I really hadn't been aware of any similarities. Then I got into post-minimalism and at my first lesson with Christopher Rouse, he said, "You sound like John Adams or Michael Torke." In a way, that made me furious and I had to respond to it. There definitely were times like that in my mid-20s where I had a sort of crisis of musical identity. But, at a certain point, I stopped worrying about it and just tried to write pieces that I thought were compelling.

Since then you've had some great successes, including writing for opera.

I'm really loving working in opera. It allows me to be very broad with my style and influences. There's so much that needs to happen in opera: It's not only about me and who I am; it's about the story. So I try to bring the narrative, the story, to life.

The first opera you composed was *Silent Night*. Was it a terrifying experience to take the plunge and write that first opera?

I was actually terrified *and* excited. I came to it in a very unusual way. Dale Johnson[5] from Minnesota Opera, was looking for someone to write an opera based on the 2005 film *Joyeux Noel*. Dale heard one of my symphonies and suddenly decided I was the guy to write this giant opera in three languages, with a large orchestra. It was scary, but I thought "You know what? I've always wanted to do this." I just hadn't been proactive enough to find the opportunities to do it.

I'm now writing my second opera with librettist Mark Campbell.[6] He and I have a simple working process: He writes the complete libretto and gives it to me and I bring it to life musically. The first day that I put the libretto for *Silent Night* on the piano and I started playing and singing, a pretty traditional approach, I felt an electricity. I've always been a huge fan of drama, mainly through film, and opera gives me an opportunity to tell a story as in a film.

Do you start with simple sketches of melody and harmony, or compose in full score?

At the very beginning I had a hard time deciding how to handle the idea of a simple piano/vocal score that was needed for rehearsals. I wanted to make very specific decisions about the orchestration, yet those decisions were completely unimportant to the singers and the staging director as far as rehearsals were concerned, so I developed a method where I would often write in four staves in order to capture details. With the opera I'm writing now, *The Manchurian Candidate*,[7] I'm a little better with writing something pianistic and I'll deal with the orchestration later. But I'm still writing very detailed notes to myself. I think that orchestration is not just a second step in the composition process; it's actually very important, and can be structural, especially in an opera.

You feel that orchestration is an integral part of the process of composition as opposed to a separate step to be addressed after the fact?
Absolutely. For example, Benjamin Britten's operas will stay with one orchestral color for a long time before moving on to another. So a scene will be about one orchestral construct and the next scene will be a different one. It not only allows him to write two and a half to three hours of music without the audience getting tired of one color or another, but it also gives a very good sense of where you are in the structure of the piece.

What other parameters do you keep in mind when composing a long-form piece?
Register is another way that I maintain freshness and interest throughout a long piece of music, especially in opera. You might write an entire scene, which never goes below middle C, and follow it with a scene that is mid-ranged or bass-oriented. That can be very compelling and feel satisfying because you haven't been in that register for a while. I plan things over a long period—the contour that the piece will inhabit over the course of two hours. Of course, I also consider rhythm, harmony, melody, and texture. Texture and register are hugely important in opera. Because there is so much music, you can avoid a kind of "sonic fatigue" by varying the registeral space that the music inhabits and by varying texture.

I think composers tend to want to have a lot going on all the time. We want there to be a lot happening and things to be very involved and complex, and that's fine for a short time, but it can get very exhausting to listen to too much happening over two hours of music. So, very sparse moments can be effective. Sometime all you need is a referential tone that everything revolves around. *The Manchurian Candidate* is a thriller, so there has to be a lot happening, but it needs to have the occasional breather, because if all of the music is exciting it can become exhausting to listen to, and the audience will lose interest, the exciting moments will lose impact.

When composing an opera, the issue of length, especially when compared to writing an instrumental piece, is clearly a great compositional challenge. Are there any other considerations composers

should be mindful of when writing an opera, as opposed to instrumental music?

I think there are several parameters that have to be considered at any given moment, parameters that are all extremely crucial. If I write opera well, it's because I will, at times, place my own desires subordinate to the story. I think that you've got to do what the story needs. I might have an urge to write a huge orchestral interlude at some point that lasts three or four minutes, but if that causes the story to fall flat and it feels out of proportion, then I won't do it.

I think the listener might be more forgiving when you write a 20-minute orchestra piece. There might be sections in an orchestra piece in which the listener is not quite sure where the music is going, but it's permissible for instrumental music to be somewhat nebulous at times. However, with opera, there is a story to tell, and the timing has to be exactly right. You've got to put your ego aside and do what the story needs, no matter what, because once you lose the audience in an opera, they are gone. That's the scary thing about opera that I'm always concerned with: keeping tight, economical, and always moving forward. Getting the pacing right is the most difficult thing.

The Manchurian Candidate sounds like an interesting story to adapt into opera. Can you talk a little about that project and how it relates to your previous opera writing?

It's been observed that *Silent Night* represents a poly-stylistic approach; it has music that sounds very Impressionistic, and then suddenly something minimalist, and then a Baroque fugue, then a Schubert-sounding song, then a Mozart-style aria. The inclusion of songs that were to be sung on the stage in the opera led me to this poly-stylistic approach that felt really good to me. I wasn't doing it for shock value; the plot moves from the German soldiers, to the French and the Scottish. There are all of these nationalities involved. I had a dreamlike sensation when I read the libretto; the event that the opera is based on was fantastic and unreal, and I felt that the music needed to reflect that.

The Manchurian Candidate is much more of a thriller, you know? It's fast paced, and I think the style is more consistent in this opera. There's a lot of combining of disparate triads and a major/minor feel in much of the music. Initially, when I thought of the new opera, Stravinsky's *Symphony in Three Movements* kept coming back to me. And then a student at Peabody played some music for me by Giacinto Scelsi, a piece called *Anahit*.

It morphs around using quarter-tone trills and moves harmonically through a kind of melting quarter-tone language. That also felt right to me. I wanted the overture to convey an elusive quality, where you keep thinking things are becoming clear, and then they become obscure again. So that language works very well, and I continue to use it throughout the opera.

I almost feel I can compose *The Manchurian Candidate* as fast as I can enter it into the computer. It's going very quickly for me, but that's certainly not the case with every piece.

It seems to require a certain set of skills to successfully compose a lengthy and effective dramatic piece. Do you feel you have a particular affinity for writing opera?
I think every composer has different strengths. I've just spent three quarters of a year writing a string quartet concerto called *How Wild the Sea* for my friends in the Miro Quartet.[8] I feel good about the piece, but it was a very difficult one to compose. I kept thinking: "Should I go this way, should I go that way?" There were so many decisions to make. On the other hand, when I write for opera it's the easiest thing in the world. It's something I wish I had started a long time ago.

I believe anyone who has done it will agree that composing is tremendously hard work and emotionally draining.
You're right. Composing is very emotionally draining. I might manage a four-hour window of work, which can be difficult.

You don't have a routine of getting up at 5 in the morning and composing until noon? [Both laugh]
I wish I could. Maybe when I get older I think I might do that. I know that some composers like William Bolcom do that, but it's not like that for me. As things have gotten busier for me I do a lot of the composing by thinking about the piece, the story, the entire opera at various times in the day. Then I refine and notate those thoughts when I have the time.

You mentioned that you enter the music into the computer as you compose. I'm interested in hearing more about that process. Do you write at the piano, keep a notebook of sketches, or use a particular computer program?
I use Sibelius and I don't make any copies of the music. I have one file going the whole time; that's the opera. I have a little black notebook of manuscript paper that I take with me when I am traveling so I can

quickly capture ideas like harmony and any salient musical features. I have to capture these ideas immediately so I don't forget them, then I can use these sketches as a starting point when I'm at the piano again. I still need to feel the harmonies through my fingers. I don't think anyone's inner ear works as vividly as hearing a chord struck on the keyboard. I need to have that sound to propel me emotionally and involve me in what I'm writing. I read recently that Mozart wrote a letter complaining that there was not a keyboard in some residence where he was staying, so he couldn't compose. I felt validated! Harmony is so crucial. For me, the emotional contour of a piece happens through harmony. I think it's more important than the melody. For the most part I don't think melodically.

Do you listen to computer versions of instruments as you compose?
I do as I'm composing; I mean who can resist playing back the score? It's useful, but mostly to get the pacing feeling right. You can use these amazing sound libraries like the Vienna Symphonic Library, but to me the whole process of composition is geared toward hearing the piece played by actual people with real instruments, so it's not of interest to me to try and approximate that along the way. It really does save time, and you can easily find mistakes in the score using the computer.

Some composers use the computer to create very rough approximations, a demo if you will, for conductors or performers when presenting a new piece. Do you do this as well?
Yes, but I hate doing it. Composers are in the business of imagining sounds, with very little to go on, you know? But performers are so sensitive to exact sounds that are being made that they can be very turned off by MIDI approximations of instruments. For example, a few years ago I wrote a piece and provided a MIDI demo. When I showed up to work with the performers, they were just not into the piece at all. They had been listening to the MIDI recording, but after the first rehearsal they said with surprise, "Oh! We love this!!" They just hadn't realized that the real strings or horns wouldn't sound like the computer version, that it would all blend and be rich sounding.

Do you think there are fundamental differences between young composers today and those at the time you were a student?
I think the fact that any kind of music is available online, without much if any effort, is resulting in a very superficial education. Students hear a piece and think, "Oh yeah, I got it." They might know how to construct

the music they hear on the Internet from a very loose point of view on the piano, but in general, I think the old way of studying scores and learning the way a piece is put together in detail is how you *really* learn your craft. I think that's lost. It's too easy to superficially listen and then move on. As a result of this approach, you end up with a composer who is very eclectic and has a lot of different sounds in his or her music, but really doesn't have the understanding to craft that and put that music into something substantive. Performers, accustomed to playing the most finely crafted works in history, can sense this and it really turns them off. There are very specific reasons why we love certain music, and it takes work, trial and error, and study to uncover those elements that make great music.

You've said your *Symphony #3* was influenced by Björk.[9] **Do you feel like you have been influenced by blues, jazz, and rock—music other than classical?**

Yeah, absolutely. People have said they hear certain harmonies in my music, which might be attributed to '90s soft rock. You know, like love ballads with the 9th added to many of the chords. So, as an educator, I certainly don't try to steer my students away from anything. I think it's fascinating that everything is so accessible, that all of these sounds may be intermingled into one aesthetic that will hopefully emerge as these young composers keep writing.

Your *Flute Concerto* is the first major piece you've written for flute. Did you work closely with the soloist Adam Walker while composing that piece?

No, not at all. Adam lives in London, so I didn't see him until after I was finished and sent him the entire piece. I showed up at the Cabrillo Festival about four days before the premiere, and we had a session together. I played the orchestra part on the piano and he played his part. I had my computer with me, ready to make revisions as needed. He's an amazing flutist, and nothing is difficult for him. It's not an easy piece; it has tons of notes and it's very virtuosic, but he said, "Yeah, it is quite nice, I like it." It was so easy; the whole process was strangely seamless and free of drama.

I used a melody for the *Flute Concerto* that I wrote while I was in college, and it's very, very sentimental. The San Francisco Chronicle gave me a horrible review, but the audience responded with a standing ovation, one of the greatest responses I've had for one of my pieces. You always know that when you get a response like that, the review is going to be terrible, which is sort of disappointing to me, but I guess I read reviews too closely. I probably should just ignore them. A few days later I listened to a recording of the performance, and I thought, "This is one of my best pieces." The entire arc of the piece worked for me, and I think it comes through very clearly. The balance between the flute and the orchestra is good, which is a difficult thing to achieve. A lot of composers say they don't read reviews and they don't care what any one thinks of their music, but I'm very interested in communicating—it's very important to me. It's not something I can ignore, and it's not something I can push under the rug.

The book *The Agony of Modern Music*[10] argues that composers from the era of serial music were indifferent as to whether audiences liked or didn't like their music. I believe that attitude has changed, and that contemporary composers are much more concerned with communicating with their audience and the reaction of the audience to their music. Do you have any thoughts on this subject?

That attitude may have changed but the composers still don't feel comfortable talking about it. Some composers feel as if they're selling out if they even discuss that issue. You have to pretend like you don't care about anything. But the fact is, I want the audience to be engaged. I can sense when the audience is not interested, that I have lost them. You can tell when that happens. Of course, this is all after the fact. When I am writing the works, all I am thinking is, "Do I like this?"

It's an absurd place that we've gotten to when a composer cannot, or will not, even acknowledge the fact that what we are doing is entertainment. Certainly Beethoven wasn't shy of that concept. He was clearly trying to knock people out of their seats, trying to knock their socks off; that's what Beethoven was trying to do. I think it's what we're *all* trying to do. Of course, all we really have to go on, again, is "how would I respond if I were sitting in the audience?" It's impossible to account for taste; all I have is my own to guide me.

This issue of accessibility certainly comes into play when opera companies commission a new work. There is the one new opera on the program, and if the audience doesn't like that one piece out of the six or so productions the company does that year, they are not going to be able to sell tickets and they are not going to be able to pay for new productions. But if one is writing abstract concert music, people aren't coming to hear only the new piece, they're also coming to hear a Beethoven Concerto or his *Symphony No.7*. If there is a new piece on the concert program, the audience may or may not be interested in hearing it, but they still get to hear the Beethoven. So there is that fundamental difference between instrumental music and opera.

I've heard from many composers that they feel like the process of composing is a mysterious, mystical experience. They often have no idea where their truly great ideas come from. Does this ring true with you as well?

Absolutely, I can relate to that. I think that's what got me into composing in the first place; there *is* something mysterious about it. You may think that you're consciously in control of everything: defining the harmony, melody, rhythm, and form. But are you, really?

I compose a lot of my music at the piano while improvising. The music comes through me and into my fingers, and I play it, but I don't actually know where it comes from. I don't know how I came to a certain place in the music. I can't really explain it. This is something that sometimes happens to me when I'm composing, and it can be emotionally draining. I feel an extraordinary amount of pressure to make the music work, and then sometimes it just suddenly appears! It's like being given a gift, a moment of clarity and understanding.

Speaking of gifts, congratulations on your Pulitzer Prize. That must have been quite a thrill! Has that changed your career?

It was certainly a shock. It was out of the blue. When I heard about it, I really couldn't believe that it had happened, and I couldn't sleep. Suddenly they were announcing it and my friends were calling me because the award was announced online. I seem to be invited to do a lot more residencies and judging competitions now. [Laughs]

I think this award lends a certain legitimacy to a composer's work. If it's appropriate or not, I don't know. But winning it is something I feel a lot of pride in.

Do you think it's possible that there is a "hermit Mozart" out there whom the public will never know of?

Yeah, that's very possible. I bet there are composers we haven't really realized the value of yet. I think most composers need to communicate through music to people and have it reacted to, and those artists probably aren't going to sit at home and not share their music. But while I'm not great at it, some composers are really good at self-promotion, like being on Twitter, et cetera.

There are no doubt talented composers out there who are just terrible at all of this social media and self-promotion. So I'm sure there are talented composers out there we don't know about, and we may never hear their great music.

SELECTED WORKS OF KEVIN PUTS

The Manchurian Candidate (2014), Opera
Flute Concerto (2013), Flute and Orchestra
To Touch the Sky (2012), Chorus
If I Were a Swan (2012), Chorus
Silent Night (2011), Opera
Clarinet Concerto (2008–2009), Clarinet and Orchestra
Night: Concerto for Piano and Chamber Orchestra (2007)
Symphony No. 4: From Mission San Juan (2007), Orchestra
Two Mountain Scenes (2007), Orchestra
Credo (2007), String Quartet
Violin Concerto (2006), Flute and Orchestra
Four Airs (2004), Flute, Clarinet, Violin, Cello, and Piano
Einstein on Mercer Street (2002), Baritone and Chamber Ensemble

▶ To learn more about Kevin Puts and his music, including score and audio excerpts from his *If I Were a Swan,* and *Symphony No.4,* visit www.oup.com/us/compositioninthedigitalworld.

NOTES

1. David Lang is an American composer, performer, and educator. He was awarded the 2008 Pulitzer Prize for music. His teachers include Jacob Druckman and Martin Bresnick. He joined the Yale faculty of music in 2008. In 1987 he co-founded Bang on a Can along with Julia Wolfe and Michael Gordon.
2. Chris Theofanidis is an American composer who has taught at the Peabody Conservatory, the Juilliard School, and Yale. His awards include the Rome Prize, and a Grammy nomination. He has also received Guggenheim, Fulbright, Tanglewood, and Charles Ives fellowships.
3. Jacob Druckman (1928–1996) was a Pulitzer Prize–winning American composer. His teachers included Vincent Persichetti and Aaron Copland. In addition to Dr. Puts, his notable students include Michael Daugherty, Donald Fagen (of the group Steely Dan), Aaron J. Kernis, David Lang, and Christopher Theofanidis.
4. Samuel Adler's teachers included Aaron Copland, Paul Hindemith, Walter Piston, and Serge Koussevitzky. Mr. Adler taught composition at the University of North Texas and the Eastman School of Music and now teaches at Juilliard. His honors include the Charles Ives Award and the ASCAP Aaron Copland Award for Lifetime Achievement in Music.
5. Dale Johnson is an American pianist and graduate of the Manhattan School of music.
6. As a librettist, Mark Campbell has collaborated with many contemporary composers, including William Bolcom, Kevin Puts, and Michael Torke. His many awards include a Grammy nomination, two Richard Rodgers Awards, and a Pulitzer Prize (for *Silent Night*).

7. *The Manchurian Candidate* is a 1959 novel that was made into a film in 1962, directed by John Frankenheimer and starring Frank Sinatra.
8. The award-winning Miro String Quartet was founded in 1995 by students of the Oberlin Conservatory of Music and is currently the quartet-in-residence at the University of Texas.
9. Björk is an Icelandic singer and composer. Her accolades include an Academy Award, 14 Grammy nominations, and two Golden Globe Awards.
10. *The Agony of Modern Music* (1955) was written by music critic Henry Pleasants (1910—2000). His book was highly critical of the art music of his day (i.e., serialism). He postulated that jazz and modern popular music have usurped the importance of the traditional world of classical music.

Michael Daugherty

Photo Credit: Yopie Prins

I use every available technology to compose my music. One of the criticisms of using MIDI, computers, sampling, and other digital technologies is that this will compromise and influence the compositional process in a detrimental way. One could argue that composing at the piano, a technology used by many composers in the past, was equally as compromising. Brahms, Mahler, Stravinsky, and many others composed their music at the piano and that certainly did not do them any harm!

I interviewed Michael Daugherty (b. Iowa, 1954) by telephone from his home in Michigan. He was extremely personable and articulate and seemed particularly adept at multi-tasking: juggling arriving messengers, phone calls from business associates and family, all while retaining an impressive focus on our conversation.

Daugherty is well known for embracing 20th-century pop-Americana in his compositions, including amusing and kitschy titles for some of his works, including references to Superman, Elvis, Barbie, Liberace, and Pink Flamingo lawn ornaments, to name a few. This dose of humor is refreshing in the sometimes staid world of classical composition, but the music itself is serious, solid, and often exciting. His orchestral writing is particularly colorful and filled with vivid imagery.

Hailing from a musical family with roots in popular music, Daugherty was a keyboard player and arranger in various rock bands before focusing his education on composition, with studies at the University of North Texas, the Manhattan School of Music, and Institut de Recherche et Coordination Acoustique/Musique (IRCAM) in Paris. He then attended Yale, where he received his doctorate in composition. His numerous accolades include three Grammy Awards for his *Metropolis Symphony*, a Fulbright Fellowship, the Kennedy Center Friedheim Award, the Goddard Lieberson Fellowship from the American Academy of Arts and Letters, and numerous stints as composer-in-residence with prominent orchestras. He currently teaches composition at the University of Michigan School of Music and Dance.

His wit and his ability to bring originality and verve to the question at hand, whether musical or otherwise, are among the reasons he's one of the most prolific and successful of America's contemporary composers.

Let's begin by talking about your creative process. What inspires you to compose? Do you have a particular regimen that you like to follow or a particular time you like to compose?

For me, composing music is not a job or duty; it is an honor and a delight. I have to be "inspired" to compose music. Before I write a note of music, I need to have the concept and title for the composition I am about to create. For example, I have composed music inspired by historical figures such as Rosa Parks, Abraham Lincoln, Jackie Kennedy, Elvis, Georgia O'Keeffe; by places such as Niagara Falls, Las Vegas, Route 66, and Sunset Strip; and by icons such as Superman, the *American Gothic* painting by Grant Wood, UFOs, and Mount Rushmore. Knowing my subject matter gives me an emotional framework and a reference point from which to begin the creative process.

I have no particular work schedule I follow, but I tend to be most engaged and able to concentrate during the evenings. That's probably because I grew up playing in rock bands and jazz groups where the gigs were always at night. What also appeals to me about the evening is that there are no phone calls, e-mails, or other distractions. During the night I can really get into my zone and focus. My motto is "you have to turn off to turn on."

I usually get a surge of energy between 10 PM and 2 AM and that is when I go downstairs to my studio where all my instruments, computers, books, music scores, and collectibles—postcards, knick-knacks, autographs, and photographs—are situated. My studio is the "world according to Michael Daugherty," where I feel safe to think, let my imagination run wild, and create anything my heart desires.

Do you work on more than one piece at a time or do you concentrate on one composition?

I can only focus on composing one work at a time. However, I remember visiting Luciano Berio,[1] in the summer of 1990, at his country farmhouse near the village of Radicondoli, Italy. In his composition studio, there were three massive orchestral works-in-progress on large manuscript paper, in Berio's hand, on a long, antique wooden table. I asked him which orchestras had commissioned each work. He replied, "the first score is for the Berlin Philharmonic, the second score is for the BBC Orchestra (London) and the third score is for the Royal Concertgebouw Orchestra." I asked him how he managed composing three different works at the same time and he replied, "I compose for a while on one score and then compose for a while on the next score, and so forth." So it appears that some composers can work on more than one composition at the same time!

When you're developing a new piece do you keep notebooks, or do you use a computer to capture ideas as they come to you?

I am always thinking of musical ideas and they come to me when I least expect them: swimming, walking, driving my convertible, gardening. Whenever an interesting title, subject matter, or musical idea comes to mind, I write it down on a sheet of paper, send myself an e-mail, or record it by speaking or singing into the voice recorder of my iPhone. I also have an area of my studio where I keep future ideas such as interesting articles I read in a newspaper or magazine, a book, a knick-knack I picked up when I was traveling.

Do you compose at the computer, at the piano, or directly to manuscript?

I use every available technology to compose my music. One of the criticisms of using MIDI, computers, sampling, and other digital technologies is that this will compromise and influence the compositional process in a detrimental way. One could argue that composing at the piano, a technology used by many composers in the past, was equally as compromising. Brahms, Mahler, Stravinsky, and many others composed their music at the piano and that certainly did not do them any harm! My father always used to say, "everything in moderation" and I use computer/digital technology in moderation and in conjunction with older forms of technology such as pencil/manuscript paper, playing the piano or a percussion instrument like bongos. As far as computer/digital technology, I use composition software like Digital Performer,[2] Pro Tools,[3] Sibelius, et cetera. Like any "technology," it can be a creative collaborator or it can be a crutch, create roadblocks, and get in the way of creative thinking and experimentation. In the end, it depends on how well you know the technology you are using and to what degree you are in control of it, not the other way around. If you have mastered the technology at hand and know all the ins and outs, then technology can be a powerful creative and composition tool.

Technology was also a great tool to learn about music when I was growing up. When I was kid growing up in Cedar Rapids, Iowa, in the '50s and '60s, I learned how to play piano by pumping the pedals of our player piano and watching how the keys moved to tunes like *Alexander's Ragtime Band*. In 1984, when Ligeti introduced me to composer Conlon Nancarrow,[4] who composed avant-garde music for player pianos, we had something to talk about! In the '70s, to create the charts for my high school jazz-rock band The Soul Company, I transcribed the music of Blood Sweat and Tears, James Brown, and Thelonious Monk by hand, listening to vinyl records. What ear training that was!

Does the use of digital technology affect the outcome of your music? In other words, would the final version of a piece be different if written at the piano versus using a computer?
I think every technology, from a pencil to a computer, has a certain bias that is built into it. What I like to do is use all the technological means available. When you compose at the computer you get immediate feedback, which is a plus. I usually compose directly into the Digital Performer software by either playing the keyboard of my Kurzweil Synthesizer or "step timing" the music, one note at a time, via my Apple computer keyboard. From time to time, I will compose with pencil and paper and then enter the music into the computer. I almost always compose for solo instruments and cadenzas in this manner.

I find it productive to bring musicians to my home studio in Ann Arbor, where I have them read through music I have written. For example, let's say

I have composed a minute of music for a violin concerto. I will hire a violinist to come to my home studio to play the violin part along with the electronic orchestra performed by Digital Performer on my Apple computer. With the musician in my studio, I also experiment with timbral details of the instrument and explore extended instrumental techniques that one cannot easily realize using sampled or MIDI instruments. Or when I am writing a new orchestra, wind ensemble, or chamber music composition, I will often bring in various instrumentalists from the orchestra or band to play along live with my MIDI orchestra. During the session, I will make enhancements to the instrumental parts on the spot, such as adding trills, harmonics, glissandi, or mutes. Or I might compose the violin part in real time with the violinist standing right next to me. When I work with the performers, I might also record them using a digital recorder and upload that recording into my computer sequencing software, and then I will start writing the music referencing those recordings from the sessions of the live players.

How did you develop this process of composing concurrently with live performers and digital technology?

I think that my method of working interactively with live instruments, in conjunction with computer technology, came about as a result of my residency at IRCAM[5] in Paris during 1979–1980. At IRCAM, composers Roger Reynolds, Pierre Boulez, and Luciano Berio were composing new works for solo instruments performing in real time with computer music. These composers also collaborated closely with their soloists at IRCAM. This interactive and collaborative approach appealed to me, because this was the way I composed music with my rock bands in high school and jazz ensembles in college. Jazz arranger Gil Evans, whom I worked with in New York from 1982 to 1984, also collaborated with musicians, like Miles Davis, during the creative process. Since the 1980s at Oberlin, and then from the 1990s until now at the University of Michigan, I have been consulting and working with performers during the compositional process of my concert music.

As I mentioned before, I compose my music using MIDI and notational software such as Digital Performer and Sibelius. While the MIDI and sampled sounds are quite good, I find that I need to hear my music, with all its dynamic nuances, played by real instruments during the compositional process. I find working with real instrumental sounds, played by real performers, provides me with expressive and timbral possibilities virtually impossible to obtain, at least for now, in the computer software world.

And you've found this to be an effective and practical compositional tool?

Most practical, indeed! There are almost no question marks for me at the first rehearsal of a new composition because I know every detail of how each instrument will sound. If a performer asks me a question at a rehearsal, I know the answer. I have found that it is important to be very prepared for the first rehearsal, just like the conductor or soloist. However, there are times in a first rehearsal where I might make changes in the *tutti* orchestration. This is because I am always pushing the boundaries and trying new ideas in the orchestration of my music. Consequently, there might be a few surprises during rehearsals, which I need to attend to.

You feel that using technology has helped you to write more effectively for acoustic instruments?

Well, there is another side to your excellent question. When I was a student composer from 1972 to 1984, the philosophy among many modernist composers/teachers was that you should not write music that was "idiomatic" to the instrument. Writing idiomatically for instruments was somehow the equivalent of stepping backward in time. In my music, I try to discover the "energy zones" of the particular instrument for which I am composing. That is perhaps one of the reasons performers enjoy playing my music: I am aware what an instrument can do and cannot do; I am aware of the psychology of their instrument; I am aware of the technical aspects of their instrument. I try to create dynamic music, which allows the performer to be emotionally, musically, and technically involved in the proceedings.

I'll ask you a two-part question and let you riff on it. Do you feel that technology has, in a positive or negative way, affected composition students? Second, and in a broader sense, do today's composition students have a different approach to learning and composing as compared to the time when you were in school?

For part one, I think that MIDI playback has helped composers get a much clearer idea of the pacing and overall structure of the music they are writing, which is a good thing. One can also experiment with multi-tracking and polyrhythmic ideas, which has always been enticing to me, and an important part of my music. Way back in 1982, when MIDI and the Yamaha DX7[6] synthesizer first became available, it was composer György Ligeti who encouraged me to incorporate my love of American culture with the new MIDI/synthesizer technology. Ligeti's mantra was that a composer must create "original" music. He thought these new technologies, like synthesizers, drum machines, and MIDI, would facilitate that.

For part two of your question, I decided long ago that when I was an older, established composer/teacher, I would not criticize the younger generation of composers. When I was a student composer, I remember hearing professional composers/teachers saying: "The young composers of today don't know how to write counterpoint"; " they don't know the repertoire"; "the music they compose is too simplistic." I now realize that every generation of composers develops a different way of writing music that is often not necessarily appealing to the previous generation.

When I am in the company of young composers, I ask questions and try to keep an open mind.

That was György Ligeti's approach when I studied composition with him in Hamburg. In 1984, I brought Michael Jackson's pop music *Thriller* album, which had just been released to worldwide acclaim, to a composition lesson. He listened attentively to "Billie Jean" and commented, "This drum machine is very interesting. I think you could compose fascinating polyrhythmic music with this new technology."

Concerning the use of technology in the composition process, almost every student who studies composition with me these days at the University of Michigan brings their laptop to their lessons. They play their orchestra, wind ensemble, or chamber music composition, notated in Sibelius or Finale, on their laptop computer. After listening to what was composed that week, we carefully examine every detail of their music composition and make corrections and edits in real time directly into their Sibelius or Finale score file.

I think the new technology is a great learning tool, and it has completely streamlined the creation of scores and parts: Students can generate a whole set of parts for a 10-minute orchestra piece that looks fairly professional, in one day! The down side is that they are using the built-in computer MIDI instrument sounds as their main reference as to what the actual instruments can do. When young composers are working with MIDI instrumental sounds, they tend to have too many instruments playing simultaneously. If you hear a real oboe play alone, it sounds acoustically fantastic, dense and complex. But if you hear a MIDI oboe play, it sounds terrible! So they think, "Well, I'd better add a vibraphone or some other instruments to make it sound more acoustically interesting." I have to keep reminding my student composers to cross-reference what they hear coming from the computer with what the actual instrument is going to sound like on the concert stage. I also encourage my students to go to rehearsals and concerts with full scores of the music being rehearsed or performed so they can develop a meaningful relationship between the music they are hearing and the music they are seeing on the printed page.

What issues do you tend to focus on with your composition students during lessons?

In lessons, I offer the young composer contrasting new ideas and new possibilities to the music they are currently composing. If a composer tends to write a lot of fast music, I'll have them listen to slow music; if they write a lot of slow music I have them listen to fast music. If they write tonal music, I might have them write something that is not tonal, and visa versa. If they are using a lot of technology, I might have them write something for a solo instrument, and not use the computer. If they only compose using manuscript paper, I might suggest that they might want to learn some computer skills. I teach them to explore alternatives and to keep an open mind.

Speaking of teachers, you mentioned that you worked with Gil Evans.[7] I knew him briefly, and admire him very much. Would you share what your experience working with him was like?

When I was pursuing my DMA in composition at Yale University, I was the conductor of the Yale Jazz Band as part of my fellowship. I heard from Willie Ruff, who played French horn on *Miles Ahead* and *Sketches of Spain*, that Gil Evans was looking for an assistant, although there was no pay involved. About once a month, I took the train to New York and went to Gil's loft on the lower West Side to help him organize his music. Gil worked totally by ear; writing things down was difficult for him. He was not very interested in memorializing his ideas or cataloging his music, and only looked toward the future, like many jazz musicians of his generation. He didn't even keep copies of important historical arrangements or compositions from his past! Another thing I learned from spending time with Gil Evans was about the importance of understanding the business side of being a composer and arranger. Gil was a very impractical guy about business and naïve about money. When I met him, he was completely broke. Many people, including Miles Davis, had taken advantage of Gil by having him sign recording and arranging contracts that paid no royalties. I realized that while it is important to focus on being a creative artist, one does need to be practical and understand how to read contracts and how the copyright law works. Ignoring the business side of art can really harm you down the road, and that's what happened to Gil Evans. At the time, I didn't realize how fortunate and important spending time with Gil was. He was a real creative soul and I feel honored to have known him.

You've segued very nicely into my next question. Do you advise your students regarding the business of music: self-promotion, dealing with websites, having your music played on the Internet? The new technology is great, but there does seem to be a certain business acumen that a composer needs to survive.

Composers today are more in control of their destinies than ever before, which is a good thing. Whether a composer is represented by a publisher or is self-published, laptop computers and smart phones have created a balanced playing field where anyone in the world can discover and experience a composer's music at the touch of a button. For younger composers today, the creative process involves composing music, videos, websites, blogs, and social media. Young composers have told me that when they "compose," they multi-task and have their MIDI sequencer or Sibelius file, Facebook, website, and e-mail all up and running simultaneously on their laptop! As far as the "business of music," it is important to be savvy. However, I always tell my composition students, and myself, that the music has to come first!

Your use of humor is refreshing, both in your titles and the music itself. *Metropolis Symphony*[8] and *Dead Elvis* come to mind as examples. I find that sense of playfulness often lacking in contemporary concert music.

I'm open to the full gambit of human emotions, from pathos to comedy, and I encourage my students "to go where no one has gone before." After a tragic event in his plays, Shakespeare often turns to humor: Three buffoons will suddenly appear on stage telling off-color jokes. Tragedy and comedy work together in the theater, so why not music? I am huge fan of the "old school" comedians like Charlie Chaplin, the Marx Brothers, Lucille Ball, and Don Rickles. There is much to learn from their pacing, delivery, and timing. I suppose there are "humorous" moments in many of my earlier works such as *Metropolis Symphony, Dead Elvis, Sinatra Shag, Hell's Angels,* and *Le Tombeau de Liberace*. I was composing a kind of music that wasn't heard often at that time, especially in Europe, and using subject matter for "serious" musical composition that was considered by many as "forbidden." My goal was to be creative and original in these works and if some hear this music as "humorous" or "witty," so be it. Now that I am turning 60 years old in 2014, the tragic works are just around the corner!

How do you approach the composition of a new piece? Do you improvise or use a compositional system?

I work in an intuitive fashion, often by ear. Why? When I was a kid growing up in Cedar Rapids, Iowa, I experienced music as a collaborative process: a group of people working together and playing music by ear. Nothing was written down and music was created "on the spot." This included when I played percussion in a drum and bugle corps, performed piano in country and western bands, or played Hammond organ with The Soul Company. When I studied composition, all the music I was involved with was meticulously composed by hand on music paper. Composing by ear, as opposed to composing music on paper, are two very different worlds, but each offers interesting possibilities. Once I generate material, I switch gears and turn to a rigorous compositional mode where I begin to structure the music. I utilize all the techniques and compositional strategies I learned in the university, such as counterpoint, twelve-tone, set and Schenkerian theory, algorithmic procedures, et cetera, to extend and shape the musical material. I also create foreground, middle ground, and background layers, which I juxtapose, expand, and compress in various ways. The way the music changes reflects the shifting of those blocks either forward or backward, taking them away, or speeding up and slowing down those blocks. Structurally, I tend to start from the beginning of the composition and write in a linear fashion to its end. The structure can be intuitive—I don't work in prearranged structures. I feel creative in both worlds and I encourage my composition students to explore both the improvisational and the notational, composing by ear and incorporating pre-composition strategies.

How do you work with notation programs such as Sibelius or Finale?

First, I enter all my music into the Digital Performer sequencer program. Then I save the Digital Performer file as a MIDI file and then translate the MIDI file into Sibelius. I do a rough formatting of the Sibelius score consisting of the notes and page layout. I print out the score and then add all of the musical details, such as articulations, slurs, and dynamics into the score by hand. Then a copyist will enter that information on a computer using Sibelius to create a final score for me.

So you've been composing using synthesizers and computer technology for a while?

In 1982, I was introduced to the world of computer music first at MIT, where I attended a summer course in computer music, and IRCAM, where I spent a year composing computer music on mainframe computers. In

1984, I purchased a Yamaha DX7 synthesizer and a QX1 Yamaha sequencer. The sequencer had eight independent tracks and I was able to multi-track, compose, and work intuitively for the first time. I eventually graduated to Apple computers and then Digital Performer around 1986. At the beginning, Apple computers had very limited memory, so there were many compromises one had to accept. Today, the technology is very powerful and the sky's the limit. In my home studio, I have two 32-inch monitors, a Kurzweil synthesizer, a Yamaha Disklavier, and a rack of MIDI sound modules.

Some composers who create music for film and TV use very expensive and sophisticated sampling libraries. When it comes to composing, I personally find that these programs are very time-consuming and I tend to not use them. Do you or your students use these more advanced digital sounds?
Yes, I have a few composition students who use advanced sample libraries. They sound great but are expensive to buy, require a lot of computer memory, and can be difficult to use.

An area where technology *has* hurt music is in Hollywood. In Hollywood, film music has become relegated to click tracks, sequencers, ostinatos, and very rigid tempos. Nowadays, the process of creating a film score starts with the creation of an electronically orchestrated "temp track," using cutting-edge sampled instrumental sounds. Once the director/producer approves this temp track, the music is acoustically orchestrated and recorded by a live orchestra. The music of the live orchestra is then synced and mixed with the music of the electronic orchestra from the "temp track." Next, additional sound effects, such as explosions, are synced to the mix. That's why there is such a dependency on click tracks by composers of film music today.

The wonderful music of John Williams[9] is "old school": You hear counterpoint, melodies, counter melodies, great orchestrations, changes of tempo, and rubatos. I must say, I miss the old days of film music, the scores of Alfred Newman, Max Steiner, and Bernard Hermann, for example.[10] Composing virtuosic film music, which was the mainstay of the golden era of Hollywood, may come back someday. But at the moment, we are in a very technologically driven world that, in my personal opinion, has inhibited the creative musical possibilities.

How important should success be to a composer? Is fame truly a measure of the worth of the music that a composer creates in his or her lifetime?
Fame is a relative thing. It's funny that an example of a composer who is cited as not being famous in his day is Charles Ives,[11] which is simply not

true. Composers of note from that era knew who Charles Ives was and were aware of his music. Here is what I've always thought is a realistic way to look at fame or success: If you want to create music that is not often performed or popular, audiences and performers don't support, and as a result you aren't recognized in your lifetime, then you need to accept that. And if other people write music that is incredibly successful, and everybody wants to perform it, you can't begrudge those people. Because *you* made a decision—a conscious decision not to write music that would be popular to performers and audiences, and you should accept the consequences of that.

What advice would you give to someone wishing to pursue a life as a composer?
My advice is to compose the music you want to compose, and then find the appropriate venue to have your music realized. Go to concerts and hang out with musicians and conductors. Learn your technology and keep up with it. And when at a restaurant or nightclub with live music, make sure to leave a tip for the musicians on your way out the door!

SELECTED WORKS OF MICHAEL DAUGHERTY

> *Fallingwater* (2013), Violin and String Orchestra
> *Labyrinth of Love* (2012), Soprano and Large Ensemble
> *Mount Rushmore* (2011), Chorus and Orchestra
> *Raise the Roof* (2007), Timpani and Orchestra or Symphonic Band
> *Ghost Ranch* (2005), Orchestra
> *Fire and Blood* (2003), Violin and Orchestra
> *Bells for Stokowski* (2002), Orchestra or Symphonic Band
> *UFO* (1999), Solo Percussion and Orchestra or Symphonic Band
> *Jackie O* (1997), Opera
> *Sing Sing: J. Edgar Hoover* (1991), *Paul Robeson Told Me* (1992), *Elvis Everywhere* (1993), String Quartet and Pre-Recorded Sound
> *Dead Elvis* (1993), Solo Bassoon and Chamber Ensemble
> *Metropolis Symphony* (1988–1993), Orchestra

▶ To learn more about Michael Daugherty and his music, including interviews and video performances of *The Gospel According to Sister Aimee,* and *Viva,* visit www.oup.com/us/compositioninthedigitalworld.

NOTES

1. Luciano Berio (1925–2003) was an extremely influential Italian composer, best known for his electronic and experimental work.

2. Digital Performer is a digital audio workstation (DAW), which includes notation and sequencing capabilities among other features.

3. Pro Tools is digital audio workstation software, widely used in the music and film/TV scoring industries. It first appeared in 1984 as Sound Designer. Pro Tools 1.0 was released in 1991.

4. Conlon Nancarrow (1912–1997) was a composer born in America who became a Mexican citizen in 1955. Most of his well-known compositions are written for player piano. He was considered something of a recluse and stayed out of the mainstream of the composition world.

5. IRCAM (*Institut de Recherche et Coordination Acoustique/Musique*), a French institute for the scientific study of sound and avant-garde music, is located in Paris, and was founded in 1970 by Pierre Boulez.

6. The Yamaha DX7 was a groundbreaking digital synthesizer manufactured by the Yamaha Corporation from 1983 to 1986. It was widely used on recordings of dance and rock music.

7. Gil Evans (1912–1998) was a US jazz arranger, composer, pianist, and bandleader. He collaborated extensively with Miles Davis. He is a member of the Down Beat Jazz Hall of Fame and was awarded a Grammy in 1986.

8. *Metropolis Symphony* (1993) is based on the stories and characters of the Superman comic book series and winner of three Grammy Awards (2011).

9. John Williams is an award-winning American composer of film, television, and concert music.

10. Alfred Newman (1901–1970), Max Steiner (1888–1971), and Bernard Hermann (1911–1975), were prominent, award-winning, American composers of film music.

11. Charles Ives (1874–1954) is considered one of the first American composers to gain worldwide acclaim, although it is generally accepted that his music was not known by the public at large for most of his lifetime. He has been posthumously praised as a great influence by many contemporary composers.

Mohammed Fairouz

I believe in the role of art in humanizing "the other," therefore preventing violence against the other. The role of art in helping people to come together has been proven time and time again. The role of the artist is so important and powerful.

One of the youngest composers represented in this book, Mohammed Fairouz has already had a remarkably successful career. Acclaimed as "an important new artistic voice" by the *New York Times*, Fairouz is quickly gaining recognition and a following of devoted admirers. Not yet 30, he has written four symphonies, four concertos, hundreds of art songs, chamber music, numerous solo pieces, and an opera.

Born in New York (1985), his musical education is impressive, with studies at the New England Conservatory of Music and the Curtis Institute. His primary teachers include Gunther Schuller, Richard Danielpour, and György Ligeti.

Fairouz's music contains elements of microtonality and dissonance but feels solidly rooted in a realm of tonal centers. His orchestration often takes unexpected turns, his rhythmic writing can be ferocious, and his sense of melody is particularly striking and original. And then there is his talent for effectively composing to text.

Self-described as obsessed with text, he wrote one of his first pieces (at age seven) set to the words of Oscar Wilde. Since then, he has collaborated with a number of eminent poets and writers.

Much is made of his cross-cultural roots—his Arab American heritage has clearly informed his substantial catalog of compositions—but, his music does not exploit this in a clichéd way. While his subjects sometimes address social and political situations, and Middle Eastern modes, melodic devices, and instrumentation are at times explored, the references remain restrained—his sound is that of contemporary art music framed in Western form.

I found him to be extremely intelligent, articulate, respectful, and above all, hopeful about our troubled human race, its future, and the role that the arts might—and should—play in bringing the world together in peace. During our conversations, I found myself thinking, "He sounds so mature and wise, is he *really* still in his 20s?" His unshakable optimism regarding the future and the prospects for peace and equality in the world became, to me, contagious. Then I remembered a similar feeling I had recently experienced—it was while listening to some of Fairouz's music. It carries a similar positive attitude; even in some of his most emotional, haunting, and forlorn works, there remains a spark of hope that mirrors the attitude of optimism that he radiates on a personal level.

What is your composition process like? For instance, do you work at a specific time every day?

In an ideal world I would say that I work every day. I like to have a set time when I go to the studio and sit down and separate myself from the outside world and compose. Of course, that is the ideal world. The reality is that I might be traveling, or giving a master class, or attending a performance. Today I composed, and yesterday, and the day before that. But tomorrow I'm on a cross-country flight.

All the demands on your time do not mean the deadlines can get moved around. It means you have to make that deadline work. I have done things like lock myself up in an airplane bathroom, much to the other passenger's dismay, on a seven-hour flight just to write music. I earn my living from commissions, and I do not have a faculty position anymore. I am very much a foreigner to the traditional academic world. The politics of academia weird me out, enough so that I stay away from that environment. Sometimes it's hard for people to believe me when I tell them, "This is my job. Writing music is my small business."

Do you use a computer when you write music, or do you use pencil and paper?
I use a pencil and paper, everything by hand. People are often surprised that I am in my 20s and write everything by hand, but for me, writing music is very intuitive. There is something tactile about that manual act of putting pencil to paper that is very meaningful to me. I think it connects me to my heritage in a way, as an Arab American. In the Arabic tradition, calligraphy is a highly refined art form. There is an incredible tradition of writing poetry in a very beautiful and stylized way.

There is also a ritual to the way I work. I like composing at the piano, and I tend to sing my music as I write. I will sing a viola line while I am playing the double bass line on the piano with my left hand and the piccolo part with my right hand. Then I might sing the inner voice. I work in a lyrical enough form that I like to be able to connect vocally and physically to the music.

I know how to use notation software, but I don't use it to write music. Instead, I write my entire manuscript by hand and send it off to my publisher. They scan the manuscript, save it as a PDF, and send it to the engravers.

Do you find that the process of writing each piece follows a similar approach or does that approach change depending on the piece of music you are working on?
It depends a lot on the narrative of the piece. If I am composing a piece with narrative or with text, a good amount of my process is devoted to research. For example, I was in a meeting earlier today with a group of distinguished scholars discussing a new commission based on medieval objects. In working on this project, I will have incredible access to rare manuscripts and ancient items for research. So the process for that piece will be wildly different from composing a string quartet that has no specific program. And parts of the process are completely separate from writing music, influences that may have come years and years before.

You have quite a few performances coming up, including the premiere of *Sadat*, your ballet for percussion and chamber orchestra. How do you juggle all of these performances, interviews, traveling, and premieres and still find time to compose?

I'm working in the world of classical music, where I am following a tradition of finalizing premieres that are going to take place a season or two in the future; I am not even sure if I am going to still be alive by the time of the first performance. We have these incredible orchestras and opera houses asking to nail down a date three years from now for a premiere or production. On the other hand, a film producer might say, "We need 20 minutes of music and we need you here with the score and parts next week." It is a completely opposite way of working. I think both worlds could learn a lot from each other.

You've studied with some wonderful composers, György Ligeti for one.

He was a wonderful, generous, and kind person, and he shared quite a lot with me. I learned a lot from György's music, and from conducting his music with him in attendance to give me feedback. When I talk about my teachers, it's primarily to honor them, and in gratitude for what they have taught me. On the other hand, studying with a composer does not mean you are inheriting something from them. It does not necessarily mean that you will be good at composition. They don't have the power to bestow that upon you; you have to work and earn that yourself. Studying with a great composer does not automatically make you part of a pedigree.

So, what does it mean to have these wonderful mentors like Ligeti, Menotti,[1] and Schuller?[2] I just named three people who are wildly different from one another musically. I studied their music and got to ask them questions. I find that being direct and asking questions is the key. My orchestration skills developed a bit differently from many young composers because of the lessons I learned from Ligeti, for example, in his approach of using texture in a beautiful and functional way. I also learned a lot from his sense of humor, which I found was very Middle Eastern, very sardonic. You're crying and laughing at the same time, you are saying something that is incredibly tragic, but it is also somehow funny. He had a sense of sarcasm that a lot of people didn't understand, but I connected to that part of him.

Do you have any particular composers that you feel have influenced your writing?

Every composer must get asked that question, but for me I think that question reeks of a sort of narrow field of vision. It is like thinking about all music only in terms of, and I put this in capital letters, "THE WESTERN CANON." Of course, there are a good number of composers from that Western canon that I could list as inspiration. Schubert is extremely meaningful to me, Benjamin Britten is extremely meaningful to me, and who doesn't love Bach? I mean gosh, there are so many of them. Then at the same time, outside of that canon of dead white European men, there is so much other music that influences me on a day-to-day basis.

I recently composed a piece for the BBC World Service in collaboration with a Bollywood dancer [Hindustani Dabkeh]. Part of my process in writing that piece was to listen to a lot of Bollywood music,[3] which I had never heard before. But this is music that influences millions and millions of people every day. And then there are the great Arabic singers of the golden age in the '50s and '60s, and Arabic pop and classical music. These influences are everywhere. The music I hear in a cab in New York, everything from klezmer music[4] to Punjabi pop.[5] It is all very influential to me. The world is such a dynamic and big place; it is too limiting to choose a favorite or a particular influence.

Fair enough, but you just mentioned quite a few very interesting influences. So I have to ask you, do feel that your music can or should be categorized in any particular style?
I have literally been asked, "Are you indie-classical?" "Are you post-classical?" "Are you avant-pop?" All of these categories are like movements, and what is the point of trying to define a movement if you are in the middle of it?

When young composers say, "I am a pop savvy composer," they mean to show that they are intending to break the boundaries of classical music, but even that statement is inherently limiting. I would ask them, "Okay, but what pop?" There is Western pop music, which is the music they are generally referring to, but then there is the pop music that the majority of the human race listens to.

Music that reflects upon, reacts to, and comments on the state of the human condition is a focus of many great artists. It could be argued that much of your music deals with the relationship between the Middle East and the Western world, and all of the difficulties that involves. How would you describe the influence of politics and culture on your music?
Human beings live in a world that is political and we have to deal with that fact. If I am labeled an Arab American composer, what does that really mean? Whatever it means is magnified in a post 9/11 world. That is a very

obvious point of departure for me, where I find myself. While not all of my music is political, I've found that I have to engage these issues in my work or they would be like an elephant in the room. There is a unique chemistry that makes each composer what they are. This political dimension is part of what makes me who I am, and as such is a unique facet of my work.

So, would you say your music is politically driven—inspired by political events?

I don't like politics—politicians never get anything done—but I *am* passionate about social justice. I believe in the role of art in humanizing "the other," therefore preventing violence against the other. The role of art in helping people to come together has been proven time and time again. The role of the artist is so important and powerful. Yet artists are constantly put into a position of having to ask for money to support the humanities. Or we put the humanities and the arts into a ghetto, an academic ghetto.

The reality of the multi-dimensional situation is something I can relate to you through one experience: I had a conversation in London with a Saudi Arabian official. He said, "We are making tremendous advances in our country; in fact, we have a lot of people studying right here in London." I asked, "What are they studying?" He said, "Business, engineering, architecture, so they can come back and build cities." I asked, "How about the humanities?" His response was, "We don't have time for that! We don't have the luxury to send people to study the arts and humanities." Then these words just came out of my mouth, because that concept infuriated me so much: "Of course, because in an absolute monarchy, why would you want people studying Voltaire in France?" Naturally, that was a hotheaded and impulsive response from a younger me that was triggered in the heat of the moment. The reality is much more complex than that with the Saudi government delicately balancing the forward-moving direction of an incredibly diverse country with the deeply entrenched Ulema [the religious authorities]. Needless to say, there are many higher-ranking officials and members of the Saudi royal family (including such senior officials as Prince Turki Al Faisal, whom I admire dearly, and King Abdullah himself, much loved among his people) who realize the need for the country to move forward and spend a good deal of time thinking about the welfare of their people.

The fact that Ai Weiwei[6] in China was under surveillance in his own studio, that the massive Chinese government was scared of this one man and the artistic statements that he would make, speaks to the power of the arts in society. As long as art is delivered in the real world, and engaged by human beings, our role as artists is to speak truth to power.

You have a rich Middle Eastern musical heritage, yet you are educated in the Western tradition. Have you formally studied Middle Eastern modes and techniques, or did you learn them on your own?
Most of the books [on Middle Eastern music theory and technique] are in Arabic and have not been translated into a Western language. I learned about Arabic music because I have traveled extensively, touring as a pianist. A defining moment took place during a trip that I took to Damascus in my teens. Damascus is one of the three cities that have had a huge cultural influence in the Arab World, the other two being Baghdad and Cairo. These three cities are to the Arab World what New York, LA, and Chicago are to the United States, so you can probably understand the agitation in the Arab world right now; Cairo is destabilized, Damascus is in flames, and Baghdad is decimated. If you enter one of the gates into the old city of Damascus, you can walk through the Armenian, Jewish, Muslim, and Christian quarters and hear all those different types of music simultaneously. During that one trip, I befriended an elderly Armenian who introduced me to the great Armenian composers. I started to hear their choral music, their opera music, their musicals, and I studied this music closely. I never really musically recovered from that trip. That music is extremely sophisticated and at the same time very singable. I heard people in the streets singing these classical melodies. The music was interwoven into the cultures, and that really stuck with me.

My third and fourth symphonies are prime example of this cultural interweaving. In my third symphony [*Poems and Prayers*[7]] there is a melding of Aramaic, Arabic, and Hebrew poetic culture. I received many positive comments about my work, though there were a few nutcases who hated the fact that I did this, that I would even postulate that people should get along together.

In the third movement of my fourth symphony [*In the Shadow of No Towers*[8]], I divided the wind ensemble into two different bands, the "blue" and the "red," representing the political division in the post-9/11 United States. Although people in a concert hall would never notice, the timing of the final movement is 9 minutes and 11 seconds.

I'm interested in your use of Arabic modes and microtones. You have spoken before about the Arabic concentration on melody and how it has inspired you to constantly refine your own melodic lines.
Anyone who is familiar with the style and form of Arabic classical music knows that there really isn't any counterpoint in the traditional Western sense. There is no Bach-like harmony. There is heterophony, so there is a sort of harmony that results from the coincidence of lines happening—one

with ornamentation and one without. But there is essentially nothing except for the melody, a drone against which the melody is set, and rhythm. This is also true in much of Indian classical music.

This Arabic musical tradition is very much alive and well. In fact, ancient Arabic melodies and folk tunes are more recognizable to young people in the Arab world today than classical Western music is to young people in the Western world. It is a tradition that has survived for thousands and thousands of years, and musicians have been concentrating their efforts on the continuing refinement of the melodic line. The Arabic melodic line is instantly enriched due to the fact it employs more than the 12 notes used in Western music.

The microtonal inflections are key. It's not at all like some sort of Western avant-garde idea of microtonal composition. It's inflectional, and the inflections come from the human voice and the vocalizations we all use in our speech on a daily basis. A sigh, for example, has inflections that are extraordinarily important to the vocabulary. And because there is no formal system of notation in Arabic music, these melodies have been passed down orally from generation to generation. It is an extremely refined way of composing. If you want a testament to the power of melody, to the power of a good tune, here is a musical tradition that has sustained itself solely on the development of the melody for millennia. It's very inspiring.

How do you approach incorporating such Arabic concepts of melody into music written for a Western instrument, as in your clarinet concerto [*Tahrir*]?

It is completely conventionally notated, no graphic notation or anything like that. You will see indications of certain timbral trills, but I write out the music just as I hear it in my head. It may be the first time that someone has traditionally notated the Klezmer oral tradition of improvisatory sounding music, but it is notated using the same notation system Mozart used.

Did you work closely with performer David Krakauer[9] in developing his part for *Tahrir*?

Yes I did, very closely. When you work with a singer, you take collaboration for granted. You get into the mud with the singer. For me, that has been the case with instrumentalists and soloists that I work with, almost without exception. David is a performer who is a master of Jewish klezmer music; he won't listen to music unless it sends raging fire through his veins. He is extremely passionate about this music he is reviving and revitalizing. Of course, his passion influenced what

I was writing for him, just as Rachel Barton Pine[10] influences my violin music when I am writing for her. While that doesn't mean that another performer can't pick up and perform the piece and bring something of themselves to the work, it is a very special thing to sit down with an instrumentalist when you are composing a piece for them and really get into the details—what they are passionate about, what you are both really excited about.

I have found that some of my students put such an emphasis on technology that they risk losing sight of the reason they chose to study music in the first place. The technology sometimes makes it easier for them to create sounds while bypassing the rigors of composition. What are your thoughts on this?

People have created some wonderful things with technology and electronic music; I will be the first to agree with this. But it went without saying that Varèse honed his craft as a composer before writing a work like *Poème électronique*.[11] Many of our advanced software programs enable us to very easily create mash-ups of sound while bypassing considerations of form, structure, and above all dramatic thrust that we have to consider in all music, including electronic and computer music.

I also find that for many young composers like myself, there is, perhaps, an overemphasis on marketability. Many composers have come to the consensus that marketing yourself—having a website, Facebook, Twitter, social networking—is not a shameful thing. And it's not! If you have something to say, you want to have an audience to say it to. But opening up a shop devoid of goods is a mistake. There are young composers who know more about international copyright law, intellectual property, and advertising than they know about writing music. It is a problem.

Much of that early electronic music came out of an academic musical environment. Are you suspicious of that?

Much of it did but a lot of it also did not. Halim El-Dabh,[12] for example, once spoke to me about the tactile, physical experience of chopping up tape, et cetera. But in the end, I am not a mid-20th-century modernist. Music for me is *much* more organic than that, *much* more immediate, and *much* more a connection to roots and a connection to the audience. I think a composer's connection to the audience is something that was never in question until the epoch of modernist complexity, and the age of academic music that alienated audiences. Some composers started questioning whether or not it was appropriate or even acceptable to write for an audience. Who the hell else are we writing for? You're writing for your performers and your audience. If not, you're terribly misguided.

So much of composers' music today is available for free on the Internet. Does that impact your ability to make a living as a composer?

All art is about communicating with the widest possible group of people. The dissemination of art around the world has expanded tremendously due to the Internet, smartphones, and so on. The piece that I wrote for the BBC for string quartet, clarinet, and Bollywood dancer was watched by over 100 million people on its first airing. So someone in a small village in Africa could have taken part in that premiere. I value the idea of having a premiere in a distinguished setting like Carnegie Hall. I value its history and the experience of interacting with live musicians and audience. But if you do the calculation, we would have had to fill Carnegie Hall to full capacity every night for 17,000 nights to reach the same audience the BBC reached in one broadcast. So that's one way to look at it. Technology can vastly increase the potential audience. Additionally, audiences are able to share their comments via websites and e-mail with each other, the composer, and the performers. That dialogue is an important part of who I am, so that's another important aspect of the new technologies available to artists.

Obviously there is a flip side. I have many more commercial recordings and publications coming up in the future. All of those projects engage a team of experts who nitpick every little detail before the CD or score is released. I don't think that people expect the same quality from an unauthorized, amateur YouTube recording of a work of mine that anyone can upload with or without my permission. The quality control is just not there. So that's the other side of the equation. I believe that art produced with professional quality will survive.

I have spoken to composers who have used the Internet to explore music that they would not have otherwise been exposed to. Is this a positive trend?

While I think the Internet allows people to be exposed to things they might otherwise have no idea about, it does not replace firsthand experience. What exists online is just a fraction of what exists out there in the real world. If you live your life in the Middle East, you can get a vague idea of what American life is like by watching American YouTube or Hollywood movies. But that isn't the same as spending time in the United States and interacting with a people's culture firsthand.

Has global communication technology directly affected the composition of any of your pieces?

When I wrote my piece for clarinet and orchestra [*Tahrir* (2012)], I certainly was not in Tahrir Square; I was traveling back and forth between New York and San Francisco. But, I had instant updates on my smartphone and YouTube. I was plugged into what was happening, and it informed the piece as I was composing. The fact that the world is able to do this, to communicate within a matter of seconds what happened on the other side of the globe, is a defining element of this generation and of future generations.

Do you think the Internet will help to raise a global interest in the music of other cultures?

I think it is helping to expand everyone's palette. Traditionally, the great cosmopolitan centers of the world—New York, London, Paris, Dubai—have been the places where one could experience all different types of music and all sorts of cuisine, and live a global life. Nowadays, someone in rural Kansas or the Arabian Desert can have experiences through the Internet that they previously may not have dreamed of.

Is this new global communication technology going to change the way music is written?

I'm 27 at the time of this interview, so for a third of my life I have lived in a fully digitally connected world. Yet, some of the younger student composers in master classes that I teach have never known anything other than a totally digital world. You couldn't ask them the same questions you are asking me about the impact of digital technology on art because they have never known a life without the Internet or cellphones, without immediate access to media in every direction. This is bound to impact the way we create and disseminate all kinds of art, as well as the way we interact with people. As we increase the ability to communicate with different cultures, there also comes an increase to do so responsibly, and to be sensitive and understanding of other cultures.

I'll tell you an extraordinary experience that I had while traveling in the Arabian Desert. At the corner of the Arabian Peninsula there are cities, but outside of the major cities there is basically a vast desert, the Rub' Al Khali (Empty Quarter), with scattered villages. I visited one of these remote villages, an oasis called Liwa on the northern edge of the Quarter. I sat with the people there and talked, and met an older woman. She was in traditional Bedouin dress, and her head was covered. She was very educated, and we spoke in Arabic. She asked, "What do you do?" and, when I told her I was a composer, she replied, "What! Oh, I love the music of Bach." She had heard a concerto at the nearby Al Ain Classical Music Festival and was then able to find many more of Bach's works instantly on the Internet. Even in that village in the Empty Quarter, the Internet had brought two cultures together.

SELECTED WORKS OF MOHAMMED FAIROUZ

Violin Concerto "Al-Andalus" (2013), Violin, Orchestra
Audenesque (2012), Mezzo-Soprano, Chamber Orchestra
The Named Angels (2012), String Quartet
Symphony No. 4, "In The Shadow of No Towers" (2012), Wind Band
Anything Can Happen (2012), Solo Baritone, Mixed Chorus, Amplified Viola
Jebel Lebnan (2011), Flute, Oboe, Clarinet, French Horn, Bassoon
Native Informant—Sonata for Solo Violin (2011), Violin
Tahrir (2011), B-flat Clarinet, Orchestra
Symphony No. 3, "Poems and Prayers" (2010), Mezzo-Soprano, Baritone, Mixed Choir, Children's' Choir, Orchestra
Sumeida's Song (2009), Opera in Three Scenes
Tahwidah (2008), Soprano, Clarinet
Piano Miniatures 1–13 (2005–2013), Piano

▶ To learn more about Mohammed Fairouz and his music, including score, audio, and video excerpts from *Poems and Prayers, Anything Can Happen, Chorale Fantasy, In the Shadow of No Towers,* and *Native Informant,* visit www.oup.com/us/compositioninthedigitalworld.

NOTES
1. Gian Carlo Menotti (1911–2007) was an Italian American composer who wrote ballets, choral works, and over two dozen operas. Two of them won the Pulitzer Prize: *The Consul* (1950) and *The Saint of Bleecker Street* (1955). He also wrote the very popular opera *Amahl and the Night Visitors.*
2. Gunther Schuller is an American composer, conductor, and jazz musician. His awards include the 1994 Pulitzer Prize in Music, the 1991 MacArthur Foundation "genius" award, two Grammy Awards (1974 and 1976), and lifetime achievement awards from Columbia University and *DownBeat Magazine.*
3. Bollywood music, or Hindi film songs, refers to the music used in some Indian films. It is characterized by pop themes and usually accompanies onscreen dance numbers.
4. Klezmer is a Jewish musical tradition of Eastern Europe. Much klezmer music consists of dance songs and instrumentals for celebrations such as weddings.

5. Punjabi pop is a South Asian musical genre that includes Bollywood songs. While it contains elements of traditional Indian music, it also incorporates Western styles including reggae and disco.

6. Ai Weiwei is a Chinese avant-garde artist. He is also a political activist and is critical of the Chinese government and its position on human rights and democracy.

7. Fairouz: *Poems and Prayers*, my third symphony, is a poetic Middle Eastern journey scored for solo vocalists, large mixed chorus, and orchestra. An evening-length piece, the symphony expresses ancient and modern texts ranging from the Aramaic Kaddish to modern Israeli and Arabic poetry by Mahmoud Darwish, Yehuda Amichai, and Fadwa Tuqan, weaving together a narrative of shared loss and dispossession as well as hope and reconciliation.

8. Fairouz: *In the Shadow of No Towers* (Symphony #4 for Wind Ensemble) takes its inspiration from details in Art Spiegelman's graphic novel of the same name.

9. David Krakauer is an American clarinetist and composer known for his work in klezmer and classical music. He also plays in other styles including jazz, hip-hop, and avant-garde improvisation.

10. Rachel Barton Pine is a violinist and composer who has toured worldwide as a soloist with numerous orchestras. She plays many styles of music, including classical, baroque, heavy metal, and jazz.

11. *Poème électronique* was written by composer Edgard Varèse. It is an eight-minute piece of electronic music written for the 1958 World's Fair, Brussels. It was recorded on tape, was synchronized to a projected film, and used various sounds in addition to those considered "musical" by traditional standards.

12. Halim El-Dabh is an Egyptian-born American composer. He is known as an early pioneer of electronic music, in particular music composed for tape. He worked at the Columbia-Princeton Electronic Music Center and was associated with Aaron Copland, John Cage, and Leonard Bernstein.

Tania León

When I brought my music home my father said, "Your music sounds very interest-ing, but where are you in there?" He didn't explain to me what he meant by that, but the way I took it was that something of me was missing in my music. I started having nightmares and hearing all sorts of rhythmical twists in my mind, and my music started being affected by that emotional state. Nowadays I compose any-thing I feel like composing.

The story of Tania León (b. Cuba, 1943) is a dramatic one and, though I was familiar with the basic arc of her tale before I ever spoke with her, the details of her ascent in the music world still left me amazed at the remarkable series of events that propelled her along her path to becoming the eminent composer, conductor, and educator she is today. Clearly a deeply gifted artist, she also must have a powerful guardian angel helping to orchestrate her career, and no one seems more incredulous about it than León herself.

A pivotal quirk of fate brought her in quick succession from Havana to Miami to New York City, where her talent was embraced wholeheartedly, first as a pianist and ultimately as a composer and conductor. Her educational credits include the National Conservatory in Cuba and the New York University (NYU) School of Music, as well as studies with Leonard Bernstein and Seiji Ozawa at Tanglewood. León was one of the earliest members of Dance Theatre of Harlem, instituted the Brooklyn Philharmonic Community Concert Series, was New Music advisor to the New York Philharmonic, and served as Latin American Music advisor to the American Composers Orchestra.

Many of her early compositions were based on principles of serialism, but her music soon evolved into a much more eclectic mix of Western classical, jazz, and Latin music, with numerous influences from various other world musics as well. León both embraces technology and espouses the importance of developing the traditional practices that have served composers over the centuries. In addition to her well-honed skills in orchestral composition, Leon is well versed in popular music and has served as musical director and conductor for a number of musicals, including Broadway productions such as *The Wiz*.

Despite an already impressive list of accomplishments, León exudes a sense of passion and excitement about the future; this force of nature seems to be just getting started.

You recently won the Victor Herbert Award from ASCAP.[1] Congratulations!
Oh! That was just incredible; ASCAP is such an important institution to me.

It's quite an honor. And you have also received a commission from the New York State Council for the Arts for a new quintet. Have you started that piece yet?
I'm still in the process of gathering materials because I've never written something like this before. I've written a lot of string quartets, and I've written a lot of piano music, but the merging of the two is something very interesting to me. And because it's in the nature of something I've not done before, I'm listening to a lot of music, a lot of quintets. I try to identify myself with the sound. Even though I have the sound in my mind, it's good to listen to that sound coming from other voices as well.

So listening to works by other composers with similar orchestration is part of your pre-compositional process, at least in this case. What other methods do you use when preparing a new piece?

Usually, prior to writing a piece, I work on the music through the creation of sketches. Whenever I get an idea, I create a sketch for that idea. By the time I get ready to put the entire puzzle together, I may have 100 or 150 sketches. So it takes me a great deal of time to begin the piece, but that's how I begin structuring and ultimately writing the form of the piece.

Do you develop these sketches at the piano?

Not really. Usually I work directly from my mind to the paper. I might work a little slower than other people who write directly to the computer, but for me the computer is used at the end; it's not how I work in the beginning.

You use the computer at the end of the composition process then, to create parts?

Yes, yes. Of course, if I have a particularly strong idea, I write it down wherever I am. I usually travel around with a pad, and wherever I am when I get an idea I'll write it down. That flash can come anywhere and at any time, and it might be a really important idea for the piece, so I like to be prepared to write it down.

Several composers have alluded to a sort of "mystical," or at least mysterious, aspect of the compositional process, saying they sometimes have no idea where the creative ideas come from. Do you ever feel that way?

All the time. Sometimes I'll come back to a score days after finishing a piece and there are whole sections that I cannot identify or remember writing. I seriously wonder, "Who wrote that?" I don't know. It feels like someone else came in at just that moment and wrote that passage, or that entire section. In a way, it feels almost like getting back to a place I recognize from my own past.

Do you find that writing a new piece of music follows a familiar pattern, or is the process different for each piece that you compose?

In my case, there are two very, very different types of process. I sometimes write a piece very quickly. One piece I wrote for piano, *Momentum*, was titled that because it came to me in one afternoon. I wrote the entire piece in just a few hours. I don't know where it came from; it just came to me fully composed. At times like that, I almost feel that I am in contact with something. It is hard to define, but *something* that is driving *me*, rather than me driving *it*. Then, at other times, I have to elaborate a great deal before I am able to come up with a piece, or with particular moments of a piece. For instance, I was having a really hard time writing the ending for my opera. I was going to have to kill the main character; he was going to be executed. I remember quite well what happened to me when I finally sat down to write that passage, that final piece needed to complete the entire work. I sat down to write it, and it may sound ridiculous, but I cried all the way through the writing, because I was killing this person. It was very emotional. I was sobbing, crying for his mother and for this innocent man who was about to be shot. I have never before been in such a trance. It was interesting because what I wrote was very, very simple; a sustained drum roll and then total silence, but it came out of something very deep and I think people feel that. At the initial performance, it was about five minutes before the audience started applauding. Sometimes as humans, I think we are working on many planes, some that we don't understand so well yet.

It's a very dramatic moment in the piece. Did you find writing an opera to be a difficult creative experience?
Oh, yes; it was overwhelming, because you get so involved with every single character, and every single instrument, every word, every note.

You moved to New York City from Cuba, as a pianist really, not as a composer or conductor at the time. It can be so difficult to get a foothold and start a career, yet here you were in a new city, a new country, and you took on all of the challenges that came your way. I think young composers, perhaps most particularly young women composers, would like to hear a little about your experiences and how you developed into the successful artist you are today.
When I was studying music in Cuba, it was not really such a big deal that I was a woman; there were a lot of other women at the conservatory, specifically studying an instrument such as the piano. The fact that I excelled as a pianist also was not such a big deal because many of my classmates were incredible and they were all developing their technical skills and interpretive skills, as I was. One thing that was different about me was that I didn't come from a family that had anything to do with music, and also I was not from a neighborhood that tended to have this type of schooling for the children. Still, it is interesting that in my building there were seven other musicians, professional people who were well recognized

in the country, including the first bass of the Cuban Symphony Orchestra. He told my grandmother, after listening to me progress, that he thought I had talent.

So your first formal musical studies were in Cuba, and you received a degree there as well?

Yes. I arrived in the United States after graduating with my master's degree in piano, solfege, and theory in Cuba. I came here thinking it would be a stop on my way to the Paris Conservatoire, and that I would then study there. But based on the political situation between my birth country and the country that embraced me, things were out of hand and I had to stay here, at least for the first five years after my arrival. At that time, leaving Cuba meant a loss of citizenship. So basically, I arrived here in the United States without citizenship in any country and with a canceled passport. The authorities told me that I would have to be here for at least five years before I could even apply for US citizenship and that, at the end of that period, an analysis would be made of my behavior and my background and everything. Based on that evaluation, they would decide whether to approve my application or not.

It must have been a very difficult experience for you. Did you come directly to New York from Cuba?

I first arrived in Miami, but I immediately made the decision to move to New York. On May 29 I was in Miami, and on June 1, I arrived in New York, and the rest is history. Upon my arrival, I stayed with some friends in the Bronx, in their living room on a sofa bed. By looking in the yellow pages [telephone directories], we found an organization called the American Council for the Émigrés in the Professions, which was across the street from the United Nations. I met a very old Hungarian woman there who was in charge of the music aspect of the organization. They got someone to translate so I could explain my situation. Then she told me she wanted to hear me play. So, they took me to a piano, I played, and she said, I'm going to get you a scholarship. Just like that.

Wow! What a great story!

It was the most incredible thing. Then she took me to the New York College of Music,[2] where they made me do sight-reading, and play the piano. At the end of that audition I had a scholarship! They also sent me to learn English, and eventually I was transferred to NYU.

How did you become the first Musical Director of Dance Theater of Harlem?[3]

A friend of mine, Laura Wilson, was playing piano accompaniment in Harlem, and she asked me to replace her for a Saturday because she was very ill with the flu. She gave me the music books and explained what I should do. It was the first time I took the subway by myself to Harlem, to a church at 145th Street and Saint Nicholas Avenue. The singer Dorothy Maynor was in charge of the program. I didn't know she was a very famous soprano who was launching a program that would later be called the Harlem School of the Arts.[4]

I played for a woman who also didn't speak English—she was originally from Europe—and so we communicated using hand signals. She would show me the steps and count the rhythm of the movements so I could follow her. It just happened that this was the exact day when a gentleman went there looking for a space to start a project he had in mind. He heard me playing the piano, and he approached me, and I said yes, and it changed the course of my life. I didn't know that he was Arthur Mitchell and that the project he had in mind was Dance Theater of Harlem, and I didn't know that I would be the first musician he contracted—the first pianist—and I didn't know that I would turn into a composer. One day he invited me to write a piece and said he would do the choreography so, out of the blue I wrote my first major piece of music, *Tones*, for the ballet. And then when we went to Europe, they literally threw me into the pits and I had to start conducting. So the first time I conducted, the first time in my life, I actually knew nothing about conducting. It was all like jumping out of a plane, being in freefall, but I did it!

It sounds a bit like a movie script, to meet someone like Arthur Mitchell on such a chance encounter.

Yes! And he wasn't the only amazing artist I worked with at Dance Theater of Harlem. Jerome Robbins[5] taught me his choreography for Debussy's *Prelude to the Afternoon of a Faun*. I also met George Balanchine then. He was one of the early mentors of Dance Theater of Harlem and of Arthur Mitchell. He had given his permission for the company to dance his ballets, and so I had to learn them all—not only the music but the steps as well, so I would know what to watch for. I particularly remember him sitting with me at the piano and breaking down the score of Bach's *Double Violin Concerto* in D minor, showing me the steps he had designed for each section of the music.

That all happened pretty rapidly, and suddenly you were not only performing but also conducting and composing. I believe that composing and orchestral conducting was particularly unusual for a woman at the time.

I went to NYU and changed my major to learn composition. That's when I studied with Ursula Mamlok[6] and started understanding the situation that composers who happen to be women were in. She told me about Miriam Gideon[7] and Louise Talma[8] and I ended up meeting both of them. Before that, I had never thought in terms of, oh, I am a woman and I compose, or I am a woman and I conduct because being a woman had never been an impediment to me. When I was in Cuba, there were a lot of us doing all sorts of different things and it was all right, and when I came here, I never got even a moment of discouragement because of that either, so I didn't ever have any other reference to go by.

Now I reflect a great deal on that, and I think the one who gave me a lot of that [confidence] was my grandmother. She was very well schooled and loved to read.

She was a strong woman and an inspiration to you.

She talked to me about Marian Anderson,[9] about Josephine Baker,[10] about these luminaries of color in the world of music, as examples for me to know about. Fate made it to happen that after being with Dance Theater of Harlem, I wrote a piece and the narrator was Marian Anderson. Then we did a show at the Palladium in London, and who were we performing with? Josephine Baker. It was a shock to me. I wished I could tell my grandmother, but she had passed by then! It was very weird, like an episode of the *Twilight Zone.*

You also were the musical director and conductor for the musical *The Wiz* on Broadway in 1978. What was that experience like?

Incredible. Some people despise Broadway; I don't. I love all forms of music. I learned a lot about what goes on behind the scenes, all the coordination that goes into a production like that. And I enjoyed working with all those great artists and wonderful musicians and singers who had a different perspective on musical performance. It was a tremendous experience. Then, I did something similar, working on *The Human Comedy* with Joseph Papp at the Public Theater.[11] Then we went to Broadway.

All composers are influenced by their backgrounds, but yours is particularly interesting. Please share your thoughts on how your heritage has informed your music. For example, a couple of things often alluded to when people speak of your music are the infusion of elements of jazz in your sonorities and form and, especially, your unusual and powerful use of percussion.

None of this occurred in my life until the 1980s. The music that I wrote before, with the exception of a few things I did for Latin theater, Teatro-Latino, was, in a way, very much political. I studied composition when serialism was the thing of the moment and, therefore, I had to do that. Besides that, at a very young age I had learned that system and in order to be accepted you had to write in that style. *Haiku* came out of that period. I didn't know that I had a voice in percussion, an instinct for it, until later. I may have jazz gestures or jazz influences, but that is not an instinctive part of my music. I say that because one of the things that really captivated me when I came to this country was jazz. A Korean classmate of mine introduced me to jazz. He played me a record, and my mouth dropped. I said, "Who is this person, this piano player?" It was Art Tatum. Until then, I didn't know Art Tatum existed. When I was in Cuba, jazz, for me, was *Rhapsody in Blue*. Of course, I hadn't realized the fact that when I was improvising with other Conservatory students on the weekends, we were playing Latin jazz! We had a way of synchronizing things, a way of jazzing up a tune—any tune. We would all play Bach in school, and then we would make a Latin Bach version that we could play to entertain ourselves. I mean, it was our thing, you know? Not until I really got out of Cuba and arrived in New York, and specifically after I heard Art Tatum, did I get really, really, interested in jazz. I mean, I thought I could play well, but when I heard him I said, "Oh, my God, how can this man play this way? It's impossible!" It was tremendous for me! I started learning more about jazz, and through Dance Theater of Harlem I met a lot of jazz musicians, including Miles Davis.

I've studied as much as I can. With some pieces I deliberately lean toward certain jazz rhythms and gestures, jazz integration. An example is a piece called *Singin' Sepia* for voice and mixed ensemble, with the poetry of Rita Dove.[12]

You and I have talked about the fact that I'm originally from New Orleans and the jazz tradition of that region. When I was first in the Caribbean and Latin America, I was blown away by the incredible music there—it's *so* powerful and sensual, fantastic driving

rhythms and soaring melodic lines. So I guess I had a similar, parallel experience to your awakening to jazz. Do you consciously incorporate elements of Latin and Caribbean music into your compositions? I ask because I hear the influences there, but they are subtle and seem to be molded to your individual voice.

I didn't really go into the aspects of music from Cuba or the Caribbean or Latin America until after I went back to Cuba for the first time. People who left Cuba around the time I did weren't allowed back to the country because of travel regulations. Then in 1979, the Cuban government opened travel for family reunification, and that's how I was able to return home after 12 years of being away. I got to meet all of the new members of my family that had been born, and I saw my parents. Specifically, I remember the shock of seeing my father with completely white hair. I didn't realize it was the last time I would see him; he died several months after my visit. And that was the shock that made me reconsider what kind of music I was writing. When I brought my music home my father said, "Your music sounds very interesting, but where are you in there?" He didn't explain to me what he meant by that, but the way I took it was that something of me was missing in my music. I started having nightmares and hearing all sorts of rhythmical twists in my mind, and my music started being affected by that emotional state. Nowadays I compose anything I feel like composing. I mean I can do a very straight piece, devoid of all of that [influence of Latin music].

Not a stamp, but your heritage is in your blood and expressed in your unique musical voice, as it is in many creative people, artists and composers. . .

I very much believe that each creative person is the sum total of their experience and background. I am much more comfortable now because all of my influences—the music that I have encountered in the world—have made an impact on me and on my life. Once the music makes an impact on me, I go hunting and researching and trying to understand the specific musical aesthetic of what it is that has moved me so. For *Haiku*, I studied a lot of the theater gestures of Noh.[13] I have so many books on the music of Japan in my studio from that time. When I went to China four or five years ago, I bought scores from there as well. Historically, in those old scores the musical language and the type of notation they used were totally different from the graphics we commonly use to notate music, and it interested me very much.

You went to Madrid and Beijing as a US Artistic Director of American Culture. What an honor. That must have been a demanding and transformative experience.

That was tremendous, oh my God yes! I got a call from the embassy and they wanted to appoint me US Director of American Culture. So I went and they did performances of my work in Madrid. That was really very moving. I gave lectures and I visited universities and conservatories. I talked about new directions in music and my heritage and how the Spanish syntax is in the music of countries such as the one in which I grew up. In Cuba you can see the influences of Spain, France, Africa, and China. I was surrounded by all of that rich heritage. We are a mélange of all of it, especially in our music. That's why the music has become what it is, because it is a hybrid of all these different cultures, by the artists of each generation, you know? So that's why for me to hear someone's description of my music is always amazing. But what people really hear in my music is me, myself, trying to portray how I listen, and how all of these influences have affected what's happening within me in terms of sound.

So those influences are part of the makeup of your musical voice. When you work with your students, do they ask you or do you advise them as to how to find their own voice as composers?

All the time. I usually tell my students that at the beginning it is natural that they will lean toward sounds or techniques or influences by the creators that they admire. That is a natural step toward progression as an artist. As we move away from those first steps, I think it is important to begin thinking very profoundly about who it is we are, you see? Who am *I*? What do *I* have to say? For that you have to go very deep. That is beyond technique; it is a little bit more spiritual or subconscious, but it is a quest that we all have. Otherwise what are we doing on this planet? Everyone wants to know, "Who am I?" before we leave the planet. So I never talk to students about following anyone but themselves. I tell them to try and discover who they are.

Do you think that composition and composers today are any different from when you were a student? Has there been a change in attitude, technique, or esthetics?

I think that the computerized world has revolutionized everything. Everyone is involved in the quest for gaining speed, and sometimes we don't give ample time to whatever it is we are creating. Out of three or four works that we write, which one will be singled out? It has to have that something in a very special way. The young students and composers of this age are very prolific.

Some of them can write incredible pieces, in terms of orchestration skills and craftsmanship. How much are they saying of who *they* are though?

Do you think the computer has helped or hurt the students?
Certainly, the computer is fascinating. We have all of these notation programs now. So, voila! There is a score realized right there in front of you! On the other hand, you have to be very, very disciplined not to allow the computer to influence your writing. Cutting and pasting, or repeating something can be seductive; it's so easy to take something out of the end and stick it in the middle. With all the easy editing you can do with these programs, it might change the composition process that one would naturally follow. We are living in the computer world, and where we are heading, I have no idea. But definitely we are heading to something much more supreme than what we have right now. But we have to be careful that we don't lose ourselves and our creativity in the process.

What's coming up next for you? I know you are working on your quintet. What do you look forward to, as a composer and as an artist in the years ahead?
Well, let me see. I have been approached about writing a second opera, and that's something that interests me a great deal. I really don't know what comes next.

To tell the truth, I am always amazed that I am doing what I am doing. It's been a magnificent ride. It is like *Alice in Wonderland*: coming from Cuba and arriving as a pianist, getting into composition and conducting, being in the world of academia, doing all of these exciting things. If you asked me tomorrow if I would like to conduct *Cirque du Soleil*, I would say, Sure! And then you would see me at *Cirque du Soleil*, conducting the show! [Laughs]

I love people; I love the music of the world. I don't call it world music; I call it the music of the world because I include all the musical systems that I don't know of yet. The music of the world is fascinating to me. I was supposed to be a musician and that's what I am. Above being a composer, or a pianist, or a conductor, or whatever, I'm a musician. This is the world of music and we are musicians—and that's the only title that I'm comfortable with.

SELECTED WORKS OF TANIA LEÓN

Ethos (2014), Piano and String Quartet
Inura (2009), Voices (SATB), Strings, and Percussion

Ácana (2008), Chamber Orchestra

Alma (2007), Flute and Piano

Toque (2006), Clarinet, Alto Sax, Piano, Percussionists, Violin, Double Bass

Reflections (2006), Poems by Rita Dove, Soprano, Clarinet, Tenor Sax, Piano, Trumpet, String Quintet, Percussion

Axon (2002), Violin and Interactive Computer

Rezos (2001), Text by Jamaica Kincaid, SATB Choir

Horizons (1999), Orchestra

Singin' Sepia (1996), Poems by Rita Dove, Soprano, Clarinet, Violin, Piano Four Hands

Scourge of Hyacinths: Full Opera (1999), Chamber Opera (1994), Libretto by León, based on a play by Wole Soyinka, Orchestra

Kabiosile (1988), Solo Piano, Chamber Orchestra

(▶) To learn more about Tania León and her music, visit www.oup.com/us/compositioninthedigitalworld.

NOTES

1. Tania León was presented with the Victor Herbert Award from ASCAP (American Society of Composers, Authors and Publishers) at its 14th annual Concert Music Awards in 2013.
2. The New York College of Music was established in 1925 and was merged with the NYU School of Music in 1968.
3. In 1969 León became the first musical director of Arthur Mitchell's Dance Theater of Harlem. She was a founding member and established its music school and orchestra.
4. Founded in 1964 by soprano Dorothy Maynor, Harlem School of the Arts offers courses in music, dance, and the visual arts.
5. Jerome Robbins (1918–1998) was an American choreographer and producer. He worked on many ballet and Broadway productions including *West Side Story, The King and I*, and *Peter Pan*. His many accolades include two Academy Awards, five Tony Awards, and the National Medal of Arts.
6. Ursula Mamlok is a German-born American composer and teacher.
7. Miriam Gideon (1906–1996) was an American composer who studied with Roger Sessions. She was the second woman inducted into the American Academy and Institute of Arts and Letters (1975).
8. Louise Talma (1906–1996) was an American composer and educator. She studied at Juilliard, NYU, Columbia University, and privately with Nadia Boulanger. She was the first woman to be inducted into the American Academy and Institute of Arts and Letters (1974), to receive two Guggenheim Fellowships, and to receive the Sibelius Medal (1963).
9. Marian Anderson (1897–1993) was an American contralto. She was the first African American to perform at the Metropolitan Opera. Her awards include the Presidential Medal of Freedom (1963), the National Medal of Arts (1986), and a Grammy Lifetime Achievement Award (1991).

10. Josephine Baker (1906–1975) was an American-born dancer, actress, singer, and world-famous entertainer.
11. The Public Theater was founded in 1954 by Joseph Papp (1921–1991), and produced numerous award-winning plays and musicals including *Hair*. León conducted *The Human Comedy* produced by Joseph Papp on Broadway in 1984.
12. Rita Dove is an American poet. She served as Poet Laureate Consultant in Poetry to the Library of Congress from 1993 to 1995. She received the Pulitzer Prize for Poetry (1987), and was the Poet Laureate of Virginia from 2004 to 2006.
13. Noh theater is a form of classical Japanese musical drama whose origins date to the 14th century.

Bright Sheng

Photo Credit: Alex Cao

When you think about American contemporary music, there are so many differ-ent possibilities. . . .When artists get to this country, partially because there's no government funding for art, it's totally free artistically. You don't owe anybody anything; you just do your own thing. If one group doesn't like you, another group will. It's all about your talent, and that's really great soil for artistic development.

Bright Sheng (b. Shanghai, China, 1955) is in great demand as a com-poser, conductor, and concert pianist across the United States as well as in Europe and Asia. My first conversation with him took place via Skype over the Internet while he was in Hong Kong, conducting and supervising the performance of one of his new pieces. When we spoke again several weeks later, he was back in the United States at work on a completely different project.

Sheng moved to New York City from Communist China in 1982 and soon became a protégé to no less a musical giant than Leonard Bernstein, with whom he continued to study and work until Bernstein's death. Among Sheng's many honors in China and the United States are fellowships and awards from the National Endowment for the Arts; and a Charles Ives Scholarship Award from the American Academy and Institute of Arts and Letters.

Sheng is one of the leaders among contemporary Chinese American composers who have helped bridge the cultural gap between the United States and China; his music is highly respected among composers and is often cited as an example of exemplary craft and artistry. His works have been performed by most of the great orchestras and conductors of the world and by eminent soloists ranging from Yo-Yo Ma to Peter Serkin. Championed both for his dramatic gifts and for the historic significance of many of his works, Sheng has been composer-in-residence for opera and ballet companies, in addition to several orchestral organizations, and was chosen by President Clinton to compose a piece played in honor of Chinese Premiere Zhu Rongji's visit to the White House.

A master of both Western and traditional Chinese art music, he has established his own musical voice, in part by melding a unique hybrid of these two traditions. Nevertheless, Sheng is decidedly modest about his accomplishments and takes great pains to express his gratitude for "luck" and the support of fellow musicians—and to credit both in explaining his success. Intense and formal during our conversations, Sheng was thoughtful, yet receptive to my questions, and deeply passionate about the seriousness of his mission as an artist.

It must have been quite an experience to be in your 20s, living in New York City, and studying music with Leonard Bernstein. Can you please talk a little bit about that time?
I think there are many great things about Bernstein, but perhaps the most important was his talent as a teacher. He was like a magnet, doing all of these great projects, including recording the Mahler symphonies at the time I studied with him. In the beginning, I would simply look at everything that he did in awe. But then, he made it such a simple thing for me to learn a particular technique. He would say, "Oh, this is easy. You can do it this way too, I'll show you." In five minutes I would feel like, "Yeah, I can do this with a little practice." When you were around him you didn't realize that you were learning, just having a great time. After only

a few years of studying with him, I had learned so much. I would have lunch with an old musician friend, and I'd realize that on certain issues, we were no longer at the same level musically. I'm so grateful that I had the opportunity.

How did you meet him?
He usually spent some time at Tanglewood every year. He had stopped going for a while but went back again in 1985, when I was first there, and I met him then. All of the composers were very excited when he spent time with us. He brought his entourage of about 20 people, including his manager, his publicist, and his cook. They all came to a dinner where the composers cooked for him. It was quite something. I remember I made a Peking duck for him. [Laughs]

Afterward, he invited all of us to go to his rehearsals. We were on the private list of persons who were allowed to attend his orchestral rehearsals.

Attending those rehearsals was a wonderful opportunity.
In those days he would have the Vienna Philharmonic come to New York to rehearse with him, rather than him going to the orchestra! I attended rehearsals every week. Not all of the young composers went. I mean the first few times they went, but they didn't continue. I assume they thought that since he was doing Mahler, Beethoven, and Brahms, they had heard this music before, and there was no point in attending. But those were great opportunities to me, and I learned a great deal. I was a student at Columbia, and I would skip classes and go to his rehearsals. The first time I went he said, "Do you happen to have a score in your briefcase you can show me?" I said, "Sorry, no." The second time I made sure there was something in my briefcase. [Laughs] So then we became friends.

How did you become his student?
I wanted to officially study conducting and composition with him. He said, "I've studied conducting with Fritz Reiner,[1] so I know what to do, but I've never studied composition. I don't know how to teach it." I said, "You've never had a composition lesson?" He said, "No, never. I just taught myself. The closest to a composition lesson that I ever had was with Copland. Copland would look at my music and say something really harsh: 'You can't do this, don't do this.' You know, critical and harsh." I said, "Oh, well, can you do that to me?" He said, "O.K." So that's how I became his student.

As busy as you are, how do you organize your schedule so that you can still compose, find time to be with your family, and meet all of

the other demands that life throws at you, like this interview. It must be very difficult.

Well, composition is something that I think about constantly, so I can compose any time. It's not always about sitting at the piano and writing it down. I think about a piece I'm working on for quite a long time. I think about it a little bit every day, so by the time I finish the preparation period, I can actually sit down at the piano to write it down. It usually goes rather fast at that point. My wife recently said, "You know, you do a lot of sitting there doing nothing." [Both laugh]

But I'm not sitting there doing nothing. I'm always thinking about the new piece. I could be driving, or doing some chore, but I will be thinking about the piece, or the next few pieces that I'm doing. This is especially true if it's a work with a large scope, like an opera or orchestral work. I will form what the piece is like in my head, and then I can write it all out. The same thing is true with my conducting. As part of my preparation I will hear the piece in my head before I conduct.

You've spoken about having a dream, a vivid dream, in which you visualized an entire orchestral score in detail. That dream turned into *China Dreams*.

Yeah, but, unfortunately, that doesn't happen often. [Laughs]

It has happened a few times—a handful of times in my 30-year writing career that a dream actually helped my composing.

When the inspiration does come to you, do you feel that there's some spiritual element involved?

There's always a spiritual element in creativity. You never know how or where inspiration may come from. You know, it just comes to you. But— you have to be ready. You have to be open and receptive for the ideas to come, and then boom, it comes. Sometimes at the least expected moment.

I know how that feels—it can be a challenge when unexpected inspiration comes while you are in the middle of completing a piece.

Yes. For example, I just finished a violin concerto. I thought there should be three continuous movements in one. The second movement being the slow movement, the last one is fast, and the first one is built upon big gestures. I composed the main thematic materials for each movement first, and the theme of the slow movement was related to the opening theme. I thought it was a good tune, but I felt that it could be more inspiring. But, in the middle of writing, I suddenly had an inspiration. A new tune just came to me. It was gorgeous and beautiful, but it didn't quite fit the section that I was currently working on. I didn't want to waste it, but I couldn't use it later, so I worked on it more and was able to incorporate it into the section for the second movement. Sometimes ideas come that you don't necessarily expect or want to come. At other times, you work very hard and the ideas will just not come to you. So you compromise. You do the best you can, using your technique and your experience to compose.

Looking back over my work from the last 10 years or so, there are some works I have written that I feel are inspired. But then, there are also some that I could live without.

I've heard you talk about the fact that in the past you've doubted your own talent. I know that I've certainly felt that way—I think a lot of composers have those feelings from time to time. It seems that you overcome that doubt though and complete your work. What advice would you give to young composers about believing in their art?

Yeah, I know what you mean, but I don't think you ever overcome it. You just live with it. Insecurity is part of the game. You have to be truthful with yourself. If you're completely confident, if you believe you can do anything, without any fear, without any insecurity, I think you're being complacent really. I think you must have some insecurity, but you overcome it and do your best. That's what counts.

If you don't have *some* insecurity, you're probably not trying anything new. If you're always doing something safe, you are not moving into new territory. Great artists always try to get into water they have never tested, and there is a danger in that that creates insecurity.

And did you find that Leonard Bernstein had to deal with insecurities as well?

At the end of his life he was such a famous, gigantic conductor and composer, some people might say he could be arrogant. For example, I remember a young conductor from Paris saying to him, "I know every piece you've ever written." Bernstein said, "I'm not surprised," He could appear to be arrogant, but once you really knew him, you realized he also had insecurities. So I don't think it's something that you can overcome. It's a healthy thing. It's part of the package.

Do you work with your students to help them find their own musical voice? Is that something that you emphasize?

People confuse individual voice with style. They think if you find the right style, that's your voice, and that's a misconception. I really think people's individual voice comes from their personality. How the music carries you as a person; that's unique. It's not your style. Look at Stravinsky and how many styles he went through. In the very beginning he was imitating Rimsky-Korsakov, or Debussy, or Ravel, but he already had his own stamp. It was *him*, he had the personality. He never worried about losing his voice when he switched from one style to the other. I think, in this day and age, there are so many styles available that people are afraid of losing their voice, so they stick to one style. That's really wrong thinking, because musical styles are just like languages, just different ways of writing. It doesn't matter what language you write in. Some writers can write in many different languages—that doesn't define their voice. Musically it's the same thing—your voice is in your personality. How do *you* get angry? How do *you* get happy? How do *you* fall in love? How do *you* pour your emotions and your personality into your art? Everybody's personality is slightly different. That's what is unique about you; it's in your DNA.

How do you convey this philosophy to your students?
In talking to students, the short answer is "be yourself." I like to make the analogy of food with culture: Some people like to stick to what they already know, while others are more adventurous. Personally, I like to venture out and try ethnic food I'm not familiar with; at least I like to try it once. Whenever people ask, "Do you want to try this new food?" I always say, "Sure!" I may or may not like the new taste, but I'll try it, and I find that I like a lot of different types of food. From European food to all Asian and Central Asian foods, I love it all. On the other hand, some people are more interested in staying comfortable and are happy with the food they are familiar with, the food they were brought up eating, and they stick with that. It's a personal choice, which is fine. So, being true to "who you are" as a creative artist, to me, means pursuing whatever you're interested in.

I have moved around a lot since I was very young. I was exposed at an early age to many different places and cultures. Throughout my life those experiences have helped to broaden my interests, so I can truly be a migrant in every sense of the word. In turn, those experiences have broadened my perspective as a composer, and this is naturally reflected in my works.

Many of your pieces refer to Asian themes in the title, the music itself, or both.
That's part of my upbringing, you know. It's part of me. But many of my pieces are completely not Chinese subjects at all, like *Northern Lights*. These are big pieces, and I venture into different territory.

In your essay "Never Far Away,"[2] you say writing music is like searching for the garden of treasure, and that perhaps the purpose of composing, of being a creative person, lies in the searching itself. To me, this seems to be a very important concept for composers to think about. Is this a philosophy you try to instill in your students and adhere to yourself as you compose?

Yes, I do that all the time. One composer, no matter how talented, is only one person. So you do your best. I remember when Leonard Bernstein and I were working together, he would often say, "You do your best, and you feel better." Basically, he put it in a colloquial sense, and it remains true.

That's also one reason I feel so strongly that it is very important that a composer knows the past, the works and history of the great composers. You build on what other people have done before you. No matter how smart you are, you cannot be smarter than the hundreds of composers who preceded you in history. You have to build on what they've done—just like a scientist does in his work. They don't start from scratch when they invent something without knowing what other people have done before them. Being a creative artist is the same thing. Think about the core classical repertoire for chamber music, opera, and symphonic music. This repertoire has a long lineage where any composer who has made it into that line knows their past really well. These composers were all masters of the past, as well as masters of the future. You have to be both. Otherwise, you cannot enter this line. You can go around this line, or above it, or below it, or hang around the edges, but unless you know the work of the masters who came before you, you will not really be a part of that core repertoire. Mahler believed that a composer has only made it into the repertoire if people are still playing his music 50 years after the composer's death.

Now, I understand that not everybody who wants to be a composer is going to enter that repertoire. To me, working toward making it into that repertoire is the searching for the hidden treasure. Maybe the searching itself is the purpose in the end. You may or may not make it into the repertoire, but at least you look for it. So that's my philosophy.

You were the first composer-in-residence for the New York City Ballet.[3] What was that experience like? Was it a new challenge to write for dance?

Yes, and I'm a slow learner. My learning curve is very slow. The same held true when I was the composer-in-residence of the Lyric Opera in Chicago for three years.[4] By the time I left there, having just finished my first opera there, I had just begun to have an inkling of what it was like to be an opera composer, the difference between writing for concert music and opera. My experience at the New York City Ballet was a little bit like that, too. By the time I left New York City Ballet, which was after about two years, I had just started to get an inkling of what dance music is about: the things that choreographers and dancers are looking for in music.

What do you think choreographers and dancers are looking for musically?
Think about the great ballet composers like Tchaikovsky and Stravinsky. I believe what they are truly looking for is a strong pulse. There are composers who write with a strong rhythm, but that doesn't mean those composers have the pulse. Dance needs the pulse. The body listens to the music and the rhythm helps them to feel, to fulfill their movement.

So do you approach composition for dance differently, with an extreme focus on that pulse, which you might not have had if the piece was for concert music?
I think yes, you need to. It's totally different. If I was commissioned today to write a dance piece, I would be a lot more experienced at it than when I was composer-in-residence, which is ironic. But it's a learning experience. You learn.

Take Stravinsky, for example. His music has always had a great hold in the world of dance. The meters are changing constantly, but you feel this great pulsation that goes on, and so his music is very dance-able. That's why Balanchine[5] was so much in love with Stravinsky's music.

And writing for opera, is that yet another challenge, another musical world for you to explore as a composer?
Yeah. That's a completely different story. It's quite different from writing for ballet, another ball game. [Laughs] Look at Verdi. He mostly composed opera in his lifetime, and not much else. His first opera success was his third, *Nabucco*, which is less often produced nowadays. I mean, people do it for novelty reasons, or when they do centennial celebrations. That's because that piece, compared to his later works from his middle or later operas, sounds young and naïve. My favorite line is, "It took Verdi three tries to get it right." So, in composing for opera, almost no one has success with their first effort—you know, hits the jackpot. There are people who do hit the jackpot, but that doesn't mean that they will be able to repeat it again. The composer might not realize what made it work, or perhaps it was just pure luck. So, you never know. This was true even for Puccini and Strauss. None of them got it right the first time. Beethoven never got it right. Beethoven only wrote one opera, and it was a big problem for him.

I find it fascinating that so many wonderful composers have come from China to the United States in recent years. Like you, many travel back and forth between China and the United States. You're an example of a talented artist who has come to this country and now goes back to share your experiences in China. There seems to be an artistic connection between our two countries. Am I wrong?
Well, thank you, but if you ask other Chinese American composers, you'll realize we are all thinking quite differently. We do share one thing: our life experiences in China have a similar pattern. During the time we all grew up in China, our lives were molded by the government. Everybody was forced into this mold, so our life experiences are similar. But, once the Cultural Revolution was over, the mold was broken and we started to do our own things. We all think very differently, and our life experience from that point on is quite different. We all came to the United States, some of us even studied with the same teachers, but everybody's experience is unique, and therefore our music is quite different from each other's. Yes, we are all Chinese American, so there is some Chinese in us, but the Chinese have a famous saying: "Eight gods cross the water, but each uses their own tricks."

Once I left China, my perspective changed. In China it is believed that China invented everything: the wheel, paper, gunpowder, everything. But that's simply not true. Once I could look at China from a different angle, I could see that China, as a whole civilization, was also influenced by its neighboring cultures, and that included the musical influence of these other cultures. With this in mind, my musical interest was broadened to include Central Asia and, in fact, all of Asia. Most importantly, the culture that resulted from the Silk Road influenced China in a very powerful way. In a broader sense, Chinese music embraces the cultures of all of the countries surrounding it.

Now my interest includes cultures beyond Asia. For instance, I've written pieces with influences from Scandinavian cultures. Ultimately, you find that there are cultures that have been really connected for a long, long, time. This cultural connection is not just a recent development. The globalization of the world that we are all experiencing is not a new thing. Yes, the world is getting smaller and smaller because of technology, especially over the last hundred years, but it is not new. It has been going on for thousands of years, ever since communication between cultures existed. Of course, until relatively recently, it has been a very slow process, but as long as communication was there, cultural exchange was taking place.

The United States is a fascinating country: its immigration policy, its openness. It embraces everybody. So, when you think about American culture, American music, it's very hard to define whether something is American music. Today everything is American music.

Obviously, you're all unique individuals, but there is a long history of composers coming from Europe to the United States, and of Americans looking to Europe for new talent and creative ideas and trends. It seems as if there is now a surge of musical talent and creative energy from Asia in general, but especially from China.

To a great extent, this is due to the American open policy. In Chinese history, there are peaks of prosperity, and one of them was during the Tang Dynasty, which was during the seventh century to the tenth century, and that was a peak in China, economically, culturally. Everybody could come to the Chinese capital as long as you were talented—and they could do well. There was no agenda. You could have a different religion. It was open. I think the United States now is a bit like that, so that's why it's very good for artistic development; that's why people are coming here from China.

When you think about European contemporary music—French, German, Italian—you can sort of get a sense of what's going on stylistically. But when you think about American contemporary music, there are so many different possibilities. It's a wonderful policy. When artists get to this country, partially because there's no government funding for art, it's totally free artistically. You don't owe anybody anything; you just do your own thing. If one group doesn't like you, another group will. It's all about your talent, and that's really great soil for artistic development. I think I'm lucky that I came to the United States rather than to a country in Europe. The people who went to Europe [from China] have also done quite well, but it's not as free there as in the United States. So again, I feel very lucky, and I feel very American.

To me, one of the most fascinating things about your story is the inspiring transition you made when you moved to this country. You came to the United States from China without money, didn't speak the language, and yet your career as a composer swiftly soared. What do you attribute that to?

I don't know. Looking back now, I think there were a few things in my early life in China, before I came to the United States, which played very important roles in my later life. The first took place during the Cultural Revolution. I suffered and lived through that, but I'm not unique. In China, millions of people suffered through that period. Many Chinese composers we know who thrive in the West went through similar experiences. When I arrived in the United States, I wanted to learn all I could, and

I was passionate about my music career. I met teachers and other musicians, and I had many opportunities that broadened me, that brought me experiences and wonderful opportunities. Not just career development, but also development as a composer. I had pieces being performed by different orchestras. I was able to figure out what worked when writing for the orchestra, and I learned some things I should not do in the next piece. Those kinds of experiences were very important.

And the other part was luck. I have been very lucky, it's true. I've had great teachers, and I've had a lot of wonderful musicians perform my music. My career has been very good because performers and institutions have given me these chances. They perform my music; they have faith in my music.

Much of your music is available, for free, on the Internet. Is this phenomenon going to make it even more difficult for composers to make their living writing music?

I've been asked this question a lot lately. I think that eventually, technology and the law will be up to date with each other. Technology has developed very quickly, but the law is catching up now. I'm not worried. I don't think my life is affected or that I've lost a lot of income opportunities because of the Internet or technology. I think it has helped me to spread my influence—even to different countries. Many more people now have access to my music if they are interested in looking into it, so it's all for the better. It's just like everything else; nature will fall into place eventually. I'm optimistic.

SELECTED WORKS OF BRIGHT SHENG

Let Fly (2013), Concerto for Violin and Orchestra

The Blazing Mirage (2012), Violoncello and Strings

Never Far Away (2008), Concerto for Harp and Orchestra

Zodiac Tales (2006), Concerto for Orchestra

The Nightingale and the Rose (2006), Ballet Score

Phoenix (2004), Soprano and Orchestra

Madame Mao (2003), Opera in Two Acts

The Song and Dance of Tears (2003), Quadruple Concerto for Sheng, Pipa, Violoncello and Piano

Nanking! Nanking! (2000), Threnody for Pipa and Orchestra

Red Silk Dance (2000), Capriccio for Piano and Orchestra

Flute Moon (1999), Flute/Piccolo, Percussion, Piano, Harp, and Strings
The Silver River (1997), Musical Theater Work
China Dreams (1995), Orchestra
H'un (Lacerations): In Memoriam 1966–1976 (1988), Orchestra

▶ To learn more about Bright Sheng and his music, visit
www.oup.com/us/compositioninthedigitalworld.

NOTES

1. Fritz Reiner (1888–1963) was an eminent Hungarian-born American conductor. He led several orchestras including the Chicago Symphony Orchestra. His students included Lukas Foss and Leonard Bernstein.
2. The essay "Never Far Away" was written by Bright Sheng in 2011 and is available on his website.
3. Bright Sheng was the composer-in-residence for the New York City Ballet from 2006 to 2008.
4. Bright Sheng was the composer-in-residence for the Lyric Opera of Chicago from 1989 to 1992.
5. George Balanchine (1904–1983) was a Russian-born American choreographer. Considered one of the greatest choreographers of the 20th century, he founded the New York City Ballet and worked with many leading composers of his day including Stravinsky.

Ladislav Kubík

It's true that the technological possibilities are getting more and more sophisticated, and thus more and more tempting. Yet, in the arts, one idea should be always clear: What is a job for a human and what is a job for (even the most sophisticated) machine?

"I swim in the notes" is one of my favorite colorful quotes from Ladislav Kubík (b. Czechoslovakia, now the Czech Republic, 1946) as he described his current approach to writing music and explained how his compositional process has evolved from the "tyranny of a set musical system." A former teacher of mine, Kubík is still one of my greatest role models, not only in matters of musical structuring but also as a worthy example of one who lives the life of a truly dedicated musician and educator.

Born in Prague, Kubík earned his degrees in composition and theory from the esteemed Prague Academy of Music. His work began attracting the attention of the music literati when he was still a teenager and has since been performed in more than 24 countries. He continues to reap awards and honors, including a Guggenheim Fellowship, a UNESCO award, First Prize in the International Franz Kafka Composition Competition, and the Intervision Prize, and he has three times been awarded the Florida Arts Council Individual Artist Fellowship.

Kubík's music is dense and complex, ranging from the achingly beautiful to fiery dissonance. Compared stylistically to other prominent composers of Eastern Europe, such as Penderecki and Lutosławski, Kubík's work is particularly distinctive in its use of poetry and text.

Kubík has held his position as professor of composition at the Florida State University (FSU) for many years and, since 1994, also has been artistic director and lecturer of the yearly CASMI International Summer Program in Composition in Prague, Czech Republic. Since 1995, and with the support of FSU, he has sponsored the *Ladislav Kubík International Prize in Composition*, a major composition contest that has attracted young composers from more than 30 countries.

Profoundly intellectual and a consummate gentleman, he also possesses a wicked and sophisticated sense of humor and a deeply felt, hearty laugh. He is a superb teacher of composition, as totally immersed in his students' challenges and successes as in his own. He gives such concentrated time and attention to his students that his own muse must be a bit jealous.

Quite a few American artists were born elsewhere and then became citizens. You were born in Prague, Czechoslovakia, now the Czech Republic. What influence did Prague have on your development as a composer and artist?

The city of Prague had a tremendous impact on me. It is an old city in which the musical culture has been developed through centuries. Everyone who has lived there, or even just visited Prague, knows what I mean. I obtained a very solid education there, not only at the college level but also before that at the high school, and as a composer and pianist with private lessons starting from childhood. My teachers at the [Prague] Academy were very erudite yet conservative. We, as the composition students, looked also at neighboring Poland where a cluster of modern composers emerged in the 1960s and where the yearly Warsaw Autumn Festival[1] established an important connection with the world. And of course, despite the political restrictions, we tried to travel and participate in the music events in Western Europe and later in the United States.

What was the first important step for you in moving from being a student to a professional composer?
My composition received an award at the UNESCO[2] International Rostrum of Composers in Paris, when I was 27. This work was immediately broadcast by the radio stations of 17 countries, followed by numerous broadcasts and live performances. Even recently, two ensembles from Holland and Belgium included it in their concerts. So, it is a pleasant feeling for a composer to see that your work, even after almost 40 years, is still attracting somebody.

You had quite a lot of success in Europe with CDs and performances of your works after the UNESCO award, including in France, Germany, Austria, Sweden, Italy, and Spain, as well as in Australia and the United States. Wasn't it also around that time that you were invited to Florida State University as a composer in the FSU Biennial Festival of New Music?
Yes, that's right. Then I was asked to teach there, originally for one semester, and that was extended by another year. After that, the mutual satisfaction was so intense, I was offered a permanent position as a full professor, which I have been holding since 1992.

How would you describe your music, your influences? Do you use any particular composition system?
Even though I have never used any strict system, my first legitimate opuses were influenced by the aesthetics of the Second Viennese School, and later by Polish aleatorism of the 1960s. Yet, the seed of tonal music, coming from the heritage of ages and represented by some equally strong streams of the 20th-century music, was still in me. To connect and even unify both of these traditional "enemies" was a challenging but very attractive goal. If you look at the progression of my music over the last decades, you might notice the increase of tonal rooting, melodic invention, and focus on formal architecture of the work; it means in the final effect more emotionality, lyricism, and clarity of communication.

I'd like to hear more about your specific composition process and how your ideas develop. For instance, some composers have

commented that the process of creating a piece of music is somewhat mystical or at least indescribable. Are you one of them?

What happens in any human brain is always quite mystical. I like the first stages of working on the piece, before it comes to technical elaboration. This phase is more abstract and has to be very creative. It's like trying to catch and embrace a balloon flying in the air—seeing the contours, contrasts, and shapes, which are still more independent of any particular pitches, harmonies, or instrumental colors. This I can do anywhere where there is a silence. Then I go to my piano and "translate" this image into a fully musical language. It is obvious that some elements are continuously changing in this process, but the major idea remains.

Is the process for writing each piece different or do you generally follow a similar approach to each new composition?

I would say that I use a combined approach. Over the years, I have developed my own style, which is characterized by certain choices of pitches, intervals, harmonies, rhythms, and instrumental or vocal colors. This remains general for various compositions. On the other side, each piece is unique. The context of its form differs from other works. In each work there is a particular idea, inspiration, and a specific stylistic element or setting. It determines the procedure of composing. Moreover, I write a lot of vocal music too. I believe that this area requires a very different approach than we can apply to any instrumental music. There is a presence of poetry, the verbal meanings, the structure, idiom, and grammar of a particular language, and, last but not least, we have to respect a very special medium—human voice.

Many of your pieces have been inspired by—or at least reference—literature, such as works by Rainer Maria Rilke,[3] Boris Pasternak,[4] and Franz Kafka.[5] What are the connections that you see between the written word and music that move you to compose music with words in mind?

I have always read and liked poetry as a kind of "parallel" imagery to music. And it always has been exciting for me to see how the poem as an autonomous creation vanishes, being absorbed by music in the process of composition setting, yet at the same time gains its "second life" when interpreted and emphasized by music. I always feel this "semiotic curiosity" and an active engagement in this transformation, no matter if I am setting a text in Czech, Latin, German, or English.

This might be seen as a continuation of the tradition of the composer as an intellectual. Do you think that young composers still feel this connection, or is that missing from much of modern art music?

Some do, some don't. Generally, the culture of reading is diminishing. And it is a pity. Good literature and poetry can give us a lot of emotional and intellectual satisfaction and help us to better understand ourselves. And even though the intuitive procedures are an important part of any creative activity, the broader educational and emotional basis of an artist, his or her knowledge and overall experience, certainly influence the quality of the ultimate artistic output and the contents of its message.

Do you have a composing routine that you follow, such as working at a particular time each day?

I like composing in the morning with my fresh brain. But I also write a lot of music in the nights when my concentration might be deeper. As an individual who teaches full time and also organizes musical events, and, of course, as a normal human being who cannot escape the practicalities of our lives, I just have to be very pragmatic in this matter. Simply, I compose whenever it's possible.

I think people who aren't musicians don't realize that many composers do a lot of creative work throughout the day, not just when they are in front of a piano or computer. Is this true for you?

No doubt about that. We carry our work-in-progress in ourselves during the entire process of working on it. Of course, the composer has to interrupt this process many times for different reasons, and then come back. I think this is one of the most difficult aspects of composing. That's why we try not to "forget it," not to lose a connection to that material we already have. Moreover, the composition process goes through various phases. Some are more abstract, some more elaborative, which requires different levels and character of concentration. In a way, the work is growing and maturing in us at least during the parts of our days (and nights) when we can enjoy silence. Of course, it doesn't happen when we are dealing with other music, teaching, or fully concentrating on something else. Then, at least I believe, this process continues to some extent even during our sleep through the subconscious processes.

How do deadlines affect your composition process?

Oh, very positively. A deadline is an ultimate inspiration.

Do you work with music technology programs such as notation or sampled instruments in your creative process?

Concerning sound samples, I am using them when I work in the electronic studio. It is rather rare, but some of my works contain an electronic component. For example, when I was working on my *Sinfonietta No.3, Gong*, I had the pre-recorded samples of choral sound in various modifications, and sounds of many gongs selected from digital sonic libraries. All of this was manipulated in the electronic studio according to my musical ideas and contexts with the live performers on the stage, in order to get an electronic component reproduced in the hall through a 5.1 surround sound system. With the notation programs, I am a little spoiled because my publisher is doing the computer typesetting for me. [Laughs]

I also believe that in the composition process there is a warmer relation between our brain and the hand writing music than any keyboard can offer. I like sketching not only the pitches on the staves but also using some graphic representation of the emerging ideas, sometimes very unconventional. I can't imagine finding immediately an adequate graphic language on the computer. Of course, with the finalization of the work it is different. Programs like Sibelius and Finale are very useful, reaching an admirable clarity and overall perfection of notation.

With the Internet we can now instantly send our music, ideas, audio files, et cetera, anywhere in the world. Is there really a center of music anymore? Or has technology made it unnecessary for a composer to live in Paris, New York—or Prague—in order to have a successful career?

It is true that the Internet has changed the world. We definitely live in a more cosmopolitan and universal society now. It means that the "club" of the people who need our music is not any more traditionally located at a few places but goes more widely across the borders of the countries and ethnic characters. I feel this is a distinctly positive feature of technology. A professionally produced and distributed CD still has an important role in the contemporary culture, but uncontrolled access to music through the Internet is already a reality, which we should adjust to.

Do you see some major shifts in contemporary music that might develop into more fundamental changes of artistic communication in the future?

Yes, indeed. For example, some forms of contemporary music tend to expand beyond the function of concert halls. The traditional setting of the stage and the audience might be insufficient, especially for multi-media

<blockquote>

</blockquote>

works and productions. The musical sphere is responding to the amazing technologies offered in our time. It gives an enormous stimulation for new types of artistic invention, of which we might be standing right at the beginning now.

Do you think talent alone is enough to allow a composer to gain recognition or are there other factors that are just as important?
In a sphere as sophisticated as music composition, there are multiple factors involved. Talent is part of that, but also an academic knowledge and professional experience, combined with general orientation in the technical and communicational phenomena of our current world. All these components should work together in the formation of a strong artistic personality of a composer. In addition, the individual communication skills and collaborative potentials in the processes such as performances, recording, and promotion are very important. And, of course, a little bit of luck as well. [Laughs]

It concerns some composer-educators that students no longer seem to put as much emphasis on learning the basics, like ear training and orchestration, because they are relying on instant computer playback, which can be unrealistic and not idiomatic. Is this a valid concern?
My students are selected intelligent individuals. They know what they have to do in order to develop their compositional skills and through this progress broaden their creative possibilities. It's true that the technological possibilities are getting more and more sophisticated, and thus more and more tempting. Yet, in the arts, one idea should be always clear: What is a job for a human and what is a job for (even the most sophisticated) machine?

You devote a lot of your time and energy to teaching young composers. In addition to your FSU professorship, you also lead the CASMI program in Prague, which has a strong international reputation.
CASMI (the Czech-American Summer Music Institute) is an international event that I have founded, organized, and taught 17 times during the last almost two decades. Students from five continents have attended this program, which includes master classes, individual lessons, and public performances of the participants' works. The majority of them come from universities in the United States. Students are immersed in European history and culture and move closer to their professional goals in a very friendly, creative, and inspiring atmosphere. We all love it.

How do you manage to balance your creative time between composing and teaching? It sounds like quite a dilemma.

You are right, it is a dilemma. Sometimes, I am pushed to the wall with the deadlines, but sometimes I can decide on it more freely. I have to say that I really like teaching very much. The permanent contact with younger, capable people is a very important source of my own energy. Students are my blessing.

Do you find that young people today are motivated enough to devote themselves to becoming professional composers? It's quite a commitment.

From my perspective, yes. I am always surprised how many young people want to become composers. All of us know that it is, euphemistically expressed, not the most practical decision. And still, something is so attractive there. I guess, it is the primarily creative character of this profession: to do something from nothing, to create a beauty of music from silence, and the score of the work from a blank page. The level of self-realization and emotional sharing is, through this activity, incredible. By composition, we can really become better people, better humans.

SELECTED WORKS OF LADISLAV KUBÍK

Flashes of Light (2013–2014), Concerto for Two Solo Trumpets, Four Pianos, Trumpet Ensemble, and Percussion

Concerto No.3 (2010), Piano, Orchestra, and Electronics (Dedicated to the memory of Bohuslav Martinů)

Sinfonietta No. 3, Gong (2008), Solo Mezzo-Soprano, Mixed Choir, Orchestra, and Electronics (Based on the poetry of Rainer Maria Rilke)

Songs of Zhivago (2006), Tenor and Orchestra (Tenor and Piano) (Based on the poetry of Boris Pasternak)

Trio for Clarinet, Cello, and Piano: Metamorphoses (2004)

Sinfonietta No. 2, Jacob's Well (1999), Large Orchestra

Sinfonietta No. 1 (1999), for Nineteen Instruments

Triptych (1996) (Based on Texts by Franz Kafka)

1. *The Way*, Contratenor and Five Instruments
2. *The River in Spring*, Mezzo-Soprano and Percussion
3. *In Night*, Baritone and Seven Instruments

Concerto Grosso (1987), Violin, Piano, Percussion, and String Orchestra

String Quartet (1981)

Concerto for Violin and Orchestra (1980)
Concerto No. 1 for Piano and Orchestra (1974)

▶ To learn more about Ladislav Kubík and his music, including audio excerpts from his *Concerto No. 3, Sinfonietta No. 1*, and *Sinfonietta No. 3, Gong*, visit www.oup.com/us/compositioninthedigitalworld.

NOTES
1. The Warsaw Autumn Festival was founded in 1956 and presents new music from Poland and around the world.
2. UNESCO (United Nations Educational, Scientific and Cultural Organization) promotes international collaboration through education, science, and culture.
3. Rainer Maria Rilke (1875–1926) was a Bohemian-Austrian existentialist poet and novelist.
4. Boris Pasternak (1890–1960) was a Russian poet and novelist and the author of *Doctor Zhivago*, for which he received the Nobel Prize in Literature in 1958.
5. Franz Kafka (1883–1924) was born in Prague and was a tremendously influential existentialist novelist.

Chen Yi

Photo Credit: Jim Hair

I think the combination of Chinese music and Western music is really fruitful; you can hear the rich colors, you can see the whole picture is moving into a flourishing stage right now.

Prolific composer Chen Yi (b. China, 1953) is an extremely active educator, promoter of new music, and advocate of young composers in the United States and China. I first met her at the Florida State University School of Music when she was attending a concert of new works by student composers. After the concert, she spent a generous amount of time commenting on the pieces that had been performed, cheerfully offering her insights and suggestions with the awestruck composition students gathered to meet her after the concert.

Chen was the first woman in China to receive a master's degree in composition and she has garnered many awards since, including a Grammy Award, the ASCAP Concert Music Award, and the Ives Living Award from the American Academy of Arts and Sciences; she also was a Pulitzer Prize finalist for *Si Ji (Four Seasons)* in 2006.

For this interview, she spoke to me from her home in Kansas City, where she lives with her husband, Pulitzer Prize–winning composer Zhou Long (they are both professors of composition at the University of Missouri-Kansas City Conservatory of Music and Dance).

All of my conversations with Chen were extremely cordial and relaxed, but her laid-back attitude does not extend to her music. Her astonishing array of compositions and powerful musical voice point to a fiercely determined, uncompromising, and sharply focused artistic ethic. Her music is filled with emotion—vibrant, colorful, and expertly crafted.

Like many Chinese American composers of her generation, her story is full of hair-raising tales of struggle and survival through the years of the Cultural Revolution. Against that background, her ultimate artistic triumph upon joining the American creative community is both deeply moving and inspirational.

You've just returned from a trip to Asia. How did that go?
The trip was really extensive, very busy. I am a visiting Distinguished Professor at the Tianjin Conservatory of Music. Tianjin is a city about 90 miles from Beijing. I have a three-year contract with them: I spend two months per year there teaching, giving lectures, and helping them plan for their upcoming music festival. I also participate in various departmental academic business matters and teach master classes. While I was there this year, a full orchestral piece of mine was performed by the Conservatory Symphony, and they were excellent. I also attended the Beijing Modern Music Festival, where one of my choral works was presented. I am on the advisory committee for that festival and advise on programming, so I have introduced American performing groups and composers to the festival. I've been doing this annually for about 10 years. On this trip, I also visited the Sichuan Conservatory of Music, which is in Cheng Du in South West China. They have two campuses and over 10,000 students! This conservatory is very good. Their composition department is very strong, and they're very good at promoting new works.

That sounds like an exciting but exhausting itinerary. Your husband [Zhou Long[1]] is also a very distinguished composer. Was he on this trip with you?

Yes. In fact, I attended the premiere of my husband's new piece, *Beijing Rhyme,* which was performed by the Beijing Symphony Orchestra. They commissioned this four-movement symphony, which premiered in June [2013] and is scheduled to go on tour in Europe this fall. The symphony is based on scenes of traditional Beijing—folklore, landscapes, that kind of thing.

After that, we went to Thailand, for the Thailand International Composition Festival, held at the Mahidol University College of Music. My symphonic works *Momentum* and *Dragon Rhyme* were performed for the first time in Thailand at this festival [2013]. After that, I went Taiwan, to teach at the Chai Found International Composition Workshop. At least 15 new chamber works by young composers were premiered in this workshop by the Chinese instrumental ensemble.

Do you see many contemporary Western composers showing an interest in learning to write for Chinese instruments?
Oh, yes! In fact, there were composers attending [the workshop in Taiwan] from all over the world who wanted to learn how to write for traditional Chinese instruments. I met every single composer there, and I gave lectures, lessons, and master classes. I used to go to Taiwan very often, but until this year's conference I had not been back for many years. You can really see the growth; they've made very good progress among the next generation. I also found this progress to be the same in mainland China, after the open policy began. Over the last 10 years, people in China have made great strides with open minds and the exchange of ideas. There has been a great improvement in modern techniques learned from Western new music. I think the combination of Chinese music and Western music is really fruitful; you can hear the rich colors, you can see the whole picture is moving into a flourishing stage right now.

How would you compare the music schools, the students, and the musicians in the United States to those in China? Are they very similar or are there big differences?
The differences are becoming less and less. Many Chinese students are coming to the States to study, and I urge many of my American students to broaden their minds culturally. I've been teaching a university course for more than 10 years at UMKC Conservatory [the University of Missouri-Kansas City Conservatory of Music and Dance] that covers an introduction to non-Western culture for our undergraduate students. I also have a class for graduate students to write for traditional Chinese instruments and for mixed instrumentation of Chinese and

Western instruments. It's been a very good experience because many of my American students are learning how to write, how to think, how to use their imaginations in their own compositions.

So this is a cultural exchange of sorts. Do American students also attend the Asian workshop?
Yes, some American students attend the workshops in Asian countries. In recent years, American students have accompanied me to Beijing, Thailand, Taiwan, and other festivals around the world as well. So I think this cultural exchange is a very promising improvement. Americans always have an open mind. It has been part of the culture here for years and years, a part of who we are. We need to do more of this, we shouldn't hold back. We want to continue to exchange ideas with other cultures as situations around the world change and other societies begin to develop broader minds.

Many of your pieces are available on the Internet. I believe many young American composers these days use the Internet to discover music that they might not otherwise be exposed to. Do student composers in China also use the Internet in a similar way?
Yes, it's about the same. But for Chinese students, they cannot go to YouTube.[2] Instead; they can use similar Chinese Internet services like Youku, Tudou, or Baidu. I do encourage my students to learn from the Internet because that is a huge resource, and they can get this information for free. However, I also buy a lot of DVDs to show my American students because among Internet postings I have to spend a long time selecting the best ones, those that are educational and authentic. Just because a video is posted on the Internet does not necessarily mean it is a good source for learning. So I take a long time to select the right ones to use as references in my classes. This can be very effective in teaching students quickly and intensively; otherwise it would take hundreds of hours searching the Internet for worthwhile content.

Many composition students in the United States use computers to write their music, both to compose and to notate. Is this also true of students in China?
It depends on the composition departments at the various conservatories in China. Some teachers encourage students to start learning the computer programs right away. In the past eight years, the technique of using the computer with musical composition and notation has improved dramatically. It has risen from being absolutely amateur

to professional-publication quality. I'm happy to see that musical publication has been flourishing and that composers in China are publishing their music professionally. This includes new pieces as well as older pieces that are being re-notated, extending the repertoire of instrumental performance. Of course, if you don't have the background knowledge of basic and fundamental notation rules, you cannot provide a high level of publication. But in general, the whole country has started to deal with computers extensively. My students who came from China 10 years ago had to start learning musical computer programs as beginners. But the ones who come now are very much at a professional stage when they arrive to study with me. Some of them are winning international competitions, and their scores are very high quality.

Some composers and educators have told me that while they believe the computer is wonderful, they are very concerned that students are not learning the fundamentals. Instead, some students rely on computer playback, sometimes unrealistically. In some cases actual acoustic instruments are not physically capable of playing what is composed on the computer. Do you find that some of your students are relying too much on the sounds of the computer instead of developing their ear and fundamental musical skills?
I have several students who have this problem. They play back their compositions from their computer, and some of what they write is playable only by their computer program. I have only a few students like that though. I push them to fix this, and 90 percent of them have already corrected these mistakes. A couple of my students are still struggling with this problem because they are so used to the system of using their computers in this way, having done this since they were young. In our conservatory program we have about 60 students. We have many programs to encourage students to attend orchestra readings, band readings, and chamber music. We also have chamber music concerts hosted by students in which they find their own players. So they can find out what the music they have written sounds like in a live setting. We also have some programs led by students to hook up instrumental studios volunteering for our composers. For example, one semester we might focus on two instruments, say, flute and tuba. Then our student leaders can hook up the performers and the composers one-on-one, and at the end of the semester we will premiere those works after their collaborations. The performers need new works to premiere in their recitals, and our composers need to learn the basic techniques of writing for each of the instruments. Of course, in the instrumentation and orchestration classes, we also invite performers

to do demos of their instruments for our student composers, so that helps as well.

You travel a great deal, and you are so busy with your concerts and teaching, how do you find time to compose? It must take great discipline.

I now take commissions about two years ahead of time. I use these two years to conceive ideas, to generate ideas, imaginations for those commissions. I do this gradually in my mind until I can find time to sit down for one or two weeks in a concentrated period to focus those ideas and write them down. Then it goes quickly. This is the way I do my composition.

You don't keep notebooks or sketches, all of the composing takes place in your head?

For some pieces, I have to take a long time to just think about a new piece I am composing, like a whole month. When I am on vacation I'll be very quiet; I don't make plans to go anywhere. During winter vacation when everyone goes to New Year's celebrations, to parties, I will instead hide in my room in order to compose. It is always the cruelest time, a very hungry time. It's in times like these when I have composed my biggest works. Now, many of my holidays are occupied by visiting programs, and with more and more Chinese students coming to the States, we have to host many dinners for these homeless students [Laughs], so now I have to figure out how to make time for my composing. Once in a while, I will be very tired and I cannot open my eyes, but I still have to meet a deadline, so I have to work anyway. That's why I have to conceive, connect ideas, and get inspiration ahead of time. That way, when I have time to sit down and write it out, I already have the ideas. I had to do this recently with a piano solo piece. I worked on it for quite a while; now it is in its final form, but it took me over a month to get there.

At one point, I did not have to teach for three years, and so I was able to produce three big works.

Was that when you won the Charles Ives Living Award from the American Academy of Arts and Letters?

Yes, that's right.

That's a wonderful honor, and it also gave you time to be a full-time composer during that time from 2001 through 2004, isn't that right?

Exactly. All of my time was dedicated to composition. I only did some visiting teaching and some workshops, but not full-time teaching. It made a huge difference.

Your spouse, Zhou Long, is also a very successful composer. What's that like to have a partner who works in the same field? My wife is an artist and I am a musician, so we have our own worlds [Both laugh], but you and your husband are both composers; is that difficult at times?

Well, I certainly think it's good for me. First of all, my husband is really a great supporter of my composition. When I complete a work, I show it to him first. Sometimes, he is not satisfied, and he will say, "This structure is not ideal," or "This section needs to be longer," those kinds of comments. Sometimes he has suggestions on my concepts, sometimes on my technique. It's very helpful for me to have his input. For many years we've given help to each other. I also comment on whatever he writes. I'm so happy to see that he has won the Pulitzer Prize for his opera *Madame White Snake*. He is the kind of a person who has a tremendous focus. When he composes, he ignores everything else. He spent a full year composing that opera. When he finished, he received very good reviews from critics, from audiences, and from musicians as well. That piece has been performed again and again, not always in the opera version, but in a concert version, because it would cost so much to have the stage setting for every performance.

You must be very proud of him.

I am, but I must say, that he is also a good cook. [Both laugh]

He cooks at home. I work too much at school, full time—more than full time—not only composition classes but also arts-exchange projects, administrative duties, and many different programs. So, my husband helps me a lot. He not only cooks every meal, he also drives me. I usually walk to school, which is not too far away, but if we go to meetings or concerts he will drive me.

So he is a good friend then. What are you working on now that is new?

I've just completed a piano solo piece for pianist Susan Chan at Portland State University,[3] I'm working on a violin concerto commissioned by Kennesaw State University in Georgia for violinist Helen Kim, and I'm working on a saxophone piece for the Prism Quartet.[4] I also have to complete—in a hurry—a new work for guitarist Xuefei Yang[5] to be performed at Wigmore Hall in London. So, right now, that is my plan for the rest of this year.

You're very busy.
That's right. In fact, this week I am hiding at home so that I can compose [Laughs], but I also have to host a couple of new students who have shown up early for orientation at school.

Are there wonderful composers out there who will remain obscure because they may not promote themselves well, or they have bad luck, or they just don't have the opportunity to have their music performed?
Some composers who teach become very busy mentoring and promoting their own students. I'm thinking of one composer I know who teaches in a university. He told me that just the time he takes to write recommendations for his students could eat up half of his life. Sometimes it feels as though the students' deadlines are more important than your own deadlines, if you are truly a dedicated teacher. This can greatly affect one's efforts to promote one's own music. Still, it's important for composers to have their works collected, performed, and recorded. The most important thing, though, is to write great music . . . for the next generation and for the culture in general. If our music is performed and audiences can hear what we are doing, that is good enough for us as composers. I don't expect to ever write commercial music, because life is too short to do all of these things.

Should student composers be thinking about ways to promote themselves and their music?
Yes, absolutely. I teach my students to start promoting themselves when they are young. When they have good work in hand, they need to seek their professional life, or I should say, their career. It's very important to achieve as much recognition as possible; that's why I push them hard. I think that artists need to be heard. The Internet is wonderful for doing this; I don't know of any more aggressive way of promoting yourself. You can pay for services, companies, or individuals to promote your work, though, and I'm not against that either. Some of my very successful students have hired agents. But in the end, if the quality is there in your music and people hear it, they will honor you. If you do good work, and you continue to do good work, you will be recognized, eventually.

You've also written for symphonic band. I'm thinking of your pieces *Wind* and *Suite from China West*. Is it a very different process for you to write for symphonic band as opposed to orchestra?

I'm a violinist, so what I am really good at is writing for strings. The band works don't use strings. [Laughs]

Right, so is writing for an ensemble without strings a special challenge for you?

We are professional composers so we don't limit ourselves to particular sections of instrumentation. For example, if I write for saxophone quartet, I am dealing with saxophones, I don't deal with strings. If I write for band, I also don't deal with strings. I don't consider it a loss, just a special instrumentation that I am writing for. So I don't think that it's a problem or a strange thing for me to do. When I got those commissions from bands, I just considered the specific instrumentation I was asked to write for. In recent years, the band repertoire has been expanded quite a bit with many different styles of music. I've written a lot of band works, including some transcriptions of my symphonic works, and I have adapted some of my chamber works for band. This is a new field for me to explore.

Speaking of instrumentation, do you consider orchestration to be a part of composition or a separate discipline? How do you approach your orchestration?

Orchestration is a part of composition; I never separate them. When I teach my orchestration course annually, I'm teaching composition; I'm just focusing more on the orchestration technique or concepts of constructing form in terms of orchestration. Orchestration is an important part of composition; it really defines the image and the whole concept of a piece. If the structure of a piece is planned well, with an orchestration plan, the piece will be an organic whole. If you don't have the orchestration skillfully planned and written, then the piece will be in parts and not have a logical structure. That's why I always consider orchestration technique to be an important part of composition. However, our teaching of orchestration needs to be more flexible these days. The traditional way of teaching orchestration is not going to prepare our students for the time when they leave school and need to be able to write with balance and flexibility for a great number of instrumental combinations.

Are there special challenges that you face when you write for traditional Chinese instruments in conjunction with a traditional Western orchestra?

If you use specific instruments that are nonstandard in the setting of Western orchestral instrumentation, you have to learn those instruments completely: the playing skills and the musical style. Traditional Chinese instruments use different temperaments, and they use different techniques, that you may not see in your typical Western instrumentation. So once you learn both worlds very well, you can combine them naturally. If you have learned one side very well, but for the other side you just know how to indicate the pitches, it doesn't work. The two instrumental groups will not combine naturally. So, my way is to learn both cultures as deeply as possible. I want to know the language of each . . . the gestures, the expressions. I incorporate Chinese instrumental techniques and styles into my writing for Western instruments, and I also borrow Western performance techniques when I write for Chinese instruments. I feel that this expands the palette for each. So that is the experience that we have earned during the past 20 years.

For young composers—for *any* composer—it can sometimes be so difficult to continue composing and to keep moving forward as an artist. Do you have any advice, especially for student composers, as far as sticking to their art and believing in themselves?
I advise younger composers to become a part of the musical community around them. If you are not willing to become a part of that community and participate, you are not going to have your works produced. Participating will have an impact on you and stimulate ideas in your own creations. If you don't have a love for nature, the community, and people, you are not going to be creative.

Some composers have commented that they find the process of composition mysterious or mystical, that they're not sure where some of their inspirations actually come from. Do those comments make sense to you? Is composition strictly an intellectual process, or is there some spiritual element at work when you are creating your music?
[Laughs] I understand. Some people do have these feelings, because they may have a need to get into a specific mood in order to compose. That is understandable, but it is not how it works for me. In my case, I am always very clear. Even though sometimes I may not know the next texture, still, I am clear with my imagination, in my concept. I always get into the mood of the specific poem, or scene, or idea that inspires my composition. But I always know where I'm going.

SELECTED WORKS OF CHEN YI

> *Fountains of KC* (2011), Orchestra
> *Dragon Rhyme* (2010), Symphonic Band

From the Path of Beauty (2008), Choir and String Quartet
Suite from China West (2007), Symphonic Band
Si Ji (2005), Orchestra
Happy Rain on a Spring Night (2004), Mixed Quintet
Symphony No. 3 (2004), Orchestra
Chinese Folk Dance Suite (2001), Violin and Orchestra
Ning (2001), Violin, Cello, and Pipa [15 min.]
Chinese Poems (1999), Children's Choir
Sound of the Five (1998), Cello and String Quartet
Fiddle Suite (1997), Huqin and String Orchestra

▶ To learn more about Chen Yi and her music, visit
www.oup.com/us/compositioninthedigitalworld.

NOTES

1. Zhou Long is a Chinese American composer and is the spouse of Chen Yi. He was awarded the Pulitzer Prize for music in 2011 for his opera *Madame White Snake*.
2. Chinese authorities blocked access to YouTube and other sites. There are officially sanctioned Chinese equivalents of Internet sites such as Amazon (Dangdang), eBay (Taobao), and Wikipedia (Hudong). In 2013, China had one of the world's largest online populations, with over 600 million Internet users.
3. Pianist Susan Chan commissioned several composers to write pieces for a performance at Portland State University in the fall of 2013. The concert featured music from several Chinese American composers, including the world premiere of Chen Yi's *Northern Scenes* for solo piano.
4. The Prism Quartet was formed in 1997 and plays new music for saxophone quartet by both classical and jazz composers.
5. The piece *Shuo Chang*, for solo guitar, was commissioned by Wigmore Hall for guitarist Xuefei Yang. The world premiere was in the fall of 2013.

Jose Bevia

Sometimes you are not composing with your brain when you write from the piano; you're composing with your fingers, and that's terrible. . . for me, especially with the great computer tools we have now, it's easy to move across the piano and capture that. Yes, it can be an advantage to play the piano, but you need to be very careful and really think, and not just let your fingers "compose."

Reflecting an historic tradition that has lost prevalence among modern composers, Jose Bevia (b. Spain, 1972) lives within that time-honored tradition of the composer who often performs his own music, as well as that of others. An accomplished pianist, Bevia already has a successful career as a teacher and jazz performer, but in recent years critical attention to his classical works for orchestral and chamber groups has begun to snowball as his work is being widely performed in Europe, the United States, and Asia.

Chafing at what he found to be a restrictive social structure in his native country, Bevia first came to the United States to study jazz at Boston's Berklee College of Music, where he discovered a passion for composition in addition to performance. Completing his education at Florida State University under the guidance of internationally recognized Czech composer Ladislav Kubík, Bevia's accolades include the Lee Ettelson Composer's Award, the International Music Prize for Excellence in Composition, and the BMI Foundation Charlie Parker Composition Prize.

I got to know Bevia well several years ago, while sharing both working and living space with him during an intensive composition program in Prague. His soft-spoken but passionate nature and his deep commitment to his craft are personified in his music, which is sonically rich, filled with emotion, and skillfully crafted.

Bevia's life is dedicated entirely to the art of creating new music, in all its facets, through teaching, performing, and composing. With a recently successful Kickstarter campaign to record his next orchestral work, Bevia in many ways represents an iconic example of the contemporary working musician/composer.

What is the setup that you use when you compose? Do you work at the piano with pencil and paper when you work, or do you use a computer?

I use both at the same time; I have a piano and then close by I have a desktop computer connected to a digital piano. I'll start to sketch on the piano, with pencil, but when I have a substantial amount of music done, I'll transfer it to the computer. Once I start to use the computer, I may go back to the piano to check things and do a little more sketching, but most often once I go to the computer, that's it; I usually don't leave.

Quite a few composers are pianists, and you're an excellent one. It's something of a tradition for composers to also play the piano. Do you think your keyboard skills give you an advantage as a composer?

It can be an advantage, but sometimes it can also be a disadvantage. Sometimes you are not composing with your brain when you write from the piano; you're composing with your fingers, and that's terrible. I used to do that, because it's very easy to move across the keyboard and write some virtuosic stuff that is not necessarily good music. I'm quite skilled at the piano, because that was my first interest. I didn't start composing until my early 20s, while I began playing the piano very early on, at around five or six. So for me, especially with the great computer tools we have now, it's easy to move across the piano and capture that. Yes, it can be an advantage to play the piano, but you need to be very careful and really think, and not just let your fingers "compose."

When you're writing for an orchestra, do you send the conductor a written score or do you ever provide a MIDI demo version for rehearsals and such?
It depends on what the conductor wants. Some conductors I've worked for want to have a MIDI recording. Most of them don't have a lot of time to learn the score so it helps them to have a MIDI recording to refer to. For MIDI demo recordings though, I don't use Sibelius [computer music notation program]. Instead, I'll usually transfer the information from Sibelius to Logic,[1] and work from there.

So you create the score using the Sibelius notation program, then you export a MIDI file, and render it in Logic.
Right. And it works great. Of course, we all wonder when we are going to finally have a program that does both functions really well. Actually, I've heard something like that is being worked on right now and that it might be available within the year.

Ah. More money to spend.
Hah! Yes, it never ends. [Both laugh]

If you were to write a piece using only a piano and pencil and paper versus writing the same piece using only the computer, do you think the end results would be the same or would there be a difference?
I believe they would be absolutely different. Using the computer you can listen to all of your different lines at the same time, even if *is* just a MIDI recording. I think you can get a much better idea of what's going on. Even though I'm skilled at the piano, when you're composing orchestral music, you can't necessarily play everything at once. At least for me, it helps tremendously to have the computer as another tool.

In addition to being a composer and a pianist, you're a college music professor. Do your students use computers to compose, and if so, is that a positive thing?
They do use computers, and I think it does help them to an extent. But, at the same time, it can be kind of dangerous. Some students think that they

can create music without being able to read music or understand theory, because its so easy with programs like Logic.

So you feel some students don't necessarily understand how to write idiomatically for various traditional instruments?
Yes, exactly; it takes time to really know the instruments. A lot of our students come with a good set of technology skills—they are familiar with computers. But while some of them don't necessarily think that being able to read music is important, we insist that they learn. I see technology as a tool that helps me successfully realize my ideas, but I couldn't compose if I didn't have all the music knowledge I've gained from studying over the years.

Do you have a set time that you like to write? I know you teach a lot, do you set aside time to write, or do you just compose whenever you can find time?
I do what I can during the year because of my teaching obligations. During the summer it's different because the teaching load is smaller; then I can manage five or six full days of composing each week. I usually wake up in the morning, exercise, then I eat lunch and spend the whole rest of the day composing. I find that schedule to be very important, because for me composing is about doing it regularly. I don't have to wait for a special moment to be inspired. Of course, those moments happen, but it's like any other job; you have to do it every day, and I love that. In the winter, when I have to stop and teach for four days, I find it extremely difficult to go back to composing, because I kind of forget what I was doing the previous weekend, and it can be frustrating. Summer is much better because of the freedom to do it regularly, every day.

You've said you usually work on one piece at a time. Why is that?
It's a choice. When I start a piece, I get obsessed with it. I don't like to leave it in the middle and have to go back later; I just like to start the piece, spend whatever time it takes me—six months, a year, two years—and then finish the piece. I did work on a couple of pieces at the same time at one point because of a deadline, but I don't usually do that.

When you present a new piece to a player, how do you work with the performer? Do you just give them the score and say good luck or work closely with them?
I think dialogue, that give and take, is extremely important. I actually like to talk to the performers, and I really appreciate their feedback, because they are the experts on their instruments. As composers, we study all of

these instruments, but they have spent their whole lives learning these instruments, so it's very important to listen to their comments. I tell them, "Listen, this is a first draft. Go over it, play it, and if you have any suggestions, just let me know; I have no problem with that." And I find it is actually a very important part of the creative process; their feedback can add a lot to a piece. Performers bring a lot to the table.

Speaking of the creative process, do you have a system that you use when you are writing? Some composers work inside of a very strict system, while some don't have any system at all. Do you start a piece by thinking, this is going to be an octatonic piece, or section, or 12-tone, or blues, or do you let the piece lead you where it may?
I usually try to find a set of pitches first that make sense to me, and then I try to derive from those pitches the harmonic material, the melodic material. That to me is part of the sketching process. I studied with a great teacher [Ladislav Kubík], who taught me so much about form, and how to write an extended piece by using musical drawings. I spend a lot of time thinking about the form, and how the piece will develop and how and where I am going to have climaxes, where I will have my valleys. Of course this is a kind of a pre-compositional stage where I might establish my macro musical shapes, but these can change during the creative process. I can also be quite spontaneous; I sometimes use my improvisatorial skills to compose. I may improvise on the piano, record it, transcribe it, and then start working from there.

One very important thing, and I think this is crucial: I always try to use my ears. I believe I have pretty good ears, which I use a lot to guide me. I don't like to compose by using a mathematical process; I am not that type of composer. I just use my ears and let them take me wherever they will take me.

For me, one of the most important and challenging aspects of composing is to establish an effective form. Sometimes it falls into place, but sometimes I get really lost and it takes a lot of hard work to get it untangled. If I think, this piece is just not making very much sense, I can almost always look back and see that the logic of the form is not in place, so the "story" I am telling doesn't build and reveal itself properly. Can the computer help you with that?
I don't think the computer helps me with form, but maybe it does for some people. I create musical drawings of the form on paper: shapes that show the textures and the energy levels of the music. It helps me define the different textures throughout the piece, and where there is a climax in

the piece, or a valley. I also include a lot of timing information in those pictures—for instance, this section that is going to be about three minutes with this kind of music. These pictures are an effective way of creating a diagram of the whole piece.

Speaking of technology, how important is the Internet to your music? When you lived in Spain was it harder to find out about other composers or to do research, than it is now [in this country] with the Internet?
It makes a huge difference. I moved to the United States in 2000, but before that I didn't have access to the Internet, so I only started using the Internet when I moved to this country. I don't think I could live without the Internet now. All of the composer opportunities are available online, and they are very well organized. I belong to several music associations including Chamber Music America,[2] and the College Music Society.[3] They all have a lot of useful information online for composers: competitions, lessons, and grants.

Do you feel that the Internet makes it easier for you to listen to new music that you might not otherwise hear?
Absolutely. I've got to be honest though; I don't find the process of downloading music as appealing as having a *real* CD, or even vinyl. I have to have my library of CDs at my home. Sometimes, though, if you need to find a certain piece by a composer, it's much easier to download it but, and maybe I am old fashioned, I would much rather have a copy of my own.

You're originally from Spain, and like so many composers from around the world, you decided to settle in the United States. Why is that? You come from such a rich culture.
The main thing is the opportunities that are here in the United States. Yes, there is a rich culture in Spain, a rich tradition, but I think it's much easier to find your way to do whatever you want to do here, not only because of the opportunities, but also because of the freedom. It's something we all take for granted. I found that there was a lot of social pressure against musicians [in Spain]. Plus, being in such a huge country [the United States], you find a lot of people doing what we do. That can be very helpful. I felt isolated in Spain; I was this kind of weird person, very strange, surrounded by a lot of people who didn't understand what I was doing, and I find here it is so much easier to reach other people in the same boat.

Is it difficult for you to find the time, the money, and the courage to do what you do, even when you have not *yet* received public accolades, huge awards and wide recognition of your work? How do you keep going?

It is difficult. As you say, it takes a lot of time, a lot of money, a lot of courage, but I don't see myself doing anything else. I love doing this. And whether I get the awards or not isn't relevant to me; I just want to keep composing. Of course, everyone loves to get these wonderful prizes, and I wouldn't mind, but if I don't get them, I will continue composing because that's what I love to do. I think that everyone is here on this planet for one purpose, and I think that you and I are here to compose music.

Are there talented composers the world will never hear, or do you think if someone's talented they will be recognized?

I think that fame is relative. Some people who are famous are not necessarily the greatest artists and vice versa. Actually, I am glad that I'm not famous. I really enjoy my privacy. I don't want to be one of those people who can't go out and just get a cup of coffee; I would hate that. Of course, I wouldn't mind getting to the point where I have a respected reputation in our field. I think that for us it's easier, because I don't think composers like us will be on MTV any time soon, so I guess it's a good thing that I really like my privacy! [Both laugh]

What are your plans for the future if you look out five or ten years from now?

My short-term goal is to release a second album. I just finished my second symphony and I still have to finish proofreading that piece and have to simplify a few things here and there, but essentially that piece is completed. I also have several chamber pieces that need to be recorded; those are my short-term goals. Long term I want to continue to develop and compose. I love chamber music and orchestral music, so I just want to keep writing, writing. I see myself writing several symphonies down the road, more chamber music, string quartets, trios. Also, I've quite recently become very interested in electronic music. I was mostly an acoustic composer but now, with all of this wonderful technology available, I find it very exciting to also incorporate electronic sounds in my music.

Are you referring to a finished piece completely realized on the computer, or electronic elements used in conjunction with acoustic instruments in performance?

No, a combination of both. For example, I just finished a piece for harp, percussion, and electronics, so it will be a combination of acoustic instruments and electronic sounds. I've been playing with the idea of writing just for electronic instruments, but I like to have real players playing the music. I see computers as more of an extension of acoustic music rather than as a substitute for real instruments. Even though, as I said, maybe in the future I will write some pure electronic music. I don't have any problem with that.

Do you have any advice for composers who are just getting started with their careers?
For beginning composers, yes: Work hard. Work very hard and don't stop.

I find a lot of my students get discouraged very quickly when they find out how hard it is, how much there is to learn. If you love what you are doing, you have to give your life to it, that's all. Just work hard and there will always be something for you to learn every day. Try to absorb influences from everyone. Throughout my life so far, I have met so many composers from all over the world, great composers from all different countries, different backgrounds. I've learned so much from all of them. I would say, "You will find some who will be significantly influential to you." Ladislav Kubík was one of them for me, Marcus Roberts was one of them, and I had a wonderful teacher in Spain, Jose Luis Prado. He was from Uruguay and was very influential to me. I think that it's extremely important for young composers to talk to different teachers and absorb new ideas and different kinds of music from all over the world. I love stealing ideas from everybody, jazz music, classical music. [Both laugh]

One of my favorite Stravinsky quotes is "Good composers borrow, great composers steal."
I totally agree with that, I steal from everybody, and I think you take those ideas from everybody and you reinterpret them, and you find your own voice.

How does a composer find their own musical voice?
I used to really worry about finding my voice, but I was at a seminar a while ago, with the great jazz composers and performers Jim McNeely,[4] and Stefon Harris.[5] Harris said something that changed my way of thinking about my voice: "Don't even think about finding your voice; it's already there." So, I don't think about it anymore, I just let it happen and I think it is there.

I've been obsessed with many composers over the years: Stravinsky, Ravel, most recently Lutosławski. But at the same time, I go back to Schoenberg, I go back to Ligeti or I go back to my jazz composers like Chick Corea,[6] Marcus Roberts, even Spanish folk music; that's very much in my blood. I don't think about it, but it's there. I try to find contrasting styles so as not to be influenced or sound like somebody in particular. Those influences are all part of my personal musical voice.

SELECTED WORKS OF JOSE BEVIA

> *El Puente de las Almas. . .* (2012–2013), Two Pianos
> *Noit-Alimissa* (2012–2013), Orchestra
> *Trio No. 3* (2011–2013), Piano, Violin, Cello
> *Cenizas y Fuego* (2012), Harp, Percussion, and Electronics
> *Symphony No. 2* (2010–2013), Orchestra
> *Al Final de la Oscuridad* (2010–2013), Harp, Chamber Orchestra, and Electronics
> *Swingurus* (2009), Jazz Orchestra
> *Three Enigmas* (2009),Two Pianos
> *B's Nightmare* (2008), Jazz Orchestra
> *Donde el Viento nos Lleve* (2008), Harp and Percussion
> *Abstractions* (2008), Jazz Orchestra
> *Symphony No. 1* (2007), Orchestra

▶ To learn more about Jose Bevia and his music, visit www.oup.com/us/compositioninthedigitalworld.

NOTES

1. Logic Pro is a Mac music software program that provides MIDI sequencing and digital audio workstation functions.
2. Chamber Music America is a non-profit organization founded in 1977 that supports small ensembles with a variety of programs including networking, funding, and education.
3. The College Music Society is an organization that promotes music teaching and learning through a variety of programs and activities.
4. Jim McNeely is an American pianist and composer. He has played with and conducted numerous jazz ensembles and has earned nine Grammy nominations and won a Grammy in 2008. He teaches at the Manhattan School of Music and is the Director of the BMI Jazz Composers Workshop.
5. Stefon Harris is an award-winning American jazz vibraphonist and composer.
6. Chick Corea is an American jazz pianist and composer. He has been nominated for an astonishing 59 Grammy Awards, winning 20. He has been an extremely influential musician, performing and composing in a wide range of styles including jazz, fusion, and classical music projects.

Daniel Wohl

Photo Credit: Shawn Brackbill

If you're making purely electronic music, you can live in a cabin in the woods and make your album and still have a huge impact, though I think it is harder. And I think that's why a lot of people are still in New York or other big cities—to meet and have access to many performers.

When I asked the composer David Lang who he thought were some of the most promising of young American composers, the name of Daniel Wohl (b. France, 1980) was one of the first he mentioned. Born in Paris, Wohl now lives and works in Brooklyn, a thriving 21st-century center for new art. Four of the established composers in this book were teachers of his, and he holds degrees in composition from some of the most prestigious music schools in the United States: Bard College, the University of Michigan, and the Yale School of Music.

Also active as an educator, Wohl has taught courses in composition, orchestration, and theory at Sarah Lawrence College and at Yale. His honors include grants from Meet the Composer/Commissioning Music USA, the American Composers Forum/Jerome Foundation, Composer Assistance Program (CAP), the Barlow Endowment, and MET Life Creative Connections, and awards from the Finale National Composers Competition and ASCAP's Morton Gould Young Composer Award.

Acclaimed by NPR as one of the young artists "shaping our contemporary music scene and defining what it means to be a composer in the 21st century," Wohl's compositions seamlessly blend the use of traditional instruments and all manner of digital sound creation and modification.

When I interviewed him for this book, he had just released a CD of his new music, to wide critical acclaim. I found him to be unpretentious and excited about the fact that his career is quickly gaining momentum. An archetype of his generation of composers, Wohl accepts technology as a given, both for performance and composition, and incorporates a wide variety of sounds, techniques, and styles into his works.

The famous quote (and there are several versions) attributed to Mozart when he met the young Beethoven comes to mind: "Mark that young man; he will make himself a name in the world!" Wohl seems well on his way to doing just that.

You live in New York now but you were born in Paris. How did you get from Paris to New York?
I'm a dual citizen because my father was born in the United States and I was born in France. When I was 18, I had the opportunity to study in the States. It was something that I was really excited to do, and New York was specifically a kind of dream. I think it still is for a lot of Europeans. I was lucky that I was able to do that, and I stayed after my studies.

When you were in France did you have a traditional music education? I think you play keyboards, don't you?
I started off playing classical piano when I was very young. I didn't really feel a connection to that music at that age, and I stopped playing classically when I was about nine or ten. Then my family found a piano teacher who was a brilliant improviser, which is what I was also into at the time. We had informal lessons where we would write or improvise music, and that was my musical education until I got into jazz piano when I was 16.

I also played in bands throughout high school. Then when I came to the States I studied music theory and composition more formally.

You've had some pretty impressive teachers including Martin Bresnick, David Lang, Joan Tower, Bright Sheng, Aaron Kernis, Ingram Marshall,[1] and William Bolcom. What was it like to study with them?

Until about a year ago, I was in a doctoral program at Yale, which was an amazing experience. Most of it was spent studying with David Lang. I also spent a semester with Martin and then another with Ingram and Aaron. They're all incredible composers in their own ways, and it was great to get their opinion on what I was doing. That's not something that you have an opportunity to do if you're not in a program, so I felt very lucky just to be able to talk to each of them for an hour a week. I love David's music, and I feel that I continue to be very influenced by it. I admire the way he thinks about music. It's fascinating. Every time I had a compositional issue he would find an original way of looking at it, a way that would never have occurred to me. Martin Bresnick is an amazing thinker and composer. He has such an incredible knowledge of music history and theory, and can bring it to bear on so many aspects of what you're doing and can totally change your perspective. Aaron, of course, is a musical genius and I felt that Ingram and I had a ton in common aesthetically. Joan Tower is an inspiration and an amazing lady, and definitely the composer who taught me the ins and outs of composition and inspired me to become a composer myself.

How did you become interested in, for lack of a better term, electronic music?

Electronic music is an important part of French culture—it's arguably where it started [France] and there is of course a huge electronic movement in Paris. Also, I think if you like interesting *sound*, it's impossible not to like all forms of sound. Electronic sounds or acoustic sounds, it's all interesting in terms of timbre. I feel that I can't limit myself to just playing around with acoustic sounds, but at the same time I love the warmth of acoustic instruments, so I became interested in combining both of those elements.

Your combination of acoustic and electronic sounds is often noted as a characteristic of your music. Of course you are not the first composer to do this, but you're known for being adept at effectively mixing electronic and acoustic sounds in a unique way.

That's what I have been focusing on doing for a while. I find it satisfying. You get the warmth of acoustic instruments and you also get the incredible sonic possibilities of electronic music. I also love the live performance aspect of acoustic music, where performers give a physical presence to the music: that's an aspect that you often don't get in electronic music performance. If you go to see an electronic artist, sometimes you're not exactly sure what they're doing. I'm fine with that, but some people do have a problem with not knowing how the sound is produced; as far as the audience is concerned, the performer might just be checking their e-mail. I tend to like having access to both of those worlds. More and more young composers are taking part in these new possibilities, and I think it brings music into a sphere that is really refreshing.

When I was in school, electronic music was more—and I don't mean this in a derogatory way at all—but it was more academic and very intellectualized. Over the last couple of decades there has been a huge explosion of "popular" music using electronic sounds. Now with a generation of new composers, I hear an acceptance and embracing of electronic music, especially when used in a live context with acoustic instruments.

I think when it started out there was more of an experimental approach. People were trying to find out the capabilities. The personal computer revolutionized all of that. Those synths used to take up a whole room that you would have to sign into. I think you'd have to go to Columbia University or Princeton to get access. Now we all have a computer that's far more powerful than any that they may have been using at the time. Basically, the miniaturization and democratization of technology made it possible to have many more unique perspectives—more of a layperson's outlook—and electronic sounds have become part of our everyday vocabulary. Computers have made it so simple; you only have to push a button to get complex processing. Some of the older pieces, the early experiments [in combining electronic and acoustic sounds] were really interesting and extremely well composed. But at the same time, it was a different approach to that combination; there was more separation in the dialogue of electronic and acoustic instruments. Personally, I'm trying to make that more of a hybrid than a separation. There are still people who keep these elements separated: here are the electronics and here are the acoustic sounds. They're playing in parallel but not necessarily melding into one another, but that [integration of the two] is what I'm attracted to. I usually derive a lot of the electronics from acoustic sounds, and that's probably why they fit together.

Previously, most composition students were expected to stick to the music as defined by their curriculum. If you were interested in some other type of music—whether it was African, or cosmic-jazz, or whatever—it was really not okay to talk about that, much less compose or perform it. That seems to have changed—the eclecticism of composers now is so exciting.

I did my dissertation at Yale studying works by Mario Davidovsky[2] and Kaija Saarihao,[3] but also using tracks by Lucky Dragons[4] as examples, and that was totally acceptable. Some of the examples I used were definitely not academic. It's really opened up in that way.

How do you approach the melding of electronic and acoustic instruments? Do you consider this an orchestration technique or a compositional technique, or both?

It's different for every new piece. Generally I have to find a sound that I'm interested in. If I don't have a strong interest in the timbre, then I'm not going to be able to compose. Obviously, there are also many different aspects of composition that you need to take into account besides timbre: harmony, structure, rhythm, et cetera. All of these parameters have to be as exciting as possible and be interesting in their own way. I don't think you can have a great piece of music, no matter how appealing the timbres, if the structure is falling apart. But definitely the first thing, for me, is the sound itself; if I'm not really fueled by that, then I'm not going to feel inspired. So I start with sound and then I try to find interesting ways of combining the acoustic instruments with the electronic sounds. So I guess it's sort of an orchestration technique to begin with, then all of the other parameters start falling into place.

So conceptually, you start with timbre. What about the "nuts and bolts" of composing? Do you use a laptop, do you write exclusively on the computer? Or do you sit at a keyboard? Do you have a notebook where you write things down?

I do sit at the keyboard, but that's not where I begin. To begin with, I use a music notation software program and sequencers: mainly Digital Performer, Ableton, and MAX. I'll use whatever seems to work for the particular process. I might record things, use found sounds, or use instruments and then process them. Once I find the sound that I am looking for, then I go into Sibelius [notation software] or to the keyboard and work out the harmonic and formal structure. Then I'll bring what I wrote on Sibelius back into the sequencer so I can figure out the interaction between the electronics and the notated music.

I can hear the care and craft of your process on your new CD [*Corps Exquis*]. It's had some great reviews. Steve Smith of the *New York Times* said that he loved your CD but couldn't imagine it being played live because it is so intricate. But I believe you *have* played it live, am I correct?

Yes, we have played it live. Of course, it is slightly different—there are some things you can do in the studio that you can't really do in a live context—but generally, with electronics anything is possible. The same way that an electronic artist produces sound at a performance—some of it is produced live, and some of it has been pre-recorded. When I was making that album, I didn't want it to be just a document of a live performance. I wanted it to be its own experience. When you go see a band play, the music doesn't sound exactly like the album—of course they still play the same material, but it is slightly amended to fit the live format.

I'm interested in how you put together the team that made this project possible, and how you used technology in the form of Kickstarter[5] to raise funds for your new CD. Composers have always found various ways of getting funding for their music, but this is a new approach.

New Amsterdam Records wanted to put out the album, and they were going to pay for the cost of publicizing and promoting it, and they were going to put a little money into the production, but not nearly enough to pay performers or pay for a studio. So in that situation, there are a couple of different options: First, you could get a grant to produce it, but that also means you have to work on their timeline and, of course, you may or may not get the grant. Then you can also use crowd-sourcing, or crowd-funding, options that are available out there. Kickstarter is the most famous one, but there are a couple of others that people use a lot. It worked well for me. I think we raised $12,000 in about a month. The Internet is definitely a game changer for that kind of thing; this project might not have been possible before.

Several composers have mentioned how important it is for a composer to either get their own ensemble together the way Steve Reich and Joan Tower did, or to hook up with an existing ensemble. Please talk a little bit about how you met Transit,[6] the ensemble on this CD, and how you started working together.

I met them at the Bang on a Can Summer Institute. We were in this international environment, with composers from all over the world, and we came up with the idea of starting an ensemble dedicated to bringing the music of young composers from different parts of the world to New York. I'm mostly in charge of helping curate for Transit. We choose a city, like Amsterdam, for example. We get in touch with composers, or ensembles from there to co-curate the concert, and they send some recommendations for three or four young composers that we have probably never heard of, either because they are not well known in this country or they are in the early stages of their career. Once or twice a year we bring their music to New York and perform it alongside the music of other young New York composers. That's a way of getting that dialogue going. This year Transit is going to do programs based in Stockholm and Berlin. We're currently talking with some ensembles about having the same program played over there, so we're really promoting a cultural exchange of ideas and performances. I don't feel that happens enough in new music. There are definitely sounds that are unique to particular places, certain ways of looking at music that are specific to those cities, but the music should be played everywhere. That just doesn't happen enough in new music. It is still very much, "She is an 'American' composer," or "He's a 'French' composer."

You have a unique perspective having lived in Paris as well as New York. At one time, Paris was the "center of the world" for new music, and New York was too—maybe it still is. I wonder, though, with the arrival of the Internet, with people being able to instantly hear music from anywhere in the world, is there still an artistic center at all, or has the world of contemporary classical music become more homogenized because of digital technology?
First of all, I don't think New York is necessarily *the* center, though it is *a* center. There are many important cities in terms of new music. I think the Internet is clearly changing things. It's definitely possible to be a composer living in some remote area and still make a name for yourself in new music. The issue is that, since in new music we are dealing with performers and not just recorded music, we have to have access to performers who are going to play our music. If you live anywhere outside of the big city centers, it will necessarily be harder to find enough performers. If you live in D.C., you're going to find performers, if you live in L.A., or New York, you're going to find performers, but if you don't live near some city, that becomes a challenge. Because new music depends on live people, I think it would be difficult to live in a completely remote area.

The aspect of live performance is very important for a composer.
It's very important. If you're making purely electronic music, you can live in a cabin in the woods and make your album and still have a huge impact,

though I think it is harder. And I think that's why a lot of people are still in New York or other big cities—to meet and have access to many performers.

You've also written for traditional orchestra, without electronics. An example is your piece *Helium*. Was composing that a challenge for you?

For me, it's a challenge to write music without electronics, just because that's where I find the timbres that I'm really interested in. By no means is it impossible to write exciting new music with acoustic instruments—there are people doing it very, very well, but I find it more challenging sonically. That's why most of my work includes electronics. Maybe I'll swing back around and do more acoustic music later, I don't know.

Some composers have expressed a concern that today's students may be relying too heavily on electronically created sounds rather than developing their "ear." They fear that those young composers will not be able to hear orchestration in their head or be able to hear the music by reading a score. They are concerned that some student composers don't fully grasp the idiosyncrasies of acoustic instruments because they rely too much on built-in sounds from computer programs. Do you think these are valid concerns?

They are valid concerns in the sense that there is nothing that can replace the immediacy that you get from playing or improvising at the piano. It's a very different flow. If you're being creative in the moment at the piano, I think you are accessing a different part of your brain than you use when you're composing. It's perhaps a more spontaneous part of the brain. Though you can get the same effect with a computer, the sequencer tends to access the organizational part of my brain more than the purely creative part. Also, composing with a sequencer is a much more passive experience than playing an instrument where your fingers are active in producing the sound. That's very different than passively receiving information back from speakers. On the other hand, it's also true that the medium changes the music. You're getting information in a different way, and you're processing it differently, and it is going to result in different music, which does not mean it is better or worse.

It's been suggested that if someone sits at a piano or uses pencil and paper to write a piece, that piece would sound different when completed from a version that was created on a computer. Do you agree?

I think so. Again, I don't think it would make it better or worse, but it would absolutely be different. It's interesting to think about. I've read articles about how notation software has changed composition; for instance, I don't think we would have David Lang's music without notation software. I think he talks about how his use of notation software really influenced his way of thinking about rhythm. I think that would go for Michael Gordon too.

What about the fact that I can go on the Internet and listen to your music and I don't have to pay a penny? That whole paradigm has changed the way composers have traditionally made a living— through publishing, royalties, and the like. Has this new model of free music on the Internet impacted your ability to have a viable career as a composer?

I think it has affected recording artists more than contemporary classical composers. Traditionally we have never relied on album sales. There are very few contemporary classical albums that have sold enough to have a sizable financial impact on someone's life. But I do think many streaming services, like Spotify,[7] can be problematic because they can negate album sales by portraying themselves more as a promotional tool for artists. I believe Spotify and other similar services should pay a larger cut to the artists who create the content that they sell. They currently pay some tiny fraction of a penny for every listen.

Many of the composers I have talked to are very concerned about it, but others have said, "You know, it is a great promotional tool." It's an interesting and important debate.

Yes, musicians are using that platform as a promotional tool, but Spotify should have a sense of responsibility towards the artist. However, I do think it is a great program. I love it and use it all the time. You can't fight against it, but there has to be a way for them to help the musicians who are creating their content.

This is an exciting time to be a composer, don't you think?

Yeah! It is. Like you said, it can be challenging with the musical landscape shifting the way it currently is. It takes a lot of hard work to make it a successful career, but when it is going well, then of course it's amazing to be able to work on projects that you're excited about.

SELECTED WORKS OF DANIEL WOHL

Progression (2013), String Quartet, Five Percussionists, and Electronics

323 (2012), Violin, Cello, Organ, Three Voices, Two Percussionists, and Electronics

Microfluctuations in Plainchant (2012), Saxophone Quartet and Electronics

Neighborhood (2012), Violin, Cello, Organ, Clarinet, Two Percussionists, and Electronics

Corpus (2012), Violin, Cello, Piano, Bass Clarinet, Percussion, Optional Mezzo-Soprano, and Electronics

Ouverture (2012), Violin, Cello, Piano, Bass Clarinet, Percussion, and Electronics

Found Object–Faded Music (2011), Orchestra and Electronics

One Piece (2011), Cello, Piano, and Electronics

Pixelated (2010), Piano, Toy Piano, Glockenspiel, and Electronics

Aorta (2010), Piano and Electronics

Glitch (2009), String Quartet and Electronics

Plus ou Moins (2009), Bass Clarinet, Cello, Violin, Percussion, Piano, and Electronics

▶ To learn more about Daniel Wohl and his music, including audio excerpts of *Corpus, 323, Plus ou Moins, Neighborhood, Fluctuations, Glitch Mvt 1, Skip, Glitch Mvt 3, Old Timey, Glitch Mvt 4, I drone, Cantus, Ouverture, Saint Arc, Limbs,* and *Pixelated,* visit www.oup.com/us/compositioninthedigitalworld.

NOTES

1. Ingram Marshall is an American composer. His music often includes the use of electronics, tape loops, and elements of world music.
2. Mario Davidovsky is an Argentine American composer. His most well known works use both acoustic instruments and electroacoustic sounds. He studied with Aaron Copland and Milton Babbitt. His awards include a Pulitzer Prize, a Guggenheim Award, and Koussevitzky, Guggenheim, and Rockefeller fellowships.
3. Kaija Saarihao is a Finnish composer. She studied composition in Helsinki, and in Paris at IRCAM. She often combines acoustic instruments and electronics. Her awards include a Grawemeyer and a Grammy.
4. Lucky Dragons is a duo (Luke Fischbeck and Sarah Rara) based in Los Angeles who perform experimental music.
5. Kickstarter was launched in 2009 in New York and is an Internet-based service that helps creative projects solicit funding.
6. Transit is a New York City–based new music collective focused on performing works by emerging composers in New York and around the world.
7. Spotify is a music streaming service that currently has more than 25 million users. Great controversy has arisen over claims that Spotify is not adequately compensating composers and performers for the use of their music.

Eve Beglarian

We only get to be here as we are now, right now. And so, we might as well do what we want to do with this life. It's that simple, really.... What I want to do is hang out with joy, experience it, both giving it and taking it. I'm doing my best to figure out how to do that; that's what I'm concentrating on.

I Will Not Be Sad, the title of a piece by Eve Beglarian (b. Michigan, 1958), describes not only the music itself, which is ethereal, gentle, and mysterious, but also captures the essence of Beglarian's personality. During our conversations, I found her to be unpretentious, individualistic, and unapologetically optimistic.

A graduate of Princeton and a pioneer of using digital music technology, she quickly dismisses both academic approaches to composition and high-tech innovations if they are not working in the service of her art. She's much more interested in results than in flashing her educational credentials or owning the latest computer music gadgets.

Raised for the most part in California as part of a prestigious musical family, Beglarian is now a New Yorker, part-time Vermonter, and a recognized denizen avatar of the art music community. Yet she remains a free spirit and steadfastly refuses to be easily categorized by labels such as "post-minimalist" or "electroacoustic composer." Her works are greatly varied in instrumentation and compositional technique, and each has a distinctive personality and style, yet the entire body of music is clearly imprinted with Beglarian's unique voice. Many of her projects, for example, *Book of Days* and *The River Project,* are fundamentally and brilliantly conceptual as art performance pieces, and others are more reflective of her intellectual curiosity, yet all bear her mark of individualism, emotion, and eager curiosity. Beglarian and her music look forward in all joyful optimism, and her lucky audience is swept right along with her.

You've composed in some unusual places—for instance, on a trip down the Mississippi river—but let's cover that later. Tell me a little about how you usually work. For example, do you have a particular space where you like to compose or a certain time of day that is most productive for you?

I like to compose early in the morning, definitely. I sometimes wake up spontaneously, really early, and because I'm a freelancer, there's no reason why I can't just get up and get my day started. I really love those early morning hours when nobody's going to call, and even e-mail is quiet. I can really concentrate and, somehow, I feel more fluent, more flexible, more like the boundaries between the universe and me are thinner at that time of the day.

In terms of places, I can work anywhere, although I have two favorite places. One is a cabin I built out in the woods in Vermont. It has electricity, but no plumbing. It has a view of the mountains that's really beautiful, and there's no one around: You can sing and make noise and you'll only be disturbing the birds. That's a place where I can turn on my creative tap. I'll spend a night there and get up in the morning, and stuff just happens. It has everything I need and nothing I don't need.

The other place is my studio in New York, which is a back room that overlooks a bunch of air-conditioning devices that generate a huge amount of white noise, so that in a way, it's the urban equivalent of the Vermont cabin. It's a small room—there's nothing fancy about it, but it's blocked off from the world. You feel the hum of the city, but the individual noises are lost in that air-conditioning white noise. I've lived there for 30 years, so everything is exactly at hand and there isn't anything I don't need. It's just ideal. Those are my two favorite spaces to compose.

Your academic background is very substantial, with studies at Princeton and Columbia, and your father was a dean at the University of Southern California [USC].[1] How did you transition from that world into being the independent artist that you are, as opposed to becoming part of the academic world you came from?

My father started out as a composer and then became enmeshed in academia on a pretty major scale. He was the dean of the School of Performing Arts at USC. In my teenage years, I watched as his composing life withered while his administrative life blossomed. I didn't need to replicate that path. It's not a bad thing necessarily; it's just not what I wanted to do with my life. The normal path, especially at that time, when I was coming up, was to become a professor.

The other possibility was something I didn't really have a lot of role models for. There was Philip Glass, who's famous for having to drive a cab after the premiere of his opera, *Einstein on the Beach*. OK? [Both laugh] But I thought, Hey, if that's what I have to do, cool. I quit school after I received my master's degree and deliberately didn't get a doctorate so that I wouldn't be tempted to get an academic job, because without that credential, I wouldn't be able to follow that academic path as easily. Then, I looked for freelance work. I got lucky because it was the dawn of the audiobook industry. I directed and produced audiobooks, and that subsidized my composing life for 15 years or so until my composing and performing got to the point of generating enough income that I could live on it. It was a very conscious and pretty risky decision. But I don't have a family that I'm supporting, so it was easier to make those choices. If I want to live on beans and rice, I can do that.

Milton Babbitt[2] was a family friend and so you were around the world of established composers at an early age. How did that affect you?

It was an intense time, a really exciting time. Heifetz[3] and Piatigorsky[4] taught at USC when my father was the dean. In Los Angeles there were all of these émigrés, refugees from World War II who ended up settling in Los Angeles. It was a very interesting place at that time because you had this collision of Hollywood and really high European culture in exile in

Los Angeles. It was a very, very interesting time. John Cage came up in the early part of that time as well. As you know, he studied with Schoenberg[5] during that period. California became a crossroads for all of these threads of 19th- and 20th-century art coming together in one place and getting reshuffled in a fresh way. It's fascinating.

How have you developed your personal style of writing? Is that something you have to work at, or does it just come to you?
To me, the question of style is artificial. The more tools you have, the more flexibility you have in figuring out what you need to do, what you want to do, what needs to happen. I put it in the passive because to me that's very much how it feels. It's not up to me what needs to happen; what needs to happen is up to the piece, and the more technique I have to bring to bear on letting the piece be what it needs to be, the better the piece is.

The more technique you learn, the more confidence you have and the more ability you have to take risks and to simplify what you're doing.

Simplification is important to you then. Why is that?
To me, a weakness I see in many young composers' work isn't a lack of ideas, or a lack of talent, but an insecurity that leads them to try to do everything in one piece of music, and to show that they know what they're doing. But nobody cares. I don't care. I care what you have to tell me, not how much you know.

Ironically enough, the more technique you have, the more you've learned all of these complex things, the easier it is to let them go, because you don't have to prove to anybody that you "know it all"; it's obvious what you know. For me, those Princeton-Columbia credentials gave me a kind of freedom to not act according to type because I had already shown that I could do it.

Hans Beer[6] was a teacher of yours. I'm paraphrasing, but I believe he told you in your first lesson to not worry about being original, because as long as you are true to yourself, you are, by definition, original. Along those lines, one of my favorite quotes is from Martha Graham[7] where she says, "Because there is only one of you in all of time, this expression is unique. And if you block it, it will never exist through any other medium and it will be lost." it seems like that's the same message Mr. Beer gave you: Be true to yourself.
That's beautiful. Not just, "Don't try to be like everybody else," but also, "Don't be anxious about being yourself." It's a dual thing. Obviously, the world doesn't need another sound that is like one that already exists;

there's no point in doing that. But there's also no point in straining after newness for the sake of newness. If you do your personal thing fully and intensely, it will, by definition, be new. As Martha Graham says, the uniqueness of you in the history of the world means that your creativity will be new. You don't have to fret.

I think that, to some degree, the present time doesn't seem to have that anxiety; "Oh, I need to be sure that I'm really avant-garde." That doesn't seem to be the anxiety of our time the way it was in 1976. Maybe I'm wrong, but I don't think that's as big a concern today.

You've been called a rebel, eclectic, idealistic, and a free spirit. You seem to be completely relaxed and free with your exploration of creative expression: music, visuals, and words. You've said that sometimes you don't feel like you're a "real composer." Obviously, you are a real composer, even if you don't fit some stereotypical image. It takes courage to do that, to just be yourself.

Well, I hate to be a downer after you said all of those lovely things, but for me it's really not hard. Even if we all live to be 92 or whatever, we're going to be dead, comparatively speaking, really, really soon. We only get to be here as we are now, right now. And so, we might as well do what we want to do with this life. It's that simple, really. I think we are given messages on a million different levels from the time we're born that there's something else we're supposed to do: make money, or get respect from society. Those things don't really, necessarily, have anything to do with enjoying your life, giving and taking joy from the experience of being on the earth today.

What I want to do is hang out with joy, experience it, both giving it and taking it. I'm doing my best to figure out how to do that; that's what I'm concentrating on. It's harder when you have responsibility for other people. But if you're not responsible for other people, then it seems to me that it's a no-brainer. Why wouldn't you choose joy over responsibility?

Let's talk about your *River Project*. I'm originally from Louisiana, and that region of the country is closely tied to the Mississippi River; it's a huge part of the culture, the mythology, and the art of the delta. Quite a few composers and authors have been inspired by the powerful metaphors of time and life associated with rivers.[8] How did your *River Project* originate?

My interest started with Hurricane Katrina and a book called *Rising Tide*.[9] The book is about the Mississippi flood of 1927 and how it changed

America. Part of that change included the African American migration to the North after the flood: Chicago, New York, et cetera. As a result, the blues and jazz went from being fundamentally regional art forms to urbanized ones. I began to realize that the line between nature and culture is actually a little more complex than we think of it as being. We think of nature as being one thing and culture another, but in fact, they influence each other all the time. Perhaps Hurricane Katrina had the kind of impact that the flood of '27 had culturally, but we just can't see it yet.

Then there was the recent financial crash, which created a tremendous amount of stress for everyone, myself included. I started thinking, "How am I going to get through the next year?" I thought, "I can sit in New York and bite my fingernails, or I can do something interesting." I had an idea to create a kind of one-person WPA project, traveling the length—the core—of the country, via its spine: the Mississippi.

I traveled at a 19th-century pace by paddling and biking. Unexpectedly, I became really interested in 19th-century America—the history of the country, its settlement, and how it is that things came to be the way that they are. The whole journey has generated a great deal of new music from me, and that's ongoing. This is four years later and I'm still working on projects that were generated by going down the river.

It sounds like technology—the Internet in particular—played a significant part in making this project a reality. You not only composed while on your journey but also created an Internet blog where you kept in touch with your musical audience, sharing your experiences and inspirations with them.

Yeah, technology was definitely a key part of the project. I kept a blog as I was going down the river and that blog created a community. As I traveled, I met various people who then commented on the blog or gave me ideas of where to go next.

As a young composer, I was an early adopter of technology and would test beta versions of early sequencers before there were any commercial ones available. I purchased Pro Tools in 1993: I could afford it because I could justify it on my taxes; I used it to edit audiobooks. But I also used it to compose music on my own time. I had just finished grad school when the MIDI specs[10] got approved in 1983. I'm a little better now than I used to be, but I'm still a pretty bad piano player, so being able to use MIDI was a great help. It was just perfect timing for me.

You've also said that it's important to not fall in love with technology, that a composer doesn't have to have all of the latest toys. An inexpensive little keyboard can be an effective tool for composition if it does the job you need to get done.

Again, it ties in to the academic snobbery that says, "In order to be taken seriously, you must write your own algorithm to generate sounds that have never before been heard by human ears." That's great if that's what you're really interested in doing—all power to you. But I'm interested in writing music and giving people an experience. In that sense, I'm not an experimentalist. For me, finding the odd corners of commercial software, or commercial gear of any kind, is where my creativity feels like it is put to its best use. Having to learn C++ [computer programming language], or whatever it is that people have to learn nowadays in order to create academic electronic music, just does not seem like a good use of my time and talent. Don't get me wrong; I'm not dissing the people who do that [programming]. There are people who do it in interesting ways. I'm thinking of the composer Luke DuBois, for instance, who comes up with really interesting things using academic software. But his work is not a standard cliché of academic music or art music. I think that's really great. So, it's not that I'm dismissing those tools; it's just that they aren't particularly my tools.

Another very creative project is your *Book of Days*. That's one of those ideas I wish I had thought of. [Both laugh]

Oh, thanks. I had the idea for *The Book of Days* around 2000: there would be one piece for each day of the year. It's related to the medieval Book of Hours, where you have a prayer and an illuminated visual to help focus the mind on the prayer. I thought of using this format by taking various texts that I had collected over the years and setting them to music along with a visual component for each.

The Book of Days is a collection of work that isn't chronologically in order with the year per se. That is, the pieces get mapped onto the year in whatever order seems appropriate. For instance, it might be somebody's birthday so I'll assign a particular piece to that day, or it'll be a day that has meaning in the world, and I'll assign a piece that I feel is appropriate for thinking about that day. Gradually, I'm filling out an entire calendar year with pieces that I've written. All sorts of projects feed into it in one way or another. Let's say, for example, I'm composing a piece for *The River Project*. It may be appropriate for it to be a part of *The Book of Days* too. *The Book of Days* is specifically a compilation of pieces to mull over. They are meditations.

In addition to live concerts of your music, you interact with your audience in a nontraditional way by using the Internet to blog, post your work, and solicit input from your listeners. On the flip side of the coin, many composers speak about how the Internet has helped them to discover all kinds of music they might not otherwise have been exposed to, an experience that influences their own compositions. Is that true for you as well?

I love the Internet. I think we're in a time of transition, though maybe every generation feels like that. During the Renaissance, people talked about being in a time of transition. But there's a certain literacy required in order for the Internet to be the fabulous tool it can be. You can go to the library and there's trash that will waste your time, and then there are books that will change your life. You yourself have to have the curatorial skill to say, "No, I'm not going to spend my life reading trash that doesn't do anything for me. I'm going to seek out the stuff that's going to change my life." The same is true when using the Internet, but greatly multiplied, because you can spend your day whiling away your time with garbage. But on the other hand, you can easily find incredible treasures online. The difficulty is how to curate that for yourself—how to make the decisions about what you're going to spend your time searching for and looking at and listening to. I don't know that any of us have really mastered that yet.

You've said that the Internet has not brought us together and I thought that was a very insightful comment. Please elaborate.

When the Internet first showed up, I think all of us felt like, "Oh, yeah. This is going to do everything for us, get us all talking to one another." But no. It's shocking to me, shocking. If you only looked at my Facebook timeline, you would not know that there is anyone on the planet who wants American individuals to be able to own an AK-47. But when I held a yard sale in my little town in Vermont, a man came and asked me, "Do you have any guns for sale?" He then informed me that he had just bought an AK-47, AT A YARD SALE!

It's important for us to know that this issue of Internet perspective is a real danger. I look at my Facebook timeline, and what's reflected back through the prism of my Facebook friends is me: my choices, my proclivities, my political point of view, my cultural interests. And that's great, because I don't have to wade through somebody else's preferences. But on the other hand it's terrible. It's dangerous, because it makes me think that *my* choices reflect the choices of the world. The moment I go outside in my little town in Vermont, I know my Facebook timeline is not the world. I'm forced to confront that, and we need to be confronted with that. That scares me badly; that we're just going to become more and more sheltered from others, and we will be in shock when we are forced to confront the fact that there are other people in the world who aren't like us and who don't see things the way we see them. Wow, I don't know how that's going to take shape. I have no idea, and it scares me badly.

Historically, composers have made their living through publishing, performing, and selling recordings of their music. A lot of your music is available for free on the Internet. Is that a good thing? Is it a bad thing? How does that affect your ability to make a living and to continue composing new music?

I don't know that contemporary music composers have ever made a living from sales of recordings of their music. Maybe Stravinsky did, and maybe Steve Reich did for a while, but that has always been really exceptional. The average contemporary music composer, or whatever terminology you want to use, has never paid rent with record sales in the way that a pop music composer or songwriter might. And so the collapse of the record industry did not affect our income to the same degree that it affected the income of a pop music composer or artist. For me, the loss of income from record sales has been counterbalanced by the increase in publishing, both royalties and sales, because as the music is more available, then more performers know about it and they buy the scores in order to perform them. That cycle of income production is working better for me than it did 20 years ago.

For me, having my scores online, as a free download is a really good idea as well. The more my music gets out there, the more sales I get. Many of my pieces are available online: You can download the score and the parts for free. But you can't play the piece without the electronic part, so people have to pay me to get the electronic part in order to perform the piece. That's working out pretty well for me as a source of income. Streaming [on the Internet] was going to be the best way of promoting new music. It turns out that isn't really true in many domains like in pop music. Free is free. Free is a loss of income. If you can't sell a CD because everything is online and you previously made your living selling CDs, you're not going to make a living anymore.

I mean, let's be real, it just doesn't work. But for me, who was sort of marginal anyway, it actually works. The loss of income from record sales is counterbalanced by publishing sales. I still sell CDs at gigs, as many as I ever did, so it's fine. I think people buy a CD at a gig as a memento of the gig if the performance was meaningful for them. It's a different thing.

I don't mean to put you on the spot, but I believe you are a very talented and creative composer: You seem to hear a different drummer, and step to the music that *you* hear. I thought that was an interesting comment you just made about yourself being marginal, so please forgive me, but I'd be interested in hearing why you feel that way.

Wow, you're really bringing something up for me. Years ago, when I was working with Stephen King, I learned that his wife and most of his children are all writers also. His wife, Tabitha, does not have 20 million selling blockbuster books, but Stephen King does. But he has complete respect for Tabitha and her work. All of us have the things we're passionate about. Each one of us has our thing that keeps us up at night, in a good way. The things that keep Stephen King up at night happen to be ones that are shared by millions of people all over the globe.

Perhaps my interests, obsessions, and passions don't speak to millions of people. But that doesn't make them any less important or any less passionate. It may be that instead of 50 million people, there are only 50 thousand people who are interested in what I create. Maybe I'm selling myself short and it's 5 million and not 50 thousand people; I don't know, my own insecurity might be at work there. But the way I see it, it's the quality of the passion that's important, and that keeps me going. It's not the number of people who are getting off on what I'm doing that matters to me; it's the quality of attentiveness that gives it value. Tabitha King's work is not of a lesser value than Stephen King's work just because only 5 million people want to read it instead of 50 million or 500 million or whatever it is. It's not a numeric thing. If it turns out that what I do speaks to fewer people, it doesn't feel like a failure to me as long as the quality and passion of engagement are at a level as intense as they can be.

The act of creating—painting, writing a novel, or composing music—is often described as mystical, inspiration as a mysterious and almost religious experience. Does this resonate with you at all?

When creating is good, it doesn't really feel like I'm in the driver's seat. It feels like I'm channeling it, and it's coming from outside of me, from a mystical place. There's this wonderful quote from, I think it's George Bernard Shaw, who was asked whether he thought the Bible was the inspiration of the Holy Spirit and his answer was, "Every book is the inspiration of the Holy Spirit." I just totally love that quotation. I think he's right. I think everything that gets to me creatively is connected to the ineffable, that core energy that you can call God if you want to, or whatever you want to call it if calling it God makes you allergic. That just seems like fact to me. There's no proof, but I feel it.

SELECTED WORKS OF EVE BEGLARIAN

Building the Bird Mound (2013), Mixed Chorus and Organ

Waiting for Billy Floyd (2011), Chamber Ensemble and Pre-Recorded Tape

I am really a very simple person (2010), Multiple Voices and/or Instruments

Sang (2007), Large Chorus, Santur, and Percussion

I am writing to you from a far-off country (2005), Cello and Pre-Recorded Electronics

The bus driver didn't change his mind (2002), Chamber Ensemble and Pre-Recorded Electronics

Creating the World (1996), Chamber Ensemble and Pre-Recorded Electronics

Wonder Counselor (1996), Organ and Pre-Recorded Electronics

Landscaping for Privacy (1995), Actor, Piano, and Small Ensemble

FlamingO (1995), Chamber Orchestra

Making Sense of It (1987), Chamber Ensemble and Pre-Recorded Electronics

The Garden of Cyrus (1985), Guitar Quartet

▶ To learn more about Eve Beglarian and her music, including audio and video excerpts from *In and Out of the Game, Brownie Feet, Flood, Testy Pony, Well-Spent,* and *Worried,* visit www.oup.com/us/compositioninthedigitalworld.

NOTES

1. Grant Beglarian (1927–2002) was the father of Eve Beglarian. He was a composer, foundation executive, and the dean of Performing Arts at the University of Southern California. He studied with Aaron Copland.
2. Milton Babbitt (1916–2011) was an American composer, teacher, and theorist, particularly known for his electronic and serial music. He was awarded a Pulitzer Prize lifetime achievement award.
3. Jascha Heifetz (1901–1987) was a Lithuanian-born American violinist. He was a member of the "Million Dollar Trio" along with William Primrose, Arthur Rubinstein, and Gregor Piatigorsky.
4. Gregor Piatigorsky (1903–1976) was a Russian-born American cellist. Composers who wrote pieces for him include Stravinsky, Prokofiev, and Hindemith.

5. Composer John Cage studied with Arnold Schoenberg in California in the 1930s at the University of Southern California, University of California-Los Angeles, and privately.
6. Hans Beer (1927–2010) studied with Carl Orff and was a professor of opera and conducting at University of Southern California (USC).
7. Martha Graham (1894–1991) was an influential American dancer and choreographer. Her work was compared in importance to that of Stravinsky and Picasso. In 1976 she was awarded the Presidential Medal of Freedom.
8. Works that have used the river as a metaphor include Homer's *Odyssey*, Twain's *Huckleberry Finn*, and Hemingway's *Big Two-Hearted River*. Musical works focused on rivers include Wagner's *Rheingold*, Smetana's *Die Moldau*, Strauss's *Blue Danube*, and *The Mississippi River Suite* by American composer Florence Price (1887–1953).
9. *Rising Tide: The Great Mississippi Flood of 1927 and How It Changed America*, John M. Barry, Simon & Schuster, 1998. ISBN-10: 0684840022.
10. In 1982, manufacturers agreed on a common system to allow all MIDI-equipped hardware and software to communicate with each other.

Glenn Branca

Photo Credit: Paula Court

I don't like being seduced into abandoning my original idea about a new kind of piece simply because what's coming out of the computer sounds cool. Later I regret not carrying out what I really wanted to hear and hate the piece of garbage that grabbed me at first but then became boring very quickly. . . . The mind is the motor of creation and I believe the more primitive the instruments the more creativity is demanded. Music is an expression of the abstract (that which cannot be articulated or in some cases even understood). We can experience what we do not yet know by accessing the part of our mind that has not yet been explored. This new kind of TV set [the computer] is just a toy, at best a tool. So is a hammer.

The Oxford University press dictionary defines a symphony as "an elaborate musical composition for full orchestra." While the instrumentation of the symphony orchestra has changed dramatically over the past 400 years, most people still would not think of orchestral instruments as including microtonal harpsichords, trash can lids, or custom-made string instruments, let alone 100 electric guitars. Glenn Branca (b. Pennsylvania, 1948) says, "Why not?"

Branca's music is written for traditional orchestra and chamber ensembles as well as for large groups of heavily amplified guitars. Angry, visceral, naked, and defiant, his musical approach is a healthy slap in the face to conservative concepts of music making. Described by some as a renegade composer, Branca upholds the historical tradition of the creative nonconformist who pushes aside the comfortable and redefines concepts of artistic expression.

He can be acerbic and curmudgeonly, but I soon learned that he is a fiercely intelligent, thoughtful, and driven artist, with a cutting sense of humor and a don't-waste-my-time impatience with the banal. He is dismissive of most digital technology.

A member of New York's downtown music scene since the 1970s, Branca was heavily involved with the post-punk music scene while becoming increasingly absorbed with creating large-scale works.

I first experienced a Branca performance in the 1980s when I attended an avant-garde art installation in New York's Chelsea district. In a darkened back room of the loft space, Branca stood in front of a large group of mostly young electric guitarists. He gruffly commanded their attention and then began to conduct them in an astonishing sonic onslaught that was huge and very loud, but also precisely organized and controlled. It was truly an original sound and, like Branca himself, stirred his audience in a way that was incredibly exhilarating and uncomfortable at the same time.

Is the process for writing each piece different, or do you generally follow a similar approach with each new composition?
It's different for almost every piece. Over the decades I've developed a large catalog of systems and processes that I work with and am adding to constantly.

Do you work on more than one piece at a time?
I'm always making notes for new pieces. I simply don't have the resources to produce them. Plays, music, theater, and novels as well. But yes, working on two or more pieces at a time (when I've got two commissions at the same time) can make the work of writing much less boring, and of course you find yourself coming up with ideas for new pieces as well since you'd rather do anything but write this monster sitting in front of you on the desk.

Do you have a composing routine that you follow (such as working at a particular time each day)?

I only work late at night and on deadline. I've done it for so many decades I can't do it any other way now.

How difficult is it to find time to compose?

Not difficult—that is, if I have something that I'm being paid to compose. This is how I've made my living for more than 35 years. When I don't have a gig I do a lot of reading, go online, watch TV, drink, take drugs, and generally waste a lot of time thinking about music that will never be produced.

What about the act of composing itself? Some composers have commented that the compositional process is mystical or at the least indescribable. Comments?

Ridiculous. Composing is very technical and hard work. The conceiving of a piece is easy for me. I have too many ideas. Writing it is the opposite of mystical. If any mysticism or anything indescribable is involved it happens in the performance.

When communicating with performers, for instance, in rehearsal of a new piece, do you completely rely on your score—or is personal interaction important?

Both when possible. Rehearsal time is expensive.

How do your ideas develop? Do you keep notebooks or computer sketches?

Piles and piles of notebooks, tablets, index cards. But I rarely refer to them. The ideas worth remembering stay in my memory. My work is an ongoing process and my mind always seems to be working on it even when I am not even consciously thinking about it. When I do, it appears in a newly advanced state seemingly still attempting to resolve a variety of problems that need to be solved. For decades I have been seeking a complex and evolved music that continues to elude me.

Your work is arguably unique when compared to most other contemporary composers. Has your experience/interest included jazz, folk, pop, or rock music? If so, how and to what extent?

All and more. Everything I hear, whether it's music, sound, or noise it affects the development of my project, as well as everything I read, see, and experience.

Do you consciously use a compositional "system" when composing?

I use many, many, compositional systems. At this point I have developed so many I could easily fill a few books but I feel writing music is more important to me than writing about it. I believe the music itself must succeed. The ideas, no matter how interesting, fail if the music does.

How do deadlines affect your compositional process? Good or bad?

Deadlines allow me to complete work that otherwise would simply remain as ideas. But they also force me to rush and cut corners. This invariably compromises the work. As Stravinsky said to a Hollywood producer who offered him $40,000 (in 1930s dollars) for a soundtrack, "How much time would I have?" The producer said, "Maybe a few weeks or a month." Stravinsky rejected the offer saying he would need at least a year to write that much music. I can't afford to turn down such offers—although I've found that when I write anything my work progresses even when it fails.

You've worked extensively with electric guitars, percussion, and custom-designed instruments. Do you also work with music technology programs such as notation or sampled instruments in your creative process?

I have, and in most cases have felt that it tended to compromise my work. I don't like being seduced into abandoning my original idea about a new kind of piece simply because what's coming out of the computer sounds cool. Later I regret not carrying out what I really wanted to hear and hate the piece of garbage that grabbed me at first but then became boring very quickly. I have plenty of ideas about how new technology can be used but they are all very time-consuming and my interest has become more and more in the primitive. The mind is the motor of creation and I believe the more primitive the instruments the more creativity is demanded. Music is an expression of the abstract (that which cannot be articulated or in some cases even understood). We can experience what we do not yet know by accessing the part of our mind that has not yet been explored. This new kind of TV set is just a toy, at best a tool. So is a hammer.

Do you *ever* use technology in the creation of a piece, for instance, sampled sounds or MIDI?

I now only use the computer for score copying. I write out all of my scores by hand—usually using staff paper but sometimes using graph paper for more complex ideas.

Do you have a "tech assistant" who helps with tech issues when you do use digital technology?

I have no tech issues. When I was working with computers I wrote my own programs. As far as score copying is concerned my wife enters most of my scores onto the Encore[1] notation program. That's about as far as my interest in the computer music goes, except for iTunes, of course. I remember when the Moog[2] came out. It was going to revolutionize music. If it did, it was a pretty lousy revolution. There have been many new music technologies since then. I used to wonder when all of this great music would start coming out. It never did, and it still hasn't. The guys in the Bronx did more with two turntables and a microphone than all the "electronic composers" combined.

Is technology making concert music more or less a collaborative art?

I am no longer interested in concert music in any conventional sense. But my answer would be no. Collaborating with a machine? I've said many times over the years: Marvin Minsky's[3] absurd idea of computer consciousness is like saying that if you pile enough lawn mowers on top of each other they will become conscious. The brain may be somewhat understood but the mind is far, far from being understood if it ever can be. Take Kurt Gödel,[4] for one.

Do you deliver electronically created parts and score to your publisher?

I have no publisher and have never been approached by one. I could if I did have one.

If you do work with electronic versions of your music, either in the composing process or as guides for your performers, how do you address the current limitations of individual instruments' idiomatic renditions?

Again, I don't use this crap. Every instrument, electronic or otherwise, is different and has its advantages and limitations. Actually, I have always loved the sound of acoustic instruments and even when electronics are involved I am more drawn to the acoustic properties inherent in the instrument and how they can be affected by manual manipulation in an acoustic space.

Do you ever use the computer to help you develop composition ideas?

Never. Computers do not develop ideas. When I have used it, I've used it the same way I would use any other tool or instrument.

There has been a steady march of development in music technology over the last several decades: tape, MIDI, digital sound, and computer-assisted composition. What's next?
More crap I would think.

OK, well, switching gears a bit, what about the business of being a composer? How do you survive by writing music?
I'm broke. As far as business, I have a good booking agent.

How important is fame? Are there talented composers the general public will never hear due to lack of marketing savvy on the part of the composer or other issues?
How could I possibly know if I haven't heard them?

Interesting point. On the same topic, many contemporary composers promote themselves via the Internet, but it can be time-consuming to build and maintain a site, or keep up with your posts on social media. How have you approached using the Internet for self-promotion?
I have a website, of course. Who doesn't? It's a pain in the ass and needs to be updated constantly. I don't consider this kind of thing part of my work but we've all been forced into having to deal with it.

Has interacting on the Internet, specifically, social networking sites like Facebook or video sites like YouTube, helped your career?
I'm not registered with any social networking sites and I never intend to be. I have much, much better things to do with my mind. This is just the Stone Age with computers, iPhones, and dishwashers.

Has technology made it less important to be located in a particular geographic region?
Of course.

Business-wise, have things changed for today's young composers as compared to when you started your career?
When I was a young composer I was 5'10" and I weighed 112 pounds, I was broke and lucky if I got to eat one piece of bread a day. I wouldn't know if things have changed. Well, to tell the truth, I do. If you want to compose music for a living you have to come from a rich family. That's why so much new music sucks. Rich kids don't need to make good music. I had no choice.

What 21st-century advice would you give to a person wishing to pursue a life as a composer?

I think I just answered this question. Although if you want to get laid it might help. Other than that, you'd have to be nuts to do this. I'm not, but of course I didn't know that I would die a poverty-stricken loser. Although the satisfaction of changing lives and making magic on stage makes up for a lot.

Are composition students different today from when you began your career?

I was never a composition student and I didn't meet one, or even want to, until after I had been writing music for at least 10 years. When I did start meeting them I found that they had been brainwashed. Their ideas about music were totally boring and unoriginal. I taught them more than they had ever learned in school. If you want to know about old music you can just listen to it, and there are plenty of books as well. You don't need to spend all your daddy's money supporting an outdated and corrupt system.

Anything else you'd like to add?

I'm done with it now, thank you.

SELECTED WORKS OF GLENN BRANCA

Symphony No. 16, Orgasm (2014), 100 Electric Guitars, Basses, and Drums

Symphony No. 14 "The Harmonic Series" (2008), Orchestra

Symphony No. 13, Hallucination City (2001), 100 Electric Guitars

Symphony No. 10, The Mystery, Part 2 (1994), Guitars, Bass, and Drums

Symphony No. 9, L'eve Future (1993), Orchestra and Chorus

The World Upside Down (1990), Orchestral Music for Ballet

Harmonic Series Chords (1989), Orchestra

Symphony No. 7, Graz (1989), Guitar Orchestra

Symphony No. 5, Describing Planes of an Expanding Hypersphere (1984), Guitar Orchestra

Symphony No. 3, Gloria: Music for the First 127 Intervals of the Harmonic Series (1983), Custom-Made Instruments

Symphony No.1, Tonal Plexus (1981), Multiple Guitars, Keyboards, Brass, and Percussion

Lesson No. 1, for Electric Guitar (1979)

▶ To learn more about Glenn Branca and his music, visit
www.oup.com/us/compositioninthedigitalworld.

NOTES

1. Encore is one of the first computer notation programs, originally released in the 1990s.
2. Robert Moog developed one of the first analog synthesizers that could be utilized by the public. It was introduced in the late 1960s at the Monterey Pop Festival, and by artists including Wendy Carlos, the Doors, and the Beatles.
3. Marvin Minsky is an American scientist working in the field of artificial intelligence. He has won numerous awards for his work and co-founded the AI (Artificial Intelligence) Laboratory at the Massachusetts Institute of Technology.
4. Kurt Gödel (1906–1978) was an Austrian-born American mathematician and philosopher. *Gödel, Escher, Bach: An Eternal Golden Braid,* by Douglas Hofstadter (1979), ISBN-10: 0465026567, is a fascinating book which compares the ideas and works of mathematician Kurt Gödel, artist M. C. Escher, and composer Johann Sebastian Bach.

Marcus Roberts

The blues component deals with the musical symbolism of life, the tensions of life, the difficulties of life, and the resilient attitude that you must have to overcome it. That's an important component of music to me. It heals people, gives them a blueprint of how to have a positive attitude even though the circumstances of life may be completely messed up. Completely messed up. Being civilized means that we don't become barbaric just because our situation is difficult. We still must maintain grace under pressure.

It is not unusual for "classical" composers to write music inspired by jazz. Examples that come to mind include Stravinsky's *Ebony Concerto* and *Ragtime*, Gershwin's *Rhapsody in Blue*, and Darius Milhaud's *The Creation of the World*. More recently, jazz musicians are turning the tables and writing in classical forms and for classical ensembles. Marcus Roberts (b. Florida, 1963) is one such example. A celebrated and innovative jazz pianist and composer, he's also been performing classical music for more than 20 years with orchestras all over the world and conductors including Marin Alsop, Robert Spano, and Seiji Ozawa.

Roberts's formal training includes a degree from Florida State University. In his early 20s he was recruited as a sideman for Wynton Marsalis, with whom he has released a number of recordings. His highly acclaimed albums include collaborations with such artists as Béla Fleck.

His awards include First Prize, Thelonious Monk International Jazz Piano Competition; Artist-in-Residence, 2002 Winter Olympic Games (2002); and commissioning awards from ASCAP and the Atlanta Symphony Orchestra. He teaches at Florida State University.

I first met Roberts in Florida some years ago and was struck not only by his gifted playing but also by his gentle nature and deep spirituality. Blind since childhood, he has spent 20 years experimenting and working with technology experts to help develop a program that would allow blind composers to write a complex orchestral score. His first piano concerto, *Spirit of the Blues: Piano Concerto in C Minor*, is a direct result of those years of effort and premiered in 2013 with the Atlanta Symphony Orchestra under the direction of Robert Spano. With digital technology freeing him from any constraints on his art, Roberts may better foreshadow the untapped potential of digital technology for composers than any other creator included in this collection.

Let's start by talking about your *Piano Concerto in C Minor*. How did you go about writing that piece, and what have the performances been like?

The idea for writing a piano concerto had been percolating for a long time, since 1997 or 1998. I was talking with Seiji Ozawa[1] and he expressed that he didn't feel there was enough music written that brought jazz and classical music together. At that time he encouraged me to learn Gershwin's *Concerto in F*, and he suggested that I write a piece for piano and orchestra. He wasn't necessarily suggesting a concerto, but some kind of piece that would incorporate an improvisational component inside of a formal structure. I had worked a little bit on orchestrating *Porgy and Bess*, but I really had no clue about what it really would take to compose an orchestral piece at that time. So I worked on some sketches and brought them to Seiji. He looked at my score, and I mean, he could figure out what was going on with the entire piece in a matter of minutes. He said, "A score needs to have a lot of information." Mine didn't have dynamic markings or anything. There was not enough information to allow a conductor to shape the piece or understand what I was getting at musically. So I set the concerto aside for a while after that. I learned Gershwin's *Piano Concerto in F* by late 2002. I rearranged it a bit, and we premiered it in Tokyo in February of 2003, followed by performances in Berlin [with Seiji Ozawa conducting].

That must have been a great experience to perform Gershwin with Seiji Ozawa conducting.

It was a lot of fun and very successful. I've been performing *Rhapsody in Blue* since 1996, and the more I played all this Gershwin music it hit me that it would be very good to write a piece where I could develop my own formal structure that I could improvise on.

I met Robert Spano in 2005 when I was doing five concerts of *Rhapsody in Blue* with the Chicago Symphony Orchestra, and he was guest conducting. We hit it off very well, and we started talking about having the Atlanta Symphony Orchestra commission me to write a concerto for piano and orchestra. The Atlanta Symphony officially commissioned me to write the piece in 2010. I started improvising and capturing ideas. It's important to me that my themes are singable, and for people to understand what they are hearing. I don't have anything against avant-garde or abstract forms and themes, but I want people to be able to listen to my music and understand it.

That initial period of starting a new piece can be difficult, and pulling together a large piece like a concerto is quite a challenge.

For me personally, there was a lot involved in writing this concerto. As a blind musician, the technology that I needed did not really exist until about 2009 or 2010. I had to have a way to work on the music in a large-score format.

So, at least at first, the lack of proper technology you needed in order to compose a large score presented an added hurdle for you. How did you overcome that?

The technology was one of the major hurdles. There's a program called Cakewalk SONAR[2] that I use to record my ideas with a keyboard and capture them on the computer. There is a company in Philadelphia called Dancing Dots[3] that specializes in music technology for blind musicians. They came out with an adaptive program by creating an interface that allows me to use SONAR to write music—without that interface, it wouldn't be possible. When I hook up a MIDI keyboard to my computer, the program provides the audio feedback that I need to compose. It tells me what instrument I am on in the score, the track names so I know if I'm on the track for violin, oboe, piano, et cetera. It tells me what measure I am on, what beat I am on, every detail. In this way, I can confirm exactly where I am in the score and what I am editing or writing. Honestly, having that software was a huge part of what made it possible for me to compose and orchestrate this piano concerto. The Dancing Dots company spent years working on this software and it really has matured and become something that enables blind musicians to orchestrate and compose large scores.

It sounds like the fact that this software made it possible for you to access all of the powerful digital music programs that are available now was a huge breakthrough for you.

The development of this technology was a big deal. The same company has similar scripts for Sibelius that allow me to play the notated score and isolate the tracks I want to edit. When I first started using this technology I thought, "Oh my goodness, blind musicians have been struggling with this stuff for years trying to figure out how to get their music written down, and finally, here is the solution." I can tell you it's been a major, major problem for blind musicians to use computers to compose until this technology was developed.

How did you go about composing the concerto after you had your thematic material and the technology was in place for you?

The next big challenge was to determine the formal structure I wanted the concerto to have. I have maybe 10 or 15 favorite concertos that I constantly listen to: the two Brahms concertos; Beethoven's C major, C minor, and Emperor Concertos; Mozart's Piano Concerto No. 20 in D minor, K. 466; and of course the Bartok concertos. I started to study these works closely in order to understand the formal structure used in each of these pieces. I felt that if I was going to write a concerto of my own that I needed to follow a solid structural outline. Some people were telling me, "Well, it doesn't really have to have a formal structure at all, it can be like this, or it can be that." But I feel that the form of a concerto is key. So, I was struggling with several big issues: the formal structure, the key relationships, the improvisational component that I want to have, and the fact that I decided to have bass and drums involved too. All of those were really huge problems to solve.

Having defined the large-scale parameters, how did you approach moving on with the composition within those parameters you set for yourself?

To me, composing is kind of like slow improvisation. The music goes where it needs to go. Your control of the composition is limited; it is driven both by intuition and spontaneity, but also by rules and sticking true to the formal structure as well as the thematic material that you're working with. At the same time, I wanted a piece that had a certain flexibility that could be expanded in terms of improvisation. The most important thing is that I wanted it to be able to stand alone as a composition without bass and drums. I didn't want this to be a piece that could not be played as a traditional piece for piano and orchestra.

The inclusion of jazz instrumentation, especially a trio, in an orchestral setting is a bit unusual. Were there any particular challenges in writing for those instruments in this situation?

I completed the entire piece before I figured out the part that my trio would play because I wanted the concerto to be able to stand on its own as a work of art.

I spent a lot of time composing this piece. I would compose parts of it and then my assistant and I would review it together. He and I have worked together for a number of years, and he knows a lot about the compositional process *and* he plays jazz piano, so I respect him and trust his judgment. For me, another important part of composing is collaboration. I gather other people's opinions when I compose. Is the texture too thick or thin? Is the tempo correct? This is the same way I work with my trio; we play a section over and over and discuss options. Should the drums play here or should they sit out? What kind of groove should we go after? Caribbean? African? or a New Orleans groove? That's how I started to gradually shape each section of the concerto. Writing, listening and gathering input.

The dedication of the piece seems to me to be particularly significant.

I wanted this work to have cultural relevance. I dedicated it to Dr. Martin Luther King and to Seiji Ozawa. Without Seiji's encouragement I certainly would not have composed this concerto. He is one of my most important mentors and I have such respect for him. Over the years, he has arranged many significant concerts that allowed me to explore the relationship between jazz and classical music. As for Dr. King, to me he is the ultimate symbol of what one individual can do to influence the larger structure of society.

While I don't think of this piece as programmatic, there is an overall title for the entire work, and then titles for each movement. I'm interested in the origin of those titles.

I titled the piece *The Spirit of the Blues*. It has to do with affirmation. It has to do with the general optimistic belief system that I always operate from. I want my music to uplift people, to give them a sense of hope, to give them a sense of purpose and enlightenment.

The first movement is called *The Blues*. It represents the struggle for freedom that African Americans have had in this country, but it's not just about African Americans. It could be any group within the larger population that has issues that the bigger structure of the culture is not really dealing with.

The second movement is called *A Dream,* and it is inspired by the great speech that Dr. King gave, in which he talked about creating a world where there's no racial tension, where people are actually able to function side-by-side, and put aside their differences instead of allowing people's differences to be a basis for strife and anarchy.

The third movement is called *Freedom*. It has a lot more snare drum and it deals with the power of rhythm and harmony working together. It delves into the Latin and jazz worlds, and resolves a lot of the tensions that have been introduced in the first and second movements.

It's clear to me that you feel strongly that art has a function beyond "art for art's sake." Do you consider the audience and its participation in your art to be critically important?

To me, any creative process, all art, has to tie into people, and to nature. If we just write something that is purely a theoretical abstraction, honestly, I'm not interested in that. The audience is always important to me. Even if it's only 10 people who hear it, I want those 10 people to hear it because that process of getting a spontaneous reaction from them helps to shape what we write and what we play—especially in jazz. The blues component deals with the musical symbolism of life, the tensions of life, the difficulties of life, and the resilient attitude that you must have to overcome it. That's an important component of music to me. It heals people, gives them a blueprint of how to have a positive attitude even though the circumstances of life may be completely messed up. Completely messed up. Being civilized means that we don't become barbaric just because our situation is difficult. We still must maintain grace under pressure. I have great respect for blues and jazz, from the high standards of creativity and virtuosity that were established in its early origins to the continued evolution of modern jazz.

I hear your respect for the blues and jazz, and I share that with you. But you are also open to, and interested in, so many other styles of music. For instance, you met Béla Fleck and ended up making some very interesting music together. How did that come about?
We met at the Savannah Music Festival at a jam session. He just came up to me with his banjo and we played a blues in G. When he started playing I couldn't believe it was a banjo. I mean, he was playing with such ease and freedom, like any jazz musician on a trumpet or a saxophone would.

So we decided after the concerts to go ahead and make a record together. He really wanted us to write all new music for the project, which I had initially been resistant to because I was so busy. But I made the time, and we both wrote a bunch of music. We went into the studio for 10 days and we rehearsed and recorded all this new music. Each piece has a different character. They range from bluegrass, to bebop, ragtime, early New Orleans style, and some modern music, so we had a lot of different colors to explore. Béla is a virtuoso. He likes jazz and I've always liked bluegrass music; it just felt like we both loved the full spectrum of American music and we are both open-minded.

Your mom sang gospel and you had a lot of interest in jazz and blues, of course. How did you get into classical music? Do you encourage your students to listen to blues and jazz as well as classical?
Yes, absolutely—I definitely encourage my students to listen to all great music. In terms of my own background, my mom was in charge of the church choir and she and my dad bought me a piano when I was about eight years old. I started learning how to play in church, literally making up stuff behind whatever I heard in the choir. They allowed me to do that. I developed my aural skills first; I couldn't have told you what key I was playing in, or anything else at that time. I was self-taught until I was 12, so in my early years I was a true "folk" musician. I started lessons at age 12 and my first piano teacher worked with me to correct a lot of problems with my technique. He also taught me harmony, a lot about chord progressions, and introduced me to Art Tatum,[4] and he made me learn how to read braille music notation. Literacy was very important to him. As I was a blind musician, he insisted that I become musically literate. But he never tried to interfere with my innate sense of the music, my ability to be able to just play. I will always be grateful to him.

You've talked about technology and how important it has been to you as a composer. As a composer and educator myself, I embrace technology—I think it can be a wonderful tool. But, at the same time, I worry that some of my students can become distracted, too dazzled by music technology, because it can be a lot of fun to play with, you know? I believe that working through the difficult process of learning your craft is so important. A composer needs that foundation in order to really cut loose and write some great, original music. Do you agree?

Oh yeah, absolutely. Because the technology in and of itself does not do anything. The technology just evens the playing field; it makes things accessible to everyone—that's the main value of technology as I see it. So, for example, braille is a technology. Louis Braille[5] wanted to be able to play organ music, so he came up with a notation that was completely different from traditional staff notation and could be read by blind people. So technology can allow something that wouldn't otherwise be possible to become possible for a group of people.

Now the danger with technology is that it can eventually become a system unto itself, and that's not a good thing. You want the technology to automate a manual process that still is being studied manually, that's the key to it. So a composer should be able to conceive of a piano part in his or her head, hear themes, and hear the music, and then the technology serves to help you bring that music out. It can't cover up the fact that you don't know anything about music or that you have no process or a true, innate understanding of music.

So in terms of technology, I see it as just one of the tools that we have. And believe me, I am fanatical about technology, computers, all of these elaborate phones, et cetera, but I have tried a lot of technology that did not work out. I've spent months and months trying some technology and then had to scrap it because I realized it was just not going to work for me. But that's part of the process, the R&D [research and development] that will help you discover any means you can get your hands on that will help you to become a better musician and to build your audience. I'm for that.

I encourage students to use technology. They can go out on YouTube now and find amazing music and do research. But it's good and bad. I think one bad thing about the Internet is that there is so much content and music out there now that the question becomes, how can you steer a young person toward something that they should actually be focusing on and gain specific individual knowledge about? Instead, they often will just get fragments of a bunch of stuff they don't really understand. Assuming a teacher or mentor can guide them, there's a tremendous amount of wonderful knowledge on the Internet. It can be a great tool.

As busy as you are, you are also associate artistic director for the Savannah Music Festival, where you direct an annual high school band competition and educational programs for students from all over the country.
The thing that we have to focus on in jazz and classical music right now is to become relevant again. We have to provide people with the opportunities to participate again and to develop their understanding of the music. Of course, our educational system, which is a whole other discussion, is in shambles. Young people are not even given the opportunity anymore to play musical instruments in most schools. I want to do what I can to keep jazz music relevant. We have to work on innovative ways to teach the principles of jazz and approaches to performing. Jazz is an art form that in its history has always been about mentoring. Older musicians were the ones to teach the next generation to play. So we try to bring a lot of gifted teachers and performers together each year in Savannah to work with these young people so that they will continue to be excited about the music. And so we as musicians will continue to create great music that audiences will want to hear.

SELECTED WORKS OF MARCUS ROBERTS

> *Spirit of the Blues: Piano Concerto in C Minor* (2013),
>   Piano and Orchestra
> *Play the Blues and Swing* (2013)
> *The Spanish Tinge* (2013)
> *Athanatos Rhythmos* (2012)
> *Searching for the Blues* (2009)
> *Express Mail Delivery* (1997)
> *Late Rehearsal* (1997)
> *Exploration* (1996)
> *Ferdinand Lementhe* (1992)
> *Angel* (1992)
> *Nebuchadnezzar* (1990)
> *The Truth Is Spoken Here* (1989)

▶ To learn more about Marcus Roberts and his music, visit www.oup.com/us/compositioninthedigitalworld.

NOTES

1. Seiji Ozawa is a Japanese conductor whose many awards include the Koussevitzky Prize, a Grammy, two Emmys, and the Praemium Imperiale, presented to him by the imperial family of Japan.
2. Cakewalk SONAR is a digital audio workstation used for recording, editing, mixing, mastering, and outputting digital audio.
3. Dancing Dots Braille Music Technology was founded in 1992 and creates music technology for the blind and the visually impaired.
4. Art Tatum (1909–1956) was an extremely influential, blind, virtuoso jazz pianist. He was noted for his perfect pitch, improvisational skills, and stunning technique. He posthumously received a Grammy Lifetime Achievement award and was inducted into the DownBeat Hall of Fame.
5. Louis Braille (1809–1852) was a blind French musician and educator who developed a new system of reading for the blind or sight-impaired. The Braille method has been widely in use for over 200 years.

R. Luke DuBois

People who are professionally engaged in creating music understand the contin-
uum of technology, and understand the value of live performers, and the human
spirit in composition. You can get all the samples you want, but nothing sounds
like a real musician playing a real instrument. But, there is a huge role for the
computer in the world of contemporary music production in conjunction with real
instruments, and I think that's a really positive dialogue.

What is a composer? After meeting with R. Luke DuBois (b. New Jersey,
1975), I would argue that the answer to that question has become fluid and
elusive, due in part to the impact of digital technology. Only by expanding the definition of the word "composer" could one hope to categorize

this creator of original music who is also a contemporary visual artist, performer, laptop musician, software programmer, artistic interpreter of data and statistics, educator, record producer, and videographer. R. Luke DuBois is truly a composer for the digital age.

Dubois earned his master's and doctoral degrees in composition from Columbia University. Early on, he demonstrated a prodigious flair for computer programming and digital technology, which he seamlessly and naturally interwove into the composition of his music. He worked as a staff researcher at Columbia's Computer Music Center and was the director of the Princeton Laptop Orchestra for its 2007 season. He is the director of the Brooklyn Experimental Media Center at the NYU Polytechnic School of Engineering and is on the board of directors of the ISSUE Project Room.

Dubois spoke to me for this interview from Florida, where he was preparing the opening of an exhibition of his work at the Ringling Museum of Art. I can't remember the last time I laughed as much or enjoyed talking with someone about such shared experiences as performing at CBGBs, musical academia, and our mutual love affair with technology and the visual arts.

DuBois uses brilliant conceptual foundations to explore our sense and perception of time, translate our boggling information overload into a human artistic experience, and reposition our visual perspective on mundane events, while creating music that is both intellectually attractive and emotionally resonant. His concepts are always clever, but never at the expense of the music. If there is a composer in this book who best represents the creative possibilities that digital technology currently offers and foreshadows its untapped potential, DuBois is that composer.

You're not only a composer but also a visual artist. Currently you're at the Ringling Museum of Art[1] for a few months. What are you working on there?

I have a big retrospective show at the museum, in which I'm showing a whole bunch of my visual art, and four performances of my music. I've also been commissioned to create a new piece for the show, so I'm doing portraits of local circus performers. They're going to look like those old 19th-century circus posters where the guy is holding his barbells up and it says, "THE WORLD'S STRONGEST MAN"!

Reminiscent of *Being for the Benefit of Mr. Kite!*[2]

Yeah, exactly. But on video, sort of like the pictures on the wall at Hogwarts in the Harry Potter books: They're going to move and make sound. I'm working with a brass ensemble in New York called TILT Brass,[3] and we're going to make some really twisted circus music. I spent the last two days filming a really great local circus group called Circus Sarasota. A lot of them are ex-Ringling Brothers people, or ex-Big Apple Circus people: hand balancers, jugglers, a Texan rope guy, and a ringmaster, so they will be referenced in the project.

We have a similar background in that I've always been involved in visual arts as well as music and technology, but it's still a bit unusual for a composer to work in multiple fields. Fifty years ago there was a very rigid definition of what it meant to be a composer, which typically included having expertise as a pianist. Has the definition of a composer shifted, and are you an example of that change?

It is all getting really fuzzy these days. I think computer technology sort of aids and abets it a little bit, you know? And the amount of money it takes to make a record, or a film, or a website is so much lower than it used to be. If you wanted to be a record producer 30 years ago, that was your gig, man: You could only afford to follow one career path, and on top of that, the corporate structure channeled you in one direction.

Things are different now. I teach engineering at NYU, I run a digital media program, I make music, I make art, and I write software. All of that is part of who I am as a creative person. The contemporary music scene is much more comfortable with technology than scenes like the New York visual art world are. Visual arts tend to put us into a ghetto. True, there are ghettos in music as well, like academic computer music and really serious electroacoustic music. But by and large, new music composers (or whatever you want to call them) all have laptops and write music with electronics. They might write chamber music, but they will often amplify it and add effects. They're comfortable in a recording studio and they are comfortable onstage. These stupid machines that we have now have made it a lot easier to do all of these things. But there's a net positive effect because we're not as locked down, and this direction totally makes sense to me.

I have seen you referred to as a "laptop musician." What does that mean to you?

I started out as a bass player, but when I got to college I worked at the Electronic Music Center at Columbia University, which is a really beautiful place. It was originally the Columbia-Princeton Electronic Music Center,[4] founded in the late 1950s. They have these beautiful machines, like the RCA MARK II synthesizer, which is the size of your back wall and is made out of all of these vacuum tubes; the thing is ridiculous. It makes about four notes at once, and has a shellac record lathe for recording your work. It's amazing. Since then they have added a lot of solid-state synthesizers like Buchla,[5] Moog, and Serge Modular[6] synthesizers.

I started out splicing tape, working on a Buchla, and touring with a little portable rig I put together. At a certain point, I realized that the equipment was not robust enough to tour with. But it wasn't like I decided to hop on the whole laptop-computer-musician bandwagon. I've had a computer since I was nine years old: I knew how to program, and I was pretty functional with computers. I was playing a gig in the '90s at a little club down on Bleecker Street, and something was wrong with the stage power: It only worked if the light switch was on in the women's room or something crazy like that. If the light switch got turned off, my entire Buchla rig would suddenly drop some really terrible musical interval, like a minor 9th. It was terrible. [Laughs]

How did you make the transition to using a computer and digital sound in your live performances?
That year MAX had just come out with MSP, the addition that made it possible to work with audio on the laptop using MAX. I had first worked with MAX as a lighting designer (I was a theater technician for awhile), but when it was just MAX by itself, it could only control hardware devices. Once I got MSP, I learned that I could create real-time sound synthesis. I got myself a Macintosh G3 PowerBook and taught myself enough so that I could create all of the sounds I wanted and tour with that setup. Once I had the laptop, we could also search the web on tour, check e-mail. It just made the business of being in a group so much easier. Then I started working for the guys who make MAX: I was a product manager and an engineer for Jitter, which is the video part. So I became pretty embedded in the computer culture. But it's not really that I so much identify myself as a laptop musician. In a way, we're all laptop musicians now; all of us are computer musicians. Unless you're some audiophile bluegrass dude, you're not going to make a record without touching your computer anymore. It's just life: The computer is here to stay and it's very difficult to dislodge it. So that label kind of sucks, but when I am onstage, yeah, I type! [Laughs]

For the most part, computer music technology was previously confined to academic settings or recordings. There were some early computer or synthesizer ensemble performances, but in my opinion, and to put it kindly, they were rarely successful. Perhaps as a result of new technologies, that has changed a lot. Now I hear

live performances incorporating computers and digital technology that sound fluid and powerful. You're part of a new generation of composers who are using digital technology to write and perform as a matter of course. Is being tech savvy a must for contemporary composers?

The way music is performed now and the amount of effort it takes to get an ensemble off of the ground have also changed a lot. It all involves these machines now. If you want to get a gig, you can't just have a tape demo anymore. You've got to have a MySpace page or a Facebook page or you send them MP3s over the Internet. Some fellow composers may think I'm a super-technology kind of guy, but I'm not, I'm just like everyone else using new technology. The history of music is the history of technology. Unless you're singing a cappella in the desert, you are using technology. Acoustics is technology. Notation is technology. Instrument design, amplification, analog recording, and broadcasting are technology. It's ALL technology. So yeah, it's important to keep up with developments and know your gear.

The piano and the metronome are examples of technology in musical history, but do you think the technology of today will still have such a lasting impact as the piano has had?

Good question. An experience that recently got me thinking about this issue was when I took a group of my students on a tour of the Steinway factory up in Queens, New York. The guy who gave us the tour said, "Okay kids, let's talk about the Industrial Revolution. A hundred years from now no one is going to want a diesel engine or a telegraph or a cotton gin: They'll all be in museums. But everybody is gonna want this piano." So we started a little discussion about what people are going to value from our current generation in a hundred years. Everybody came up empty. Nobody is going to want a 2013 MacBook Pro in 2113, but a 1936 Steinway Model M? Everybody is going to want one of those. You see what I am saying? It's an interesting reality check of the space we are in now.

Is the laptop the new piano? Is that a fair comparison?

With the laptop, you're sitting onstage with this thing that is meant to help people do their taxes: It's got an 18-month obsolescence cycle, it's made out of plastic and silicon, and unless you program it to, it doesn't make any sound. It can make any sound you want, but at the same time it doesn't really make any sound of its own at all. It's all sort of fake. So how do you get people behind the idea that musicianship can exist on a laptop? That's the challenging thing, because you see people onstage with laptops all of the time now, but the audience may be thinking the musicians are DJs or that they are posing or they are checking their e-mail, right? [Laughs]

Or the laptop musicians go to these elaborate, pointless lengths to prove to the audience that it's a real performance. They're like, "I've got all this weird stuff, knobs and slider screens, and I'm going to wave my arms around!" Like that is going to prove to anyone that you are a musician.

When I first saw people performing with computers about 10 years ago (myself included), I was like, "Oh, man this sucks." But now I think we are either getting used to it or getting better at it, I'm not really sure. I hope we are getting better at it though.

What about writing music on the computer that is to be performed by acoustic instruments as in a chamber or orchestral setting? Some composers have expressed skepticism as to the efficacy of using computer-music programs for this purpose.

I understand their reservations. If the objective is to write something idiomatically for acoustic instruments, you need to spend a lot of time with people who play those instruments. You can't just plunk down some notes into Sibelius and download some library of string sounds and then declare, "Now I know how to write a string quartet!" You don't. You just know how to make a bunch of cool string sounds on your computer, which is not the same thing.

My composition teacher in graduate school wouldn't let me get away with anything that I couldn't play myself on the piano. He would tell me, "If you can't play it, you can't expect the performers to play it, so cut out the stupid psycho triplet-thirty-second-note crap. Get your own chops up."

I think computers have had a huge influence on the rise of complexity in certain types of musical writing. It's weird, because I hang out with all of these post-minimalist cats that are kind of unaffected by that, like David Lang and Michael Gordon[7] and all of those guys. They are influenced by rock and roll; they are not influenced by sequencers.

Are some composers writing traditional performers out of the picture by composing music that only a computer can play?

There are composers who are writing music on a computer that maybe six people on the planet can play, barely. These composers say, "Why shouldn't I write this psychotically impossible and complicated piano trio?" [Laughs]

But I don't think the computer is a bad thing. As we were saying earlier, everything is technology. This fear of the computer taking the place of musicians who play traditional acoustic instruments is just a silly panic, that whole thing: "We're all gonna get laid off because of the computer!"

The invention of the piano caused the same kind of panic: "Oh no! We can't allow an instrument to have 88-note polyphony! The whole orchestra will lose their jobs!" And then with the saxophone: "You can't have an instrument that can be produced on an industrial scale; it will cost the jobs of all of the people who build clarinets and flutes!"

And the computer will ultimately take the place of the composer? That, I think, is a fear some people have as well.
Exactly. But that's nonsense. I think that's why a lot of people are afraid of computer music: We let the genie out of the bottle when we created software that could do algorithmic composition[8] and compose without us. There is a fear that 300 years from now all of us are not going to be able to create anything; we'll just let the computer do it. Maybe I am full of it, but I don't see that happening at all. People who are professionally engaged in creating music understand the continuum of technology and understand the value of live performers and the human spirit in composition. You can get all the samples you want, but nothing sounds like a real musician playing a real instrument. But there is a huge role for the computer in the world of contemporary music production in conjunction with real instruments, and I think that's a really positive dialogue. Any working musician nowadays needs to understand and control the technology of their music production: They need to be able to record and mix themselves and get their music online.

Is the traditional role of composers and performers of music for acoustic instruments going to go away?
The answer, I think, is in two parts: One, the instruments are here to stay; two, the institutions within which those instruments are used to operate may not be here to stay. The symphony is a very, very expensive problem. People who want to hear Beethoven live are going to have to adapt. Opera companies are trying to adapt. Hip, young composers are in there doing creative things with film and electronics or cutting an orchestra piece into a sequence of small chamber pieces. You can do something in a warehouse or outdoors, and if you want to hear *Don Giovanni,* maybe you'll hear a really funky, weird version of *Don Giovanni.* I think those are really interesting things to do, really visionary, and might let people rock it out for a few more years within that huge structure.

Let me ask you about a particular piece of yours in a bit of detail: *Vertical Music*. How did the piece come to you conceptually, how did you come to write it and bring it together?

I've been doing two things that are kind of fun. One is about performing arts and portraiture. I did a piece in 2011 based around a performance for a bunch of marching bands that were in different parts of New Orleans converging on a park. I made a big cross-cut remix DVD, so you never see everything all at once. It's a new technique, something different I think. If you were there that day, you saw one thing, but I'm showing you a totally different perspective of the whole experience. I think a really interesting way to make a portrait of a musician is to play around with time like this. If you take a photograph of a musician, you have captured their image but you haven't captured their sound. So how do you deal with that?

I bought myself a cheap high-speed camera that can shoot 300 frames a second, so when you play it back at 30 frames a second, everything—the video and the sound—lasts 10 times as long. I can capture this stuff into the computer and stretch it without too much of a quality loss. I wrote a four-minute piece of music, applied this technique to it, and that's the 40-minute piece called *Vertical Music*.

That's an intriguing process; it must provide you with unusual material to work with.

So many interesting things happen when you stretch sound: Vibrato becomes microtonal and when the violinist is going eh-eh-eh, you hear ahh-ahh-ahh instead, that kind of thing. Visually you can see strings vibrate, the pitches drop below 150 Hertz, when played at that speed, you see the strings vibrating. This really weird thing happens with acoustic space when I use this method of slowing down: I shot the whole piece in my apartment, but it sounds like it's in a church, the echoes get bigger. That's an old Motown trick, you put Diana Ross on the tape deck and then you play the tape deck sped up while in a stairwell and then when you slow it down again it sounds like she is in a big church. It's the oldest, dumbest record production trick in the book, but it works. If all of your reverbs and reflections get 10 times bigger, then my tiny New York apartment ends up sounding like a cathedral. I thought it was a really cool way to make this portrait.

So, before you wrote the music at all, you were thinking of this as being a piece that presented a musical idea 10 times as long as originally notated and performed?

Vertical Music was originally a test of a concept that ended up working out so well that I released it as a piece in its own right. I had a bunch of students come into my apartment, one at a time, and then lit them and filmed them playing four minutes of music.

Once I had finished and stretched it all out and hit play, I went, "Whoa ... Awesome!"

Was this approach conceptually related to your piece *Billboard*?
Yeah, but *Billboard* is the same concept backwards. It was part of a trio of pieces looking at American cultural media. We seem obsessed with asking, "What's the best? What is the number one song or movie? Blah, blah, blah."

When I composed this piece in 2004, we were still at that absurd moment where there were four record labels and only eight songs played in the entire year. But now, nobody pays for music anymore, so what the hell is a number one song these days? It was a little bit of a piece about that; I wanted to track that trajectory of change. So I started with songs from 1958, which was when they deracinated the pop chart. When we went from having a "race records" chart and a separate white "pop" chart to having "The Hot 100s" chart.

So this piece traces the music that was listed on the Billboard charts over a period of time.
Yeah, and the way that listing of hit records has changed because of cultural influences. Hip-hop became so dominant that the "big four" record labels lobbied to reorganize how the charts were determined so the rock acts could start having number one songs again. They hadn't had a number one song since 1996, because many black people don't buy white records. So the charts have been resegregated by a really disturbing, cynical, corporate move. Now we actually have multiple number one songs at any given time, which is weird.

So I selected music by determining how many weeks a song had been at number one, and I sped that music up to one second per week. If you string all of the pieces together and play them back-to-back, it equals something like six days of music.

Some composers still write their music with pencil and paper and compose for traditional chamber groups or for the orchestra. Do you consider yourself a continuation of that tradition, or do you represent something else, a turn away from that paradigm?
Well, I am unusual, an exception in a way. I am part of that lineage because I have a doctorate in composition from Columbia, so I can play that game. I understand the traditional musical language and am comfortable

working in that world, but that game is not very relevant to my act, the kind of music I'm interested in now.

How has the computer facilitated making the music that you *are* interested in, and does composing with the computer constitute a break with the traditional method of composing?

Once you get yourself into the head-space of writing music on the computer, leveraging the computer to write the music, then you're talking about a new set of possibilities that people didn't have before. But this is not a break with tradition; there is such a continuation here. It disappoints me when people imagine that there are these clean breaks in history instead of seeing the continuation that exists. Music is algorithmic all of the time: A scale is an algorithm, a key is algorithmic, all of Western music is based on algorithms, and so is Balinese gamelan music. Mozart made music with dice.

Harmony is our ace in the hole here. You need to know how chords work, and that takes a little bit of time. There is no cookbook; it's more like learning how to mix paint. It's a craft, and it's hard. That is my conservative rant.

Schoenberg's music was a really fascinating experiment that had an important historical point: If you're going to write music that everyone is going to fight a war over, it's got to be abstract, mathematical, cool, clean, and totally modern. It shouldn't reference anything about your race, your religion, or where you're from. A fascinating concept, but the problem is that the resulting music is unlistenable.

You're referring to serial music?

Right, and it's unlistenable. Twelve-tone music is like Esperanto,[9] and who wants to listen to poetry in Esperanto?

What about composing using algorithms and a computer? Is that a valid form of composition? Does that process have anything to do with the musical traditions that preceded it?

I've written a lot of pieces where I'll use the computer to come up with a good part of the piece, or sometimes I'll surrender the process to the computer completely. But it can be hit or miss: I usually throw out about 20 computer-generated ideas for every one that I think is going to make sense for the piece I'm working on. So I'm ultimately still in charge as the composer in a traditional sense. Another example is a piece I composed using data about the Iraq war. My concept was to compose an emotionally resonant piece out of facts that are getting spewed out on television and the Internet about the war. I selected the facts that I believed relevant and constructed the piece. So again, I was the composer of that music, no matter how untraditional the approach may seem. There are many approaches composers can take to putting together a work, but to me there is a continuation of the tradition of composing that came before us, so yeah, there is a lineage.

SELECTED WORKS OF LUKE DUBOIS

CLOUDS (2013), Film Soundtrack
Vertical Music (2012), Twelve-Piece Chamber Ensemble
The Marigny Parade (2011), Five Marching Bands
Star Wars and Modernism (2010), Film Soundtrack
a year in mp3s (2009–2010), 72 hours of electronic music in 365 days
Moments of Inertia (2010), Violin and Electronics
Hard Data (2009), Amplified String Quartet
Entanglement (2004), Ten-Piece Chamber Ensemble
Biology I-IV (2003–2005), Violin and Electronics
Growing Pains (2003), Guitar
Repeat after Me (2003), Flute and Electronics
Plant (2002), Violin, Double Bass, Bass Clarinet, Piano

▶ To learn more about Luke DuBois and his music, visit www.oup.com/us/compositioninthedigitalworld.

NOTES
1. The Ringling Museum of Art, located in Sarasota Florida, was established in 1927 by the Ringling family of circus fame.
2. Being for the Benefit of Mr. Kite is a composition by John Lennon of the Beatles, which was included on their seminal 1967 album Sergeant Pepper's Lonely Hearts Club Band. The piece includes avant-garde tape-collage techniques and surrealist lyrics and was inspired by a 19th-century circus poster.
3. TILT Brass, located in Brooklyn, was formed in 2003 and presents works for brass by living composers.
4. Founded in 1950, the Columbia-Princeton Electronic Music Center was the first facility in the United States dedicated to electronic and computer music and multi-media research. Luciano Berio, Wendy Carlos, and Edgard Varèse are among the prominent composers who made use of the facility.
5. Buchla Electronic Musical Instruments was founded by Synthesizer innovator Don Buchla in 1963 and manufactures synthesizers and a variety of electronic musical instruments and controllers.
6. Serge Tcherepnin, a professor at Cal Arts, developed an affordable and powerful analog modular synthesizer system in the 1970s. Artists who have used Serge Modular instruments include John Adams, Todd Rundgren, and Stevie Wonder.

7. Michael Gordon is an American composer and co-founder (along with Julia Wolfe, his wife, and David Lang) of Bang on a Can. His compositions are often labeled post-minimalist and are influenced by his experiences with rock music in New York. Gordon's teachers include Martin Bresnick at Yale.

8. Algorithmic composition usually refers to the use of chance procedures or computers in the composition of music without human intervention. Strictly speaking, an algorithm is simply a formal process with a set number of steps used for making calculations. A cooking recipe is also an example of an algorithm.

9. Esperanto is an artificial language meant to facilitate international communication. It is based on roots from the chief European languages and was developed in 1892.

Greg Wilder

My greatest aspiration is to design software that writes music that is so compelling, the music is successful and nobody can detect that a computer created it.

While perusing the web site of Greg Wilder (b. Ohio, 1973), images of Einstein playing the violin came to mind. Part musician, part scientist, Wilder is a conservatory-trained pianist and composer who also happens to be a successful inventor and entrepreneur. The holder of several patents, he is the founder of the Isomer Project, a suite of intelligent software tools that is, in Wilder's words, "exploring the limits of computational creativity." Wilder was also instrumental in the creation of Clio Music, a musical analysis platform widely in use by the music industry.

I must admit that I unfairly projected the image of a mad scientist onto Wilder before we spoke for this interview. I expected him to be able to wax poetic about software and business models, but I wasn't at all sure we would speak the same language when it came to music. That preconception was overturned within moments of beginning our conversation. Wilder is articulate, friendly, supremely intelligent, and fully focused on creativity.

An experienced speaker and educator, he taught at Dickinson College and West Chester University. His many music honors include awards from the American Composer's Forum, ASCAP, the William Penn Foundation, the Society of Composers International, and the American Academy of Arts and Letters.

Wilder's music varies from avant-garde electronics to pieces for traditional instruments; many of his works evoke a sense of introspection and complexity. It's difficult to pin a label on his music, a compliment in my opinion. His collaborators include visual artists, filmmakers, theater directors, and animators. While he approaches music from a decidedly intellectual slant, his own compositions are filled with surprise, ingenuity, and passion. Wilder, though, is not satisfied with simply bending technology to the service of human creation. Rather, his goal is a true melding of music and technology: He wants to teach a machine to write true "music of substance." He may have a bit of the mad scientist about him after all, but what great innovator doesn't?

How did you begin your musical life? And what influences helped you evolve into the composer you are today?
I started playing the piano when I was about three years old and began writing my own little melodies pretty soon after that, which is a fairly typical thing for many composers. I eventually took the university and conservatory route, but I spent a lot of time in my high school and undergraduate years playing all different types of music, jumping into the deep end of the pool. I would throw myself into a situation where I didn't know the tunes or didn't have written music, and would just have to sink or swim. It was a good way to learn musicianship in an applied way.

I also began working with technology early on, as primitive as it was in the 1980s. I did a lot of multi-track cassette recordings, and I collected early synthesizers and learned how to program them. From a very early age I was interested in building my own creative space outside of the concert stage. I grew up in the Midwest, in a small town where there weren't ensembles just sitting around waiting for new composers, so I was sort of isolated in that sense. My interest in technology gave me a way to realize my earliest musical ideas.

You had some significant teachers, mentors who helped you to find your musical path.

As an undergrad at Bowling Green State University, I met Sam Adler who became a mentor of mine. I then met George Rochberg[1] in 1995 at a seminar that Sam had organized. When I first met George, I was 20 or maybe 21, and I was a sponge, just as we all are at that age. When George spoke about music, it felt as if someone was reading my mind; there was an immediate alignment aesthetically. After that program I wrote to him and said, "You have really changed my life; may I come visit you?" He accepted, so I drove my (barely functioning) vehicle 11 hours to Philadelphia and spent the day with him. That sparked a friendship that lasted until his death in 2005. In fact, he became one of my primary mentors, both musically and in life. While I was studying at Eastman, I traveled to Philadelphia to visit him regularly, and after I graduated I moved to Philadelphia in order to continue meeting with him. My time with George had a very important role to play in my musical thinking. I was still a young musician, so I didn't have the experience, the breadth and depth of understanding that he had. His ideas that had the greatest impact on me were about understanding music through practice, through applied studies, and what makes certain music memorable. What gives music identity? Why is it that we repeatedly go back to certain great works again and again? And that was what set me on the path of working with computers—to try and understand what it is about the great masterpieces of music that make them last.

Would you say that as a composer you use the computer differently now from the way that you did when you first began as a student?

Absolutely. At first, I was drawn to the computer as a way of orchestrating, of essentially giving a performance. I could realize a performance without having access to an ensemble. Once I was at Eastman, there were numerous ensembles that could perform my music, so my focus changed. I had a love/hate relationship with technology for a while. I felt the computer was not musically expressive enough—it was very frustrating trying to make this inanimate box of chips feel musically expressive. I am a pianist, so I had a physical command over musical materials, but I couldn't get that same sense of musicality or urgency from the computer that I could from a live instrument. But then, technology improved; computing speed improved dramatically, and it continues to improve. Slowly, advances in technology appeared that allowed me to capture more of the ideal that I was after musically.

You've taken your skills and your ideas about programming and composition to a whole new level. You're not just using a computer to generate sounds or notate your music in a traditional way. Can you please elaborate on that?

When I left school and moved to Philadelphia to work with George, I was involved in many different musical activities. Eventually, I started building software to perform musical analysis. At first, it was very intuitive; I was thinking about how I internally process music, as a performer, a theorist, and as a composer. How was it that I understood musical grammar? How did I process it and translate it into sound? At that time I was a regularly performing pianist, and I found myself in many different musical situations where I wasn't familiar with the lexicon, so I would have to adapt what I understood to fit certain projects. As I thought about my own process, I began imagining ways that I might be able to get a machine to replicate that process. I discovered a considerable amount of research in this area and I absorbed as much as I could. I began building the software and eventually made enough progress with my work that there was a commercial option available. At that time I was essentially supporting my own research through teaching, composing for theater and performing on the piano. I would work for a month and then I'd have three months of down time to develop my ideas, program, and conduct research. Ultimately, I formed a company called Clio Music, which is now operating out of San Francisco. Clio Music creates data about the musical patterns that are present in a music track, compares those patterns against large catalogs of music, and then finds music that functions in similar ways. Along the way, I became quite proficient as a programmer and as a researcher. So, now that my programming chops have caught up to my musical thinking, I'm able to write software to help me compose.

How do you use the software you've programmed to help you with your composition?

My software is listening to musical models that exist, and it is learning things about those models from a cognitive perspective. It then applies those principles to new music. In other words, the software looks for perceptual trends and patterns. Instead of simply looking for the order of notes and rhythms and the harmonies that are present, it searches for the tendencies and the function of the individual events. Then it tries to adapt those trends, those musical expectations, into a new language, a new musical idea. Does that make sense?

Yes, it does. It's fascinating, but it's far ahead of the curve of the way that computers are usually used in composition. Do you think that composers as a whole have learned to take advantage of recent developments in computer music technology?
There are many, many fantastic composers who do interesting work with computers, but my approach is fairly unique. I'm interested in trying to unlock musical meaning, the musical essence behind classic works, works that have stood the test of time, to try and discover those qualities that are worth repeating. For many composers who use computers in their work, it is a matter of applying known transformations to lists of musical events. My own journey involves trying to understand the old language, trying to understand why Bach is Bach, and not Vivaldi and not Telemann. There are things about Bach's musical ideas that are inherently different—and better—than others. We composers think about that all the time, but there are things about those ideas that are not immediately obvious from a standard theoretical perspective. I wanted to know whether a computer could listen to the music of these composers and identify elements that we react to as listeners and as musicians, but can't easily codify. The most obvious quality to consider from this perspective may be timbre. In music theory, we spend a lot of time on melody, harmony, and pitch, and we do some work with rhythm. We don't really codify timbre, but because of the way computers "listen" they absolutely have to deal with and codify timbre. So, the starting point for me was getting computers to dissect musical models to see what makes them successful. My goal today is to translate those analyses into original music that is compelling in new ways, but musical in ways similar to those models the computer is looking at.

Many composers seem to feel that the process of creating music is a mysterious, if not mystical, experience. They say they often have no idea where their ideas come from, and may sometimes find themselves amazed at the creative output that they have produced. It almost sounds as if you are attempting to codify that process. Am I on the right track or is that a separate issue?
That is very insightful of you. But of course you are a musician and a composer yourself, so those would be experiences you are familiar with. I think everyone who loves and deals with music, especially in a creative capacity, understands that feeling. That "magic" is a human thing, and not

something that a computer can create, at least not today. On the other hand, our brains do all sorts of amazing things—we have evolved and adapted over the years to process sound in very specific ways. For example, what is it that determines the line we draw between a sound we hear on the street, versus a musical sound? Research shows that just as there is a framework for how our brains perceive visual stimuli, there is also a framework for how we perceive aural stimuli, and how we make sense of the sound patterns that we call music. Those patterns are not necessarily simple, but they can be understood and codified. That work is still under way and certainly we have not unlocked all of those secrets, but I'm convinced that there must be patterns in Bach, for example, that tend to create favorable reactions in humans. I believe, and I think most scholars would agree, that there are musical reasons beyond the standard trappings of history that can explain why the music of certain composers has survived. So, my goal is to try and codify why those things have stood out, why they have persisted. If I can define some of these principles, I can use them to my musical advantage by applying them to the music that I create.

Can you talk about a specific piece of yours where you have applied these principles to your own compositional process?
Yes, absolutely. I'm currently working on a large-scale piece for piano and computer that makes heavy use of my software. There are nine movements, and each of the movements has very specific influences. For each movement, I am pulling from specific works of Beethoven, Brahms, Chopin, and Handel—music that I love—and in each of these movements I am extrapolating certain aspects of those composers' personalities as I see them, and applying some of the patterns that exist in their music to the music that I am feeding into the machine. In a sense, I am building a bridge between my own musical thinking and the music of the past. The piece is called *Elysium*[2] in honor of the omnipresent ghosts of the composers that I reference. Those musics are alive, and they continue to influence us both in subtle ways, and in some ways that are pretty obvious.

Let's look at another example, for instance, your piece *Interlude for Marimba and Computer*. How did you work with the performer Nathaniel Bartlett [percussionist] on that piece?
At the time, I very much wanted to integrate the software that I had been working on into *Interlude*, but the software just wasn't sophisticated enough. I couldn't achieve the kinds of things that I can do now, with machine learning and artificial intelligence processing; I wasn't quite yet up to snuff from a programming point of view. So what I did with Nate was

to follow him to a number of venues where he performed and spend a lot of time with him. He has a very beautiful and unusual way of approaching music and it was very important to me to understand that approach so that I could really write to his strengths. Although the computer wasn't functioning as a direct collaborator at the time I wrote *Interlude*, I was very much thinking then about the things I am actually able to do now with the software tools I have developed.

Have you developed any particular processes or habits that help you work? For instance, do you have a specific place that you prefer to work when composing? How do you find time to compose music while running a business, teaching, and programming?

I used to be very particular about my environment before my business experience. I had many rituals while I was writing, as many composers do. But the experience of having to so fiercely manage my time, and having to be so ultra-efficient in what I do has changed that for me. Now I think about the music I'm writing at very odd times and in odd places, whether it is on the train or in the shower or whatever. I work out problems away from the studio, so when I sit down to compose, I can just go about the business of composing. Because I don't depend on music to make my living, I'm able to take the time that I need to compose. I used to imagine that if I had that sort of flexibility, all I would ever want to do is compose and play the piano. What I have found instead is that, in fact, I still want to teach, I still want to program, and I still want to develop business relationships, all in addition to continuing my composing.

When I was a student many of us listened to all kinds of music, rock, jazz, blues, whatever, but we would never mention those interests to our teachers because we feared being ostracized. It seems that's not the case anymore. Students may be interested in hip-hop, or computer music, or Bach, and it is all OK. There is a great musical diversity that is acceptable now. I suspect that a lot of the worldliness that we see in today's students is due, in part, to the Internet and the ability to go on the Internet and find music they might otherwise not be exposed to.

I agree completely. In fact, I was just remarking the other day that Eastman had one of the best music libraries in the world, and I remember digging around in the dark corners to find the exciting things that were happening in Europe. In the generation before, that stuff was almost outlawed. Even when I was at Eastman in the '90s, finding decent recordings of Xenakis[3] or Stockhausen was kind of tough. Today it is amazing; on YouTube that stuff is everywhere, often with the score following along. I think that does help a lot with teaching because you can throw resources at students, and they are savvy enough that you can let them sort through and find their own path. I think that is actually quite a benefit.

I have heard from several composers who teach, that many of their students come to lessons with their laptop, and they are using a notation program and generic computer sounds. There is a concern that students aren't developing their ear or their musical fundamentals because of over-reliance on this easy playback; they haven't learned the nuances of the instruments, their idiomatic properties, and they don't really know how to read a score. Do you think that is a valid concern?

I certainly do. As I mentioned before, when I was a student I threw myself into these situations where it was sink or swim, where I was sitting with an instrument in my hand and I had to play along with the "adults," and there is no better ear training than that. It's something that I always encourage students to do as well, especially when I am teaching theory. It's really important to do something musical, whether it is singing or playing an instrument. The attitude of students is often, "I don't play the piano so, you know, I can hear the recording or whatever, I don't need to look at the score." I often draw the parallel to a creative writing major: Imagine a conversation with someone who says, "I am a creative writing major." And you ask, "Can you write English?" They say, "No." "Okay. Well, can you read English?" "Well, sort of . . . a little bit, I'm learning a few words here and there." If you are not literate and you don't have facility, you are limited to what it is you can understand and what you can actually do as a musician. So, I encourage students to throw themselves into situations where they risk being embarrassed. Show up at the local open mic night and be the pianist who accompanies everybody. If you don't know the piano very well, you are going to learn real fast when you start making mistakes onstage. You will find ways to cover your mistakes. You'll find ways to cope with reading scores quickly. I think that's one way to do it.

Absolutely, I've certainly done some learning in that way. Painful, but effective. [Both laugh] How do you think the Internet has affected the ability of more isolated musicians to get their music heard? For example, do you think there are talented composers in some remote locations that the general public will never hear because the composer lacks marketing or social skills? Or has the Internet changed that also?

I don't think the Internet has changed that yet. For years I dealt with the music industry, the business side of things, so I know exactly how they view all of that and what it means. The great promise of the Internet was to democratize, to let everyone join in. But just because you get your music on YouTube or it shows up on Spotify doesn't mean you're going to be selling more than a couple hundred copies of your CD. You can't really do a whole lot of sophisticated music searching at this point, for a number of reasons. Part of what I was hoping to do in my business was to provide a tool that would allow music to, on its own merit, rise to the top. I wanted to build a search tool that listened intelligently, so a user could find great music that wasn't being promoted. It turns out the industry doesn't work that way, and it isn't interested in working that way. I hope that in the future, these tools will become savvier and that custom content and user-generated content will become more manageable, so that you can actually find the things that you are interested in. I think the tools are starting to have the power to do that, but I am not sure if the real power—the dollar muscle—will support that.

One of those tools may include Isomer, the suite of intelligent software you are working on. What is the origin of that concept and what are its goals?
I would really love to offer Isomer as an open-source suite of tools to composers, musicians, and the greater music community that gives them the kinds of benefits that I am getting from the work that I am doing. The biggest challenge is that Isomer is a framework that can do a wide variety of things—it is a difficult piece of software to use. I'm experimenting with ways to make the interface manageable so I can provide access to it. Also, Isomer requires a lot of computing power. I suspect that it will ultimately become a cloud-based Internet tool, providing one big version of the software that is always up to date. A user could log in to an Isomer account, see the materials, and get a response from the system.

Are there any other exciting technologies that you see on the horizon, as far as music composition is concerned? A technology that composers will all be using in 10 or 20 years?
I do. I have an affiliation with Drexel University in Philadelphia, which has a new facility called the ExCITe (Expressive and Creative Interaction Technologies) Center, run by Dr. Youngmoo Kim. One of the things that Dr. Kim's current and former students are working on is the magnetic resonator piano (MRP),[4] which is a hyperextension of the acoustic properties of the piano. Other people are doing things like this for other instruments

and I think that sort of interdisciplinary thinking, that fearless desire to cross boundaries, is going to have the biggest impact in the near future. We will see what will stick and what will fall away. Technology also provides the potential for completely new media. We already know audiences are becoming directly involved with performances in the classical concert hall, where they can wave lights around so that a machine will adjust the outcome of a live performance and that sort of thing, but I think this kind of interaction is going to get much more sophisticated. I'm not sure a lot of those experiments are musically satisfying, but I think that will change. I hope that intelligent listening technology finds its way onto the stage and into the presentation of large dramatic works as well.

What are your aspirations personally as an artist for the upcoming years? Do you have any goals that you hope to achieve as an artist? My greatest aspiration is to design software that writes music that is so compelling, the music is successful and nobody can detect that a computer created it.

SELECTED WORKS OF GREG WILDER

Sonification Studies (2013), Computer

Valley of the Tharsans (2012), Radio Play (in collaboration w/Alison Conard)

Moment of First Awakening (2012), Piano and Video (in collaboration w/Alison Conard)

Elysium (rev. 2012–2013), Piano and Interactive Computer

Infernum (2012), Computer

Fabulation (2009), Theatrical Score

Elysium (2008), Marimba and Interactive Computer

Daughters of Genius (2006), Theatrical Score

Interlude (2006), Marimba and Computer

Crime and Punishment (2004), Opera for Interactive Computer and Live Cast

Vyšehrad (2003), Computer

Concerto for Piano and Computer (2002), Piano and Computer

⊙ To learn more about Greg Wilder and his music, including audio excerpts from *Interlude, Isomer Study No.1,* and *Vyšehrad,* visit www.oup.com/us/compositioninthedigitalworld.

NOTES

1. George Rochberg (July 5, 1918–May 29, 2005) was an American contemporary classical music composer and educator. Rochberg abandoned his practice of writing serial music and included tonal sections in his music, a practice that drew ridicule from some composers and educators of the time.

2. Elysium is an ancient Greek mythical concept of the afterlife, as reserved for those chosen by the gods: "the souls of the guiltless passed to the Elysian Fields, where each followed the chosen pursuit of his former life in a land of spring, sunlight, happiness, and song. And by the Fields there flowed the river Lethe, from which the souls of those that were to return to the earth in other bodies drank oblivion of their former lives." (From *The Classic Myths in English Literature and in Art* by Charles Mills Gayley, Ginn and Company, 1893,1911, pp. 51, 359).

3. Iannis Xenakis (May 29, 1922–February 4, 2001) was an avant-garde Greek composer. His compositions employed the use of mathematical models including set and game theory. He also created multi-media performances and wrote many theoretical texts.

4. The magnetic resonator piano is a grand piano that is modified to allow characteristics of some digital synthesis instruments. These extended characteristics include indefinite sustain, pitch bend, variable timbre, and the ability to perform crescendos.

Pamela Z

I think a lot of people worry about the machinations of how to function in the world as a composer, and you have to figure that out, but all of that is useless if you're not creating anything. To be an artist, you've got to be making art. I always tell people, "Focus on your work and make really good work." That work will help you to find your way. Get your work out there in some way or another and go see or hear other people's work. Be engaged in the community, and support the community. Make art.

Composer/performer and media artist Pamela Z (b. New York, 1956) found her passion for music playing in a rock band and went from there to earning a degree in classical voice from the University of Colorado. Ultimately, her interest in music technology led her to San

Francisco, where she became immersed in the contemporary music and performance scene. Recognized as an early innovator of live digital looping techniques, Z is perhaps best known for her sonorous multi-media performance pieces, which often involve processing her voice through MAX/MSP software using a MacBook computer, extended vocal techniques, percussion, and sampled sounds. In addition to her solo works, she composes for chamber ensembles, including commissions from the Kronos Quartet, Bang on a Can, and the St. Luke's Chamber Orchestra. She also tours extensively, with performances at such prestigious venues as Lincoln Center, the Kitchen, Japan's Interlink Festival, and La Biennale di Venezia in Italy.

Our interview was a lot of fun as she shared her effervescent spirit and wicked sense of humor, liberally peppering her comments with laughter. Her curiosity and excitement about the use of technology as a compositional tool are contagious. Her live performances are hypnotic as she gracefully manipulates her electronics like a dancer while producing unusual and beautiful vocal sonorities.

While other performance artists also use technical manipulations of the voice in concert, Z's music seems to most solidly reinforce the traditions of the composer/artist by expanding the boundaries of traditional composition while still embracing and furthering the art form. In a number of ways Z exemplifies the new composer—no longer bound to traditional expectations, she sets an example by creating her own path, defining her own values, and continuing to grow the legacy and art of creating concert music.

How did you make the decision to become a composer? Did your interest in music begin in childhood or develop later in life?
I had a love of music from the very beginning. I can't remember a time not having that. My first public performance was when I was five years old, singing with my sister in an elementary school talent show. My parents bought my sisters and me classical guitars and recorders (German block-flutes), and we played with those when I was pretty little. Then I began to write songs in junior high school and formed a folk music club, in which people played guitars and sang songs. I also played the viola throughout my younger years, up until junior high school.

In high school I sang in the choir while studying voice and learning opera arias. My parents were divorced, and one year my father sent us a cassette tape deck, then he sent us a second one a little later. I started immediately experimenting (not knowing what I was doing at all) with overdubbing. I would record with one of the tape decks, then play that back as I would speak or sing into the other. I began creating all of these things with multi-layers when I was pretty young.

Did you pursue your interests in music technology in college?
I attended the University of Colorado and it was pretty conservative at that time. I learned later that if I had gone somewhere more progressive, like Mills College in Oakland, for example, I could have been studying with someone like Robert Ashley[1] or Steve Reich, but as far as I knew, there was no one like that at my school. I later learned that in the basement of the school there was a whole center set up for computer music. But at the time I was unaware of it. It seemed like it was a big secret. The only people who really knew about it were the people in Dr. Richard Toensing's program.

How did you become interested in composing and make the transition from being a vocal major to focusing on composition? You also played in rock bands while studying traditional Western music in college didn't you?
When I was in music school, everybody made a big distinction between composers and performers. But outside of school I was also a singer-songwriter, so I was already comfortable with the concept of a person who actually composes the work that they perform. Throughout music history this has been an important concept: The composer-performer was not invented in the era of Steve Reich or Philip Glass. All of the composers in the old days performed their own works. But somehow in the modern classical music world, some people have a desire to separate that concept as if it's an anomaly. I started out composing the music that I performed, even if it wasn't the classical music part of what I was doing. So there was nothing strange to me about that idea. I was writing songs when I was in music school and I was playing my music in clubs.

And then in the early '80s, after I was out of college, it was the New Wave and punk rock era. I was exposed to all of these new rock music artists who were art school dropouts but were consorting with these people who were from the world of "serious" classical music. For example, David Byrne,[2] Brian Eno,[3] and Laurie Anderson[4] were collaborating with the likes of Philip Glass and creating work that straddled the edge of new music. The classical music avant-garde and the visual art world were a part of this movement. I was very interested in all of those people. I felt inspired to try to expand what I was doing and became more interested in experimental music. My work was coming from a performance-art sensibility, and I realized that I could combine these two worlds in my own work, so I began practicing other styles of singing and of making vocal sounds.

I started playing with electronics, processors, and multi-track tape recorders to compose music.

I think that's when I first started calling myself a composer. People who come from the popular music world write songs and sing and perform their music, but usually don't refer to themselves as composers, you know what I mean?

When you were in school, was your interest in genres other than traditional classical music accepted and taken seriously by your peers and teachers?

It was not accepted by most of the instructors at my school. They were the types that don't even believe that there are any living composers of value. There were teachers from the vocal faculty who wouldn't even allow the students to sing show tunes. [Laughs] Had I studied with them, I would have had to hide the fact that I was playing in clubs at night.

Luckily, my voice teacher was not so restrictive in that regard. Even though he didn't really care for popular music, or even contemporary classical music, he didn't forbid me from playing whatever I wanted to on my own time. So the basic climate was that there was this big separation between "popular music" and "classical music," but it was a problem for me because I was interested in both, and I couldn't quite figure out how to make both of those work with each other. But there were just as many people in the club world that I was dealing with telling me that my voice sounded too trained. So it wasn't just the classical people rejecting the commercial music or whatever but it was the popular music people too. Now they use the word "pop," which I really hate. When I was younger, pop was not hip. If you called something pop music that was the bad stuff you would hear on the variety shows at night. People wearing sequined outfits sang pop music. [Both laugh]

It's an important distinction that seems to have been lost.

Right! We didn't think of Joni Mitchell, or Tom Waits, or whoever it was that we might like as pop artists: "Pop" was a dirty word. I'm a little bit allergic to that word just because of what it used to mean to me when I was coming up. I didn't think of the music I was playing at night as being pop music. But really, in truth, pop is just short for popular, and nowadays, I think it refers to anything that's in the mainstream.

A real turning point for me was finding a third ground: experimental music that crosses all music genres. I became interested in experimental music in the '80s, no matter what genre the music came out of. There were these great collaborations like Robert Wilson[5] working with Philip Glass.

Before that phrase "electronic music" was co-opted by the dance-music world, electronic music used to refer to something very academic, like Stockhausen.[6]

I've read that you trace your legacy to John Cage and Terry Riley. Would you say that's accurate?

When people ask me whom I'm influenced by I always mention Cage almost immediately. A lot of people say, "I am influenced by Cage, but more his ideas than his music." But I'm influenced by both. I think that his ideas were amazing, but I also really like his music. So yeah, I think Cage is extremely important—not just to the origins of my work and my thinking, but for all of us, even the people who won't admit to it. I think he was a pillar.

And then the minimalist composers. Of course, none of them like to be called "minimalist" composers. When I first started listening to contemporary classical music, they were some of the composers I listened to the most: Philip Glass, Steve Reich, I really liked Terry Riley and I love *In C,*[7] but I didn't listen to him very much early on; I just wasn't as aware of him and I wasn't in California yet. I think of Terry Riley as a very California composer in a way, but I listened to Steve Reich. I was also really interested in Alvin Lucier[8] and in his very conceptual pieces—these really long, long, pieces, all based on really simple concepts, like this piece called *Music on a Long Thin Wire.* It was just this wire in a space that picked up the ambient frequencies of the space, and that was the whole recording, an hour of this wire reflecting the ambience in a simple space. Steve Reich's early works in which he worked with tape loops were also huge for me. I worked with looping my voice and digital delays, creating very short phrases and then building layers with them. I didn't get that idea from Steve Reich: I was ignorant of his music before I started doing that, but later people compared me to him so I then went and investigated his music. I remember when I first figured out how to create out-of-phase loops with three different digital delays set at slightly different tempos. When I first discovered that technique, I was just over the moon: I thought I had invented the technique! Seriously, I didn't know that Reich had done it 20 years before with tape.

We both lived in New York and there has been a healthy "downtown" music scene there for decades. I know you played at the Kitchen, and you may know some of the pioneers of that scene, for instance, composer Phil Niblock?[9]

Yeah, I know Phil. I've played at his venue, we've been in festivals together and we hung out in Italy together when we were both performing at the same festival. I'm one of the organizers of the San Francisco Electronic Music Festival, and we've had him in the festival.

I believe that there is still a mainstream image of a composer being someone who writes music in a familiar form, with traditional notation and instrumentation. But some composers, including you, have taken different paths from that expectation. Has the definition of what makes someone a composer changed? If not, should it change to embrace those who have less traditional ideas of music making?

This reminds me of an experience I had. I was touring in Japan with a group of composers and we went to the University at Kyoto. Coincidentally, the guy who was the head of the music department there used to be on the music faculty at Boulder, where I went to school. He was part of the hard core group who believe, "If you don't make little black marks on pieces of paper then you're not a composer." As we gave our presentations, and a Q&A for the students, he kept asking us, "Why do you call yourselves composers?" And I finally said, paraphrasing Truman Capote, "That's not writing, that's typing." That's my opinion of the idea that composing is making little black marks on staff paper: That's not composing, that's just notating. Composing is the actual coming up with the musical content. That's composing. I've always been a staunch crusader about trying to make people understand that notating is not the same as composing. You can be a copyist and never compose a note in your life.

For some people, their composition process deeply involves the process of writing down the music, and they probably wouldn't be able to separate the two. Then there are others who don't connect their process to writing music down at all. It's a broad spectrum, and no one way is right or wrong; there are just different approaches. I happen to move in circles where most people tend to agree with my philosophy so I don't have to argue that point with people very often. But it did happen when I went to that university in Japan.

Are there any circumstances where you do use notation?

I sometimes notate music, but only when I'm writing a piece for other people to play. I compose 90 percent of my music for myself to perform, so there's really no reason to write anything down; I'm the only person who needs to know how to do it. For me, the writing it down is all about conveying to someone else what I want them to play. When I get commissions from chamber ensembles, of course I notate the music.

You've written for dance and film as well as for chamber groups. Do you take a different approach to composing when writing for a particular setting for your music?

They are very different. When I write for dance and film, it is usually a studio activity in front of my Pro Tools station. A very typical way for me to start a new piece is to do what you're doing right now: I interview a bunch of people. I have to do this with really high-quality audio, so I get them to sit in the isolation booth in my studio to interview them so I can get a really good recording. I'll ask people a bunch of questions about the subject that the piece is based on. Then I'll take all of those interviews, which will sometimes be hours and hours long, and edit them in Pro Tools. I'll literally make hundreds of regions,[10] which I will then use to sculpt a text collage, which I will then use as the armature for the piece. Oftentimes there will be sections of the piece that are made out of the text collage, or sometimes the text collage is used all the way through the entire piece. Sometimes, especially for a dance piece, I'll derive pitches and rhythms from the text collages. I record all of this in my studio and manipulate it in Pro Tools: I actually sculpt it, almost like I was making plastic art.

How is the process different when you're composing for film or a chamber group?

When I'm working with film, I'll get a copy of the film and import the movie file into Pro Tools so I can see the image as I'm creating the sound for it. When I compose for a chamber ensemble, it's a different approach: It then involves my making sound for acoustic instruments to play. I will sometimes start by singing and then taking what I've composed and arranging it for different instruments. The piece I wrote for the Kronos Quartet is about speaking accents, so I recorded about 30 different people who all had different regional or foreign-language accents. I cut up little bits and pieces of the words those people said and created a text collage that I composed string parts around. So I'm actually sitting in front of the computer with a MIDI keyboard playing the string parts into the computer. Sometimes it can be a time-consuming and painstaking process to capture and transcribe the pitches that are found in an individual's speaking voice. Then I open that up in Sibelius and tweak the file to create a score and parts for performance.

It's a very different process when I compose for myself to perform: something that is not for film, not for dance, not for chamber ensemble. I often do that by setting up the gear that I use to perform live and then improvising until I do something I like.

So they are really different processes. There is a lot of overlap between them, but they are very different processes for each of those three ways of composing.

Please talk a little bit about how you got into MAX/MSP,[11] and why that's important for you as an artist?
When I first moved to the Bay area, I had friends who were using MAX. I wasn't interested in MAX for myself, because the people I knew were using it just for MIDI stuff, and maybe some synthesis. My work was all about signal processing: taking an acoustic signal and manipulating it. Since MAX didn't have MSP [Max Signal Processing] yet, there was no relationship between what I was doing and what the program offered at that time.

Then they added MSP to the program, which meant I would actually be able to do signal processing. Around that time, I was starting to tour a lot. I had a residency in Japan and I was carrying a six-space rack of gear, bags of cables, and all of the power-supply equipment with me whenever I would go play gigs. My gear was so cumbersome and heavy I would put it on wheels, but I could barely lift it myself. I was getting charged hundreds of dollars in overweight luggage fees every time I flew. In the middle of my residency in Japan, I was invited to go play at a festival in New Zealand and had to fly from Japan to New Zealand all by myself. The flight stopped over in Korea, and they made me take out at least half of my luggage, and then charged me again for it being overweight. By the time I got back to Japan I was like, "That's it, I've gotta use MAX! I've got to figure out how I can do this on a computer so I don't have to carry all this stuff with me."

How did you tackle learning how to use MAX? It's quite a daunting program to master.
When I was in Japan, I met these two really great MAX geeks, and I called them and said, "You've got to help me to start learning MAX." I started working a little bit on it when I was in Japan and when I got back to the United States, I did a short residency at Dartmouth. But it took about four or five years to completely port over from using this big stack of hardware to having everything on the laptop.

I decided I wouldn't try to replace everything at once with software, I would just replicate whatever features I was using, one at a time. It took me several years, little by little. I was able to take one thing out of the rack at a time until I had them all replaced with software versions. I wanted to create a software instrument that would replace my stack of digital delays, a multi-effects processor, and a sampler: All of that stuff was my instrument. I needed to replace that so I could play all of my compositions and have one master MAX patch that would encompass all of that. It took a long time but I accomplished it.

What advice would you give to young composers who are just getting started and looking at the horizon ahead of them?

The answer is really simple and important: Create the work. I think a lot of people worry about the machinations of how to function in the world as a composer, and you have to figure that out, but all of that is useless if you're not creating anything. To be an artist, you've got to be making art. I always tell people, "Focus on your work and make really good work." That work will help you to find your way. Get your work out there in some way or another and go see or hear other people's work. Be engaged in the community, and support the community. Make art.

There are so many people I know who stay in their studio and they quietly and very slowly make very few things. They're grumpy and ask, "Why is no one inviting *me* to a festival?" Well, because NOBODY KNOWS WHO YOU ARE! You are not out there, you're not going to see other people's work, you're not generating anything, you're just agonizing over details that no one but you hears for, like a year, and then you're not even showing what you *have* done to anyone.

So, I would just say make work, be prolific, and follow your creative instincts. Share your art with people, and be a presence in the world by going out and participating and supporting. Do whatever it takes to get it out there.

It's easier now that we have the digital ability to stick our work up on the Internet, but you really want to be out there doing actual physical performances, making things happen. When I came to San Francisco, I started organizing events, producing concerts in which I could present my work and other people's work. I didn't want to wait around for somebody else to invite me to be in their concerts, so I made my own. There are a lot of things you can do. You just have to make the work and the other stuff follows.

What do you look forward to in your career? What do you hope to accomplish creatively as an artist?

What is important to me is that I continue making work and doing what I want to do. I'm really expansive in what I like to do. I don't want to just stick to doing things that are sonic; I also like doing things that are visual. I'm always expanding my concept of myself as an artist: I make a lot of my own video for my work, I like doing large-scale performance work, I like doing installation work. I want there to always be opportunities for me to make art and to experiment and to try new things, to expand what I do. That is my hope as an artist, that I can keep making my work. I'm inspired by people like Phil Niblock, and I respect people who continue to create new work and are able to figure out ways to keep it going. I'll be happy if I am able to continue the path that I am on.

SELECTED WORKS OF PAMELA Z

And the Movement of the Tongue (2013), String Quartet, Tape
Carbon Song Cycle (2013), Voice and Electronics, Bassoon, Viola, Cello, Percussion (With Multi-Screen Video Projections by Christina McPhee)
Flare Stains (2010), Solo Voice and Electronics
Baggage Allowance (2010), Multi-Media Performance Work for Solo Voice and Electronics, Multi-Channel Interactive Video
Sonic Gestures (2008), Multi-Channel Video and Surround Audio
Wunderkabinet (Co-Composed with Matthew Brubeck) (2004), One-Act Opera for Solo Voice, Cello, Electronics
Syrinx (2003), Surround Sound "Tape" with Human and Bird Voice Samples
Ethel Dreams of Temporal Disturbances (2004), String Quartet, Tape
Gaijin (2001), Multi-Media Performance Work for Solo Voice and Electronics, Multi-Channel Video, Four Butoh Dancers
The Schmetterling (1998), Voice and Electronics, Clarinet, Cello, Contrabass, Electric Guitar, Piano, Sampler, Percussion
The MUNI Section (1995), Solo Voice and Electronics, Samples, Bodysynth™ Controller
Bone Music (1992), Solo Voice, Electronics, Five-Gallon Water Bottle
Pop Titles "You" (1986), Solo Voice, Delays, Found Text

▶ To learn more about Pamela Z and her music, including audio excerpts from *Flare Stains, Pop Titles "You," Carbon Song Cycle, Bone Music, Badagada, Timepiece Triptych,* and *Feral,* visit www.oup.com/us/compositioninthedigitalworld.

NOTES

1. Robert Ashley is a contemporary American composer known for his use of synthesis, electronics, and extended-instrumental techniques.
2. David Byrne was the lead singer and main songwriter for the band Talking Heads. He has won awards for his music for films including a Grammy, an Oscar, and a Golden Globe Award.
3. Brian Eno is an English composer and producer. He is considered one of the main innovators of ambient music. His many awards include two Grammys.
4. Laurie Anderson is an American composer and performance artist. She is most widely known for her performance art and her use of technology, including the vocordor [which produces robotic voice effects].
5. Robert Wilson is an American avant-garde playwright and theatrical director. One of his best-known collaborators is Philip Glass. Their work together includes the opera *Einstein on the Beach*.
6. Karlheinz Stockhausen (1928–2007) was a German composer known for his revolutionary work in serial, aleatoric, and electronic music. He studied with Olivier Messiaen.
7. Terry Riley's piece *In C* was groundbreaking and is an iconic anthem of the Minimalist School of Music. The first performance took place in San Francisco in 1964 with players including Steve Reich and Morton Subotnick.
8. Alvin Lucier is an American composer best known for his experiments in auditory perception and sound installations. One of Lucier's best-known works is *I Am Sitting in a Room* (1969).
9. Phil Niblock is a composer, filmmaker, and director of the avant-garde Experimental Intermedia Foundation, based in New York and Belgium. I recall attending his early concerts in his New York loft with my father Charles Raines who was a colleague of Niblock. Many of his pieces were played at high volume while a film of his was projected in the room accompanied by recordings of acoustic instruments playing very long tones via circular breathing. Gradual shifts away from unison tones in microtonal increments produced dramatic beating effects as the pitches moved closer or further from each other. He taught at The College of Staten Island, the City University of New York (1971–1998).
10. In Pro Tools, regions are sections of audio that are selected by the user. These regions can then be manipulated in numerous ways.
11. MAX is a programming language for multi-media and music applications. It is used in a wide variety of creative applications including performance, recording, and art installations. MSP is an add-on for MAX that allows for the real-time manipulation of digital audio.

Eric Whitacre

I had a conscious realization that I had to either find a way to make a living writing music or I was not going to make it. I am pretty dramatic, so I probably said to myself, "I will die. I've got to make a living composing music, or I will die." So I just started hustling. I took every damn commission I could take, it didn't matter how much it was for, and I wrote and wrote and wrote, and I was sending out scores left and right, entering contests—I didn't win a thing, but it didn't matter—I kept going just trying to make something happen.

A few years back I was working at some routine task in my studio when my ears pricked up at the music that had come on the radio. I stopped what I was doing, mesmerized by what I heard. It was music of Eric Whitacre

(b. Nevada, 1970), specifically one of his early Virtual Choir projects, which have since become a worldwide musical and Internet phenomenon.

If contemporary classical music can be said to have a "superstar," Whitacre is probably it. Not only does he look the part, but his charismatic persona is backed up by a fierce talent and finely honed technical and business savvy. His website could serve as the prototype on how Internet self-promotion should be done. All of that aside, his triumph really lies with his music. His persistently uplifting instrumental and choral work is contemporary but for the most part tonal, lush, and accessible to modern audiences; it's not difficult to understand his enormous popularity.

Whitacre earned his master's degree at Juilliard, where he studied with John Corigliano. His career began its meteoric ascent shortly after graduation and has continued unabated. He won a Grammy Award in 2012 and is currently composer-in-residence at Cambridge University.

I spoke to Whitacre from his studio in London. To say he was charming is an understatement. His contagious enthusiasm for the work he is doing had me rejoicing for his successes and wanting to jump in and get involved. By the time the interview was over, I felt I had just spent time with an old friend and regretted having to end the conversation. Despite his accomplishments, he verges on being self-deprecating: He's very modest and does not miss an opportunity to praise others, give credit, and express wonderment and gratitude at his own fate. It will be interesting to watch and see where he turns his talents next: One gets the feeling that this is only the beginning of Whitacre's fruitful career.

I'm very glad that you were able to take the time to do this interview, but with so many demands on your time, how do you balance your success with finding time to compose?
That's a great challenge these days. Over the last few years it's become really difficult. I'm a very slow composer and my normal composition process was to let an idea take months and months of gestation. There was a lot of time where it might not have looked like I was doing anything, then after a couple of months it would suddenly all pour out of me. These days I might have 10 days of down time, but even those 10 days aren't really down time—there's always something happening, but at least I'm in one place. It's only within the last year that I sat down with my great manager, Claire, and said, "Okay we need to cut out blocks of time so I can compose." So right now, for instance, I'm here in London and I'm doing very few things except sitting here in the studio and trying to put a couple of notes together.

Do you have a space where you like to compose? A particular set of habits and rituals you use when you work?

I didn't think I did. I've always wanted to be the kind of composer who could bring a laptop and a small MIDI controller with me and compose in hotels and on planes. But the reality is that I still compose everything with pencil on paper. We have been in London for two years now and we just moved to this new place, which is big enough that I can take my grand piano out of storage and have it here. I realized after a week of being here, that this is it, this is what I need: an actual piano in a quiet room with pencil and paper sitting in front of me, wearing my slippers; it's the only way I can really get anything done.

I mostly compose with pencil and paper too, at least when starting a piece.

There are not many of us left. I wonder if you get the same thing out of it that I do; a part of it is just the tactile sensation. But even more than that, it doesn't matter how big of a computer screen I have, with Sibelius or Finale I feel claustrophobic. I just can't get a sense of the scope of the piece; do you know what I mean? The best thing you can expect is to be able to look at 8 or 12 pages at a time. But with paper and pencil I use 11 × 17 pages, and I can lay them out in a row down on the floor. I can walk from one to the other and get a physical sense of how this thing works. I feel like this is the biggest part of why I don't compose on the computer. The other part of it is that I want to feel like I've *worked* at the end of the day, like I've produced something. There is just nothing so completely unsatisfying as working at a computer all day. I turn it off and say, "What is this thing? Where's the work?" Even if I spend 12 hours writing crap—which happens all the time—at least when I'm writing by hand at the end of the day there is a big stack of paper, and my arm is hurting, and I've got lead all over my hands. So at least I can feel like I've done something with the day, even if it wasn't something good.

I've read that Stravinsky would tape up his scores all over the room and use scissors and chop parts out and move them around, so I know exactly what you're talking about.

Yeah! Yeah that's it, I studied with John Corigliano[1] and he used to say to me, "Back in the day, when we would cut and paste something, it literally meant cutting and pasting." That really stuck with me. He liked that aesthetic because with the computer you can cut and paste very easily, and sometimes you don't really consider it before you do it. Doing it by hand used to be such a pain in the ass—in fact it still is. You would take some time to really consider your decisions; you would think, "Before I write out these 30 bars by hand, do I really want to do this"? I want to be a thoughtful composer, and I'm hoping that the constraints of my process actually force me to do that.

What was it like studying with John Corigliano?
Oh it was the best. They were by far the most successful composition lessons I had. I studied with David Diamond[2] right before John, and David is a legend, but he was also a legendarily difficult teacher. Just brutal.

You studied with David Diamond at Juilliard?
Yeah, that's right. And I felt he was especially brutal with me. He kind of paralyzed me that first term, so when I switched over to John I didn't know what to expect. With David I used to bring in pieces that I was working on and he would take his "infamous red pen" and he just would violently chop it up. He had very strong opinions. He might ask, "Why did you do this?" And you could never say, "Well, I liked the way it sounded." That was never enough. You had to have some sort of reason, some intellectual answer. On the other hand, from the beginning John was not interested in anything that I had finished. He felt there was no need to go back to finished work, because all that would happen is that I would end up defending work that I had already completed. And so we would start at the very beginning of a new piece. I would say 95 percent of the time we never spoke about notes or harmony. We spoke about architecture—he had me do these crazy drawings, which I still do. Drawing the emotional architecture of the piece from start to finish without writing a note. I found it thrilling, because not only did I then have a sense of where this piece was going, but also I was free from the tyranny of harmony. If you sit at the piano, your hands want to do certain familiar things, and it is easy to micromanage early on. With this drawing technique, it was all about having fun, having a sense of being creative for the sake of being creative. It was revelatory to me really.

Your career has had an amazing trajectory. Over a period of a very few years, you've gone from playing in rock bands and not being able to read music to getting your master's degree at Juilliard, and you're now a successful composer. What lit that fire in you?
Looking back, I think I just had "the music brain." I was built for music. I remember being in high school and sitting and listening to '80s pop, or Pink Floyd, or the Beatles and having these mystical experiences through the music. Even though I didn't know, technically, what I was

listening to, I was putting names to it on my own and playing it by ear. When I first joined a choir in college, it was like having those same mystical experiences, but I just couldn't believe the depth of it. Not that I don't think pop music has depth, but—my God—singing Mozart and Bach: A new world opened up to me. Frankly, I still just stand in awe, especially of Bach.

Not of this world.

Right, not of this world. Especially given how much he wrote—I still can't imagine how he did it. In the first couple of years after I discovered choral music, and concert music in a wider sense, I just wanted to be a conductor; I wanted to swim in that world. I loved it and I knew I wanted to be there. I don't think I've ever told this story: There is a composer, Kirke Mechem,[3] who writes mostly choral music, and we were singing one of his pieces. I guess I was maybe 20; I hadn't written any classical music yet, and someone in the choir asked a question of the conductor, something like, "I don't know if this note should be short or long." The conductor said, "Well, I'm not sure. Let me call Kurt and see what he wants." It was like someone had turned on a light for me. First, I couldn't believe it was possible. I was like, "Oh my God, there are people alive doing this?" And then second, I remember thinking, "Wait, so the conductor is not the top of the food chain?" [Both laugh]

I think that was the first time I thought that maybe I should try this. I was just giddy with the possibility of it all.

What was the transition like from the time you got your master's degree at Juilliard to winning a Grammy? I'm interested in what happened once you got that piece of paper and walked out in front of Lincoln Center [location of Juilliard] onto Broadway and really began your career.

By the time I graduated, I had had a number of pieces published, but I wasn't really making any real money. My fiancée, now my wife, and I were living in Nevada with my mother and I didn't know what to do; I was 27 years old living at my mom's house. A friend called from Los Angeles and said, "Listen, the choir director down here just left. Do you want to take the choir program over?" So I went down and taught 4th through 12th grade choir for a semester. On paper, it seemed like it would be the easiest gig ever. You know, 8:30 to 3 o'clock Monday through Friday, and I get the summers off. I thought, "This will be a piece of cake." As it turned out, it was the hardest thing I have ever done in my life! I really think there is nothing nobler, and more difficult, than being a good teacher. I didn't write a note during that time, not a note. I was so creatively wiped out from teaching.

I got to the end of that year—I guess this would be 1998—and that's when I had a conscious realization that I had to either find a way to make a living writing music or I was not going to make it. I am pretty dramatic, so I probably said to myself, "I will die. I've got to make a living composing music, or I will die." So I just started hustling. I took every damn commission I could take, it didn't matter how much it was for, and I wrote and wrote and wrote, and I was sending out scores left and right, entering contests—I didn't win a thing, but it didn't matter—I kept going just trying to make something happen.

What is interesting to me now is that during those three years, I wrote, easily, 50 percent of my entire catalog. It was just flooding out of me. And then, I would say around 2000, Napster[4] hit. I could track my pieces that had been recorded, and I could see on Napster that they were being shared quite a lot, and I saw a noticeable kind of blossoming awareness of my music by the public. I think that was right around the time I realized that the Internet wasn't just a fad.

So I built my first, very simple, very humble website. For the next few years I was just hustling. I called every single person I could think of in order to promote my music. I played a game with myself that I called "fishing." Every day I would throw out 20 lines into the water, it didn't matter how crazy they were; I would write to Hans Zimmer[5] and on the same day I would write to the high school conductor in some little town in California. I was just throwing out lines; you never know when one is going to get a bite. It could sometimes be two years before someone would write or call back. And then something happened around 2004 or 2005, where it felt like it all flipped over. For the first time, people were contacting *me*. And I don't know why that was, if it had just reached the tipping point from all the "fishing," or because the pieces were out there doing their work, or the combination of publicity and hustle. Since then it feels more like riding the wave than making the wave.

Your current website is exceptionally savvy and well designed in every respect. How much do you have to do with that? I ask, because building and managing an effective website can be a tremendously challenging and time-consuming undertaking.

Up until four or five years ago, I was trying to manage it myself, and it was a disaster. Early on, I sort of fashioned myself as a web designer, and then at some point, I threw in the towel and said, "You know what? You don't know what you're doing!" Hah! So I found this guy to take that over for me. He still does all of the heavy lifting and the design, but I'm obsessed with it. I could never let someone else take over altogether, especially in terms of the content including posts on Facebook and Twitter. I would never let someone else post on my behalf. It's something that I love doing and something that I see as an extension of what I do.

You mentioned Hans Zimmer in passing. You worked on the film *Pirates of the Caribbean* with him. Some composers have really excelled working in the film medium while others have found it terribly difficult. What was your experience on that project like?
Well, the process is interesting. I had never collaborated with anyone before. First, you've got to see his studio to believe it. It is just so over the top. He owns an entire compound, called Remote Control Productions. There are probably 20 to 25 full-time composers working there, all with their own studios. There are big, elegant recording studios, with secretaries and lobbies, and then there is his personal writing room. It must be 100 feet long; all custom designed and made to look like a 19th-century brothel. [Laughs]

I'm a huge fan of some of the things he has done; I loved the *Gladiator* soundtrack. So I was intimidated to say the least. But he's a sweetheart. He gave me a big bear hug, we sat down, and we just kind of chatted. Then he put two pianos together, and he took out a bottle of rum because it is a pirate movie. [Laughs] We drank and jammed for a couple of hours, and after 20 minutes it wasn't Hans Zimmer across from me anymore, just another musician. So, my part of the process felt so effortless. We came up with this "theme" and then he sent it off to his team and the team orchestrated it, put it all together, and made it into all of this beautiful music. Weirdly, it was the easiest thing I had done in a long time—you know, compared to the stuff you and I normally do, which is just agonizing over every damn note, for months and months.

It sounds like he has quite an organization there, certainly the antithesis of the cliché of the lone composer who is not very business savvy.
What I really learned from Hans, which was big for me, was that as much as the "business" is around him—and my God, is it around him—he values and protects his creativity. We had a session where the directors and producers came in, and there must have been 40 people in the room. There were people from sound, from effects, from production and studio heads. All of them were freaking out; it's a $300 million movie. But Hans is able to actively protect the part of him that is creative; he really honors

that part. He goes way further than I ever do in nourishing his creativity; he really makes sure that he gets to be a kid in there, that it always feels like playing, that it always feels like fun. It was a great lesson for me to see that.

I would like to do more film, but I'm a little worried because I do get precious about every note, and you can't be like that in film. Hans told me this great story: He was working with a 90-piece orchestra playing his music, and the director was listening and said, "What's that instrument right there?" They said, "Well, that's the flute." And the director says, "Oh, oh, the flute. Can we hear that up an octave?" Now everybody is terrified because, you know, when a director says something like that, you think he must have read that in a book somewhere, you know, "up an octave." You just know he has no idea what that means. So the orchestra takes it up an octave, and now the flute is in the stratosphere, so the director goes, "Oh, yeah, yeah, lets go back to the other way." So a little while later he says, "Wait, wait that note there. What is that instrument?" "Well that's an oboe." He says, "Ah, can I hear that up an octave?" It gets kind of quiet, and the orchestrator says, "Actually, it can't go up an octave; that's as high as it will play." So the director says, "Well then, let's hear it up half an octave." [Both laugh]

When you're surrounded by that, and the pressure, you have to have the kind of personality where you don't take it personally, you just have to think, OK, the director doesn't like oboes: NO OBOES. I would like to think that I could manage that kind of situation, but I can imagine parts of me dying quickly in that environment.

Do you have specific techniques that you return to when you set out to compose a new work?

When I'm writing choral music especially, it is always about the text. I feel like all I'm really trying to do is illuminate the poetry with sound. I always feel incredibly guilty for getting the credit for these pieces, because I really feel like the poet did all the work. I'm just doing what the poetry says to do—I will work very literally according to what is said in the poem. In *Water Night* there is a line that goes, "And if you close your eyes, a river, a silent and beautiful current, fills you from within." So on "fills you from within," I had the soprano starting at D-flat at the top of the staff, and everybody else starting at a low E-flat. Then they come toward each other, on a diatonic scale, holding each of those notes, literally "filling" the chord "from within." I did what it says to do.

What about when the ideas don't come, or you get stuck on a particular piece? How do you work your way out of those situations?

When I get lost, or I'm struggling, I need to quit thinking so much and go back to the poetry. Almost every time, it's right there in the text; "Oh, of course. Just do that."

Lately I've been working with the poet Charles Anthony Silvestri building pieces from the poem up; we write at the same time, so it's a little bit like writing the script and scoring the film at the same time. We will talk a lot about dramatic beats, and "the emotional architecture" of the work, and what needs to happen dramatically. We send drafts back and forth to each other, until something kind of locks. Then the architecture of the piece starts to become evident.

You've also written wind symphonies and orchestral works; do you enjoy composing those as much as your choral works? Do you take a different approach with those instrumental pieces?

Yeah, profoundly different. The truth is, I haven't written enough orchestral music yet to think I really have my own voice, or even my own concept of that music. I think what I am doing is just writing in styles. A piece like *October,* to me, is very much written like Edward Elgar or Ralph Vaughan Williams, with a little bit of Thomas Newman[6] thrown in. *Equus* to me sounds very much like John Adams with a little bit of Stravinsky here and there. I feel more like I am learning the "cloak" of another composer, but I don't say that with any self-deprecation. I think there is great honor in learning that way, to get inside and figure out what a great composer is doing.

Would you say that pop and rock has influenced your writing a lot?

Yeah. It is almost impossible to avoid. One of the things I seem to do, which so far nobody has called me out on, is to have parts of my music land on a hook. Do you know what I mean? Pop music and rock music does that in such a satisfying way. The hook is always set apart in some way. It is either shinier, or the bass kicks in; whatever it is, the hook is the destination and it's the moment of satisfaction. With most of my music, I always feel like I've got this big build and then—here we go, we're into the "Hey, Jude" part of the anthem. [Both laugh]

Yeah, you know exactly what I'm talking about, don't you?

Absolutely.

The other thing I tend to do, especially with choral music, is to punch certain words and ideas. By punch, I mean to illuminate the idea with a cluster or a chord, in what feels like a very "pop" way. The prosody of the text is almost conversational in the way that it is set, in a similar way to rock music.

I would be remiss if I didn't ask you about the concept for your *Virtual Choirs*. I believe this is one of the most artistically creative uses of digital technology I've encountered in a long time.
A young woman posted a video on YouTube hoping that somehow I would see it. She was singing the soprano line to a song I had written called *Sleep,* and I teared up when I saw it. It gave me a very simple idea, which was that if we could get 50 people like her to all sing their part in tempo and in the same key, and if we started all the videos at the same time, it would make a choir. I was excited because I thought it would be a cool thing to do. And so we tried it, at first on a very small scale. Everybody was listening to the same recording, so everybody was singing along to an existing recording. We edited it all together and I thought, "Oh my God, this actually sounds like music." Then we pushed for the next level: I uploaded a video of me conducting the next piece and made a conductor track underneath it. When I heard the results I got chills all over my entire body. It wasn't until that moment that I realized that this was actually much bigger than traditional choral music. This was something else entirely. The poetry of the experiment really struck me. And then it went very viral when we posted it, and my whole world turned upside down.

It's a remarkable concept. I don't know exactly what is involved technically, but I've read that *Virtual Choir 2.0* had something like 2,000 voices on it. How do you manage that?
The most recent one, *Virtual Choir 4*, has 8,400 videos from 101 countries. Can you imagine? It started with a young man, Scott Haines, who put it all together, and me online saying, "All right singers, I need you!" There is no money being made, but it is becoming a small cottage industry. I think the last one had about 35 people working on it, divided up into teams. It is a massive, massive undertaking. Just managing the files alone is a nightmare. But it is also, for us, less about the music—although we want it to be of the highest possible standard—and more about the social phenomenon of the thing, about connecting people from all over the world. Some of the participants haven't ever sung before and would do anything to be a part of this project. That is the most thrilling part for me.

You currently live in London with your son and your wife [Hila Plitmann].[7] She is a very talented and successful singer.

Yes, she is the real musician in the family. She is a freak of nature. She is. And she sings everything from memory. It doesn't matter how big or how contemporary.

There are a couple of composers I have spoken with whose spouses are also musicians, and that's an interesting dynamic.
Is your wife a musician?

No, she's a visual artist.
Oh! See, that's good. Because you both get to be crazy—you both understand crazy, but you're crazy in different ways, right? [Both laugh]

My career has enough overlap with Hila's that there can sometimes be some real tension. The biggest issues can arise when we're working together—when I'm conducting and she's singing. We joke about it all the time, but if I say to her, "Baby, ah, that was a little bit flat," what she hears is, "I don't love you anymore." [Both laugh more than is strictly necessary]

On the other side, and I don't know if you feel this way as a composer, but I wish I had an editor the way writers have editors. Contemporary composers are often treated with such reverence; nobody will really speak truth to power and say, "Listen, that doesn't really work," or "It's three minutes too long." The only person who will speak to me like that is my wife. So having her around may be another source of tension—I can imagine her saying, "Yeah, well, I don't know, I've heard you do all of that before." It can be hard, tough medicine, but it's *good for me*, and I really trust her opinion, both as an artist and as a musician. I've been very lucky to have her as a partner.

Some composers have expressed a real concern about their music being available for free on the Internet. Are composers still going to be able to make a living?
That's a big question. I guess, first of all, whatever I think of it doesn't really matter. The whole paradigm is crumbling day by day. That's the new reality, that's what's happening and we're not going to change it.

I've always felt that the most important thing is to get the music out there. I don't care what the vehicle is: TV, radio, Spotify, or the Internet. If the music is communicating like it ought to, if people hear it and connect to it, then it is doing what it is supposed to do.

In terms of the "making money" part of it, the golden days of making a ton of money on records is gone. It was great for those people who were in it while it was hot, but it's just not that way anymore. But that's okay. There are very smart people who have figured out all kinds of ways to make money with music in the past, and they will figure out how to make it some other way in the future.

One of the things that I love seeing with pop music is that the order has flipped. It used to be that an artist would release a disc, and then they would tour to promote the disc. But now, they release a disc in order to promote their tour. You want people to know you and love you so they will come see you live, because live performance can't be replicated yet. Of course, some of the *really* pop acts are basically just lip-synching up there, and okay that's fine, whatever it is. But I think there is a renaissance of real musicians performing again, and it's becoming a "thing" again to go to a live show, and marvel again at that live experience. For me, that's worth the whole thing. You said it best when you asked, "Can you make a living?" It's definitely not about making a killing. As long as I get to compose and that's my job, I don't really care how much money there is.

What are your goals and dreams for yourself as a composer?
I would love to do more work in film, and I'd like to write and conduct more orchestral music. Just to be swimming in the deep end that I'm totally uncomfortable in, to force myself to grow. And I have this dream that I can start to collaborate with some of my heroes in the pop world. I would love to work with Peter Gabriel, Paul McCartney, Radiohead, and Björk. That would just be perfect, that would make it all worth it, frankly. Actually, I think if I just shook Paul McCartney's hand, I'd retire. What else is there after that?

SELECTED WORKS OF ERIC WHITACRE

Sainte-Chapelle (2012), SATB

Alleluia (2011), SATB

The River Cam (2011), Solo Cello and String Orchestra

The City and the Sea (2010), SATB Chorus and Piano; Solo Baritone and Piano

The Seal Lullaby (2007), SATB; SSA; TTBB; Wind Ensemble; String Orchestra

A Boy and a Girl (2002), SATB

Leonardo Dreams of His Flying Machine (2001), SATB

Paradise Lost (2001), Music Theatre

Equus (2000), Wind Symphony

Sleep (2000), SATB; Wind Symphony

Lux Aurumque (2000), SATB; TTBB; Wind Symphony; String
  Orchestra
When David Heard (1999), SATB
Cloudburst (1992), SATB; Concert Band

▶ To learn more about Eric Whitacre and his music, visit www.oup.com/
us/compositioninthedigitalworld.

NOTES

1. John Corigliano is an American composer and educator whose father was con-certmaster of the New York Philharmonic. He studied at Columbia University and the Manhattan School of Music, and was an assistant to Leonard Bernstein. His awards include a Grammy, the Grawemeyer Award, and the Pulitzer Prize. He also won an Academy Award for his film score for *The Red Violin*.
2. David Diamond (1915–2005) was an American composer and educator. His teachers included Roger Sessions and Nadia Boulanger.
3. Kirke Mechem is an American composer particularly known for his choral works. He studied with Walter Piston at Harvard and is composer-in-residence at the University of San Francisco.
4. Napster was a peer-to-peer file sharing service started in 1999 that focused on sharing audio files over the Internet. At its zenith the company had over 70 million users. The company was shut down by court order in 2001.
5. Hans Zimmer is a German-born musician and film composer. His scores often integrate electronic and traditional orchestral sounds. He has received numerous awards for his film scores including four Grammy Awards and an Academy Award.
6. Thomas Newman is an American composer. Awards for his film scores include five Grammy Awards, three Golden Globe nominations, and eleven Academy Award nominations. He comes from a family of musicians and composers whose members include Alfred and Randy Newman.
7. Hila Plitmann is a Grammy award-winning soprano who has worked with top orchestras and conductors. She has sung contemporary compositions by composers including David Del Tredici, Eric Whitacre, John Corigliano, and Aaron Jay Kernis.

ACKNOWLEDGMENTS

As a composition student I greatly enjoyed a book entitled *The Muse that Sings* by Ann McCutchan (Oxford University Press, 1999). It's a wonderful collection of interviews with composers (some of whom are also included in this book) and has been an inspiration to me, and my students, over the years. I owe Ms. McCutchan a debt of gratitude, both for her outstanding book and for sparking the idea for *Composition in the Digital World*.

When I set out to write this book, I was—in a word—naïve about the amount of work it would involve. Luckily for me, I come from a family of artists, writers, and readers, so I was able to impose on them on a regular basis to assist with transcriptions, loving criticism, and editing. My wife, Kate Raines, spent countless hours reading, re-reading, and editing my work. I am for this (and many other things) forever in her debt. My sincere thanks also to my mother, Mary Bozeman-Osborn, not only for her freely given hours helping me on this project but also for the example she has always set for living the creative life, and to my son Devon Raines and my friend Stacy Shannon for their help in turning taped recordings into transcriptions I could work with. Warm thanks to Dr. Peter Spencer, former director of the composition and theory departments at Florida State University for his sage counsel and steadfast support. And I thank my Father, Professor Charles Raines, who was my most enthusiastic supporter and reader on this project. Sadly, he died shortly before the manuscript was completed.

This book would not have been possible without the many hours of work my family donated to this project.

My sincere thanks to my editor at Oxford University Press, Norman Hirschy, whose eyes lit up when I suggested the subject of this book to him over coffee. His enthusiasm and support for this project have never wavered and I thank him most sincerely.

I also offer my appreciation to the crucial individuals who work with the composers and who helped to make these interviews happen: Patrick Gullo, Cheryl Lawson, Lynn Moore, Elizabeth Dworkin, Isabelle Deconinck, Jennifer Wada, Claire Long, and Joanne Steward.

Last but not least, my deep gratitude goes to the composers who graciously took time out of their busy schedules to share their experiences and wisdom in this book. I thank them for their time, their altruism, and most of all for their music, which brightens our world.

RECOMMENDED READING

Braun, Hans-Joachim, ed. *Music and Technology in the Twentieth Century*. Baltimore: Johns Hopkins University Press, 2002.

Bredeson, Carmen, and Ralph Thibodeau. *Ten Great American Composers*. Berkeley Heights, NJ: Enslow Publishers, 2002.

Duckworth, William. *Talking Music: Conversations with John Cage, Philip Glass, Laurie Anderson, and Five Generations of American Experimental Composers*. New York: Da Capo Press, 1991.

Hinkle-Turner, Elizabeth. *Women Composers and Music Technology in the United States: Crossing the Line*. Burlington, VT: Ashgate, 2006.

Hoover, Tom. *Keeping Score: Interviews with Today's Top Film, Television, and Game Music Composers*. Course Technology PTR, 2009.

Katz, Mark. *Capturing Sound: How Technology Has Changed Music*. Los Angeles: University of California Press, 2010.

Mazzola, Guerino, Joomi Park, and Florian Thalman. *Musical Creativity: Strategies and Tools in Composition and Improvisation*. New York: Springer, 2012.

McCutchan, Ann. *The Muse that Sings: Composers Speak about the Creative Process*. Oxford and New York: Oxford University Press, 2003.

Rockwell, John. *All American Music: Composition in the Late Twentieth Century*. New York: Da Capo Press, 1997.

Simmons, Walter. *Voices in the Wilderness: Six American Neo-Romantic Composers*. Lanham, MD: Scarecrow Press, 2006.

Slayton, Michael K., ed. *Women of Influence in Contemporary Music: Nine American Composers*. Lanham, MD: Scarecrow Press, 2010.

Stickland, Edward. *American Composers: Dialogues on Contemporary Music*. Bloomfield: Indiana University Press, 1991.

Watson, Scott. *Using Technology to Unlock Musical Creativity*. New York and Oxford: Oxford University Press, 2011.

ABOUT ROBERT RAINES

Photo Credit: Dallas Raines

As a composer, musician, educator, and creative director, Dr. Raines's career has spanned both music and the visual arts, creating award-winning work in both fields. Born in Louisiana and raised in New York City's Greenwich Village by parents who were active in the arts, he was immersed in music, theater, literature, and the visual arts from an early age. Educated first at Berklee College of Music in Boston, his early career was spent as a guitarist and composer in New York City, producing as well as performing on many recordings of jazz, blues, and popular music. Simultaneously following a graphic design arc, he also made a name for himself in the commercial art world, ultimately leading the creative department as vice president at America Online, before choosing to focus entirely on music. Since earning a master's degree from Shenandoah University in Winchester, Virginia, and a doctorate from Florida State University in Tallahassee, Florida, Robert's music for concert, theater, ballet, and film has been performed and appreciated worldwide. He lives with his family in the foothills of Virginia's Blue Ridge Mountains, where he composes full time.

INDEX

creativity. *See also* inspiration
  Aaron J. Kernis on, 105–6
  Bright Sheng on, 205
  Eric Whitacre on protecting, 323–24
  Glenn Branca on, 267
  Jennifer Higdon on, 124
  John Anthony Lennon on, 128–29, 137
  Kevin Puts on, 160
  Martin Bresnick on, 50
  Tania León on, 191
Crumb, George, 35, 41n1, 117
culture
  Bright Sheng on, 207, 210–11
  Chen Yi on American open-mindedness and, 226
  Eve Beglarian on nature and, 258
  influence of, on Mohammed Fairouz, 180–81
Currie, Colin, 30
Curtis Institute of Music, 117–18
cutting and pasting, 72, 136, 199, 319–20
Czech-American Summer Music Institute (CASMI), 220

El-Dabh, Halim, 184, 188n12
Da Capo Chamber Players, 59–60, 63n2
Daedalus Quartet, 61, 64n9
Damascus, Mohammed Fairouz on trip to, 182
Dance Party on the Disco (Kernis), 103
Dance Theater of Harlem, 194, 200n3
Dancing Dots, 275, 282n3
Daugherty, Michael, 163–74
  advice of, 174
  on business and technology, 171
  on fame and success, 173–74
  on humor, 171
  process of, 164–68, 172–73
  on sample software, 172–73
  on technology, 166–69
  technology use of, 172–73
  on working with Gil Evans, 170–71
  works, 174
    Dead Elvis, 171
    Hell's Angels, 171
    Metropolis Symphony, 164, 171, 175n8
    Sinatra Shag, 171

    Le Tombeau de Liberace, 171
  on young composers, 169–70
Dead Elvis (Daugherty), 171
deadlines
  Ellen Taaffe Zwilich on, 17
  Glenn Branca on, 268
  John Anthony Lennon on, 135
  Ladislav Kubík on, 218
  Michael Torke on, 88
  Mohammed Fairouz on, 177–78
Debussy, Claude, 48
Diamond, David, 320, 329n2
Different Trains (Reich), 21, 22, 29
difficulties in composing
  Bright Sheng on insecurity, 206
  Eric Whitacre on getting stuck, 325
  Jennifer Higdon on hitting a wall, 118–19
  Joan Tower on terrible pieces, 57–58
  Steve Reich on pieces that aren't working, 25
  William Averitt on getting unstuck, 74
Digital Performer, 166–67, 172, 175n2
Dixon, Willie, 49–50
Dog Days (Little), 140, 141, 146, 147
Dolphy, Eric, 26
Doppler shifts, 46
Double Sextet (Reich), 21, 22, 29
Dragon Rhyme (Yi), 225
Dream of a Morning Sky (Kernis), 112, 113n7
dreams, Bright Sheng on, 205
Dreamsongs (Kernis), 108–9
Drexel University, 303
Druckman, Jacob, 152, 161n3
Drumming (Reich), 24, 26
drums, 24, 26, 38, 141–42, 145
DuBois, R. Luke, 283–93
  on algorithmic composition, 292–93
  on becoming a "laptop musician," 285–86
  on composing with computer, 292
  Eve Beglarian on, 259
  on fear of technology, 288–89
  on laptop musicianship, 287–88
  on piano as lasting technology, 287
  on Ringling Museum of Art projects, 284–85

poetry, Ladislav Kubík on connection between music and, 217–18
poker, parallels between composition and, 87
politics, influence of, on Mohammed Fairouz, 180–81
pop music
  Eric Whitacre on, 328
  as influence on Eric Whitacre, 325–26
  as influence on Pamela Z, 308–9
  as influence on Steven Reich, 26–27
  John Anthony Lennon on, 131
  Mohammed Fairouz on, 180
  Pamela Z on separation of classical and, 309
Prado, Jose Luis, 241
Prague, Czech Republic, influence of, on Ladislav Kubík, 215–16
pre-recording, 21–22, 145
Prism Saxophone Quartet, 229, 233n4
Professional Composer, 70, 76n1
Prokofiev, Sergei, Second Symphony, 33–34
proofreading
  Ellen Taaffe Zwilich on MIDI playback for, 10
  Michael Torke on, 85–86
  William Averitt on, 71
Pro Tools, 166, 175n2, 258, 312
Pulitzer Prize
  Jennifer Higdon on, 122
  Kevin Puts on, 160
pulse, 95
Puts, Kevin, 150–61
  on compositional process, 160
  on engaging audience, 159
  on finding voice, 152–53
  on Flute Concerto, 158–59
  influences on, 158
  process of, 156–57
  on Pulitzer Prize, 160
  teachers of, 152
  on technology, 157
  on transition to composing, 151–52
  on unknown composers, 160
  work habits, 156
  works, 161
    Flute Concerto, 158–59
    How Wild the Sea, 156
    The Manchurian Candidate, 153–54, 155–56

    Silent Night, 151, 153, 155
    Symphony No. 3, 158
  on writing opera, 153–55
  on young composers, 157–58

Radiohead, 30
Radio Rewrite (Reich), 30
Rapids (Tower), 61
Reason, 24, 31n11
recording and record label, Michael Torke on, 79–80
record sales, 261. See also CDs; royalties
register, Kevin Puts on, 154
Reich, Steve, 19–31
  current projects, 30
  on demos, 24
  on finding voice, 27
  influence of, 28, 310
  influences on, 26–27, 30
  on location and finding time for writing, 20–21
  on pieces that aren't working, 25
  pre-recorded and live performances, 21–22
  process of, 24, 29–30
  rock composition of, 29
  on sound engineers, 22
  on style and 12-tone music, 25–26
  on styles interesting student-composers, 28
  on success, 29
  technology use, 21, 23–24
  works, 30–31
    The Cave, 21, 29
    Different Trains, 21, 22, 29
    Double Sextet, 21, 22, 29
    Drumming, 24, 26
    It's Gonna Rain, 22, 31n5
    Music for 18 Musicians, 24
    New York Counterpoint, 21
    Radio Rewrite, 30
    Tehillim, 24
    Three Tales, 21
    Triple Quartet, 21
    2X5, 21, 29, 30, 31n1
    Vermont Counterpoint, 21
    WTC 9/11, 21, 23, 31n3
Remote Control Productions, 323
repeating sections, 72, 136, 199, 319–20

starting over
  Steve Reich on, 25
  William Averitt on, 74
St. Matthew Passion (Averitt), 66, 74
Stravinsky, Igor
  Bright Sheng on, 207
  defines composer, 1
  as influence on Joan Tower, 60
  rejects commission, 268
  Rite of Spring, 35
  and 12-tone music, 25
Stroke (Tower), 60
student-composers. *See also* music
    education; young composers
  Aaron J. Kernis on, 107
  Chen Yi on American versus Chinese,
    225–26
  Chen Yi on self-promotion of, 230
  Chen Yi on technology and Chinese,
    226–28
  Christopher Rouse on, 37–38
  David T. Little on influences
    on, 146
  Ellen Taaffe Zwilich on, 14–15
  Ellen Taaffe Zwilich's advice for,
    15–16
  Glenn Branca on, 271
  Greg Wilder on, 302
  Internet use by Chinese, 226
  Jennifer Higdon on musical taste of,
    123
  Joan Tower on technology and, 59
  Joan Tower's advice for, 56–57
  John Anthony Lennon on, 134
  Jose Bevia on computer use of,
    236–37
  Libby Larsen on, 98–99
  Martin Bresnick on technology and,
    44–45
  Steve Reich on styles interesting, 28
style
  of Aaron J. Kernis's teachers, 106
  Bright Sheng on voice and, 206–7
  David T. Little on, 141–42
  English-speaking versus European,
    28
  Eve Beglarian on, 256
  evolution of, 2–3
  of Ladislav Kubík, 217
  of Mohammed Fairouz, 180

success
  of Bright Sheng, 211–12
  Christopher Rouse on, 37–38
  Jennifer Higdon on, 122–23
  Ladislav Kubík on, 220
  Michael Daugherty on, 173–74
  Michael Torke on, 88
  Steve Reich on, 29
  William Averitt on, 75
Super Star Etudes (Kernis), 103
Symphony No. 3 (Puts), 158
Symphony No. 3 (Rouse), 33–34
Symphony No. 4 (Rouse), 40

Tahiti (Torke), 79–80
Tahrir (Fairouz), 183–84, 186
talent
  Christopher Rouse on success and, 38
  Ladislav Kubík on success and, 220
  Michael Torke on success and, 88
  William Averitt on, 75
Talma, Louise, 195, 200n8
tape loops, 307–8, 310
taste, evolution of, 2
Tatum, Art, 196, 279, 282n4
teaching
  Aaron J. Kernis on, 104
  Chen Yi on, 230
  Eric Whitacre on, 321–22
  Jennifer Higdon on, 117–18
  Joan Tower on, 58, 62
  John Anthony Lennon on, 129
  Ladislav Kubík on, 221
  Libby Larsen on, 91, 98
  Martin Bresnick on, 50
  William Averitt on, 67–68, 73
technology. *See also* Internet; software
  Aaron J. Kernis on, 109–12
  Bright Sheng on, 212
  Christopher Rouse on, 36–37
  Daniel Wohl on, 246
  Daniel Wohl's use of, 247
  David T. Little on, 144–45
  Ellen Taaffe Zwilich on impact of, 16
  Eve Beglarian on, 258–59
  Glenn Branca on, 268–70
  Greg Wilder on, in composition, 299
  Greg Wilder on future of, 303–4
  Greg Wilder on students and, 302
  Greg Wilder's early use of, 296–98

mentors of, 297
software of, 298–99
on technology use in composition,
  299
work habits, 301
works, 304
  Elysium, 300
  Interlude for Marimba and Computer,
    300–301
Willy's Way (Bresnick), 43–44, 49–50
Wilson, Laura, 194
Wincenc, Carol, 57, 63n5
Winchester Musica Viva, 69
Wind (Yi), 230
Wohl, Daniel, 243–52
  on center of music, 249
  on combining acoustic instruments
    and electronic sounds, 245–46,
    247
  on computer use in composition and
    notation, 250–51
  education of, 244–45
  on electronic music, 245
  on live performance, 249–50
  on live performance of *Corps Exquis*,
    248
  on non-curricular music, 247
  process of, 247
  on producing *Corps Exquis*, 248
  on technology, 246
  on Transit, 248–49
  works, 251–52
    Helium, 250
Woodard, James, 66–67, 69–70, 76n1
world music
  as influence on Steven Reich, 26–27
  Tania León on, 199
Wrinkle in Time, A (Larsen), 92, 96–97
Writings on Music 1965–2000
  (Reich), 23
WTC 9/11 (Reich), 21, 23, 31n3

Yale University, 152
Yang, Xuefei, 229, 233n5
Yi, Chen, 223–33
  advice for young composers, 232
  on Charles Ives Living Award,
    228–29
  on computer use in composition and
    notation, 226–27

current projects, 229–30
on inspiration, 232
on Internet, 226
on MIDI playback, 227–28
on music schools in United States and
  China, 225–26
on orchestration, 231
process of, 228
on recent trip to Asia, 224–25
on self-promotion, 230
works, 232–33
  China West, 230
  Dragon Rhyme, 225
  Momentum, 225
  Northern Scenes, 233n3
  Shuo Chang, 233n5
  Wind, 230
on writing for Chinese instruments
  and Western orchestra, 231–32
on writing for symphonic band versus
  orchestra, 230–31
on Zhou Long, 229
young composers. *See also*
  student-composers
  Aaron J. Kernis's advice for, 112
  Chen Yi's advice for, 232
  Ellen Taaffe Zwilich on, 14–15
  Ellen Taaffe Zwilich's advice for,
    15–16
  Glenn Branca on situation of, 270
  Glenn Branca's advice for, 271
  John Anthony Lennon's advice for,
    134–35
  Jose Bevia's advice for, 241
  Kevin Puts on, 157–58
  Ladislav Kubík on, 220
  Libby Larsen on, 93–94
  Libby Larsen's advice for, 98
  Michael Daugherty on, 169–70
  Pamela Z's advice for, 314
  Steve Reich's influence on, 28
  Tania León on, 198–99
YouTube
  Aaron J. Kernis on, 108, 109
  in China, 226, 233n2
  David T. Little on, 143
  Ellen Taaffe Zwilich on, 16
  Greg Wilder on, 301–2
  Michael Torke on, 82–83
  Mohammed Fairouz on, 185